"TWO FRIENDS ROWED ME ACROSS THE CHARLES RIVER, A LITTLE TO THE EASTWARD WHERE THE SOMERSET MAN-OF-WAR LAY. IT WAS THEN YOUNG FLOOD, THE SHIP WAS WINDING, AND THE MOON RISING. THEY LANDED ME ON THE CHARLESTOWN SIDE."

Thus Paul Revere writes of the beginning of the ride that would trigger the shots at Concord heard around the world. His is but one of the magnificent chorus of eyewitness testimonies that bring history to life and turn men too long viewed as marble statues into vibrant flesh and blood. This is the American revolution as it really was. These are the people on both sides as they really were.

"Extraordinarily good reading."
—*Book-of-the-Month Club News*

"Comes closer to the nitty-gritty of the struggle for independence than is possible in school textbooks. Highly recommended." —*San Francisco Examiner-Chronicle*

"An intriguing perspective on the war and the people who participated on both sides." —*Houston Post*

A Christopher Award Winner

RICHARD WHEELER is a former Marine and a full-time author, with fifteen other books to his credit, among them the prize-winning *Voices of the Civil War* and *Witness to Gettysburg*, both available in Meridian editions.

D0032258

George Washington in 1772, by Charles Willson Peale. For this portrait, the only one made of him prior to the Revolution, he donned his uniform from the French and Indian War. *(Washington and Lee University)*

VOICES OF 1776

RICHARD WHEELER

A MERIDIAN BOOK

MERIDIAN
Published by the Penguin Group
Penguin Books USA Inc., 375 Hudson Street, New York, New York 10014, U.S.A.
Penguin Books Ltd, 27 Wrights Lane, London W8 5TZ, England
Penguin Books Australia Ltd, Ringwood, Victoria, Australia
Penguin Books Canada Ltd, 10 Alcorn Avenue, Toronto, Ontario, Canada M4V 3B2
Penguin Books (N.Z.) Ltd, 182-190 Wairau Road, Auckland 10, New Zealand

Penguin Books Ltd, Registered Offices: Harmondsworth, Middlesex, England

Published by Meridian, an imprint of Dutton Signet, a division of Penguin Books USA Inc.

First Printing, October, 1991
10 9 8 7 6 5 4 3 2

Ⓜ REGISTERED TRADEMARK—MARCA REGISTRADA

LIBRARY OF CONGRESS CATALOGING-IN-PUBLICATION DATA:
Wheeler, Richard.
    Voices of 1776 / Richard Wheeler.
        p.   cm.
    Reprint. Originally published: New York : Crowell [1972].
    Includes bibliographical references and index.
    ISBN 0-452-01078-0
    1. United States—History—Revolution, 1775-1783—Personal narratives.
    2. United States—History—Revolution, 1775-1783—Campaigns.
    I. Title.
    [E203.W45   1991]
    973.3—dc20   91-20121
                                                                CIP

Printed in the United States of America
Original hardcover design by Stan Drate

BOOKS ARE AVAILABLE AT QUANTITY DISCOUNTS WHEN USED TO PROMOTE PRODUCTS OR SERVICES. FOR INFORMATION PLEASE WRITE TO PREMIUM MARKETING DIVISION, PENGUIN BOOKS USA INC., 375 HUDSON STREET, NEW YORK, NEW YORK 10014.

To my nearest four:
Margaret Wheeler, my mother
Margery and Henry Mattox, my sister and brother-in-law
And Kathleen Bross, a much-valued friend

FOREWORD

One of the greatest narratives in our history is the story of the American Revolution, and there is just one thing wrong with it. It is too familiar. We know it by heart, and the people in it have come to seem remote and unreal. They are figures out of a pageant, rather than sorely beset mortals whose desperate efforts to cope with immense problems provided history with one of its greatest turning points, and although the pageant is noble and inspiring it contains no surprises. We know how it is going to come out, and it is all too easy to feel that the outcome was predestined all along; we feel that we can detect the presence of a character standing just offstage with a script in his hands, making sure that the prepared events follow one another in proper order. From George Washington down to the humblest Continental private, the people in the pageant have come to look like figures from a gigantic frieze, moving across the stage with majesty but without much dramatic impact. They were hot, passionate men, but the years have turned them to marble.

The historian who wants to present this story to the general reader faces a formidable task. It is up to him to turn the men in the frieze back into human beings; to make it clear that the men who made the Revolution were not following a script but were simply improvising, going one step at a time as people do today, trying to meet each morning's problem without giving a thought to destiny. In a sense, the challenge is to turn the majestic pageant into a moving, suspenseful melodrama.

It seems to me that Richard Wheeler, the author of this book, has done this job very well. He has done it in the simplest way imaginable—the simplest, and the most effective. He has let the men of the Revolution speak for themselves. They do not declaim, or recite carefully contrived lines; they just talk, and as they do they reveal themselves and the nature of the struggle they were engaged in; and suddenly we find ourselves getting a fresh understanding of the men and events involved. Mr. Wheeler presents his material in short takes, quoting everyone and anyone, providing enough bridge material and connective tissue of his own to tie the narrative together, and in the end he produces a compact, integrated narrative that has a realistic freshness.

Everything is here, from Paul Revere's ride to the climactic scene at Yorktown. For the reader who cannot keep his Revolutionary chronology straight and has trouble remembering just how the incidents in the long sequence dovetailed together, this is just the book; which is to say that it will tell him what happened when and where, and how it tied in with the final outcome. For the more discursive reader, who appreciates the value of the seemingly irrelevant anecdote, he offers excellent fare.

It is interesting, for example, to know about the militiaman who, growing weary of military life and deserting, carried with him a cannon ball because he felt that his mother could use it when she was pounding mustard.

Everybody knows, of course, that Washington gave a blistering rebuke to General Charles Lee at the battle of Monmouth; but the business somehow gets added point when we find a Virginia officer, who was within earshot, writing that Washington "swore till the leaves shook on the trees." (Apparently a connoisseur of forceful language, this officer added: "Charming, delightful!")

Then there was a joint Franco-American assault on the British lines at Savannah, in the fall of 1779. An advanced French battery was vigorously bombarding the British position, and the officer sent back for a keg of beer to refresh his gunners, the action being hot. By mistake someone sent forward a keg of rum, instead; the cannoneers got all awry-eyed and began bombarding their own lines; and in the end the assault had to be called off.

A Pennsylvania Quaker stands by the road to watch Lord Howe's Britishers approach Philadelphia, and notes that the ranking officers are "short, portly, well dressed and of genteel appearance," with skins so white and delicate that it is hard to believe that they have really undergone any hardship; and one of them calls out to the Quaker, "You have got a hell of a fine country here."

Incidents like these have no real importance, to be sure, but they do help us to see the real people back of that marble frieze. And that, it seems to me, is what the story of the Revolution needs more than it needs anything else. We understand the significance of the Revolution, the forces that led up to it, the tremendous events that it finally set in motion; what Mr. Wheeler tries to do is re-introduce us to the men who were immediately involved. This he does admirably, and *Voices of 1776* is a joy to read.

—Bruce Catton

PREFACE

Voices of 1776 was first published in 1972 in anticipation of the Revolution's bicentennial. The present edition anticipates the year 2000 with the view that the war deserves remembrance as one of the millennium's greatest events. The year 1776 launched an experiment in democracy that has shown a remarkable aptitude for survival and, in spite of its imperfections, has functioned to the greater good of the world.

Those who were part of the Revolution's clamor and violence left behind them millions of words: histories, autobiographies, personal narratives, journals, diaries, reports, letters, and newspaper items. *Voices of 1776* endeavors to link together a selection of quotations from this vast record in such a way as to present an authentic eyewitness account of the military side of the war from the first shots at Lexington, Massachusetts, in 1775 to the surrender of Cornwallis at Yorktown, Virginia, in 1781. The editor has had to intrude as author, adding words of his own for the sake of illumination and continuity, but the greater part of the book belongs to the war's participants.

The quotations were chosen first for veracity, and only second for interest and color. Not all are presented exactly as they were first penned. Many original manuscripts of the period are so heavily laden with abbreviations and intrasentence capital letters that they strain the eye. Happily, early scholars who studied this material passed much of it down to us in a reliably edited form. They made no embellishments. The syntax wasn't improved. Often they allowed even serious misspellings to stand. Their only intention was to make the material a little easier to read. For the same reason, in the present work some alterations have been made in paragraphing, capitalization, punctuation, and, occasionally, in spelling. Any other tampering that has been done—for the sake of clarity and conciseness, and also to rid certain passages of faulty information—is clearly indicated by brackets and ellipses.

CONTENTS

ILLUSTRATIONS

MAPS

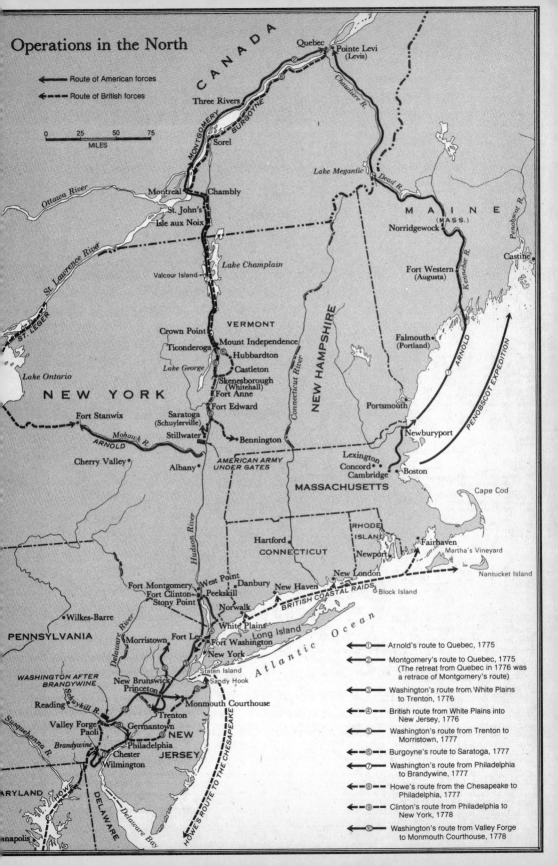

Operations in the North

Legend:
→ Route of American forces
⇢ Route of British forces

0　25　50　75
MILES

CANADA

Quebec
Pointe Levi (Levis)
Chaudière R.
Three Rivers
MONTGOMERY
BURGOYNE
Sorel
Lake Megantic
Dead R.
Montreal
Chambly
St. John's
Isle aux Noix
MAINE (MASS.)
Norridgewock
Ottawa River
St. Lawrence River
ST. LEGER
Lake Champlain
Valcour Island
Fort Western (Augusta)
Kennebec R.
Castine
Penobscot R.
VERMONT
Crown Point
Mount Independence
Ticonderoga
Hubbardton
Lake George
Castleton
Skenesborough (Whitehall)
Fort Anne
Falmouth (Portland)
ARNOLD
PENOBSCOT EXPEDITION
NEW YORK
Lake Ontario
Fort Stanwix
Mohawk R.
ARNOLD
Saratoga (Schuylerville)
Stillwater
Fort Edward
Bennington
Portsmouth
Newburyport
NEW HAMPSHIRE
Connecticut River
Cherry Valley
Albany
AMERICAN ARMY UNDER GATES
Lexington
Concord
Cambridge
Boston
Cape Cod
MASSACHUSETTS
Hudson River
RHODE ISLAND
Hartford
CONNECTICUT
Newport
Fairhaven
Martha's Vineyard
Nantucket Island
Block Island
Wilkes-Barre
Fort Montgomery
West Point
Danbury
New Haven
New London
BRITISH COASTAL RAIDS
Fort Clinton
Stony Point
Peekskill
Norwalk
PENNSYLVANIA
Delaware River
Morristown
White Plains
Fort Lee
Fort Washington
Long Island
New York
Atlantic Ocean
WASHINGTON AFTER BRANDYWINE
New Brunswick
Princeton
Staten Island
Sandy Hook
Reading
Schuylkill R.
Trenton
Monmouth Courthouse
Valley Forge
Paoli
Germantown
NEW JERSEY
Susquehanna R.
Philadelphia
Brandywine
Chester
Wilmington
DELAWARE
Delaware Bay
HOWE'S ROUTE TO THE CHESAPEAKE
HOWE
MARYLAND
napolis

Legend (right side):
① Arnold's route to Quebec, 1775
② Montgomery's route to Quebec, 1775 (The retreat from Quebec in 1776 was a retrace of Montgomery's route)
③ Washington's route from White Plains to Trenton, 1776
④ British route from White Plains into New Jersey, 1776
⑤ Washington's route from Trenton to Morristown, 1777
⑥ Burgoyne's route to Saratoga, 1777
⑦ Washington's route from Philadelphia to Brandywine, 1777
⑧ Howe's route from the Chesapeake to Philadelphia, 1777
⑨ Clinton's route from Philadelphia to New York, 1778
⑩ Washington's route from Valley Forge to Monmouth Courthouse, 1778

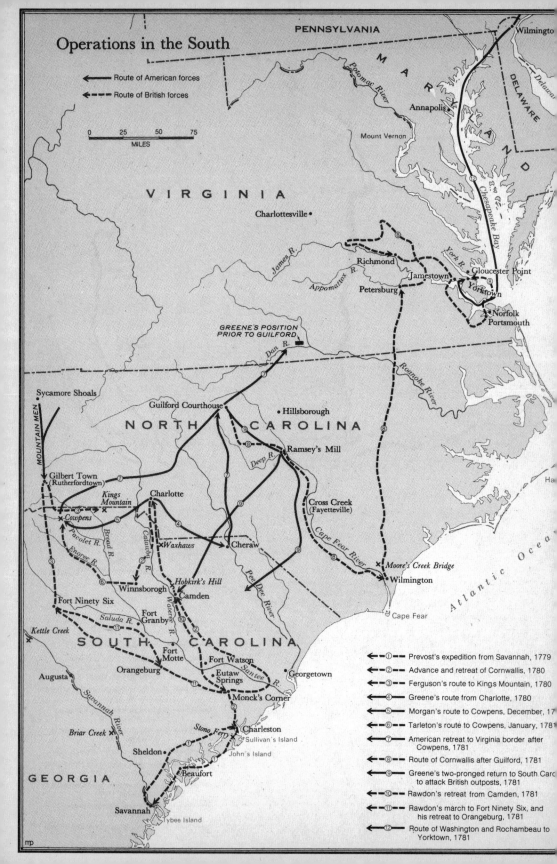

Operations in the South

→ Route of American forces
⇢ Route of British forces

0   25   50   75
MILES

PENNSYLVANIA

M A R Y L A N D

Wilmington

Potomac River

Annapolis

DELAWARE

Delaware

Mount Vernon

Chesapeake Bay

V I R G I N I A

Charlottesville •

James R.

Richmond

York R.

Gloucester Point

Appomattox R.

Jamestown

Yorktown

Petersburg

Norfolk

Portsmouth

GREENE'S POSITION PRIOR TO GUILFORD

Dan R.

Roanoke River

Guilford Courthouse

Hillsborough

N O R T H   C A R O L I N A

Deep R.

Ramsey's Mill

Sycamore Shoals

MOUNTAIN MEN

Gilbert Town (Rutherfordtown)

Kings Mountain

Charlotte

Cross Creek (Fayetteville)

Cowpens

Pacolet R.

Broad R.

Catawba R.

Waxhaws

Cheraw

Cape Fear River

Moore's Creek Bridge

Enoree R.

Winnsborough

Hobkirk's Hill

Camden

Pee Dee River

Wilmington

Fort Ninety Six

Saluda R.

Fort Granby

Wateree R.

Cape Fear

Atlantic Ocean

Kettle Creek

S O U T H   C A R O L I N A

Fort Motte

Fort Watson

Orangeburg

Augusta

Eutaw Springs

Santee R.

Georgetown

Savannah River

Monck's Corner

Briar Creek

Stono Ferry

Charleston

Sheldon

Sullivan's Island

John's Island

G E O R G I A

Beaufort

Savannah

Tybee Island

mp

①⇢ Prevost's expedition from Savannah, 1779
②⇢ Advance and retreat of Cornwallis, 1780
③⇢ Ferguson's route to Kings Mountain, 1780
④⇢ Greene's route from Charlotte, 1780
⑤⇢ Morgan's route to Cowpens, December, 17[ ]
⑥⇢ Tarleton's route to Cowpens, January, 178[ ]
⑦⇢ American retreat to Virginia border after Cowpens, 1781
⑧⇢ Route of Cornwallis after Guilford, 1781
⑨⇢ Greene's two-pronged return to South Caro[ ] to attack British outposts, 1781
⑩⇢ Rawdon's retreat from Camden, 1781
⑪⇢ Rawdon's march to Fort Ninety Six, and his retreat to Orangeburg, 1781
⑫⇢ Route of Washington and Rochambeau to Yorktown, 1781

1

THE OPENING SHOTS

By the *beginning of the year 1775, the long-standing quarrel between the American colonies and their mother country had reached a point where an explosion seemed imminent. And Massachusetts was the powder keg. Boston Harbor held a forbidding array of tall-masted British warships, and the city's streets teemed with occupation troops: proud men in scarlet coats who scoffed at the resentment they stirred, for they believed themselves to be far superior to their American cousins in courage and fighting ability.*

Matters had been building toward a crisis since the end of the French and Indian War in 1763, at which time England determined to tighten her grip on American affairs. The Parliamentary measures implementing the new policy, which was strong on taxation, were seen by the colonists as violations of their constitutional liberties as Englishmen, and they responded with official protests, economic reprisals, and mob actions. Tensions waxed and waned for a decade. During a riot in Boston in 1770, five people were fatally shot by redcoats, and American radicals cried "Massacre!" Two years later, a mob of Rhode Islanders seized and burned the British customs schooner Gaspée.

It was the Boston Tea Party, on December 16, 1773, that led directly to an open break. The steeping of good English tea in American salt water exasperated not only George the Third and his ministers but most of the English people, including many hitherto sympathetic toward American complaints. Parliament retali-

1

ated in early 1774 by voting to shut off Boston's trade and to place Massachusetts under strict royal control. The office of governor went to a military man, General Thomas Gage, who had been serving for years as commander in chief of all British forces in North America.

But the general soon learned that he had little power outside of Boston. The Massachusetts Patriots—or rebels, as the British called them—defiantly established their own provincial congress and set about improving their military status. The militia was reorganized and strengthened. Companies of "minutemen" were formed. As the name implies, these were special units pledged to keep themselves ready for action at a moment's notice. In many villages the martial sound of drum and fife was heard regularly as men of all ages, wearing homespun breeches and gripping worn muskets, trained under graying veterans of the French and Indian War.

Military supplies were busily gathered and stored. A leading depot was the village of Concord, eighteen miles inland from Boston, considered to be out of Gage's reach but handy enough to provide materials for emergency use in the Boston area. Toward spring in 1775 Concord became temporarily the seat of the Second Provincial Congress. Most of the delegates were men who had a fierce will to resist British domination. Part of this will was based on the knowledge that Massachusetts had the strong support of the Patriots in other colonies, both northern and southern.

General Gage, kept informed of events by his spies, found himself in a difficult spot. The home government was urging him to establish his authority by military means, and it seemed his only choice. In mid-April he decided to send a force of about 750 men to seize and destroy the stores at Concord. Along the route, an advance patrol was to try to locate John Hancock and Samuel Adams, two of the leading incendiaries. They were lodging in Lexington, six miles from Concord, having been attending the meetings of the provincial congress. Gage hoped to avoid drastic trouble by sending his men out at night, with orders to maintain as much secrecy as possible. But the Patriots had a spy system that was just as good as Gage's. Paul Revere, who lived in Boston, relates:

In the fall of 1774 and winter of 1775, I was one of upwards of thirty . . . who formed ourselves into a committee for the purpose of watching the movements of the British soldiers, and gaining every intelligence of the movements of the Tories [the Americans siding with the Crown]. We held our meetings at the Green Dragon

Tavern [in Boston]. We were so careful that our meetings should be kept secret that every time we met, every person swore upon the Bible that they would not [reveal] any of our transactions but to Messrs. Hancock, Adams, Doctors [Joseph] Warren, [Benjamin] Church and one or two more. . . . In the winter, towards the spring, we frequently took turns, two and two, to watch the soldiers by patrolling the streets all night.

The Saturday night preceding the 19th of April, about twelve o'clock at night, the boats belonging to the transports were all launched [from shore] and carried under the sterns of the men-of-war. (They had been previously hauled up and repaired.) We likewise found that the grenadiers and light infantry were all taken off duty. From these movements we expected something serious was to be transacted. On Tuesday evening, the 18th, it was observed that a number of soldiers were marching towards the bottom of the Common. About ten o'clock, Dr. Warren sent in great haste for me and begged that I would immediately set off for Lexington, where Messrs. Hancock and Adams were, and acquaint them of the movement, and that it was thought they were the objects. When I got to Dr. Warren's house, I found he had sent an express by land to Lexington—a Mr. William Dawes.

The Sunday before, by desire of Dr. Warren, I had been to Lexington, to Messrs. Hancock and Adams, who were at the Rev. Mr. Clark's. I returned at night through Charlestown. There I agreed with a Colonel Conant and some other gentlemen that if the British went out by water, we [in Boston] would show two lanthorns in the North Church steeple; and if by land, one as a signal; for we were apprehensive it would be difficult [for a messenger] to cross the Charles River or get over Boston Neck.

I left Dr. Warren, called upon a friend and desired him to make the signals. I then went home, took my boots and surtout, went to the north part of the town, where I kept a boat. Two friends rowed me across Charles River, a little to the eastward where the *Somerset* man-of-war lay. It was then young flood, the ship was winding, and the moon was rising. They landed me on the Charlestown side. When I got into town, I met Colonel Conant and several others. They said they had seen our signals. I told them what was acting. . . .

I set off upon a very good horse. It was then about eleven o'clock and very pleasant. After I had passed Charlestown Neck . . . I saw two men on horseback under a tree. When I got near them, I discovered they were British officers. One tried to get ahead of me, and the other to take me. I turned my horse very quick and galloped toward Charlestown Neck, and then pushed for the Medford road. The one who chased me, endeavoring to cut me off, got into a clay pond. . . . I got clear of him, and went through Medford, over the bridge, and up to Menotomy [now Arlington]. In Medford, I awakened the captain of the minute men; and after that I alarmed almost every house, till I got to Lexington.

The people of Lexington already suspected that something momentous was stirring. Among the first to take the alarm was Orderly Sergeant William Munroe, of the militia company commanded by Captain John Parker:

. . . early in the evening of the 18th of . . . April, I was informed by Solomon Brown, who had just returned from Boston, that he had seen nine [mounted] British officers on the road, travelling leisurely, sometimes before and sometimes behind him; that he had discovered, by the occasional blowing aside of their topcoats, that they were armed. On learning this, I supposed they had some design upon Hancock and Adams, who were then at the house of the Rev. Mr. Clark, and immediately assembled a guard of eight men, with their arms, to guard the house. About midnight, Col. Paul Revere rode up and requested admittance. I told him the family had just retired, and had requested that they might not be disturbed by any noise about the house.

"Noise!" said he. "You'll have noise enough before long. The regulars are coming out."

We then permitted him to pass. Soon after, [another messenger] came. These gentlemen came different routes . . . and both brought letters from Dr. Warren in Boston to Hancock and Adams, stating that a large body of British troops had left Boston, and were on their march to Lexington.

According to Lieutenant John Barker, of the King's Own Regiment, the British expedition had trouble getting started:

. . . between 10 and 11 o'clock all the Grenadiers and Light Infantry of the army . . . (under the command of Lt. Col. Smith of the 10th and Major Pitcairn of the Marines), embarked and were landed upon the opposite shore on Cambridge Marsh. Few but the commanding officers knew what expedition we were going upon. After getting over the marsh, where we were wet up to the knees, we were halted in a dirty road and stood there . . . waiting for provisions to be brought from the boats and to be divided, and which most of the men threw away, having carried some with 'em.

Ensign Jeremy Lister, of the 10th Regiment of Foot, adds:
We . . . was on our march by one, which was at first through some swamps and slips of the sea till we got into the road leading to Lexington, soon after which the country people begun to fire their alarm guns [and] light their beacons, to raise the country. . . .

Shortly after midnight, Paul Revere and William Dawes rode toward Concord, spreading the alarm as they went. They were soon overtaken by a young doctor named Samuel Prescott, a Concord man who had been in Lexington visiting his sweetheart. He decided to aid them in their mission. About two miles farther on, the riders suddenly were challenged by a group of mounted redcoats. Dawes and Prescott managed to gallop clear, but Revere was captured. He had company, for this was the patrol that Solomon Brown had seen earlier; and now Brown and two other Lexington men, Elijah Sanderson and Jonathan Loring, were in its hands. The patrol had passed through Lexington, and the trio had been taken while trying to follow it and keep it under surveillance. Not long after taking Revere, the British began herding the four captives, astride their horses, back toward Lexington. Says Elijah Sanderson:
When we had arrived within fifty or one hundred rods of the meeting-house,* Loring . . . told them, "The bell's a ringing, the town's alarmed, and you're all dead men!" They then stopped—conferred together. One of them dismounted, and ordered me to dismount, and said to me, "I must do you an injury." I asked him what he was going to do to me now. He made no reply, but . . . cut my bridle and girth. . . .

The same was done to the horses of Loring and Brown, and the three Lexington men were released. Revere was still in custody as the ride was resumed. A moment later, some gunfire was heard in the village—doubtless an alarm volley by the assembling militia. The British stopped again, and Revere noted that they were now greatly concerned:
The major inquired of me how far it was to Cambridge, and if

---

* One rod equals 16.5 feet, or 5.5 yards; thus, Sanderson means 275 to 550 yards, or, splitting the difference, about a quarter of a mile from the meeting-house.

there were any other road. After some consultation, the major rode up to the sergeant and asked if his horse was tired. He answered him he was. . . . "Then," said he, "take that man's horse." I dismounted, and the sergeant mounted my horse. . . .

The British left Revere standing on the moonlit road. He watched them ride quickly past the meetinghouse and back toward Cambridge, seemingly intent upon joining the main expedition. Then: "I went across the burying-ground and some pastures, and came to the Rev. Mr. Clark's house, where I found Messrs. Hancock and Adams. I told them of my treatment, and they concluded to go from that house towards Woburn [and greater safety]. I went with them. . . ." Orderly Sergeant William Munroe escorted the party to the outskirts of Lexington, and then returned to the town's center:

I found Capt. Parker and his militia company paraded on the common, a little in the rear of the meeting-house. About that time, one of our messengers, who had been sent toward Cambridge to get information of the movement of the regulars, returned and reported that he could not learn that there were any troops on the road from Boston to Lexington, which raised some doubt as to their coming. . . .

Militiaman Ebenezer Munroe takes up:

The weather being rather chilly, after calling the roll, we were dismissed, but ordered to remain within call of the drum. The men generally went into the tavern adjoining the common. . . . The last person sent [toward Cambridge] was Thaddeus Bowman, who returned between daylight and sunrise and informed Capt. Parker that the British troops were within a mile of the meeting-house. Capt. Parker immediately ordered the drum beat to arms. I was the first that followed the drum. I took my station on the right of our line, which was formed from six to ten rods back of the meeting-house, facing south.

About seventy of our company had assembled when the British troops appeared. Some of our men went into the meeting-house, where the town's powder was kept. . . . When the regulars had arrived within eighty or one hundred rods, they, hearing our drum beat, halted, charged their guns, and doubled their ranks, and marched up at quick step. Capt. Parker ordered his men to stand their ground, and not to molest the regulars unless they med-

THE OPENING SHOTS 7

dled with us. The British troops came up directly in our front. The commanding officer advanced within a few rods of us and exclaimed, "Disperse, you damned rebels! You dogs, run!—Rush on, my boys!" and fired his pistol.

The British version of the encounter's opening is different. In the words of Colonel Francis Smith, the expedition's top commander:

Our troops advanced toward them, without any intention of injuring them, further than to inquire the reason of their being thus assembled, and if not satisfactory, to have secured their arms; but they in confusion went off, principally to the left—only one of them fired before he went off, and three or four more jumped over a wall and fired from behind it among the soldiers; on which the troops returned it. . . .

The contradictory statements as to who fired the first shot were never to be reconciled. The Americans, being hopelessly outnumbered, shortly began dispersing. But at least some of the men stood their ground long enough to take some British fire. One of these was Lieutenant William Tidd:

They . . . fired upon us. I then retreated up the north road, and was pursued about thirty rods by an officer on horseback (supposed to be Maj. Pitcairn), calling out to me, "Damn you, stop, or you are a dead man!" I found I could not escape him unless I left the road. Therefore I sprang over a pair of bars, made a stand, and discharged my gun at him; upon which he immediately returned to the main body. . . .

Corporal John Munroe's departure from the field was less precipitate:

After the first fire of the regulars, I thought, and so stated to Ebenezer Munroe . . . who stood next to me on the left, that they had fired nothing but powder; but, on the second firing, Munroe said they had fired something more than powder, for he had received a wound in his arm; and now, said he, to use his own words, "I'll give them the guts of my gun." We then both took aim at the main body of the British troops—the smoke preventing our seeing anything but the heads of some of their horses—and discharged our pieces.

After the second fire from the British troops, I distinctly saw Jonas Parker struggling on the ground, with his gun in his hand, apparently attempting to load it. In this situation the British came up, run him through with the bayonet, and killed him on the spot.

After I had fired the first time, I retreated about ten rods, and then loaded my gun a second time, with two balls, and, on firing at the British, the strength of the charge took off about a foot of my gun barrel. Such was the general confusion, and so much firing on the part of the British, that it was impossible for me to know the number of our men who fired immediately on receiving the second fire from the British troops; but that some of them fired, besides Ebenezer Munroe and myself, I am very confident. The regulars kept up a fire, in all directions, as long as they could see a man of our company in arms.

Elijah Sanderson was a witness to one of the fight's closing incidents:

After our militia had dispersed, I saw [the British] firing at one man (Solomon Brown) who was stationed behind a wall. I saw the wall smoke with the bullets hitting it. . . . [Brown] fired into a solid column of them, and then retreated. . . . The wall saved him. He legged it just about the time I went away.

The brief encounter left eight Americans dead and about ten wounded. Only one man had been wounded among the British, who now fired a victory volley into the air and gave three cheers. Soon afterward, while Lexington's stunned citizens watched, the red-coated men formed into columns, and, to the tune of fife and drum, started for Concord. According to Lieutenant John Barker, of the King's Own, the march there was uneventful:

We met with no interruption till within a mile or two of the town, where the country people had occupied a hill which commanded the road. The Light Infantry were ordered away to the right and ascended the height in one line, upon which the Yankies quitted it without firing, which they did likewise for one or two more successively.

The American numbers were small, and there was uncertainty as to what had happened at Lexington and as to what the British intended; therefore the militia commanders had decided against making a stand. In the words of Concord Minuteman Amos Barrett: "We marched into town [and through it] and over the north bridge

*a little more than half a mile, and then on a hill . . . where we could
see and hear what was going on."*

*With the sun glistening on their arms, the redcoats advanced to
the green in the middle of town, an area from which most of the
residents had fled. The columns drew up there, but some of the
troops were shortly given missions. One detachment was sent to
seize control of a bridge to the south. The movements of a second
detachment are explained by a British ensign named Henry de
Berniere, who was acquainted with the region, having been there
a few weeks earlier as a spy:*

Capt. Parsons of the 10th was dispatched with six light companies [about two hundred men] to take possession of a bridge that
lay three-quarters of a mile from Concord [the North Bridge], and
I was ordered to shew him the road there, and also to conduct him
to a house where there was some cannon and other stores hid. When
we arrived at [and crossed] the bridge, three companies under the
command of Capt. Laurie of the 43d were left to protect it. These
three companies were not close together, but situated so as to be
able to support each other. We then proceeded [past the rebels on
the hill] to Col. Barrett's, where the stores were. We did not find
so much as we expected, but what there was we destroyed.

*There was an excellent reason why few important stores were found
at Barrett's—or elsewhere. The Patriots had been alerted early
enough so that, working urgently, they were able to transfer some
of the things to safer towns, and to hide other items in cellars, attics,
and nearby patches of woods.*

*At the North Bridge, meanwhile, the situation was becoming
taut. The Americans who had occupied the hill—men of Concord
and neighboring Lincoln—were being joined by militia units from
other villages scattered about Concord; and as the force increased
in size it increased also in aggressive spirit. Among the British
officers who anticipated trouble was Lieutenant Barker:*

During this time the [rebels] . . . taking advantage of our scattered disposition, seemed as if they were going to cut off the communication with the bridge, upon which the two companies [near-
est the rebels] joined and [fell back] to the bridge to support that
company. The three companies drew up in the road the far side
the bridge . . . [facing] the rebels on the hill above, covered by a
wall. In that situation they remained a long time, very near an hour,
the three companies expecting to be attacked. . . .

Capt. Laurie, who commanded these three companies, sent to Col. Smith begging he would send more troops . . . and informing him of his situation. The Col. ordered 2 or 3 companies, but put himself at their head, by which means [he] stopt 'em from being time enough, for being a very fat heavy man he would not have reached the bridge in half an hour, though it was not half a mile to it.

An incident that was to affect matters at the bridge was now occurring in the center of the town, where several hundred of Colonel Smith's men remained. One of the few residents who hadn't fled this area was an elderly and poor "widow woman" named Martha Moulton. A large party of redcoats had invaded her home beside the green and had made it their headquarters. Mrs. Moulton's involvement in the day's events was later to prompt her to petition Massachusetts for a financial reward (which she was granted):

. . . all on a sudden they . . . set fire to the great gun carriages just by the house, and while they were in flames your petitioner saw smoke arise out of the Town House higher than the ridge of the house. Then your petitioner did put her life, as it were, in her hand, and ventured to beg of the officers to send some of their men to put out the fire; but they took no notice, only sneered. Your petitioner, seeing the Town House on fire, and must in a few minutes be past recovery, did yet venture to expostulate with the officers just by her, as she stood with a pail of water in her hand, begging of them to send, etc. . . . [T]hey only said, "O, mother, we won't do you any harm!", "Don't be concerned, mother!" and such like talk.

The house still burning, and knowing that all the row of four or five houses, as well as the school house, was in certain danger, your petitioner (not knowing but she might provoke them by her insufficient pleading) yet ventured to put as much strength to her arguments as an unfortunate widow could think of; and so your petitioner can safely say that, under Divine Providence, she was an instrument of saving the Court House, and how many more is not certain, from being consumed, with a great deal of valuable furniture, and at the great risk of her life. At last, by one pail of water after another, they sent and did extinguish the fire.

Seeing the smoke rising from the village angered the Americans at the bridge. Those who lived in Concord decided that it was time they made a move to defend their homes. At this point, a militia company from Acton, commanded by Captain Isaac Davis, joined the muttering troops. Among the newcomers was Thomas Thorp:

We found a great collection of armed men, from Concord and other towns. There were several hundreds, cannot say how many. The officers seemed to be talking by themselves, and the British were then at the bridge. Our officers joined the others; and in a few minutes . . . Captain Davis returned to his company and drew his sword, and said to the company, "I haven't a man that is afraid to go," and gave the word "March!"

With fifers and drummers playing an especially lively tune called "The White Cockade," the aggregation headed down the hill toward the bridge. There was a general determination "to march into the middle of the town for its defence, or die in the attempt." Major John Buttrick, of Concord, was in charge. The leading unit was the thirty-eight-man Acton company under Isaac Davis. Lieutenant Barker, of the King's Own, describes the British reaction:

. . . Capt. Laurie made his men retire to this side the bridge. . . . As soon as they were over . . . the three companies got one behind the other so that only the front one could fire.

A few of the redcoats had been ordered to linger on the bridge and try to make it impassable by removing some of the planks. This caused Major Buttrick to protest loudly, and he and the other leading Americans quickened their step. The British effort, begun too late anyway, was abandoned. According to Lieutenant Barker, the British next sent a "dropping shot" toward the Americans. Minuteman Thaddeus Blood confirms this:

I saw where the ball threw up the water about the middle of the river, and then a second and third shot [did the same]. . . .

These were intended as warning shots. But the Americans didn't stop. Now the British fired for effect; and Major Buttrick, hearing a young Acton fifer cry out that he had been hit, shouted excitedly, "Fire, fellow soldiers! For God's sake, fire!" In a general exchange that lasted but a few minutes, two Americans and two redcoats were killed. The Americans had only two or three wounded, while the British had about ten. One of the Americans slain was the gallant Captain Davis. His widow was later to write:

He was then thirty years of age. We had four children; the

youngest about fifteen months old. They were all unwell when he left me in the morning; some of them with the canker-rash. . . . My husband said little that morning. He seemed serious and thoughtful; but never seemed to hesitate as to the course of his duty. As he led the company from the house, he turned himself round, and seemed to have something to communicate. He only said, "Take good care of the children," and was soon out of sight.

Outnumbered by the Americans, and poorly deployed, the redcoats retreated in confusion; and the Americans swept across the bridge and occupied the abandoned area. An overexcited American youth, wielding a hatchet, split the skull of a redcoat lying wounded on the ground. Now a large number of the enemy were seen approaching from town. Minuteman Amos Barrett relates:

We were ordered to lay behind a wall that run over a hill, and when they got nigh enough, Major Buttrick said he would give the word fire. But they did not come quite so near as he expected. . . . The commanding officer ordered the whole battalion to halt, and officers to the front. . . . Then we lay behind the wall, about 200 of us, with our guns cocked, expecting every minute to have the word fire. Our orders was if we fired, to fire 2 or three times and then retreat. If we had fired, I believe we could have killed almost every officer there was in the front; but we had no orders to fire. . . . They staid about 10 minutes and then marched back. . . .

Solomon Smith, of Acton, tells of another incident:

After a short time, we dispersed, and without any regularity went back over the bridge. While we were there, the [British] detachment which had been to destroy stores at Col. Barrett's returned and passed us. . . . It was owing to our want of order and our confused state that they were not taken prisoners. They passed . . . two of their number who had been killed, and saw that the head of one had been split open. It was said this circumstance gave them the impression that the Americans would give no quarter.

Observing the scene of action from his home (the Manse), which stood near the bridge, was the Reverend William Emerson, grandfather of the more famous Emerson:

For half an hour, the enemy, by their marches and countermarches, [showed] great fickleness and inconstancy of mind, sometimes advancing, sometimes returning to their former posts; till at length they quitted the town and retreated by the way they came. In the meantime, a party of our men (150) took the back way through the Great Fields into the east quarter and had placed themselves to advantage, lying in ambush behind walls, fences and buildings, ready to fire upon the enemy on their retreat.

These Americans were joined by many others, some of them newly arrived in the Concord area; and the British suddenly found themselves in serious trouble. Says Ensign De Berniere:

All the hills on each side of us were covered with rebels . . . so that they kept the road always lined and a very hot fire on us without intermission. We at first kept our order, and returned their fire as hot as we received it; but when we arrived within a mile of Lexington our ammunition began to fail, and the light companies were so fatigued with flanking [maneuvering to protect the column's flanks] they were scarce able to act; and a great number of wounded, scarce able to get forward, made a great confusion.

Col. Smith (our commanding officer) had received a wound through his leg; a number of [other] officers were also wounded; so that we began to run rather than retreat in order. The whole behaved with amazing bravery, but little order. We attempted to stop the men and form them two deep, but to no purpose; the confusion increased rather than lessened. At last, after we got through Lexington, the officers got to the front and presented their bayonets, and told the men if they advanced they should die. Upon this they began to form under a very heavy fire. ·

In the. best romantic tradition, help reached the anguished redcoats at the moment of their greatest need. It came in the form of a thousand reinforcements from Boston under Brigadier General Hugh, Earl Percy. Some lively work by Percy's two fieldpieces soon put a temporary end to the American sniping.

Elijah Sanderson of Lexington tells what happened after the British took a short rest:

. . . they set fire to Deacon Loring's barn; then to his house; then to widow Mulliken's house; then to the shop of Nathaniel Mulliken, a watch and clock maker; and to the house and shop of Joshua Bond.

It was now midafternoon. Aware that fresh American units were still gathering, Lord Percy ordered the entire British column to retire to Boston, a march of about twelve miles. De Berniere writes:

The rebels . . . kept firing on us, but very lightly until we came to Menotomy [Arlington], a village with a number of houses in little groups extending about half a mile. Out of these houses they kept a very heavy fire. . . . The soldiers shewed great bravery in this place, forcing houses . . . and killing great numbers of rebels.

De Berniere exaggerates the slaughter. He doesn't mention the looting. In the words of the Reverend William Gordon of Roxbury: "Many houses were plundered of everything valuable that could be taken away, and what could not be carried off was destroyed; looking glasses, pots, pans, etc., were broke all to pieces; doors . . . sashes and windows wantonly damaged and destroyed." Lieutenant Frederick Mackenzie, of the Royal Welsh Fusiliers, viewed the depredation with concern: "I have no doubt this inflamed the rebels, and made many of them follow us farther than they would otherwise have done. By all accounts some soldiers who staid too long in the houses were killed. . . ." Attempts were made to start more fires. One of the homes chosen was that of Deacon Joseph Adams. He had just fled, at his wife's agonized insistence. She relates:

Divers of the King's troops entered our house by bursting open the door; and three of the soldiers broke into the room in which I was confined to my bed, being scarcely able to walk from the bed to the fire, not having been to my [room's] door [since] being delivered in child-bed to that time. One of the soldiers immediately opened my [bed] curtain with his bayonet fixed, pointing the same at my breast. I immediately cried out, "For the Lord's sake, do not kill me!"

He replied, "Damn you!"

One that stood near said, "We will not hurt the woman if she will go out of the house, but we will surely burn it."

I immediately arose, threw a blanket over me, and crawled into a corn-house near the door, with my infant in my arms. . . . They immediately set the house on fire, in which I had left five children [in hiding places]; but the fire was happily extinguished. . . .

The highest-ranking American officer on the field at this time was General William Heath. Because of the disordered nature of the action, his control was limited. But he encouraged the men by riding often where the fire was hottest:

. . . I was several times greatly exposed, in particular at the high grounds at the upper end of Menotomy, and also on the plain below the meeting-house. . . . On this plain, Dr. Eliphalet Downer, in single combat with a British soldier, killed him on the spot by thrusting him nearly through the body with his bayonet.

The sniping and skirmishing continued as the British pressed on through Cambridge and today's Somerville. Daylight was beginning to fade as the weary marchers headed for the narrow neck of the Charlestown peninsula. They intended to cross from this peninsula to Boston by water. The people of Charlestown, feeling trapped on their small triangle of land, took great alarm as the column approached. Jacob Rogers and his family, among others, decided to try to beat the British to the neck, in hopes of slipping to safety on the mainland. Rogers narrates:

. . . I got my chaise, took my wife and children, and . . . drove into the main street, put my children in a cart with others then driving out of town . . . and followed after [in the chaise with Mrs. Rogers]. Just abreast of Captain Fenton's, on the neck of land, Mr. David Waitt, leather-dresser, of Charlestown, came riding in full speed from Cambridge, took hold of my reins, and assisted me to turn [back and] up on Bunker's Hill, as he said the troops were then entering the common [on the mainland side of the neck].

The cart filled with children had continued on across the neck directly into the face of the British column. A few wild shots came their way, but then they were allowed to leave the scene in safety. Jacob Rogers continues:

I had just reached the summit of the hill, dismounted from the chaise, and tied it fast in my father-in-law's pasture, when we saw the troops within about forty rods of us. . . . One Hayley, a tailor . . . with his wife, and a gun on his shoulder, going towards them, drew a whole volley of shot on himself and us, that I expected my wife, or one of her sisters, who were with us, to drop every moment.

It being now a little dark, we proceeded with many others . . . till we arrived at Mr. Townsend's, pump-maker, in the training field. On hearing women's voices, we went in, and found [Mr. Townsend], Captain Adams . . . Mr. Samuel Carey . . . and some others, and a house full of women and children, in the greatest terror, afraid to go to their own habitations.

After refreshing ourselves, it being then dark, Mr. Carey, myself, and one or two more, went into town to see if we might, with safety, proceed to our own houses. On our way, met a Mr. Hutchinson, who informed us all was then pretty quiet; that when the [British] soldiers came through the street, the officers desired the women and children to keep indoors for their safety; that they begged for drink, which the people were glad to bring them, for fear of their being ill-treated.

Mr. Carey and I proceeded to the tavern by the Town House, where the [British] officers were. All was tumult and confusion; nothing but drink called for everywhere. I stayed a few minutes, and proceeded to my own house; and finding things pretty quiet, went in search of my wife and sisters, and found them coming up the street with Captain Adams. On our arrival at home, we found that her brother, a youth of fourteen, was shot dead (on the neck of land) by the soldiers as he was looking out of a window. I stayed a little while to console them, and went into the main street to see if all was quiet. . . .

It was. The day's strife was over. The Americans had wisely decided not to attempt an assault across the neck. And during the night the British embarked in small boats for Boston.

The trip to Concord and back had cost the British 73 killed, 174 wounded, and 26 missing. American losses were 49 killed, 39 wounded, and 5 missing. In all, about 1,800 redcoats had taken part in the action. The American total is unknown, but was doubtless higher than that of the British. Military annals list few feats of endurance more remarkable than that of the redcoats of the original party. Heavily encumbered with equipage, they had, in about twenty hours, marched thirty-five or forty miles—half of the distance under almost constant attack.

When the Americans gave up the chase, they did not go home. Still being joined by fresh units, they formed a great semicircle about Boston. Thus the king's troops, who had long held American soldiers in contempt, found themselves not only vanquished by these ill-trained rustics but also solidly besieged.

2

TO ARMS! TO ARMS!

ON APRIL 21, 1775, a twenty-one-year-old doctor named James Thacher, who lived in the Massachusetts town of Barnstable, about sixty miles southeast of Boston, recorded in his journal:

Intelligence is now received that the British regulars have marched out of Boston and actually commenced hostilities against our people. . . . For the purpose of ascertaining the particular facts, I have been desired to wait on Colonel Otis [James Otis, Sr.] at his mansion in this town. It was in the evening when I found this dignified patriot in his easy chair, with several of his neighbors listening with agitated spirits to some account of this first most awful tragedy. The good old gentleman had received a letter containing a statement of some particulars, and with manifest trepidation he . . . [related them, saying in conclusion,] "The fearful day has arrived! A civil war has actually commenced in our land. We must be prepared for the worst, and may God preserve and protect our country."

This tragical event seems to have electrified all classes of people. The brave are fired with manly resentment, the timid overwhelmed in despair; the patriotic whigs sorrowing over public calamities, while the tories indulge the secret hope that the friends of liberty are about to receive their chastisement. The sword is now unsheathed, and our friends are slaughtered by our cruel enemies. Expresses are hastening from town to town, in all directions through the country, spreading the melancholy tidings and inspiriting and rousing the people *To Arms! To Arms!* . . . Never was a cause more just, more sacred, than ours. We are commanded to defend the rich inheritance bequeathed to us by our virtuous ancestors; and it is our bounden duty to transmit it uncontaminated to posterity. We must fight valiantly. . . .

The reaction to April 19 in Philadelphia, the largest city in the colonies, is described by James Wilkinson, whose scandal-charged career as a top army commander and associate of Aaron Burr in the early 1800s makes him one of the more dubious characters in American history. In 1775, he was still a student in Philadelphia's medical school. He writes:

The blow was sudden and unexpected. . . . The citizens were seen assembled in crowds at the corners of the streets. Alarm and terror were excited. . . . Men spoke in whispers, as if afraid of being overheard, and the solemn peal which issued from the bells of Christ Church gave to the conjuncture an air of mournful solemnity. . . . But this submission was short-lived. It soon gave way to indignation, resentment and denunciations.

A leading Loyalist, Judge Thomas Jones of Long Island, New York, tells how the first bloodshed affected the rebels of New York City:

They had wished for it for a long time. They received the news with avidity. Isaac Sears, John Lamb and Donald Campbell . . . paraded the town with drums beating and colours flying (attended by a mob of negroes, boys, sailors and pickpockets), inviting all mankind to take up arms in defence of the "injured rights and liberties of America." The posts were stopped, the mails opened, and the letters read.

In the afternoon, a number of the [rebel] faction . . . seized upon a sloop loaded with provisions for Boston, unloaded her and cast the cargo into the dock. On the same evening the same set of fellows . . . broke open the Arsenal in the City Hall and forcibly took away 1,000 stand of arms belonging to the City Corporation, and delivered them out to the rabble to be used as the demagogues of rebellion should direct.

The whole city became one continued scene of riot, tumult and confusion. Troops were enlisted for the service of rebellion, the Loyalists threatened with the gallows, and the property of the Crown plundered and seized upon wherever it could be found.

The Loyalists, or Tories, of whom there were many thousands, suddenly found themselves in a critical position. Some began making plans to leave the country, and some to join the British army. The majority, however, decided to stay at home, either to do what they could for their beliefs or to pursue a neutral course and try to avoid public notice. To the more ardent Patriots, a Loyalist was "a creature whose head is in England, whose body is in America, and who ought to have its neck stretched." Dr. James Thacher was shortly writing:

Liberty-poles are erected in almost every town and village; and when a disaffected tory renders himself odious by any active conduct, with the view of counteracting the public measures, he is seized by a company of armed men and conducted to the liberty-pole, under which he is compelled to sign a recantation and give bonds for his future good conduct. In some instances . . . individuals have been imprisoned or their names have been published in the newspapers as enemies of their country. It has indeed unfortunately happened that a few individuals . . . have received from the rabble a coat of tar and feathers. . . .

The tories make bitter complaints against the discipline which they receive from the hands of the whigs. Their language is, "You make the air resound with the cry of liberty, but subject those who differ from you to the humble condition of slaves, not permitting us to act, or even think, according to the dictates of conscience." The reply is, "It is one of the first principles of a free government that the majority shall bear rule. . . . We have undertaken the hazardous task of defending the liberties of our country. . . . If you possess not patriotism and courage enough to unite your efforts with ours, it is our duty to put it out of your power to injure the common cause. . . ."

Thanks to determined couriers and strong horses, the news of Lexington and Concord quickly spread to the southern colonies. "This accident," wrote Thomas Jefferson of Virginia, "has cut off our last hopes of reconciliation, and a frenzy of revenge seems to have seized all ranks of people."

Wherever the news was received, the reaction among the patriotic elements of the population was the same. The British were condemned, the woes of Massachusetts were lamented, and steps were taken to strengthen the local militia. The banners under which the men rallied were emblazoned with such mottoes as "Liberty or Death" and "Unite or Die." According to Dr. Thacher's journal:

The maxim adopted by our enemies is "Divide and conquer." We enjoin the command "Unite and be invincible." It is considered infinitely important to encourage and promote a more perfect union among the colonies, and harmony and unanimity among the people.

In fighting spirit at least, the New England states were unified by the time the news of April 19 was two weeks old. Dr. Thacher explains:

The universal voice is, "Starve them out [of Boston]. Drive them from the town, and let his majesty's ships be their only place of refuge." Our Provincial Congress have resolved that [a regular] army of thirty thousand [New Englanders] be immediately raised and established. A considerable number have already enlisted, and, being formed into regiments, have taken their station at Cambridge and Roxbury. The country militia, in great numbers, have arrived from various parts of New England; and the town of Boston is now invested on all sides. And thus is the royal army reduced to the humble position of a besieged garrison.

The British were indeed in a humble spot. Their numbers totaled only about thirty-five hundred, and they were unsure of their ability to repel an attack. In addition, they had the matter of provisions and supplies to worry about. Before April 19, many of their necessities (and luxuries) had been bought from Americans of areas surrounding the town. Especially missed was the fresh beef and mutton that had been available in abundance. The redcoats were now eating mostly salt provisions from their ships.

Boston's American residents, of course, were also unhappy. Dr. Thacher termed their situation "deplorable":

A considerable proportion of the most affluent have removed into the country; but others, from various circumstances, are compelled to remain and suffer all the calamities of a besieged town and precarious subsistence. Instances indeed are not wanting of members of families being torn from each other, women and children flying from their husbands and parents, under the most afflictive and destitute circumstances.

James Lovell, later to become a member of the Continental Congress, was one of Boston's residents at this time. His wife had just pro-duced an addition to the family. On May 3, Lovell wrote to a friend in the Massachusetts town of Newburyport:

Mrs. Lovell has suffered extremely in the head, fears a fixed disorder there; but is I hope only suffering thus through weak-ness. My family is yet with me. 4 children are prepared to go away; and Mrs. Lovell with the rest will follow when able, if I so judge proper. . . . *I* shall tarry if 10 sieges take place. I have determined it to be a duty which I owe the cause and the friends of it, and am perfectly fearless of the consequences.

An ill turn, of a most violent diarhea, from being too long in a damp place, has confirmed Dr. Gardners advice to me not to go into the trenches, where my whole soul lodges nightly. How then can I be more actively serviceable to the friends who think with me [but are gone from the town] than by keeping disagreeable post among a set of villains who would willingly destroy what those friends leave behind them?

Lovell sent another letter to Newburyport a few days later:

Mrs. Lovell begins to mend. Her alarming sweats lessen. 'Tis a miserable little baby in comparison of her former ones; but that is not to be wondered at, considering it as hitherto nurtured by Anxiety.

Elsewhere in the same letter, Lovell states:

It seems impossible that matters can remain long in such a situation as the present. God knows what will be the next alarm, but I trust He will direct it in favor of the oppressed.

3

MISSION TO TICONDEROGA

Though *substantially outnumbering the enemy, the New England troops besieging Boston were woefully short of military equipment. Especially needed were more cannon. The Patriots knew that without strong artillery batteries they had little chance of forcing the British to give up the city and withdraw to their ships. Where to get more cannon? There was a good supply, it was known, at Ticonderoga and Crown Point, two British forts that guarded the southern end of Lake Champlain. The forts were old, decaying, poorly defended, and less than two hundred miles from Boston, though on the lake's New York shore. Not surprisingly, the thoughts of Patriot leaders soon turned toward the northwest.*

Taking the initiative, some prominent members of the Connecticut Assembly authorized the raising of an expedition to attack the forts, and their agents decided to seek the aid of Ethan Allen, of the New Hampshire Grants (now Vermont). Allen was the leader of a group of fighting frontiersmen who called themselves the Green Mountain Boys. For years the group had been active in a border feud between the people of the Grants and the government of New York. To New Yorkers, Allen and his men were known as the Bennington Rioters. Allen, well over six feet tall and remarkably strong, was a man with a knavish disposition and a great capacity for alcohol. He was already a legendary figure, partly because of

bold deeds and a colorful style, and partly because of a talent for
self-promotion. He uses these words to describe his reaction to the
war and to Connecticut's request:

. . . the first systematical and bloody attempt at Lexington, to
enslave America, thoroughly electrified my mind and fully determined me to take part with my country. And while I was wishing
for an opportunity to signalize myself in its behalf, directions
were privately sent to me from the . . . colony . . . of Connecticut to
raise the Green Mountain Boys and, if possible . . . to surprise and
take the fortress Ticonderoga. This enterprise I cheerfully under
took. . . .

Colonel Allen and about 150 Green Mountain Boys, allied with
sixty or seventy men raised in Connecticut and western Massachu-
setts, had marched to a point near Lake Champlain's eastern shore
and were completing their plans for crossing the lake to Ticon-
deroga when a complication developed. Unknown to the expe-
dition's organizers, the Massachusetts Committee of Safety had
authorized Colonel Benedict Arnold to raise a force for the same
purpose. A self-assured, energetic, and impatient man with a special
aptitude for military leadership, Arnold was eager to distinguish
himself in the Patriot cause. He had assigned several officers to do
his recruiting, while he himself, accompanied by a servant, rode
in haste toward the lake to reconnoiter. Learning that he had been
preceded made Arnold unhappy. As for the frontiersmen, they were
openly curious about the smartly uniformed newcomer, who was
obviously a gentleman. One of the expedition's officers tells what
happened:

We were . . . shockingly surprised when Colonel Arnold presumed to contend for the command of those forces that we had
raised, who we had assured should go under the command of their
own officers, and be paid and maintained by the Colony of Connecticut. . . . Mr. Arnold, after we had generously told him our
whole plan, strenuously contended and insisted that he had a right
to command them and all their officers, which bred such a mutiny
among the soldiers which . . . nearly frustrated our whole design, as
our men were for . . . marching home, but were prevented by
Colonel Allen and Colonel [James] Easton, who told them that
[Arnold] should not have the command of them, and if he had,
their pay would be the same . . . but they would damn the pay,

and say they would not be commanded by any others but those they engaged with. . . .

In spite of the anger in the ranks, Benedict Arnold won agreement from Ethan Allen to accompany the expedition as co-commander. This was mainly because the orders that Arnold was carrying augmented the expedition's authority. Allen was well aware that in New York, where the forts were located, the Bennington Rioters were considered common outlaws. But Arnold receives no credit in Allen's account of the attack on Ticonderoga:

. . . I . . . arrived at the lake opposite to Ticonderoga on the evening of the ninth day of May, 1775, . . . and it was with the utmost difficulty that I procured boats to cross the lake. However, I landed eighty-three men near the garrison, and sent the boats back for the rear guard, commanded by Col. Seth Warner. But the day began to dawn, and I found myself under a necessity to attack the fort before the rear could cross the lake; and, as it was viewed hazardous, I harangued the officers and soldiers in the manner following:

"Friends and fellow soldiers— You have, for a number of years past, been a scourge and terror to arbitrary power. Your valour has been famed abroad, and acknowledged, as appears by the advice and orders to me from the general assembly of Connecticut, to surprise and take the garrison now before us. I now propose to advance before you, and in person conduct you through the wicket gate; for we must this morning either quit our pretensions to valour or possess ourselves of this fortress in a few minutes. And in as much as it is a desperate attempt, which none but the bravest of men dare undertake, I do not urge it on any contrary to his will. You that will undertake voluntarily, poise your firelocks."

The men being at this time drawn up in three ranks, each poised his firelock. I ordered them to face to the right; and, at the head of the centre file, marched them immediately to the wicket gate aforesaid, where I found a centry posted, who instantly snapped his fusee at me. [The gun did not discharge.] I ran immediately toward him, and he retreated through the covered way into the parade [ground] within the garrison, gave a haloo, and ran under a bomb-proof [shelter].

My party, who followed me into the fort, I formed on the parade in such a manner as to face the two barracks, which faced each other. The garrison being asleep, except the centries, we gave three huzzas, which greatly surprised them. One of the centries made a pass at one of my officers with a charged bayonet, and slightly wounded him. My first thought was to kill him with my sword, but in an instant [I] altered the design and fury of the blow to a slight cut on the side of the head; upon which he dropped his gun and asked quarter, which I readily granted him, and demanded of him the place where the commanding officer kept.

He shewed me a pair of stairs . . . which led up to a second story . . . to which I immediately repaired, and ordered the commander, Capt. [William] Delaplace, to come forth instantly or I would sacrifice the whole garrison; at which the captain came immediately to the door with his breeches in his hand, when I ordered him to deliver to me the fort instantly, who asked me by what authority I demanded it. I answered, "In the name of the great Jehovah and the Continental Congress."

Actually, it wasn't Captain Delaplace but his second-in-command, Lieutenant Jocelyn Feltham, who faced the Americans without his breeches. According to Feltham's account of the affair, he asked the names of the party's leaders, and what they intended:

. . . I was informed by one Ethan Allen and one Benedict Arnold that they had a joint command. . . . Mr. Allen told me . . . that he must have immediate possession of the fort and all the effects of George the Third . . . Mr. Allen insisting on this with a drawn sword over my head and numbers of his followers' firelocks presented at me, alleging I was commanding officer and to give up the fort, and if it was not complied with, or that there was a single gun fired in the fort, neither man, woman or child should be left alive in the fort. Mr. Arnold begged it in a genteel manner. . . . It was owing to him they were prevented getting into Capt. Delaplace's room, after they found I did not command. Capt. Delaplace, being now dressed, came out, when after talking to him some time they put me back into the room. They placed two sentrys on me and took Capt. Delaplace downstairs.

Ethan Allen continues:

In the mean time, some of my officers had given orders, and . . . sundry of the barrack doors were beat down, and about one-third of the garrison imprisoned. . . . [The garrison] consisted of the said commander, a Lieut. Feltham, a conductor of artillery, a gunner, two serjeants and forty-four rank and file; about one hundred pieces of cannon, one 13-inch mortar, and a number of [guns on] swivels.

This surprise was carried into execution in the gray of the morning of the tenth day of May. . . . The sun seemed to rise that morning with a superior lustre; and Ticonderoga and its dependencies smiled on its conquerors, who tossed about the flowing bowl [got drunk on the fort's liquor] and wished success to Congress and the liberty and freedom of America. . . .

Col. Warner, with the rear guard, crossed the lake and joined me early in the morning, whom I sent off without loss of time, with about one hundred men, to take possession of Crown Point, which was garrisoned with a serjeant and twelve men; which he took possession of . . . as also upwards of one hundred pieces of cannon.

Ethan Allen's satisfaction and pride weren't shared by Benedict Arnold. In a prompt report from Ticonderoga to the Massachusetts Committee of Safety, Arnold complained:

On and before our taking possession here, I had agreed with Colonel Allen to issue further orders jointly . . . since which Colonel Allen, finding he had the ascendancy over his people, positively insisted I should have no command, as I had forbid the soldiers plundering and destroying private property. The power is now taken out of my hands, and I am not consulted, nor have I a voice in any matters. There is here at present near one hundred men, who are in the greatest confusion and anarchy, destroying and plundering private property, committing every enormity, and paying no attention to the publick service. . . . There is not the least regularity . . . but every thing is governed by whim and caprice; the soldiers threatening to leave the garrison on the least affront. Most of them must return home soon, as their families are suffering. . . . Colonel Allen is a proper man to head his own wild people, but entirely unacquainted with military service. . . .

A couple of days later, Benedict Arnold was reporting in a more cheerful tone that the men he had been authorized to recruit were beginning to arrive at the fort. "I . . . expect more every minute. Mr. Allen's party is decreasing, and the dispute between us subsiding."

The campaign against the British of Lake Champlain was not yet over. Command of the lake was held by a sloop-of-war then lying at St. John's, about a hundred miles to the north, across the Canadian border. The vessel had to be dealt with. Benedict Arnold, thanks to the continuing growth of his command, got the edge over Allen as this mission began. Arnold writes:

The afternoon of [May 14], being joined by Captains Brown and Oswald, with fifty men enlisted on the road, they having taken possession of a small [Tory-owned] schooner at Skenesborough [now Whitehall] we immediately proceeded on our way for St. John's. . . .

Ethan Allen, with eighty or ninety men in four batteaux, or river boats, also started north. But he was unable to keep up with the schooner. That vessel herself soon had to cope with contrary winds. She managed to get within thirty miles of her goal by nightfall of the sixteenth, but then glided to a halt as the wind died. Benedict Arnold, however, was determined to go on. The schooner was towing two smaller boats, and he promptly armed them and filled them with crews totaling thirty-five men. According to an unnamed man who kept a journal of the trip's events:

After rowing hard all night, we arrived within half a mile of the place at sunrise, sent a man to bring us information, and in a small creek infested with numberless swarms of gnats and musquetoes, waited with impatience for his return. The man returning, informed us they were unapprised of our coming. . . . We directly pushed for shore, and landed at about sixty rods distance from the barracks. The [British] had their arms, but upon our briskly marching up in their faces, they retired within the barracks, left their arms, and resigned themselves into our hands. We took fourteen prisoners, fourteen stands of arms, and some small stores. We also took the King's sloop, two fine brass field-pieces, and four boats. We destroyed five boats more, lest they should be made use of against us.

Luck had played a considerable part in Benedict Arnold's success. About the same time that Ticonderoga was falling to the Americans, the British in Canada were launching measures to increase the fort's strength. Arnold arrived at St. John's as these measures were maturing. He explains:

The [sloop's] captain was gone to Montreal, and hourly expected with a large detachment for Ticonderoga [and] a number of guns and carriages for the sloop, which was just fixed for sailing. Add to this, there was a captain of forty men at Chambly, twelve miles distant from St. John's, who was expected there every minute with his party; so that it seemed to be a mere interposition of Providence that we arrived at so fortunate an hour.

According to the journalist, the group's departure was also especially favored:

Just at the completion of our business, a fine gale arose from the north. We directly hoisted sail and [started south] in triumph. About six miles from St. John's, we met Colonel Allen. . . .

Allen writes:

. . . [Arnold] saluted me with a discharge of cannon, which I returned with a volley of small arms. This being repeated three times, I went on board the sloop with my party, where several loyal Congress healths were drank.

Arnold's version of the meeting includes unhappier details:

I . . . supplied him with provisions, his men being in a starving condition. He informed me of his intention of proceeding on to St. John's . . . and keeping possession there. It appeared to me a wild, impracticable scheme, and . . . of no consequence, so long as we are masters of the lake. . . .

The journalist adds:

. . . Montreal was near [St. John's], with plenty of men and every necessary for war. Nevertheless, Colonel Allen proceeded. . . .

Benedict Arnold and his party, picking up the schooner along the way, returned to Ticonderoga. In the journalist's words:

It is Colonel Arnold's present design that the Sloop *Enterprise*, as she is called, and the Schooner *Liberty* shall cruise on the lake and defend our frontiers till men, provisions and ammunition are furnished to carry on the war.

Arnold's vessels were the first in history to undertake naval operations under American command.

In a report to the Massachusetts Committee of Safety dated May 23, Arnold had the satisfaction of penning these lines about Ethan Allen:

. . . on the evening of the 18th instant he arrived with his party at St. John's, and hearing of a detachment of men on the road from Montreal, laid in ambush for them. But his people being so much fatigued (when the party were about one mile distant) thought proper to retreat, and crossed the lake at St. John's, where they continued the night. At dawn next day they were, when asleep, saluted with a discharge of grape-shot from six field-pieces, and a discharge of small arms from about two hundred regulars. They made a precipitate retreat. . . .

For a time after Ethan Allen returned to Ticonderoga, he and Arnold were apprehensive that the British in Canada would assemble a fleet of small boats and come southward on the lake and try to regain their forts. The British did consider such a move, but they were not then strong enough—nor certain enough that a war had really begun—to take action. Thus the Allen–Arnold campaign, in spite of its dissensions and the relative modesty of its engagements, turned out to be one of considerable significance. Not only were the desired cannon obtained, but the Americans gained control over an important military route between the colonies and Canada.

4

AMERICA THROWS DOWN
THE GAUNTLET

Dᴜʀɪɴɢ *the activities on Lake Champlain, the Second Continental Congress convened in Philadelphia; and according to
Judge Thomas Jones, the New York Loyalist:*

The British colors were sent to Congress . . . and with great
pomp and ostentation hung up as a trophy in Carpenter's Hall,
where that illegal and unconstitutional body of people were then
sitting.

*Actually, the Allen–Arnold mission had been undertaken without
Congressional authority, and it was now decided that the British
cannon should be held in New York State, near the place of their
capture, and carefully inventoried "in order that they may be
safely returned when the restoration of harmony between Great
Britain and the colonies, so ardently desired by the latter, shall render it prudent and consistent with the overpowering law of self-
preservation."*

*Congress maintained that so far the American people had com-
mitted no acts of aggression, that they had moved solely to meet
the British threat to their security. The delegates also insisted
that they themselves had no aggressive intentions, that they had
convened in the same spirit of self-defense that had given rise to
the first Congress the preceding autumn. They averred that all England had to do to regain the loyalty of the colonists was to abandon*

*her tax schemes and her other infringements on their constitutional
liberties.*

*As if hoping for an agreeable British response, the Congress did
not immediately take a firm stand on the Boston issue. However,
some delegates were privately convinced that the time for modera-
tion was past, and that a bitter struggle lay ahead. In a letter
written late in May, 1775, a Virginian named George Washington
observed.*

Unhappy it is . . . to reflect that a brother's sword has been
sheathed in a brother's breast, and that the once happy and peace-
ful plains of America are either to be drenched with blood or
inhabited by slaves. Sad alternative! But can a virtuous man hesitate in his choice?

*The majority of the people represented by the Congress were
already on a war footing, though many were only meagerly
equipped. Most of the preparations up to this time had been made
by individual localities, working on their own. Nowhere was the
ardor for the cause more in evidence than in the city where the
Congress was sitting. A well-to-do female citizen wrote:*

Our all is at stake; and we are called upon, by every tie that
is dear and sacred, to exert the spirit that Heaven has given us in
this righteous struggle for liberty. . . . My only brother I have sent
to the camp with my prayers and blessings. . . . I am confident
he will behave with honor. . . . And had I twenty sons and
brothers, they should go. I have retrenched every superfluous expense in my table and family. Tea I have not drank since last
Christmas, nor bought a new cap or gown since . . . Lexington.
And what I never did before, have learnt to knit, and am now
making stockings of American wool for my servants; and this way
do I throw in my mite to the public good. . . . Nothing is heard
now in our streets but the trumpet and drum; and the universal
cry is, "Americans to arms!" . . . We have five regiments in the
city and county of Philadelphia. . . . We have companies of light
horse, light infantry, grenadiers, riflemen and Indians, [and] several
companies of artillery. . . .

*A newspaper writer extolled these examples of patriotism else-
where in Pennsylvania:*

The ladies in Bristol Township have evidenced a laudable regard
to the interest of their country. At their own expense they have
furnished the regiment of that county with a suit of colors and

drums, and are now making a collection to supply muskets to such of the men as are not able to supply themselves. We hear [that] the lady who was appointed to present the colors to the regiment [warned] the soldiers never to desert the colors of the ladies if they ever wish that the ladies should list under their banners.

The spirit of opposition to the arbitrary and tyrannical acts of the ministry and parliament of Britain hath diffused itself so universally throughout this province that the people, even to its most extended frontiers, are indefatigable in training themselves to military discipline. The aged as well as the young daily march out under the banners of liberty and [reveal] a determined resolution to maintain her cause even until death.

In the town of Reading, in Berks County, there had been some time past three companies formed, and very forward in their exercise. Since, however, we are well informed, a fourth company have associated under the name of the Old Man's Company. It consists of about eighty Germans of the age of forty and upwards. Many of them have been in the military service in Germany. The person who, at their first assembling, led them to the field is 97 years of age, has been 40 years in the regular service and in 17 pitched battles; and the drummer is 84. In lieu of a cockade, they wear in their hats a black crape as expressive of their sorrow for the mournful events which have occasioned them, at their late time of life, to take arms against our [British] brethren in order to preserve that liberty which they left their native country to enjoy.

As it was in Pennsylvania, so it was in the other colonies. In the words of Charles Lee, who was shortly to become one of the Revolution's top commanders:

No man is better acquainted with the state of this continent than myself. I have run through almost the whole colonies, from the North to the South, and from the South to the North. I have conversed with all orders of men, from the first estated gentlemen to the lowest planters and farmers, and . . . the same spirit animates the whole. Not less than an hundred and fifty thousand gentlemen, yeomen and farmers are now in arms, determined to preserve their liberties or perish.

The universal military preparations did not strengthen America as much as might appear. Most of the men who answered the call to arms had no wish to leave their home territory. They expected to do

Portrait of General Charles Lee published in England in 1775.
(*Library of Congress*)

Portrait of General Israel Putnam published in England in 1775. *(Library of Congress)*

their fighting when they themselves became the target of England's coercive measures.

Even in Massachusetts, the number of Patriots surrounding the British, possibly as high as twenty thousand in the beginning, had diminished. Most of the New England militiamen who had dropped everything to grab the family musket and rush to Boston had expected to begin fighting as soon as they got there. When days passed and nothing happened, many decided to return home and continue with such important affairs as the planting of crops. The assembling of a regular army under competent officers proved a slow and difficult task, and the beginning of June found the siege being maintained by a mixture of about fifteen thousand regulars and militiamen.

The English commander in chief, Thomas Gage, had by this time begun to receive reinforcements from across the sea. New arrivals included three well-known generals: Sir William Howe, Sir Henry Clinton, and John Burgoyne. But Gage's entire force still numbered only about six thousand—not enough to break the siege, let alone put down the rebellion. Hoping to win with words what he could not with arms, Gage issued a proclamation on June 12 that at once defended British actions and appealed for peace. Gage claimed that on April 19 the Americans had been the aggressors, while the British had fired only in self-defense:

Since that period, the rebels . . . have added insult to outrage; have repeatedly fired upon the King's ships and subjects with cannon and small-arms; have possessed the roads and other communications by which the Town of Boston was supplied with provisions; and with a preposterous parade of military arrangement they [have] affected to hold the army besieged. . . .

In this exigency of complicated calamities, I avail myself of the last effort within the bounds of my duty to spare the effusion of blood; to offer . . . in His Majesty's name . . . his most gracious pardon to all persons who shall forthwith lay down their arms and return to their duties of peaceable subjects, excepting only . . . Samuel Adams and John Hancock, whose offences are of too flagitious a nature to admit of any other consideration than that of condign punishment.

The proclamation closed with the warning that thereafter all persons who committed acts hostile to the Crown would be treated as traitors.

Not only were the terms of the paper ignored, but Gage was ridiculed. Dr. James Thacher noted in his journal:

. . . singular as it may appear, this same authorized governor and general-in-chief of the royal army is now cooped up in the town of Boston, panting for a country airing, of which he is debarred by his denounced rebels.

During these same June days, the Congress in Philadelphia was working on a set of measures that its members termed defensive, but which would convince England they were throwing down the gauntlet. Says Judge Thomas Jones:

This Congress . . . issued a declaration of war against Great Britain under the title of "Reasons for taking up arms," ordered [a continental] army raised, appointed generals and other officers to the command of it, struck money for its pay, its clothing and accoutering, and, in short, assumed all the powers of a sovereign state. . . .

The work of the Congress had no effect on mid-June events in Massachusetts. Immediately after General Gage issued his proclamation, he made a decision that quickly brought on another round of combat.

5

THE BATTLE OF BUNKER HILL

G AGE *was far from eager to tangle with the besiegers at this point; but the British position was precarious; it called for action. In the words of "Gentleman Johnny" Burgoyne:*

Boston is a peninsula, joined to the main land only by a narrow neck, which, on the first troubles, General Gage fortified. Arms of the sea and the harbour surround the rest. . . . On one of these arms, to the north, is Charlestown . . . and over it is a large hill. . . . To the south of [Boston] is a still larger scope of ground, containing three hills, joining also to the main by a tongue of land, and called Dorchester Neck. The heights . . . both north and south . . . command the town; that is, give an opportunity of erecting batteries above any that you can make against them, and consequently are much more advantageous. It was absolutely necessary we should make ourselves master of these heights, and we proposed to begin with Dorchester; because, from the particular situation of batteries and shipping . . . it would evidently be effected without any considerable loss. Everything was accordingly disposed. . . .

But the Massachusetts Committee of Safety, with headquarters at Cambridge, two or three miles inland from Boston, received intelligence of the British plan three days before it was to be executed. The committee decided that efforts ought to be made to deny the enemy both objectives, and a council of war was called. In charge

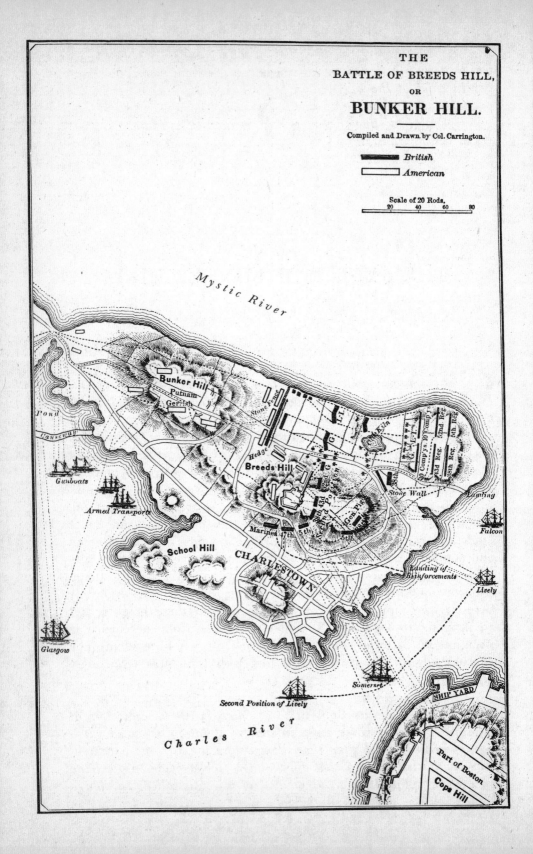

THE BATTLE OF BREEDS HILL,
OR
BUNKER HILL.

Compiled and Drawn by Col. Carrington.

British

American

Scale of 20 Rods.
20   40   60   80

Mystic River

Bunker Hill
Putnam
Gerrish
Stone Fence
Hedge
Breeds Hill

Pond
Causeway

Gunboats

Armed Transports

School Hill

CHARLESTOWN

Glasgow

10 Comp'ys 10 Comp'y 52nd Reg 5th Reg
43d Reg 38th Reg
38th

Redoubt
43d
Gen Pigot
Marines 47th 5th Gen Pre...

Stone Wall

Landing

Falcon

Landing of
Reinforcements

Lively

Somerset

Second Position of Lively

SHIP YARD

Charles River

Part of Boston

Cops Hill

*was a portly Massachusetts general named Artemas Ward, comman-
der in chief of the besieging troops. There was sentiment in the
council for caution, since the troops were poorly organized and
poorly equipped. But the more aggressive officers, rallied by Connecticut's vigorous General Israel Putnam ("Old Put"), argued for
action. The result was that plans were made to begin operations at
once with the occupation of Bunker Hill, on the Charlestown
peninsula. A suitable force was to be assembled by Colonel William
Prescott, a tall and sinewy Massachusetts farmer. Among the men
alerted was Corporal Amos Farnsworth, of the Massachusetts
militia, who kept a diary:*

Friday, June 16 [1775]. Nothing done in the forenoon. In the
afternoon we had orders to be redy to march. At six, agreable to
orders our regiment preadid [paraded] and about sunset we was
drawn up and herd prayers; and about dusk marched for Bunkers
Hill under command of our own Col. Prescott.

*Israel Putnam, eager to help run things, joined Prescott along the
route. It was well after dark when the party, consisting of about
a thousand men accompanied by wagons loaded with entrenching
tools, slipped across the slender neck of the Charlestown peninsula
and climbed to the grassy summit of Bunker Hill. Here General
Putnam urged a change of plan. It would be more advantageous,
he said, if the entrenchments were dug on Breed's Hill, a lower
mound connected to Bunker by a saddle of land and lying immediately north of the buildings of Charlestown and about five hundred
yards closer to the shore that faced Boston. Breed's Hill wasn't
really the better location. Old Put apparently wanted to make certain that the British were forced into a fight. He won his way, and
the party moved down the slope of Bunker Hill and across the
saddle to the lower summit. Breed's Hill, not Bunker, was to be the
scene of the battle, but Bunker Hill would play its part; and, since it
was the commanding height on the small peninsula, it would give
the battle its name.*

*Colonel Prescott says, "We arrived at the spot, the lines were
drawn by the engineer, and we began the intrenchment about
twelve o'clock." The diggers could hear the hour being struck by the
clocks in Boston. Lamps glowed in various parts of the town. Colonel
Prescott, worried about the noises his men could not avoid
making, soon went down the slope on the Boston side to listen for*

sounds of alarm. He was reassured by the cries of "All's well!" that carried across the dark water. On the summit, the work was pushed strenuously. A parapet, or protective barrier, of earth was raised, with the ditch being toward the enemy. One of the diggers was a youth named Peter Brown:

. . . we . . . made a fort of about ten rod long and eight wide. . . . We worked there undiscovered till about 5 in the morn, and then we saw our danger, being against 8 ships of the line and all Boston fortified against us. The danger we were in made us think there was treachery, and that we were brot there to be all slain; and I must and will venture to say that there was treachery, oversight or presumption in the conduct of our officers. And about half after 5 in the morn, we not having above half the fort done, [the British] began to fire. . . .

The shots, along with great red flashes and puffs of white smoke, issued from the cannons of a warship that had been alerted by her sentries. No damaging hits were scored. But the heavy, vibrating noise startled everyone in Boston and other adjacent areas. Many people were jolted out of their sleep. Excited groups began hurrying toward high places to try to learn what was happening.

Even General Gage heard the shots without understanding their meaning:

. . . advice was soon afterwards received that the rebels had broke ground and were raising a battery . . . against the Town of Boston. They were plainly seen at work. . . .

Actually, the surprise should not have been so complete. Sir William Howe fixes the blame:

. . . the centrys on the Boston side had heard the rebels at work all night without making any other report of it except mentioning it in conversation in the morning.

To General Burgoyne, this much was clear:

. . . every hour gave them fresh strength; it therefore became necessary to alter our plan, and attack on that side.

The day—Saturday, June 17—was dawning beautifully. The sky was a clear blue dome, and the waters to the east shimmered with sunlight. But the beauty of their surroundings meant little to the imperiled Americans. According to the Reverend Peter Thacher, a resident of nearby Malden and official historian of the battle for the Committee of Safety:

. . . an heavy fire began from 3 men of war, a number of floating batteries, and from a fortification . . . on Copp's Hill in Boston directly opposite to our little redoubt. These kept up an incessant shower of shot and bombs, by which one man pretty soon fell.

In Colonel Prescott's words:

The . . . man . . . was killed by a cannon ball which struck his head. He was so near me that my clothes were besmeared with his blood and brains, which I wiped off, in some degree, with a handful of fresh earth. The sight was so shocking to many of the men that they left their posts and ran to view him. I ordered them back, but in vain. I then ordered him to be buried instantly.

"Not discouraged by the melancholy fate of their companion," the Reverend Peter Thacher continues, "the soldiers laboured indefatigably till they had thrown up a small [additional] breastwork extending from the north side of the redoubt . . . to the bottom of the hill. . . ." This was on the redoubt's left (away from Charlestown), where Breed's Hill sloped toward the Mystic River. With the extension of the lines, command began to be a problem. The troops had few good leaders. Companies that left the immediate sphere of the able and courageous Prescott lost some of their effectiveness. In the beginning, to inspire the men in the redoubt, the colonel walked its parapet freely, in defiance of the British fire. At the same time, however, he cast an occasional glance toward the rear, where reinforcements might be expected to come from. He knew that Cambridge was aware of his situation, for the church bells were tolling an alarm.

Israel Putnam, astride a strong horse, had made himself a kind of commander at large. He was much concerned with trying to call up the needed support. At the same time, he had some of the men begin secondary entrenchments (which would come to nothing) back on Bunker Hill.

Two other popular men of high rank appeared on the field: elderly Brigadier General Seth Pomeroy, who, like Putnam and Prescott, had fought in the French and Indian War; and young Dr.

Joseph Warren, president of the Massachusetts Provincial Congress, prominent member of the Committee of Safety, and newly appointed major general. Warren was dressed in elegant civilian clothes that attracted much notice. Both men refused positions of command, wishing to serve only as volunteers.

The British, in spite of their original alarm, did not hasten to launch their attack. For a time during the morning they even let up on their cannonading. But then, laments Peter Brown,

. . . they began pretty brisk again; and that caused some of our young country people to desert. . . . We began to be almost beat out, being tired by our labour and having no sleep the night before, but little victuals, no drink but rum.

The redoubt, however, had been brought to a stage where the enemy gunners could make little impression on it. They found it a work of "an extraordinary thickness and solidity."

Our officers [Peter Brown goes on] sent time after time the cannons from Cambridge in the morning, and could get but four, the captain of which fired but a few times and then swang his hat round three times to the enemy, then ceased to fire.

The captain was presumably aiming at the artillery position on Copp's Hill. Generals Burgoyne and Clinton, who were viewing the American lines from this spot, took note of the firing. Burgoyne says: ". . . two cannon balls . . . went a hundred yards over our heads. . . ."

Spectators were now thick not only on Copp's Hill but in many other elevated places surrounding the Charlestown peninsula. There were people on rooftops, in church steeples, and even high among the masts of vessels at the wharves. One of the most spectacular shows in military history was about to begin. The redcoats were at last hurrying about Boston with obvious purpose. An anonymous citizen writes:

At twelve o'clock, the Light Infantry and Grenadiers, with the Fifth, Thirty-Eighth, Forty-Third and Fifty-Second Regiments, embarked on board the transport boats at the Long Wharf and at the north battery. . . .

Sir William Howe was in command. The boats, about forty in number, soon began pushing out from shore. Colonel Prescott, standing on his lofty parapet, watched the flotilla come gliding across the calm blue water. Dozens of oars flashed in the sunlight. Prescott soon perceived that the landing would be made at Morton's Point, about five hundred yards to his left front:

I ordered the [artillery] train, with two field-pieces, to go and oppose them, and the Connecticut forces to support [the move]; but the train marched a different course, and I believe those sent to their support followed. . . .

These detachments went down the left rear of Breed's Hill and out of Prescott's sight. Meeting General Putnam, they were judiciously assigned. The breastwork on the left of Prescott's redoubt was inadequate, since it ended more than two hundred yards short of the Mystic River. A few hundred feet behind the point where the breastwork stopped, there was a long, low stone fence topped by two wooden rails—and it ran in the desired direction. Lieutenant Thomas Grosvenor, of the support troops, was later to explain:

. . . our detachment, in advancing to the post, took [with us] one rail fence and placed it against [the other] . . . and extended our left nearly to Mystic River.

There were not enough men, however, to fill the line effectively. But there were now several hundred reinforcements approaching on the mainland side of Charlestown Neck. Some of these units hesitated when they found that the neck was under steady bombardment from British vessels. Though Colonel John Stark's New Hampshire regiment didn't falter, it didn't rush ahead either. Captain Henry Dearborn relates:

My company being in front, I marched by the side of Col. Stark, who moving with a very deliberate pace, I suggested the propriety of quickening the march of the regiment, that it might sooner be relieved from the galling cross-fire of the enemy. With a look peculiar to himself, he fixed his eyes upon me and observed with great composure, "Dearborn, one fresh man in action is worth ten fatigued ones," and continued to advance in the same cool and collected manner. When we had reached the top of Bunker's Hill . . . the regiment halted for . . . the rear to come up. Soon after, the enemy were discovered to have landed on the shore of Morton's Point. . . .

It had been necessary for General Howe's boats to make two trips to complete the landing. According to the Reverend Peter Thacher:

The brigade formed upon their landing, tho they were something galled by the fire of two small field pieces which we had placed at the [left] end of the intrenchments.

Howe was preparing to make a frontal assault, though he might have avoided this by landing in the American rear and seizing Charlestown Neck, thus bottling up the whole force. The decision to strike from the front had been made by a council of war in Boston. It was felt that the American lines should be assaulted boldly, and that they could be easily carried. But Sir William, upon observing the Americans from a closer position, began to have second thoughts:

Their works . . . were crowded with men, about 500 yards from us. From the appearance of their situation and numbers, and seeing that they were pouring in all the strength they could collect, I sent to General Gage [in Boston] to desire a reinforcement. . . .

On Bunker Hill, the New Hampshire regiment under Colonel Stark had now consolidated and was ready to make its descent to the American lines.

At this moment [says Henry Dearborn] the veteran and gallant Stark harangued his regiment in a short but animated address, then directed them to give three cheers and make a rapid movement to the rail fence which ran . . . towards Mystic River.

Shortly Stark's regiment and the other units at the fence were joined by a few more New Hampshire troops under Colonel James Reed. The men busied themselves improving their breastwork. Newly mown hay was stuffed between the fence rails; and, at Stark's direction, stones from nearby walls were used to extend the barrier down the beach of the Mystic to the water's edge.

In all, there were now fifteen or sixteen hundred Americans occupying an irregular front between the Charlestown side of Breed's Hill and the Mystic. The British were to believe that thousands opposed them, for numerous confused units would mill about in the rear, as far forward as the summit of Bunker Hill, all through the battle.

Time had finally run out for the defense-builders. The British reinforcement had arrived from Boston, and General Howe had his army deployed for action from Charlestown to the Mystic:

Our strength being then about 2200 rank and file [plus artillerymen] with six field pieces, two light 12-pounders and two howitzers, we begun the attack (the troops in two lines, with [General Robert] Pigot upon the left) by a sharp cannonade, the line moving slowly, and frequently halting to give time for the artillery to fire. The Light Companies upon the right were ordered to keep along the beach [of the Mystic] to attack the left point of the enemy's breastwork, which being carried, they were to attack them in flank.

Colonel Prescott was at this time worried about the other extremity of the American defenses. There was nothing to prevent General Pigot's wing from swinging around the redoubt. Prescott made a quick decision: "I commanded my Lieutenant-Col. Robinson and Major Woods, each with a detachment, to flank the enemy. . . ." These men hurried toward Charlestown, which lay to the right-front. Concealing themselves in buildings at the town's edge, they began a sniping fire at the British left.

To the sound of drums and fifes, and under proud banners, the British soldiers advanced with fixed bayonets toward the waiting Patriot line. The Americans lacked training, good leadership, and equipment—even ammunition was in short supply—but they had the important advantage of being hidden, while the British, their scarlet coats and white breeches vivid in the sunlit fields, made excellent targets. According to militiaman Israel Potter, of Rhode Island:

We were now harangued by Gen. Putnam, who reminded us that, exhausted as we were by our incessant labour through the preceding night, the most important part of our duty was yet to be performed, and that much would be expected from so great a number of excellent marksmen. He charged us to be cool, and to reserve our fire until the enemy approached so near as to enable us to see the whites of their eyes. . . .

Over on Copp's Hill, General Burgoyne was viewing the scene with keen attention:

Howe's disposition was exceedingly soldierlike. . . . As his first arm advanced up the hill, they met with a thousand impediments from strong fences, and were much exposed. They were also exceedingly hurt by musketry from Charlestown, though Clinton and I did not perceive it until Howe sent us word by a boat, and desired us to set fire to the town, which was immediately done.

We threw a parcel of [incendiary] shells, and the whole was instantly in flames. . . .

Actually, a British landing party helped with this work. The fire endangered few civilians, for most of Charlestown's families had left this section of "no man's land" weeks earlier. As for the sharp-shooters, they determined to stay at the town's edge, helping to protect Prescott's right flank, as long as they could.

The entrenched Americans, who were still holding their fire, were now forced to take full advantage of their cover. A long-range musketry had been added to the enemy's bombardment. Neither shells nor bullets, though nerve-racking, did much damage. At last, with the British coming through the knee-deep grass only a few rods away—their attack developing chiefly against the central breast-work and the rail fence—the order "Fire!" was shouted, and suddenly hundreds of American muskets crashed almost as one. Says General Burgoyne:

And now ensued one of the greatest scenes of war that can be conceived: if we look to the height, Howe's corps ascending the hill in the face of the intrenchments, and in a very disadvantageous ground, was much engaged; to the left the enemy pouring in fresh troops . . . over the land; and in the arm of the sea our ships and floating batteries cannonading them; straight before us a large and noble town in one great blaze—the church-steeples, being timber, were great pyramids of fire above the rest; behind us, the church-steeples and heights of our own camp covered with spectators; . . . the hills round the country covered with spectators; the enemy all in anxious suspense.

The roar of cannon, mortars and musketry; the crash of [burning] churches, ships upon the stocks, and whole streets falling together, to fill the ear; the storm of the redoubts, with the objects above described, to fill the eye; and the reflection that, perhaps, a defeat was a final loss to the British Empire in America, to fill the mind, made the whole a picture and a complication of horrour and importance beyond any thing that ever came to my lot to be witness to.

A British defeat, in fact, seemed quite possible. Connecticut's Thomas Grosvenor writes:

. . . so precise and fatal was our fire that, in the course of a short time, they gave way and retired in disorder out of musket shot, leaving before us many killed and wounded.

The Americans had surprised themselves. They had, with few losses, beaten off a heavy attack by skilled professional troops! Hats were swung enthusiastically, and a medley of cheers went ringing up and down the lines. Some of the men wanted to bound from cover and chase the foe, but they were restrained by their leaders.

The Reverend Peter Thacher noted that many of the redcoats retreated all the way to the shore where they had landed:

At this time their officers were observed . . . to come there and then use the most passionate gestures, and even to push forward the men with their swords. At length . . . the troops were again rallied. . . .

During the second advance, some of the bolder Americans tried to unnerve the enemy by shouting taunts. According to an officer in Colonel James Abercrombie's Corps of Grenadiers: "When we marched to the attack of their redoubt, they called out, 'Colonel Abercrombie, are the Yankees cowards?'" America's Colonel Prescott tells what followed:

The enemy advanced and fired very hotly on the fort, and meeting with a warm reception, there was a very smart firing on both sides. After a considerable time . . . I commanded a cessation till the enemy advanced within thirty yards. . . .

The renewed fire punished the British severely. Among the officers hit was Colonel Abercrombie. Though his wound seemed a light one, it would cause his death.

As for the British on the right: General Howe's effort to break through the line in that area in order to make a flank attack was failing disastrously. In the words of an unnamed redcoat:

Our Light Infantry were served up in companies against the grass fence, without being able to penetrate. Indeed, how could we penetrate? Most of our Grenadiers and Light Infantry, the moment of presenting themselves, lost three-fourths, and many nine-tenths, of their men. Some had only eight and nine men a company left; some only three, four, and five.

The fate of the second British attack as a whole was noted by Henry

Dearborn from his position near the center of the American lines:

. . . the fire from the redoubt and the rail fence was so well directed and so fatal, especially to the British officers, that the whole army was compelled a second time to retreat with precipitation and great confusion. At this time the ground [which had been] occupied by the enemy was covered with his dead and wounded.

A new wave of elation swept the Americans. They had managed to triumph again, and the majority of them were still unharmed. Sir William Howe, who had been directing the attack with great bravery, had been placed in a critical position. ". . . there was a moment," he was later to admit, "that I never felt before." His landing force was not only badly battered but gravely dispirited. More reinforcements were preparing to come over from Boston, but Howe decided that awaiting their arrival would give the Americans too much time to strengthen themselves. Adding to the general's woes was the carnage among his personal staff; these men had been shot down at such a rate that Howe was more than once left alone on the field. Though he himself remained unhurt, his gaiters were streaked with blood from the grass. Some of his commanders pleaded with him to abandon the attack, but this Howe wouldn't do. Both his own reputation and that of the British army in America were at stake. What he had his troops do next is described by the Reverend Peter Thacher:

. . . having formed once more, they brought some cannon to bear in such a manner as to rake the inside of the breastwork [the central entrenchment], and having drove the provincials thence into the redoubt, they determined now, it appeared, to make a decisive effort. The fire from the ships and batteries, as well as from the cannon in front of their army, was redoubled. Innumerable bombs were sent into the fort. The officers behind the army of the regulars were observed to goad forward their men with renewed exertion.

In the American lines, ammunition was now almost spent. There was enough to inflict more damage, but not to repel another attack. Only the arrival of a strong reinforcement could save the day. General Putnam galloped about among the troops milling in the rear, but all of his pleas and threats failed to send more than a few thinly manned companies forward. Putnam's chief problem was that he lacked real authority. He could expect obedience from his own Connecticut men, but the troops of other provinces were unaccustomed to taking orders from a stranger.

Farther off, a few units of reinforcements were still approaching from Cambridge, among them a spirited company of Connecticut men commanded by Captain John Chester. These men could hear the exchange of close-range musketry beginning on the battlefield as they crossed Charlestown Neck; and they themselves were fired upon by British warships. Angered at finding the approaches to Bunker Hill crowded with delinquent troops, Captain Chester forced some to go forward by threatening to have them shot on the spot.

While Chester and his company were hurrying up Bunker Hill, the Americans in the entrenchments on Breed's were expending the last of their ammunition—with deadly results. The British took drastic punishment, especially in front of the junction of Prescott's redoubt and the central breastwork, but pressed forward courageously. Francis, Lord Rawdon, a young grenadier lieutenant in the thick of the action there, tells what happened when he and the others began to close:

As soon as the rebels perceived this, they rose up and poured in so heavy a fire upon us that the oldest officers say they never saw a sharper action.

A major was among those wounded; several of his fellow officers urged a boyish ensign named George Hunter to go for medical help:

. . . I had sense enough to know that I was much safer close under the works than I could be at a few yards from it, as the enemy could not depress their arms sufficiently to do any execution to those that were close under; and to have gone to the rear to look for a surgeon would have been almost certain death. Indeed, the Major was not a very great favorite [with me], as he had obliged me to sell a pony that I had bought for seven and sixpence.

On the attack's extreme left, a battalion of British marines with General Pigot's forces had run into similar resistance as it drew close to the redoubt. According to the battalion's adjutant:

. . . we were checked by the severe fire of the enemy, but did not retreat an inch. We were now in confusion, after being broke several times in getting over the rails, etc. I did all I could to form the two companies on our right, which at last I effected, losing many of them while it was performing. Major Pitcairn [of Lexington and Concord] was killed close by me, with a captain and a subaltern; also a sergeant, and many of the privates; and had we stopped there much longer, the enemy would have picked us all off. I saw this, and begged Colonel Nesbitt of the 47th to form on our left, in order that we might advance with our bayonets to the parapet. I ran from right to left, and stopped our men from firing. While this was doing, and when we had got in tolerable order, we rushed on, leaped the ditch, and climbed the parapet. . . .

At the same time, the grenadiers were completing their assault. Lord Rawdon was surprised to find the American fire continued at point-blank range. " . . . they even knocked down my captain, close beside me, after we had got into the ditch of the entrenchment." The captain says of this: " . . . a ball grazed the top of my head, and I fell, deprived of sense and motion." Lord Rawdon himself took a ball through his hat. He goes on:

There are few instances of regular troops defending a redoubt till the enemy were in the very ditch of it. . . . I myself saw several pop their heads up and fire even after some of our men were upon the berm [the ledge just above the ditch and in front of the parapet].

The aggressive Connecticut company under John Chester was now coming over the summit of Bunker Hill. Chester saw at once that he was too late to help defend the redoubt on Breed's, but noted that there were several thin companies of American reinforcements firing effectively from a position behind the work, somewhat to the right. He decided to join them:

. . . during our descent . . . the small as well as cannon shot were incessantly whistling by us. We joined our army . . . just by a poor stone fence, two or three feet high, and very thin, so that the bullets came through. Here we lost our regularity, as every company had done before us, and fought as they did, every man loading and firing as fast as he could.

In the redoubt, ammunition had failed. The British vengefully began to surround the defenders and assault them with guns, bayonets, and swords; among those slain in these final moments was the

Death of Joseph Warren, an engraving from the painting by John Trumbull. *(Library of Congress)*

gallant president of the Massachusetts Provincial Congress, Joseph Warren. Only now that the situation was hopeless did Colonel Prescott order a retreat. Young Peter Brown, among others, took the order as a signal to fly:

... I jumped over the walls and ran for about half a mile where balls flew like hailstones and cannons roared like thunder.

Corporal Amos Farnsworth also escaped, but not undamaged:

I ... retreated ten or fifteen rods. Then I receved a wound in my rite arm, the bawl gowing through a little below my elbow, breaking the little shel bone. Another bawl struck my back, taking a piece of skin about as big as a penny. ... Oh, the goodness of

God in preserving my life althoe thay fell on my right hand and on my left!

Rhode Island's Israel Potter says that many of the Americans trying to leave the redoubt found their way blocked by redcoats:

A close and bloody engagement now ensued. To fight our way through a very considerable body of the enemy, with clubbed muskets (for there were not one in twenty of us provided with bayonets) were now the only means left us to escape. . . . Fortunately for me, at this critical moment, I was armed with a cutlass, which although without an edge, and much rust-eaten, I found of infinite more service to me than my musket. In one instance I am certain it was the means of saving my life. A blow with a cutlass was aimed at my head by a British officer, which I parried, and received only a slight cut with the point on my right arm near the elbow, which I was then unconscious of; but this slight wound cost my antagonist . . . a much more serious one, which effectually dis-*armed* him; for with one well directed stroke I deprived him of the power of very soon again measuring swords with a "yankee rebel!" We finally, however, should have been mostly cut off and compelled to yield to a superiour and better equipped force, had not a body of . . . Connecticut men . . . held the enemy at bay until our main body had time to ascend the heights [of Bunker Hill]. . . .

Colonel Prescott, one of the last to leave the redoubt, refused to run. Limiting his pace to long strides, he was obliged to turn from time to time to defend himself with his sword. His clothes were pierced in several places, but he wasn't hurt. The stand made by the Connecticut men proved costly. A lieutenant in John Chester's company named Samuel Webb was to write:

We covered their retreat till they came up with us by a brisk fire from our small arms. The dead and wounded lay on every side of me. Their groans were piercing indeed. . . . [The British] now had possession of our fort and four field-pieces. . . . Our orders then came to make the best retreat we could. We set off, almost gone with fatigue, and ran very fast up [Bunker] Hill, leaving some of our dead and wounded in the field.

The units that fought at the rail fence, which hadn't been breached, also retreated to Bunker's summit, and from there, all the survivors sped toward Charlestown Neck and the safety of the mainland. Old Put, according to one militiaman, lingered on Bunker's summit as long as he could:

General Putnam, seeing a field-piece deserted by the company, dismounted from his horse and fired the piece once or twice with his own hands, and then remounted his horse and rode off the hill with the retreating troops.

The general swore heartily as he went, and was later to say, "It was almost enough to make an angel swear, to see the cowards refuse to secure a victory so nearly won." Lord Rawdon was with the British troops who prodded the Americans down the slope: "The rebels . . . continued a running fight from one fence, or wall, to another, till we entirely drove them off the peninsula of Charlestown."

Late in the afternoon, the din of battle at last subsided. The spectators in their high places now saw only a scene of tragedy and disarray. The battlefield was littered with dead and wounded— mostly men in bright uniforms—and with all kinds of military equipment. Flames and smoke still rose from Charlestown. A Boston Loyalist named Ann Hulton describes what followed:

The rebels sheltered themselves in the adjacent hills and the neighborhood of Cambridge, and the [British] army possessed themselves of Charlestown Neck. We were exulting in seeing the flight of our enemies, but in an hour or two we had occasion to mourn and lament. Dear was the purchase of our safety! In the evening the streets [of Boston] were filled with the wounded and the dying; the sight of which, with the lamentations of the women and children over their husbands and fathers, pierced one to the soul.

The Battle of Bunker Hill solved nothing. Though the British gained possession of the Charlestown peninsula they remained in a state of siege and were still vulnerable on the Dorchester side (which neither they nor the Americans had yet tried to occupy). British losses in the battle were about 1,050 men killed or wounded, while the Americans lost, in killed, wounded, and captured, less than 450. "Upon the whole," wrote General Nathanael Greene of Rhode Island, "I think we have little reason to complain. . . . I wish we could sell them another hill at the same price." England's General Gage had been staggered: "The number of killed and wounded is greater than our forces can afford to lose." Something else lost by the British that they could ill afford was their psychological edge. Had they overrun the Americans with ease, further resistance might have been discouraged. As it was, the Americans had learned that they could do well in conventional battle. Their cause, it seemed, had a definite chance of succeeding.

6

WASHINGTON'S ROLE BEGINS

Sʜᴏʀᴛʟʏ *after the Battle of Bunker Hill, young Dr. James Thacher, of Barnstable, Massachusetts, made a serious decision:*
Participating, I trust, in the glorious spirit of the times, and contemplating improvement in my professional pursuits, motives of patriotism and private interest prompt me to hazard my fortune in this noble conflict with my brethren in the provincial army. . . . My friends afford me no encouragement, alleging that, as this is a civil war, if I should fall into the hands of the British the gallows will be my fate. The terrors of the gallows are not to be conquered, but I must indulge the hope that I may escape it. Hundreds of my superiors may take their turn before mine shall come.

The tories assail me with the following powerful arguments: "Young man, are you sensible you are about to violate your duty to the best of kings, and run headlong into destruction? Be assured that this rebellion will be of short duration. The royal army is all-powerful, and will, in a few months, march through the country and bring all to subjection. . . . What is your army but an undisciplined rabble? Can they stand against an army of regulars? Where are your cannon, your fire-arms, your bayonets, and all your implements of war? Above all, where is your treasure, and where can you look for a barrel of gunpowder? The whole country can scarcely afford a sufficiency for a battle of an hour."

Not a small portion of their reasoning I feel to be just and true. I am not certain, however, but much of it may prove erroneous. The result of the late battle at Charlestown should convince the most incredulous tory that our soldiers will face the regular troops. . . . It would be presumption in me to determine as to possibilities and prospects; but the voice of liberty cannot be stifled while the welfare and happiness of more than three millions of people now in America, and of unborn millions, are involved in the issue.

Dr. Thacher was assigned to the staff of the provincial hospital in Cambridge, and took up his duties on July 15, 1775. He found the building's facilities overtaxed:

Several private but commodious houses in Cambridge are occupied for [auxiliary] hospitals, and a considerable number of soldiers who were wounded at Breed's Hill, and a great number of sick of various diseases, require all our attention. . . .

I am informed that General George Washington arrived at our provincial camp, in this town, on the 2d July, having been appointed [on June 15] by the unanimous voice of the Continental Congress at Philadelphia, general and commander-in-chief of all the troops raised, and to be raised, for the defence of the United Colonies, as they are now termed. . . . General Washington . . . was in General Braddock's defeat in 1755, and having had considerable experience in the wars with the French and Indians . . . he is supposed to possess ample qualifications for the command of our army, and the appointment gives universal satisfaction. Such is his disinterested patriotism that he assured Congress . . . that he should receive from the public . . . no other compensation than the amount of his necessary expenses.

He has been received here with every mark of respect, and addressed by our Provincial Congress in the most affectionate and respectful manner. All ranks appear to repose full confidence in him as commander-in-chief. It is the fervent prayer of the religiously disposed that he may be instrumental in bringing this unhappy controversy to an honorable and speedy termination. He is accompanied by General [Charles] Lee and General [Horatio] Gates. . . . The former is now appointed major-general, and the latter adjutant-general, by our Continental Congress. General Washington has established his headquarters in a convenient house about half a mile from Harvard College, and in the vicinity of our hospital.

Less than a week later, Thacher wrote:

I have been much gratified this day with a view of General Washington. His excellency was on horseback, in company with several military gentlemen. It was not difficult to distinguish him from all others. His personal appearance is truly noble and majestic, being tall and well proportioned. His dress is a blue coat with buff-colored facings, a rich epaulette on each shoulder, buff under-dress, and an elegant small sword; a black cockade in his hat.

Thacher and the others who were impressed by the majesty and elegance of the Virginia aristocrat were unaware that he regarded his task with reluctance and uncertainty. Before leaving Philadelphia, he had written his wife at Mount Vernon:

You may believe me, my dear Patsy, when I assure you in the most solemn manner that, so far from seeking this appointment, I have used every endeavour in my power to avoid it, not only from my unwillingness to part with you and the family, but from a consciousness of its being a trust too great for my capacity; and that I should enjoy more real happiness in one month with you at home than I have the most distant prospect of finding [away,] if my stay were to be seven times seven years.

But as it has been a kind of destiny that has thrown me upon this service, I shall hope that my undertaking it is designed to answer some good purpose. You might, and I suppose did perceive from the tenor of my letters that I was apprehensive I could not avoid this appointment, as I did not pretend to intimate when I should return. That was the case. It was utterly out of my power to refuse this appointment without exposing my character to such censures as would have reflected dishonour upon myself and given pain to my friends. This I am sure would not, and ought not, to be pleasing to you, and must have lessened me considerably in my own esteem.

I shall rely, therefore, confidently on that Providence which has heretofore preserved and been bountiful to me, not doubting but that I shall return safe to you in the fall. I shall feel no pain from the toil or the danger of the campaign. My unhappiness will flow from the uneasiness I know you will feel from being left alone. I therefore beg that you will summon your whole fortitude, and pass your time as agreeably as possible.

If Washington really believed he would feel no pain other than

*that related to his wife's plight, he was soon undeceived. He found
his army of besiegers so deficient in organization and equipage that
he was obliged to make an urgent appeal to Congress for aid. His
aristocratic background caused him to view the Yankees as a race
apart. They seemed a seedy lot, lacking in schooling, manners, and
a proper respect for discipline, and they moved him to private
thoughts that ran like this:*

The people of this government have obtained a character which
they by no means deserved. Their officers, generally speaking, are
the most indifferent kind of people I ever saw. . . . In short,
they are by no means such troops, in any respect, as you are led
to believe of them from the accounts which are published. But I
need not make myself enemies among them by this declaration.
. . . I dare say the men would fight very well (if properly officered),
although they are an exceeding dirty and nasty people.

*Washington's sense of tidiness was offended by the casual manner in
which some of the men lived in their makeshift camps. But a frequent civilian visitor to Cambridge, the Reverend William Emerson of Concord, found the same scenes "diverting." He penned this
description of the army's shelters:*

They are as different in their form as the owners are in their
dress; and every tent is a portraiture of the temper and taste of
the persons that incamp in it. Some are made of boards, some
of sailcloth, and some partly of one and partly of the other. Others
are made of stone and turf, and others again of birch and other
brush. Some are thrown up in a hurry and look as if they could
not help it—mere necessity. Others are curiously wrought with
doors and windows done with wreaths and withes in the manner
of a basket. Some are your proper tents and marquees, and look
like the regular camp of the enemy. . . . I think that the great
variety of the American camp is, upon the whole, rather a beauty
than a blemish to the army.

*According to Emerson, Washington lost no time asserting his au-
thority over the New Englanders:*

There is a great overturning in camp as to order and regularity.
New lords, new laws. The Generals Washington and Lee are upon
the lines every day. New orders from his excellency are read to
the respective regiments every morning after prayers. The strictest
government is taking place, and great distinction is made between

officers and soldiers. Everyone is made to know his place and keep it, or be immediately tied up and receive . . . thirty or forty lashes, according to his crime.

These measures helped, but were hardly a cure-all for the problems of command, which were as evident in the upper ranks as in the lower, the vanity of New England's generals causing Washington much annoyance. He had arrived at Cambridge with Continental commissions that established their relative seniority; but he had no sooner issued the first one—to Israel Putnam—than another general left camp in a huff because he was Putnam's senior in the Connecticut service and had no wish to be his junior in the Continental. Washington wisely decided to withhold the rest of the commissions and refer the matter back to Congress for further consideration.

In spite of all his problems, Washington managed to make rapid headway with one of his most important tasks—that of improving the great semicircle of earthworks. "Thousands," Emerson observed, "are at work every day from four till eleven o'clock in the morning. It is suprising how much work has been done." Washington's second-in-command, Charles Lee, wrote on July 20:

. . . I have scarcely an hour's time in a week upon my hands. Our lines are fourteen miles in extent, and I am scamperer General. I am seldom less than twelve hours on horseback. The want of engineers has occasioned a fatigue to me scarcely credible. . . . I do not believe there is one capable of constructing an oven. However . . . three or four days more hard labour will make us so secure that I flatter myself not a single post can be forced without a loss of men too great for the enemy to spare.

Lee's general impressions of the New Englanders were more favorable than Washington's. Lee was a soldier of fortune who had seen a variety of troops in several parts of the world. He himself was described by a Yankee clergyman named Jeremy Belknap as "a perfect original, a good scholar and soldier, and an odd genius, full of fire and passion and but little good manners; a great sloven, wretchedly profane, and a great admirer of dogs." Lee says of New England's enlisted men:

. . . they are admirable—young, stout, healthy, zealous, good-humoured and sober. Had we but uniforms, compleat arms, more gentlemen for officers, I really believe a very little time and pains would render 'em the most invincible army that have appeared since the first period of the Roman Republic. . . . The more we consider the affair of Bunker's Hill, the more wonderful it appears. . . .

Troops from colonies to the south were now beginning to join the New Englanders. A letter written in Cambridge on July 25 states:

Captain Dowdle, with his company of riflemen from [York County] Pennsylvania arrived . . . about one o'clock to-day, and . . . has made proposals to General Washington to attack the transport stationed at Charles River. He will engage to take her with thirty men. The General thinks it best to decline it at present; but at the same time commends the spirit of Captain Dowdle and his brave men, who, though they just came a very long march, offered to execute the plan immediately.

Washington was able to oblige the eager Pennsylvanians with a mission a day or two later. It was described in a newspaper item presumably written by a man in one of the American camps:

Last Friday the [British] regulars cut several trees [on Charlestown Neck] and were busy all night in throwing up a line and abatis [a tangle composed of the felled trees] in front of it. In the evening [following], orders were given to the York County Riflemen to march down to our advanced post on Charlestown Neck to endeavor to surround the [enemy's] advanced guard and to bring off some prisoners, from whom we expected to learn their design in throwing up the abatis. . . .

The rifle company divided, and executed their plan in the following manner: Captain Dowdle, with thirty-nine men, filed off to the right of Bunker's Hill, and, creeping on their hands and knees, got into the [enemy's] rear without being discovered. The other division of forty men under Lieutenant Miller were equally successful in getting behind the sentinels on the left, and were within a few yards of joining the division on the right when a party of regulars came down the hill to relieve their guard. . . . The regulars were within twenty yards of our men before they saw them, and immediately fired. The riflemen returned the salute, killed several, brought off two prisoners and their arms, with the loss of Corporal Creuse, who is supposed to be killed. . . .

In return for this [raid], the regulars alarmed us last night in their turn. At one o'clock this morning a heavy firing of small arms and cannon occasioned our drums to be beat to arms, and the corps were immediately ordered to their posts. . . . Some hours elapsed before we knew the design of the enemy, which was this: We had surrounded some of their out-guard the night before, which induced them to serve our sentinels in a like manner.

They sent two flat-bottomed boats to Sewell's Point to attack our redoubt there. The boats, after a useless fire of several hours, retired. The picquet guard of the enemy on Charlestown Neck attacked and drove in our advanced guard, who [after] being reinforced by General Lee's orders, recovered their ground and beat the enemy, killed several, and brought off seven muskets without losing a man. . . .

On July 27, three and a half weeks after his arrival at Cambridge, Washington summed up his efforts and the general situation in this way:

I found part of our army on two hills (called Winter and Prospect Hills) about a mile and a quarter from the enemy on Bunker's Hill, in a very insecure state. I found another part of the army at [Cambridge], and a third part at Roxbury, guarding the entrance in and out of Boston. My whole time since I came here has been imployed in throwing up lines of defence at these three several places; to secure, in the first instance, our own troops from any attempts of the enemy; and, in the next, to cut off all communication between their troops and the country. . . . Their force, including Marines, Tories, etc., are computed, from the best accounts I can get, at about 12,000 men. Ours, including sick, absent, etc., at about 16,000. . . .

The enemy are sickly and scarce of fresh provisions. . . . I have drove all the live[stock] within a considerable distance of this place back into the country, out of the way of the men-of-war's boats. In short, I have, and shall continue to do, every thing in my power to distress them. The [British] transports are all arrived, and their whole reinforcement is landed, so that I can see no reason why they should not, if they ever [expect to] attempt it, come boldly out and put the matter to issue at once. If they think themselves not strong enough to do this, they surely will carry their arms (having ships of war and transports ready) to some other part of the continent, or relinquish the dispute; the last of which the Ministry [in England], unless compelled, will never agree to do. Our works and those of the enemy are so near and quite open between that we see every thing that each other is doing.

The British did not come boldly out. Nor did they board their vessels and leave. General William Heath, of the American forces, tells how the days passed:

August 2d: There was a considerable firing between the advanced parties; and the Americans burnt a barn near Charlestown Neck, in which the British had some hay. A British officer was wounded . . . . 4th: A [British] ship of war came up above the ferry at Charlestown, and there took a station. 6th: In the afternoon a party of the British, in two barges, covered by a floating battery, burnt the house on the other side of Penny Ferry. 11th: One of the ships which had been stationed above the ferry went down [to Boston]. 15th: There was a smart cannonade on the Roxbury side. There was more or less firing every day, but little damage done. 17th: A [cannon] shot from the British lines on Boston Neck struck among the main guard at Roxbury and damaged two muskets in a very remarkable manner, but did no other harm. The same day six or seven tons of powder arrived [in the American camp] from the southward.

Reinforcements, by units and by small parties, continued to reach Cambridge. A newspaper report dated August 14 states:

Last night, arrived at the camp . . . Swashan the chief, with four other Indians of the St. Francis tribe, conducted by Mr. Reuben Colborn, who has been honorably recompensed for his trouble. The above Indians came to offer their services to the cause of American liberty, have been kindly received, and are now entered the service. Swashan says he will bring one-half of his tribe, and has engaged four or five other tribes, if they should be wanted. He says the Indians in Canada, in general, and also the French, are greatly in favor of the Americans, and are determined [though British subjects] not to act against them.

Other new arrivals at Cambridge were additional riflemen from Pennsylvania, Maryland, and Virginia. These troops made an excellent first impression. In Dr. Thacher's words:

They are remarkably stout and hardy men, many of them exceeding six feet in height. They are dressed in white frocks, or rifle-shirts, and round hats. These men are remarkable for the accuracy of their aim, striking a mark with great certainty at two hundred yards distance. . . . They are now stationed in our lines, and their shot have frequently proved fatal to British officers and soldiers who expose themselves to view, even at more than double the distance of common musket-shot.

The riflemen, however, would soon be adding to Washington's troubles with insolent and undisciplined conduct, and he would find himself almost wishing they hadn't come. Describing his struggles to make an army out of his independent troops, Washington wrote in a private letter composed late in August:

As we have now nearly compleated our lines of defence, we [have] nothing more, in my opinion, to fear from the enemy, provided we can keep our men to their duty and make them watchful and vigilant. But it is among the most difficult tasks I ever undertook in my life to induce these people to believe that there is, or can be, danger till the bayonet is pushed at their breasts. . . .

There has been so many great and capital errors and abuses to rectify—so many examples to make—and so little inclination in the officers of inferior rank to contribute their aid to accomplish this work, that my life has been nothing else (since I came here) but one continued round of annoyance and fatigue. In short, no pecuniary recompense could induce me to undergo what I have; especially as I expect [in the end], by shewing so little countenance to irregularities and publick abuses, to render myself very obnoxious to a greater part of these people.

In another letter, Washington wrote:

. . . we now wish [the British] to come out as soon as they please; but they . . . [reveal] no inclination to quit their own works of defence; and as it is almost impossible for us to get to them, we do nothing but watch each other's motions all day at the distance of about a mile, every now and then picking off a straggler when we catch them [outside] their intrenchments. In return, they often attempt to cannonade our lines to no other purpose than the waste of a considerable [quantity] of powder . . . which we should be very glad to get.

Back in June, Washington had written his wife that he expected to return to Mount Vernon, where his heart abided, by autumn. This, of course, was not to happen. The Boston stalemate alone was to drag on till the following spring. And already Washington, as commander in chief of all operations on the American continent, was becoming involved with activities on a "second front."

7

TO THE PLAINS OF ABRAHAM

As EARLY *as June 27, 1775, just ten days after the Battle of Bunker Hill, Congress had authorized an invasion of Canada. The province was populated largely by Frenchmen, many of whom had never become reconciled to having British masters. A successful Canadian campaign would serve two purposes: It would remove the province as a base for a British invasion of America and it would gain America a valuable ally—perhaps even an extra colony. In the summer of 1775, there were only about eight hundred regulars in the whole of Canada. But the military governor, Sir Guy Carleton, could count on aid from some of the Anglo-Canadian and French-Canadian militiamen and Tories, and from certain of the Indians.*

The territory's chief fortress was the town of Quebec, on the St. Lawrence River about 150 miles above New England's northern frontier. Though Carleton was a first-rate commander and Quebec was formidable, the Americans felt they had a good chance of conquering Canada if they acted before Carleton was reinforced from England. Plans were made to move against Quebec from two directions at the same time. One expedition, commanded by General Philip Schuyler and General Richard Montgomery, and accompanied by Colonel Ethan Allen, assembled at Ticonderoga. These men prepared to boat their way northward on Lake Champlain, hoping to capture St. John's and Montreal before heading northeastward to the main fortress. The second expedition, commanded

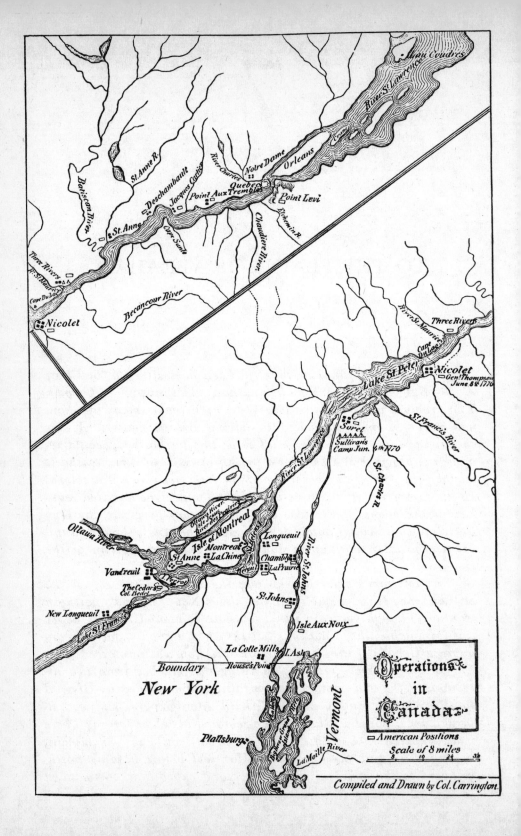

Operations in Canada

by Colonel Benedict Arnold, was organized under Washington's eye at Cambridge. Arnold proposed to take his men through a great stretch of eastern wilderness: up the Kennebec River in the province of Maine as far as the Dead River, then westward to Canada's Lake Megantic and down the Chaudière River directly to Quebec.

The Lake Champlain expedition crossed the Canadian border early in September. During the advance upon the fort at St. John's, illness compelled General Schuyler to turn full command of the expedition over to General Montgomery. The latter, finding the log-walled fort stoutly defended, made the reluctant decision that it would have to be reduced by siege. During these same September days, Benedict Arnold was making ready to march from Cambridge. Among those under him was sixteen-year-old John Joseph Henry, of Lancaster, Pennsylvania. Years later, Henry was to recall:

The detachment consisted of eleven hundred men. . . . Riflemen composed a part of the armament. These companies, from sixty-five to seventy-five strong, were from the southward: that is, Captain Daniel Morgan's company from Virginia; that of Captain William Hendricks from Cumberland County in Pennsylvania, and Captain Matthew Smith's company from the county of Lancaster in the latter province. The residue, and bulk of this corps, consisted of troops from [New England]. . . .

This little army, in high spirits, marched from Prospect Hill, near Cambridge . . . on the 11th of September . . . and on the following day arrived at Newburyport. . . . This place . . . was a small . . . [coastal] town near the border of Massachusetts. Here we remained encamped five days, providing ourselves with such articles of real necessity as our small means afforded.

The troops then went aboard a fleet of small, dirty, commercial vessels, some of which smelled strongly of fish. Private Abner Stocking, of Connecticut, says in a journal entry dated September 19:

This morning we got under way with a pleasant breeze, our drums beating, fifes playing and colours flying. Many pretty girls stood upon the shore, I suppose weeping for the departure of their sweethearts. At eleven o'clock . . . we left the entrance of the harbor and bore away for the Kennebec River.

In the latter part of the night, there came a thick fog and our fleet was separated. At break of day we found ourselves in a most dangerous situation, very near a reef of rocks. . . . We were brought into this deplorable situation by means of liquor being dealt out too freely to our pilots . . . but through the blessing of God we all arrived safe in Kennebec River.

John Joseph Henry adds: "We ascended the river to Colonel Colborn's ship yard. Here we left our vessels and obtained batteaux, with which we proceeded to Fort Western [now Augusta]." According to young Doctor Isaac Senter, of Londonderry, New Hampshire (another member of the expedition who kept a journal):

The arrangements of men and provisions [were] made at Fort Western in such a manner as to proceed with [efficient promptness]. For this end it was thought necessary that Capt. Morgan's company with a few pioneers should advance in the first division, Col. Greene's in the second, and [Colonel] Enos, with Capt. Colbourn's company . . . to bring up the rear. The advantage of the arrangement was very conspicuous, as the [first] division would not only have the roads cut, rivers cleared passable for boats, etc., but stages or encampments formed and the bough huts remaining for the rear. The men being thus arranged, the provisions were distributed according to the supposed [transporting] difficulty or facility attending the different dispositions. Many of the first companies took only two or three barrels of flour with several of bread . . . while the companies in the last division had not less than fourteen of flour and ten of bread.

Now facing the sterner waters of a narrowing river, the expedition set out from Fort Western during the last week in September. The men ·had to pit their laden batteaux and their muscles against shoals, swift currents, rapids, and waterfalls. Much of the time they had to drag and push the vessels, and there were difficult portages to be made. "When night came on," says Abner Stocking, "wet and fatigued as we were, we had to encamp on the cold ground. It was at this time that we inclined to think of the comfortable accommodations we had left at home." Dr. Senter writes that the expedition reached Norridgewock Falls early in October:

We had now a number of teams employed in conveying the batteaux, provisions, camp equipage, etc., over this carrying place. By this time, many of our batteaux were nothing but wrecks, some stove to pieces, etc. The carpenters were employed in repairing them, while the rest of the army were busy in carrying over the provisions, etc. . . . The [dried] fish lying loose in the batteaux . . . being continually washed with the fresh water running into the batteaux [were spoiled]. The bread casks not being water-proof, admitted the water in plenty, swelled the bread, burst the casks, as well as soured the whole bread. The same fate attended a number of fine casks of peas. . . . We were now curtailed of a very valuable and large part of our provisions ere we had entered the wilderness or left the inhabitants.

About two hundred miles west-northwest of Norridgewock Falls, the Lake Champlain expedition was undergoing its own set of troubles. The fort at St. John's was proving a tough objective. In a letter written on October 6, a Connecticut man named Samuel Mott reported:

Ever since the 17th of last month we have laid siege to this place. It is a very difficult place to come at, as it is almost surrounded with sunken swamps and marshy ground. . . . The enemy, it is thought, have fired six-hundred bomb-shells, besides numbers of cannon-shot and showers of grape-shot; but we have lost but about a dozen men by them all. . . .

Colonel [Ethan] Allen has been very serviceable in bringing in the [friendly] Canadians and Indians; but . . . [on September 24, without authority from General Montgomery] he . . . crossed the river about five miles below Montreal with only about thirty New England men and seventy Canadian friends . . . and intended to augment his number of Canadians, and, if possible, get possession of Montreal. But he was the next morning met by . . . about four hundred Regulars and French Tories [and Indians]. They overpowered Allen. . . .

This was a bitter blow to the proud hero of Ticonderoga. Nonetheless, his own account of the moment is filled with drama:

The officer I capitulated with . . . directed me and my party to advance towards him. . . . I handed him my sword, and in half a minute after, a savage, part of whose head was shaved, being almost naked, and painted . . . came running to me with an incredible swiftness. . . . [H]is hellish visage was beyond all description . . . and in less than twelve feet of me [he] presented his firelock. At the instant of his present, I twitched the officer to whom I gave my sword between me and the savage; but he flew round with great fury, trying to single me out to shoot me without killing the officer. But by this time I was near as nimble as he, keeping the officer in such a position that his danger was my defence; but in less than half a minute I was attacked by just such another imp of hell. Then I made the officer fly around with incredible velocity . . . when I perceived a Canadian [of the enemy's ranks] . . . taking my part against the savages. And in an instant an Irishman came to my assistance with a fixed bayonet and drove away the fiends, swearing by Jasus! he would kill them.

According to an unnamed soldier in the American lines at St. John's:
Several Canadians were taken prisoners with Colonel Allen, whom the regular officers said they would put to death; on which Allen stepped up, opened his breast, and said the Canadians were not to blame; that he brought them there, and if anybody must be murdered, let it be him. This got him great credit with all the officers at Montreal, and Carleton himself said it was a pity a man of Allen's spirit should be engaged in so bad a cause, as he calls it. Colonel Allen is prisoner on board the *Gaspee* brig, before Montreal.

News of the capture prompted General Washington to comment: "Colonel Allen's misfortune will, I hope, teach a lesson of prudence and subordination to others who may be too ambitious to outshine their general officers. . . ." Allen was to remain a captive, part of the time in England, for about two and a half years. An exchange of prisoners between the two armies would finally free him.

As the siege of St. John's wore on, with the firing from both sides being kept up "pretty briskly," Benedict Arnold and his men continued their dogged struggle through the Maine woods. By mid-October they were well beyond the last outpost of civilization and were leaving the Kennebec at the Great Carrying Place. Here they began a journey westward across three ponds (separated from one another by portages of several miles) that led toward the Dead River. "The army was now much fatigued," writes Dr. Senter, "being obliged to carry all the batteaux, barrels of provisions, warlike stores, etc., over on their backs through a most terrible piece of woods conceivable; sometimes in the mud knee-deep, then over ledgy hills, etc. . . ." Senter was speaking only of one of the earliest portages.

Many of the men began to sicken, some through drinking

yellow marsh water and some as the result of the declining quality of the rations. Curiously, not much game was taken. Perhaps most of the forest's creatures were driven into deeper hiding by the expedition's noise.

Reaching the Dead River brought the men little satisfaction, for a hurricane-like rainstorm quickly caused the river to become "live enough." The trip toward the Canadian border and Lake Megantic was another tough upstream fight. Some of the men made their way along the irregular banks, while others struggled with the heavily loaded batteaux in the water. It was necessary to portage around numerous falls. The batteaux took a further battering, and a number had to be abandoned. After the rains ended, the weather turned colder. In Dr. Senter's words:

Every prospect of distress now came thundering on with a two-fold rapidity. A storm of snow had covered the ground of nigh six inches deep, attended with very severe weather. We now waited in anxious expectation for Col. Enos' division to come up, in order that we might have a recruit of provisions. . . .

But when Enos and his men came up, they were willing to part with only two or three barrels of flour. Moreover, they were now thoroughly pessimistic about the mission's outcome. A letter written by a man in one of the more spirited units tells what happened:

. . . Col. Enos . . . with three companies and the sick . . . turned back! May shame and guilt go with him, and wherever he seeks shelter may the hand of justice shut the door against him.

Benedict Arnold wasn't on hand to deal with the crisis. He was ahead of the expedition, making all possible speed toward the first French-Canadian settlements.

The narrowing origins of the Dead River led the expedition—now beginning to suffer acutely from hunger—to another chain of ponds and across several rocky, densely wooded and snowy heights to Canadian soil. On October 28, according to Dr. Senter:

A letter per express from . . . Arnold . . . requesting as speedy a procedure as possible. That one of his expresses had returned . . . from the Canadian inhabitants informing [him] of their amicable disposition towards us; that he had received their pledge of friendship in a loaf of bread. . . . In consequence of this news, we were ordered to be in motion immediately.

When Lake Megantic was reached, there arose the problem of nego-
tiating its wild margin to the outlet of the Chaudière River. During
this stage of the journey, young John Joseph Henry (like many
others) found himself with nothing to eat but "bleary, which was no
other than flour and water, and that without salt." But he managed
to keep going. He writes of November 1:

This morning . . . we took up the line of march through a
flat and boggy ground. About ten o'clock a.m. we arrived by a
narrow neck of land at a marsh which was appalling. It was three-
fourths of a mile over, and covered by a coat of ice, half an inch
thick. Here [Lieutenant Michael] Simpson concluded to halt a
short time for the stragglers or maimed of Hendricks' and Smith's
companies to come up.

There were two women attached to those companies. . . . One
was the wife of Sergeant Grier, a large, virtuous and respectable
woman. The other was the wife of a private [James Warner] of our
company, a man who lagged upon every occasion. These women
being arrived, it was presumed that all our party were up. We were
on the point of entering the marsh when someone cried out,
"Warner is not here." Another said he had sat down sick under a
tree, a few miles back. His wife begging us to wait a short time,
with tears of affection in her eyes, ran back to her husband. We
tarried an hour. They came not.

Private Warner was to perish. But John Joseph Henry would be
pleasantly surprised to meet Mrs. Warner in Quebec "bearing her
husband's rifle, his powder horn and pouch" and appearing "fresh
and rosy as ever." Henry tells of entering the marsh:

. . . breaking the ice here and there with the butts of our guns
and feet, as occasion required, we were soon waist deep in the mud
and water. . . . Now Mrs. Grier had got before me. My mind was
humbled, yet astonished, at the exertions of this good woman. Her
clothes more than waist high, she waded before me. . . . No one,
so long as she was known to us, dared intimate a disrespectful
idea of her. . . . Arriving at firm ground, and waiting again for our
companions, we then set off. . . .

By this time some of the units had already reached the Chaudière
and were following its rugged downhill course through thick groves
of spruce, cedar, and hemlock trees. Among these men was Dr.
Senter:

We had now arrived . . . to almost the zenith of our distress. Several had been entirely destitute of either meat or bread for many days. . . . The voracious disposition many of us had now arrived at rendered almost anything admissible. Clean and unclean were forms now little in use. In company was a poor dog [who had] hitherto lived through all the tribulations [but now] became a prey for the sustenance of the assassinators. This poor animal was instantly devoured without leaving any vestige of the sacrifice. Nor did the shaving soap, pomatum, and even the lip salve, leather of their shoes, cartridge boxes, etc., share any better fate.

Thanks to the bold and indefatigable Benedict Arnold, the expedition was saved. Immediately upon reaching the first Canadian inhabitants, he sent back help. Says Dr. Senter:

Not more than eight miles had we marched [on November 2] when a vision of horned cattle, four-footed beasts, etc., rode and drove by animals resembling Plato's two-footed featherless ones. Upon a nigher approach, our vision proved real! Exclamations of joy! Echoes of gladness resounded from front to rear! . . . Three horned cattle, two horses, eighteen Canadians and one American. A heifer was chosen as victim to our wants; slain and divided accordingly. Each man was restricted to one pound of beef. Soon arrived two more Canadians in [birch] canoes, ladened with a coarse kind of meal, mutton, tobacco, etc. . . . We sat down, eat our rations, blessed our stars, and thought it luxury.

At this same time, the western expedition under General Richard Montgomery, so long stalled at St. John's, was also enjoying a change in fortune. On October 18, a three-hundred-man detachment had captured the small fort at nearby Chambly, and among the supplies gained were nineteen cannons and about six tons of much-needed gunpowder. This success gave new strength to the siege of St. John's. Montgomery received additional aid in the person of General David Wooster of Connecticut. Working together, the two generals brought about the surrender of the British fort on November 3. This further enriched the Americans in supplies, and left them free to take up the march to Montreal, their second target.

Benedict Arnold's expedition had been much depleted by desertion, sickness, and death; but the gaunt and tattered survivors, bearing what remained of their arms and other equipment, were now nearing the main objective: Quebec. In the words of an un-

Sir Guy Carleton.

Portrait of General
David Wooster
published in England
in 1776.
(Library of Congress)

named officer: "We were at least one month too late for this northern climate. . . . But our joy upon our arrival among the Canadians is inexpressible. . . ." Most of these simple French settlers were amazed at the American feat. Benedict Arnold himself was convinced that the march was "not to be paralleled in history."

The expedition soon reached Pointe Levi, located on the St. Lawrence River, on the shore opposite Quebec. Several British warships lay on the river, and the Americans who showed themselves drew cannon fire. The anonymous officer goes on:

We tarried at Point Levi near a week, during which time we were busy in preparing to cross the river, being obliged to purchase birch canoes twenty miles distant and carry them by land, the regulars at Quebec having burnt all near them as soon as they heard of our coming.

While Arnold was encountering this delay, Montgomery and Wooster were about 160 miles to the southwest, closing on Montreal, which was also on the St. Lawrence River. Though Sir Guy Carleton himself was in Montreal, he had only 150 men. No fight developed. Carleton fled the town and hastened along the St. Lawrence toward Quebec. Montgomery, leaving Wooster in charge at Montreal, soon followed.

It was on the same day as Montreal's capture that Benedict Arnold ventured to take his expedition across the river at Pointe Levi. The anonymous officer continues his account:

The men-of-war lay in such a manner as they supposed would prevent our attempt, but on Monday, the 13th inst., every thing was ready for our embarkation; and at nine o'clock in the evening, being very dark, the first division set off, and we passed between the *Hunter*, of fourteen guns, and Quebec, and landed safely at Point de Pezo. The boats were immediately sent back, and continued passing till near daybreak, while the men on this side marched up the hill at the same place the immortal Wolfe formerly did [during the French and Indian War], and immediately formed. The place we marched up is called Wolfe's cove. . . .

Near daybreak the guard boat belonging to the man-of-war was passing from the *Hunter* to the *Lizard,* a frigate of twenty-eight guns, at the time some of our boats were crossing, which made us uneasy, and as the guard boat came near the shore we hailed her and then fired upon her, and could distinctly hear them cry out they were wounded. They pushed off. . . .

After waiting some little time till all our men were over (except a guard stationed at Point Levi), we marched across the Plains of Abraham, and at daybreak took possession of some houses one mile and an half from Quebec. After fixing a strong guard we retired, but were alarmed by their seizing one of our sentinels, whom they carried off. Our army was immediately marched off towards the [city's] walls. They fired some heavy shot at us, but without any execution; and our men . . . picked up a number of [the balls], gave them three hearty cheers, and retired to their quarters.

On Tuesday they made an attempt for a second sentinel, but were unsuccessful. Our little army immediately turned out, and we took possession of a nunnery in the suburbs within point-blank shot, and fixed a strong guard there. They kept up a pretty heavy fire, but fortunately no person received the least injury. We had now in a great measure cut off all communications between the city and country, and I believe they began to feel we were not the most agreeable neighbors.

On Wednesday we had two alarms, and expected they would have turned out and ventured a battle, but [the threat] vanished with the roaring of their cannon. On Thursday evening . . . one of our men, a Pennsylvanian and a noble soldier, was wounded by a cannon ball in the leg. . . .

The man's name was Robert Dixon. John Joseph Henry was with him when he was hit:

Dixon was . . . carried on a litter to the house of an English gentleman. . . . An amputation took place. A tetanus followed. . . . The lady of the house, though not one who approved of our principles of action, was very attentive to our wounded companion. She presented him a bowl of tea.

"No, madam," said he. "It is the ruin of my country."

. . . uttering this noble sentiment, this invaluable citizen died, sincerely lamented by every one who had the opportunity of knowing his virtues.

Robert Dixon was buried on the Plains of Abraham, "a noble grave for a soldier," on Friday. Over the weekend, Benedict Arnold made the reluctant decision that he could do nothing against the walled city without General Montgomery's help. Returning again to the anonymous narrative:

On Sunday evening . . . every man received orders to parade at

Head Quarters at three o'clock in the morning, with his pack on his back. The boats were dispatched across the river and our guard brought from Point Levi. At the appointed hour we assembled and received orders to retreat [along the river road toward Montreal]. We set off, and in our march passed three different armed vessels, and . . . we expected at least a broadside; but they passed us in peace, and upon their arrival at Quebec we heard the discharge of a number of cannon, from which we concluded that Carleton was on board one of them, or that 'twas [done] for joy of our raising the siege.

We marched eight leagues that day, and the colonel [Arnold] found it absolutely necessary to halt here [at Pointe aux Trembles, where this account was being penned on November 21] till he could provide the men with shoes or moccasins, many of them being almost barefoot. It was the first time I ever wore moccasins on a march, and . . . from the roughness of the road (it being very hard) I could not, in my opinion, if my life had depended upon it, have marched ten miles next day.

It has ever been our fortune, from first marching from Cambridge, whenever we were much depressed, fatigued, etc., to hear some agreeable news that would immediately invigorate us, and enable us to proceed with tolerable cheerfulness. At this place we heard the agreeable news of Montreal being in our possession, that Governor Carleton made his escape in a birch canoe, and that he was actually in the ship that passed by here yesterday.

In short, everything once more seems to conspire in our favor. Gen. Montgomery is on his march for Quebec, and we halt here till he comes up, when we shall return to Quebec again, though whether it will be in our possession this winter or not is uncertain. We hear they are driving in all the cattle, etc., which will enable them to stand a long siege. In this part of the world, 'tis time for men to think of winter quarters rather than attacking fortified towns. However, we are *Americans* and *American soldiers.* I have not an objection to visiting the Plains of Abraham once more. . . .

According to John Joseph Henry, General Montgomery and his troops arrived on December 1:

Now new life was infused into the whole of the corps. . . . The next day we retraced the route [we had taken] from Quebec. A snow had fallen during the night, and continued falling. To march on this snow was a most fatiguing business. By this time we had generally furnished ourselves with seal-skin moccasins, which are large and, according to the usage of the country, stuffed with hay or leaves to keep the feet dry and warm. . . .

The combined forces, numbering only about a thousand men, commandeered quarters in comfortable homes in Quebec's suburbs. While Montgomery and Arnold planned their next move, the men had time to cultivate the friendlier French females, to drink and laugh and sing in the warm taverns, and to plunder a few Tories. In the line of duty, the riflemen sometimes crept close to the gray walls of their objective and picked off sentries in exposed positions. John Joseph Henry says that an attempt was also made to bring the fortress under cannon fire from the Plains of Abraham:

The earth was too difficult for the intrenching tools to pierce. The only method left was to raise a battery composed of ice and snow. The snow was made into ice by the addition of water. The work was done in the night time. Five or six nine-pounders and a howitzer were placed in it. It was scarcely completed, and our guns had opened on the city, before it was pierced through and through by the weightier metal of the enemy. Several lives were lost on the first and second day. Yet the experiment was persisted in till a single ball, piercing the battery, killed and wounded three persons. . . .

By this time Montgomery and Arnold had resolved to try to take the city by assault. They couldn't afford the delays that attended siege operations. Henry explains:

Many of the New England troops had been engaged on very short enlistments, some of which were to expire on the first of January, 1776. The patriotism of the summer of seventy-five seemed almost extinguished. . . . The patriotic officers made every exertion to induce enlistments, but to no purpose. We of the rifle corps readily assented to remain with the General . . . yet this example had no manner of influence on the generality. The majority were either farmers or sailors, and some had wives and children at home. These, and other reasons, perhaps the austerity of the winter and the harshness of the service caused an obstinacy of mind which would not submit to patriotic representation. Besides, the smallpox, which had been introduced into our cantonments [living quarters] by the indecorous yet fascinating arts of the enemy, had already begun its ravages.

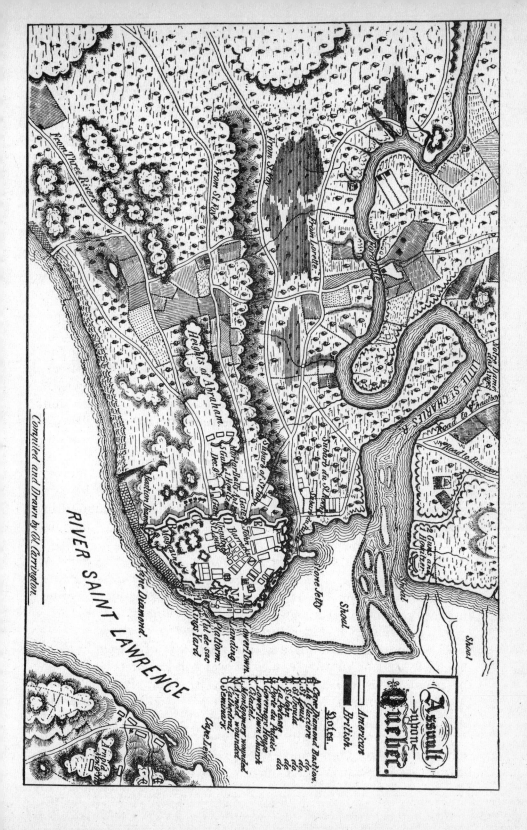

Assault upon Quebec.

American
British.

Notes.

RIVER SAINT LAWRENCE

Compiled and Drawn by Col. Carrington.

A footnote to Henry's account adds that "a number of women loaded with the infection . . . came into our cantonments." During these days in late December, the men were much engaged with contemplating and discussing the objective and General Montgomery's attack plan. The unnamed officer quoted earlier penned this description of the objective:

Quebec . . . stands upon a point between St. Lawrence and St. Charles Rivers. . . . It consists of the upper and lower town. The [lower] is immediately on the point, or water's edge, and consists of a large number of houses built thick. The upper town is upon the hill, which is prodigiously high. The town is surrounded on the country part by a wall from twenty-five to thirty feet high. . . .

Dr. Senter recorded the attack plan:

The arrangements of the army was as follows . . . General Montgomery on the right wing with the majority of troops from Montreal, etc.; Colonel Arnold on the left with his division of "Famine Proof Veterans"; Colonel [James] Livingston's Canadian Regiment [in the center] to assault the walls at St. John's Gate with combustibles for firing the gate and thereby to draw the attention of the enemy that way, and at the same time attempt the walls . . . with scaling ladders, etc. The place where the General was to assault was on the bank of the St. Lawrence at the termination of the city walls. . . . Arnold was to attack at the other extremity of the town [around the walls along the St. Charles], where he first expected to be opposed by some small batteries before he arrived in the lower town, where the two [divisions] were to form a junction.

To sum up: While Livingston's Canadians were making a noisy false attack on the city's walls in front, Montgomery was to swing around the walls on the right and Arnold on the left. Meeting in a waterfront area that was believed to be vulnerable, they were to press into the city together. In John Joseph Henry's words:

It was not until the night of the thirty-first of December . . . that such kind of weather ensued as was considered favorable for the assault. The forepart of the night was admirably enlightened by a luminous moon. Many of us, officers as well as privates, had dispersed in various directions among the farm [houses] and tippling houses of the vicinity. We well knew the signal for rallying. This was no other than a snow-storm. About twelve o'clock . . . the heaven was overcast. We repaired to quarters. By two o'clock we were accoutred and began our march. The storm was outrageous, and the cold wind extremely biting. . . .

When we [of Arnold's division] came . . . near [the wall at] Palace Gate a horrible roar of cannon took place and a ringing of all the bells of the city, which are very numerous and of all sizes Arnold, heading the forlorn hope [a party of volunteers], advanced perhaps one hundred yards before the main body. After these, followed Lamb's artillerists. Morgan's company led in the secondary part of the column of infantry. Smith's followed, headed by Steele, the captain . . . being absent. Hendricks' company succeeded, and the [New Englanders], so far as known to me, followed in due order.

The snow was deeper than in the fields because of the nature of the ground. The path made by Arnold, Lamb and Morgan was almost imperceptible because of the falling snow. Covering the locks of our guns with the lappets of our coats, holding down our heads (for it was impossible to bear up our faces against the imperious storm of wind and snow) we ran along the foot of the hill in single file. Along the first of our run from Palace Gate, for several hundred paces, there stood a range of insulated buildings which seemed to be store-houses. We passed these quickly in single file, pretty wide apart. The interstices [between the buildings] were from thirty to fifty yards. In these intervals we received a tremendous fire of musketry from the ramparts above us. Here we lost some brave men, [being] powerless to return the salutes we received, as the enemy was covered by his impregnable defences. They were even sightless to us. We could see nothing but the blaze from the muzzles of their muskets.

At this point, Henry tumbled down a steep slope on his left; and by the time he scrambled back up his friends were gone and he had to fall in with strangers:

We proceeded rapidly . . . for now we were unprotected by any buildings. The fire had slackened in a small degree. The enemy had been partly called off to resist the General [on the St. Lawrence side of the city] and strengthen the party opposed to Arnold in our front. Now we saw Colonel Arnold returning, wounded in the leg and supported by two gentlemen. . . . Arnold called to the troops in a cheering voice as we passed, urging us forward; yet it was observable among the soldiery . . . that the colonel's retiring damped their spirits.

Arnold says of his misfortune:

I received a wound by a ball through my left leg at the time I had gained the first battery at the lower town, which, by the loss of blood, rendered me very weak. As soon as the main body came up, with some assistance I returned to the hospital, near a mile, on foot, being obliged to draw one leg after me, and a great part of the way under the continual fire of the enemy from the walls, at no greater distance than fifty yards. I providentially escaped, though several were shot down at my side.

During these same moments, the troops working their way through the storm and the darkness along the St. Lawrence suffered an even graver blow. While they were assaulting a blockhouse—the first barrier beyond the end of the wall—General Montgomery was killed by artillery fire. His death stunned the whole division. The surviving officers, instead of pressing the attack and striving for a quick meeting with Benedict Arnold's division, gathered for a council of war. As for Arnold's men, they had heeded his urgings and were breaking into the lower town. John Joseph Henry resumes:

. . . enfiladed by an animated but lessened fire, we came to the first barrier, where Arnold had been wounded in the onset. This contest had lasted but a few minutes and was somewhat severe, but the energy of our men prevailed. . . . The guard, consisting of thirty persons, were either taken or fled, leaving their arms behind them. . . . From the first barrier to the second, there was a circular course along the sides of houses and partly through a street, probably of three hundred yards or more. This second barrier was erected across and near the mouth of a narrow street. . . .

Captain Daniel Morgan, of the Virginia riflemen, was now in command. He relates:

The sally port [gateway] through the barrier was standing open. The guard had left it, and the people were running from the upper town in whole platoons, giving themselves up as prisoners to get out of the way of the confusion which might shortly ensue. I went [through the sally port] up to the edge of the upper town . . . to see what was going on, as the firing had ceased. Finding no person in arms at all, I returned [through the barrier] and called a council of . . . officers. . . . Here I was overruled. . . . It

The Death of General Montgomery. From the painting by
John Trumbull. *(Library of Congress)*

was said, in the first place, that if I went on I should break orders;
in the next, that I had more prisoners than I had men, and that if
I left them they might . . . retake the battery we had just captured
and cut off our retreat. It was further urged that Gen. Montgomery was certainly coming down along the river St. Lawrence
and would join us in a few minutes, and that we were sure of conquest if we acted with caution and prudence. To these . . . reasons
I gave up my own opinion. . . .

*This was a serious mistake. According to one of Sir Guy Carleton's
officers:*

Had they acted with more spirit, they might have pushed in at first and possessed themselves of the whole of lower town and let their friends in at the other side before our people had time to have recovered from a certain degree of panic which seized them on the first news of the post being surprised.

While Morgan and his men were hesitating, the enemy was rallying. Returning again to Henry's account:

The admirable Montgomery, by this time (though it was unknown to us) was no more. . . . His division fell under the command of a Colonel [Donald] Campbell, of the New York line, a worthless chief who retreated without making an effort in pursuance of the General's original plans. The inevitable consequence was that the whole of the [enemy] forces on that side of the city, and those who were opposed to the . . . persons employed to make the false attacks [who had also retreated] embodied and came down to oppose our division.

The sally port that Morgan had used was slammed shut; and, tragically, the Americans now launched a bitter fight against the barrier that had belonged to them a few minutes before. Visibility in the snowy darkness was dim; but the shooting, says Henry, was sharp:

We were on the disadvantageous side of the barrier. . . . Confined in a narrow street hardly more than twenty feet wide, and on the lower ground, scarcely a ball, well aimed or otherwise, but must take effect upon us. Morgan, Hendricks, Steele, Humphreys and a crowd of every class of the army had gathered into the narrow pass, attempting to surmount the barrier, which was about twelve or more feet high and so strongly constructed that nothing but artillery could effectuate its destruction.

There was a [platform] fifteen or twenty yards within the barrier, upon a rising ground, the cannon of which much overtopped the height of the barrier. Hence we were assailed by grapeshot in abundance. . . . Again, within the barrier and close in to it, were two ranges of musketeers, armed with musket and bayonet, ready to receive those who might venture the dangerous leap. Add to all this that the enemy occupied the upper chambers of the houses in the interior of the barrier on both sides of the street, from the windows of which we became fair marks.

The enemy, having the advantage of the ground in front, a

vast superiority of numbers, dry and better arms, gave them an irresistible power in so narrow a space. Humphreys . . . attended by many brave men, attempted to scale the barrier, but was compelled to retreat by the formidable phalanx of bayonets within, and the weight of fire from the platform and the buildings. Morgan, brave to temerity, stormed and raged. Hendricks, Steele, Nichols, Humphreys, equally brave, were sedate, though under a tremendous fire. The platform, which was within our view, was [at last] evacuated by the accuracy of our fire, and few persons dared venture there again.

Now it was that the necessity of the occupancy of the houses on our side of the barrier became apparent. Orders were given by Morgan to that effect. We entered—this was near daylight. The houses were a shelter from which we could fire with much accuracy. Yet even here some valuable lives were lost. Hendricks, when aiming his rifle at some prominent person, died by a straggling ball through his heart. He staggered a few feet backwards and fell upon a bed, where he instantly expired. He was an ornament of our little society. The amiable Humphreys died by a like kind of wound, but . . . before we entered the buildings.

Many other brave men fell at this place. Among these were Lieutenant Cooper, of Connecticut, and perhaps fifty or sixty noncommissioned officers and privates. The wounded were numerous, and many of them dangerously so. Captain Lamb, of the . . . artillerists, had nearly one half of his face carried away by a grape or canister shot. My friend Steele lost three of his fingers as he was presenting his gun to fire.

With all hope of success now gone, Henry explains, some of the Americans, together with a number of Canadian and Indian allies, took to their heels:

. . . [They] escaped across the ice which covered the Bay of St. Charles. . . . This was a dangerous and desperate adventure, but worth while the undertaking. . . . Its desperateness consisted in running two miles across shoal ice thrown up by the high tides of this latitude—and its danger in the meeting with air holes deceptively covered by the bed of snow.

Henry laments the fact that while the rest of the men (about four hundred in number) were trying to decide what to do, a party of the enemy issued from the upper town through Palace Gate and came

around the wall and cooped them up. "About nine o'clock a.m. it was
apparent to all of us that we must surrender. It was done."

   Most of the troops who had retreated from the action returned
to their former positions in the suburbs. Expecting an immediate
counterattack, Benedict Arnold, from his hospital bed, ordered a
keen watch kept on the fortress. Shortly a small detachment came
marching toward the hospital. Dr. Senter writes that artillery fire
turned it back:

   Notwithstanding this, we were momentarily expecting them out
upon us. . . . Under these circumstances we entreated Colonel
Arnold, for his own safety, to be carried back into the country where
they would not readily find him . . . but to no purpose. He would
neither be removed, nor suffer a man from the hospital to retreat.
He ordered his pistols loaded, with a sword on his bed, etc., adding
that he was determined to kill as many as possible if they came into
the room. We were now all soldiers, even to the wounded in their
beds [who] were ordered a gun by their side. . . . An express was
sent off to Congress informing of our situation and requesting immediate assistance. . . . The prospect was gloomy on every side.

Of the situation a few days later, Senter says:

   The troops were stationed in the most advantageous position for
preventing the enemy making any descent upon us. The number
[of our men] I cannot exactly ascertain, but imagine them to be
about 400. We had now relinquished the idea of taking the city by
force till a reinforcement should arrive. Contented ourselves with
barely keeping up the blockade. . . .

As for the Americans imprisoned in the fortress, they were regarded
with disdain by many of the more gentlemanly redcoats, one of
whom scoffed in a letter:

   You can have no conception what kind of men composed their
officers. Of those we took, one major was a blacksmith, another
a hatter. Of their captains, there was a butcher, a tanner, a shoe-
maker, a tavern-keeper, etc. Yet they pretended to be gentlemen.

Sir Guy Carleton, to his credit, insisted that all of the Americans be
treated well, and gave them assurances that they would eventually
be freed. When some of his officers complained that he was being
too lenient, he said, "Since we have tried in vain to make them

acknowledge us as brothers, let us at least send them away dis-
posed to regard us as first cousins."

Benedict Arnold learned of Carleton's kindness and was im-
pressed. But he had no change of heart about his mission against
the general's forces. On January 6 he wrote:

We are as well prepared to receive them as we can possibly be
in our present situation. . . . I expect General Wooster from Montreal in a few days with a reinforcement. I hope we shall be properly supported with troops by the Congress. I have no thoughts of
leaving this proud town until I first enter it in triumph. My wound
has been exceeding painful, but is now easy, and the surgeons assure
me [it] will be well in eight weeks. . . . I am in the way of my
duty and know no fear.

The Quebec issue wasn't to be settled quickly. Benedict Arnold's
support would be slow in coming. As for Sir Guy Carleton, he had
decided to await the arrival of reinforcements from England; and
they weren't due until spring.

8

A SCATTERING OF SPARKS

Dᴜʀɪɴɢ *the latter months of 1775, while the Canadian campaign developed and the two armies at Boston continued to glower at each other, it became apparent also in other areas that the drift toward full-scale war was accelerating.*

Incidents involving the British fleet were common. The king's warships cruised the colonial coasts at will. Landings were sometimes made for the purpose of securing fresh meat for Boston's hungry garrison. These alarms prompted some of the coastal towns to take defensive measures. A Patriot newspaper, the Constitutional Gazette, *announced in an item dated September 11:*

The people of New Hampshire are building a strong fort at Pierce's Island, in Piscataqua River, in order to prevent their capital, the town of Portsmouth, from being attacked by the piratical ships-of-war which now infest this coast.

Of course, the New Hampshire Patriots were not above committing piratical acts themselves. According to an article in the New York Journal *dated three weeks later:*

This evening arrived in the Piscataqua River a ship from England intended for Boston. . . . Meeting a fisherman at the eastward of Cape Ann, the captain inquired the course to Boston. The honest fisherman, pointing towards the Piscataqua, said, "There is Boston." The crew shaped their course accordingly, and soon found themselves under the guns of a battery lately erected by the people of New Hampshire. The commander of the battery, with a number of men, very humanely went on board to pilot the ship up to Portsmouth.

"I cannot go there," said the captain of the ship. "I am bound to Boston."

"But you must," replied the other.

Then he ordered her to get under way, and soon carried her safe alongside a wharf, where she is taken proper care of. She has been out eleven weeks from Bristol, in England, and has on board eighteen hundred barrels, and four hundred half barrels, of flour intended for the use of the besieged army in Boston.

Other British merchant ships fell to the Americans as the result of a growing system of privateering, which was legalized piracy, with the captains holding government licenses. Most of the vessels being armed for this purpose were owned either privately or by the individual colonies, but Congress had placed a few directly under Washington's control. The success of these small, fast vessels depended upon their ability to elude the vigilant British warships. The warships posed a threat also to the coastal towns that produced and harbored privateers. A few of the towns were fired upon; and one —Falmouth (now Portland), in the province of Maine—was burned. But the growth of privateering wasn't impeded. A November entry in Dr. James Thacher's journal exults:

The joyful intelligence is now announced in the public papers that Captain Manly, of Marblehead, commander of one of our privateers, has captured an English ship bound to Boston, loaded with ordnance stores of immense value at the present time. Among the ordnance is a large brass mortar on a new construction, and a number of pieces of fine brass cannon. There are small arms, ammunition, utensils, etc., etc., in great abundance. An invoice, it is said, could scarcely be formed of articles better suited to our wants and circumstances. Several other store vessels have been taken by our privateers, with cargoes of provisions and various kinds of stores, to a very considerable amount, which greatly augments the distresses of the troops and people in Boston and affords us a very opportune and essential supply.

Tensions increased meanwhile in the various colonial capitals as Patriots contended with royal governors. The outcome of this strug-

gle in New York was recorded by Thomas Jones, the Loyalist judge:

In the beginning of October, 1775, the Governor [William Tryon] received information . . . that it was then proposed to apprehend him as an enemy to America, make him a prisoner, transport him to Connecticut, and there confine him till the end of the war. Alarmed at this intelligence, he prudently withdrew from the town and took refuge on board the *Asia* man-of-war, then in the harbor.

During these same autumn days, according to Gaine's Mercury *(a New York weekly), South Carolina was the scene of a similar incident:*

Lord William Campbell . . . has fled with the utmost precipitation on board the man-of-war in the harbor, the Committee of Charleston having . . . discovered that his excellency had employed . . . an Indian commissary in the interior parts of that province to engage the Indians in the [British] service.

Virginia's John Murray, Earl of Dunmore, was the most assertive of the colonial governors. Convinced that he could bring his colony's rebels to heel, he enlisted the aid of the British fleet and his Loyalist supporters; and he even went so far as to issue a proclamation offering freedom to all slaves and indentured servants who took up arms for the king. But Lord Dunmore underestimated Virginia's revolutionary spirit. The Patriot elements, led by such firebrands as Patrick Henry, were quite as aroused as their New England cousins. Virginia's militiamen won a decisive victory over Dunmore's forces in a sharp skirmish at Great Bridge on December 9. Dunmore, however, took to the sea and retaliated drastically on New Year's Day, 1776. As reported by the Pennsylvania Evening Post *in an item dated January 2:*

Yesterday, at about quarter after three o'clock, the British fleet lying off Norfolk, Virginia, commenced a cannonade against that town, from upwards of one hundred pieces of cannon, and continued till nearly ten o'clock at night without intermission. It then abated a little, and continued till two this morning. Under cover of their guns, the regulars landed and set fire to the town in several places near the water, though our men strove all in their power to prevent them. The houses being chiefly of wood, took fire immediately, and the fire spread with amazing rapidity. It is now become general, and the whole town will probably be consumed in a day or two.

Even before the ashes were cold, a citizen of Virginia who referred to himself as AN AMERICAN *penned for publication an article that included this sentiment:*

We hope our countrymen will not be at all dispirited at the destruction of Norfolk, but rather rejoice that half the mischief our enemies can do us is done already. They have destroyed one of the first towns in America, and the only one (except two or three) in Virginia which carried on anything like a trade. We are only sharing part of the sufferings of our American brethren, and can now glory in having received one of the keenest strokes of the enemy without flinching.

None of the king's governors could muster enough power to aid his cause effectively. All they managed to do was make the Patriots more intransigent. As for the Loyalists who gave active support to the governors, their chief accomplishment was to bring greater disfavor upon Loyalists everywhere. These people had become fair game for the Patriots, whose repressive measures had the secret approval of the Continental Congress. In November, 1775, the colony of New York was the scene of a mob action that won widespread Patriot applause, since its chief accomplishment was the silencing of an influential Loyalist press. As narrated by the Pennsylvania Journal:

On the twentieth of this month, sixteen respectable inhabitants of New Haven, Connecticut, in company with Captain Sears, set out from that place to East and West Chester, in the province of New York, to disarm the principal Tories there and secure the persons of Parson Seabury, Judge Fowler and Lord Underhill. On their way thither they were joined by Captains Richards, Sillick and Mead, with about eighty men. At Mamaroneck they burnt a small sloop which was . . . [used] for the purpose of carrying provisions on board the *Asia*. At East Chester they seized Judge Fowler, then repaired to West Chester and secured Seabury and Underhill. Having possessed themselves of these three caitiffs, they sent them to Connecticut under a strong guard.

The main body, consisting of seventy-five, then proceeded to New York, where they entered at noonday on horseback, bayonets fixed, in the greatest regularity, went down the main street and

drew up in close order before the printing office of the infamous
James Rivington. A small detachment entered it, and in about
three-quarters of an hour brought off the principal part of his types
[having smashed his presses]. . . . They then faced and wheeled
to the left and marched out of town to the tune of Yankee Doodle.
A vast concourse of people assembled at the Coffee House, on
their leaving the ground, and gave them three very hearty cheers.

On their way home they disarmed all the Tories that lay on their
route, and yesterday arrived at New Haven escorted by a great number of gentlemen from the westward, the whole making a very grand
procession. Upon their entrance into town they were saluted with
the discharge of two cannon and received by the inhabitants with
every mark of approbation and respect. The company divided into
two parts and concluded the day in festivity and innocent mirth. . . .
Seabury, Underhill and Fowler, three of the dastardly protesters
against the proceedings of the Continental Congress, and who it
is believed had concerted a plan for kidnapping Captain Sears
and conveying him on board the *Asia* man-of-war, are . . . safely
lodged in New Haven. . . .

Loyalist Judge Jones adds angrily:
  . . . they were all confined in a public house under a strict
guard, where every low-lived wretch for ten miles around the
country had free liberty to enter their apartments at pleasure and
to treat them with the vilest language, accusing them as enemies
to their country, as the friends of a tyrant, and betrayers of the
liberties of America. . . . These gentlemen, after being detained as
prisoners for many weeks at a heavy expense to themselves (no
provision being made for their maintenance) and absent from their
business, their families, and avocations, were discharged and suffered to return home without the least compensation being made
for the damages they sustained, and without being ever permitted
to prosecute the persons by whom they had been robbed, plundered, pillaged, insulted and imprisoned, for no other reason than
acknowledging themselves (as they really were) the lawful subjects
of the King of Great Britain.

*An example of one of the commonest things done to professed
Loyalists was noted in a December issue of the* New York Journal:
  At Quibbletown, New Jersey, Thomas Randolph, cooper, who
had publicly proved himself an enemy to his country by reviling

and using his utmost endeavors to oppose the proceedings of the continental and provincial conventions in defence of their rights and liberties; and being judged a person not of consequence enough for a severer punishment, was ordered to be stripped naked, well coated with tar and feathers, and carried in a wagon publicly around the town—which punishment was accordingly inflicted. As soon as he became duly sensible of his offence, for which he earnestly begged pardon, and promised to atone as far as he was able by a contrary behavior for the future, he was released and suffered to return to his house in less than half an hour. The whole was conducted with that regularity and decorum that ought to be observed in all public punishments.

Not all of the Patriots approved of Tory persecution. Some, in fact, were deeply distressed by the practice. But no less a person than George Washington believed that the Tories had to be subdued: "Why should persons who are preying on the vitals of this country be suffered to stalk at large, whilst we know that they will do us every mischief in their power?"

There were, of course, Patriot women who joined the campaign against the Tories. A diarist of the day recorded:

The following droll affair lately happened at Kinderhook, New York. A young fellow, an enemy to the liberties of America, going to a quilting frolic where a number of young women were collected, and he the only man in company, began his aspersions on Congress as usual, and held forth some time on the subject, till the girls, exasperated at his impudence, laid hold of him, stripped him naked to the waist, and instead of tar, covered him with molasses, and for feathers took the downy tops of flags which grow in the meadows, and coated him well and then let him go.

Writing busily at a desk in Philadelphia during the widespread embroilments of the final weeks of 1775 was the passionate pamphleteer Thomas Paine. He was completing work on Common Sense, *which soon would swirl through the colonies in something like snowflake numbers, doing much to consolidate America's revolutionary spirit. Urging the necessity of an immediate formal separation of the colonies from England, it would represent them as a symbol of the worldwide struggle against governmental oppression. Patriot readers would thrill to such sentences as:*

The sun never shined on a cause of greater worth. . . . Posterity

are virtually involved in the contest . . . even to the end of time. . . .
I challenge the warmest advocate for reconciliation to show a single
advantage that this continent can reap by being connected with
Great Britain. . . . But the injuries and disadvantages which we
sustain by that connection are without number; and our duty to
mankind at large, as well as to ourselves, instructs us to renounce
the alliance. . . . O ye that love mankind! Ye that dare oppose not
only the tyranny but the tyrant, stand forth!

9

WASHINGTON EARNS A MEDAL

IN AUGUST, *1775, Washington had believed his army, despite its many shortcomings, to be a match for the redcoats; but they made no attempt to push out of Boston, and the plans he devised for going in were voted down by his generals. Soon the army's state of readiness, so precarious in the first place, began to decline alarmingly. Short-term enlistments constituted one of Washington's chief problems. Most of the men would be free to walk out of camp at the end of the year. He knew that it would be difficult to persuade many to reenlist, especially since the chances of action seemed remote. Maintaining the siege was, for the most part, burdensome and boring work, which made it all the easier for a man to convince himself that his presence before Boston was not essential.*

Another grave problem was the sluggishness of the Continental Congress in meeting the army's needs. The delegates were intelligent and industrious, but as yet somewhat unsure of themselves— and unsure of how much power should be entrusted to Washington. They had much to learn about running a war. Moreover, their resources were limited. Washington wrote to Congress in this manner on September 21:

It gives me great pain to be obliged to solicit the attention of the honourable Congress to the state of this army in terms which imply the slightest apprehension of being neglected. But my situation is inexpressibly distressing, to see the winter fast approaching upon a naked army, the time of their service within a few weeks of expiring, and no provision yet made for such important events. Added to these, the military chest is totally exhausted. The paymaster has not a single dollar in hand. The commissary-general, he assures me, has strained his credit for the subsistence of the army to the utmost. The quartermaster-general is precisely in the same situation; and the greater part of the troops are in a state not far from mutiny [because of] the deduction from their stated allowance. I know not to whom I am to impute this failure; but I am of [the] opinion, if the evil is not immediately remedied, and more punctuality observed in the future, the army must absolutely break up.

This letter brought a Congressional committee, headed by Benjamin Franklin, hurrying to Cambridge to consult with Washington and several influential representatives of the New England colonies. Steps were taken to alleviate the pressing need for money and supplies; and plans were developed for building a new army (on the foundations of the old) of twenty thousand men. If enlistments went so slowly as to imperil Washington's strength, he was to call out the New England militia. During the drive to stimulate reenlistments among the men then under arms, copies of a patriotic appeal, written by A FREEMAN, *were passed about the camp:*

Your exertions in the cause of freedom, guided by wisdom and animated by zeal and courage, have gained you the love and confidence of your grateful countrymen. And they look to you, who are EXPERIENCED VETERANS, and trust that you will still be the GUARDIANS OF AMERICA. . . . I doubt not America will always find enough of her sons ready to flock to her standard and support her freedom; but experience proves that *experienced* soldiers are more capable of performing the duties of the camp, and better qualified to face the enemy than others. . . . Although your private concerns may call for your assistance at home, yet the voice of your country is still louder. . . . Notwithstanding the many difficulties we have to encounter, and the rage of our merciless enemies, we have a glorious prospect before us, big with everything good and great. . . . Persevere, YE GUARDIANS OF LIBERTY! May success be your constant attendant until the enemies of freedom are no more. And all future generations, as they successively tread the stage of time and taste the JOYS OF LIBERTY, will rise up and call YOU blessed.

Unfortunately, this eloquent composition inspired no stampede toward the reenlistment desk. A great many of the soldiers gave advance notice that they intended to leave camp as soon as their terms expired. New troops arrived slowly, and early in December Washington had to call out the militia. The response was good, and disaster was averted. But this was only a temporary measure. The drive for regular enlistments had to be continued.

Perhaps Washington's only real comfort, as Christmas approached, was an occurrence described in a Cambridge news note of December 14: "Last Monday night, came to town from Virginia, the lady of his Excellency, General Washington, and the lady of the Hon. Adjutant-General Gates, accompanied by John Custis, Esq., and lady, and George Lewis, Esq." Washington's friend and aide, Joseph Reed, called the ladies of the party, "no bad supply, I think, in a cold country where wood is scarce."

Action between the Americans and the British during this period was limited to exchanges of artillery fire, with the British throwing most of the missiles. The Americans were still short of artillery, though some of the best of the Lake Champlain cannon were now on their way to camp. The enemy's superiority in heavy weapons, said Dr. Thacher, hadn't gained him much:

It is stated, from the minutes of some person, that from Breed's Hill battle to the 25th instant, the British have thrown upwards of two thousand shot and shells. By the whole firing, on Cambridge side they killed only seven, and on Roxbury side five—just a dozen in the whole. At this rate, how many shot and bombs will it require to subdue the whole of his majesty's rebellious subjects?

On January 1, 1776, Washington raised the first Continental flag over the Cambridge camp. The banner held thirteen alternating red and white stripes, but in its upper left corner was a reproduction of the British Union flag. (Not until June 14, 1777, would Congress provide for the replacement of this British symbol with a blue field holding thirteen white stars.) The beginning of 1776 was a time of great change for Washington's army. "The officers and men of the new regiments," General William Heath explained, "were joining their respective corps. Those of the old regiments were going home by hundreds and by thousands. . . . Such a change, in the very teeth of an enemy, is a most delicate manoeuvre. . . ." In a letter dated January 4, Washington wrote:

Search the vast volumes of history through, and I much question whether a case similar to ours is to be found; to wit, to maintain

a post against the flower of the British troops for six months together, without [powder]; and at the end of them to have one
army disbanded and another to raise within the same distance of a
reinforced enemy. It is too much to attempt. . . . I wish this month
was well over our heads. . . . We are now left with a good deal less
than half raised regiments, and about five thousand militia, who
will stand ingaged to the middle of this month; when, according
to custom, they will depart. . . .

In another letter, the general confessed:
  The reflection on my situation and that of this army produces
many an unhappy hour when all around me are wrapped in sleep.
. . . I have often thought how much happier I should have been
if, instead of accepting the command under such circumstances,
I had taken my musket on my shoulder and entered the ranks; or, if
I could have justified the measure to posterity and my own con-
science, had retired to the back country and lived in a wigwam.

*There were some improvements in the enlistment picture during
January, with groups arriving not only from several parts of New
England but from the middle colonies. And Washington found
himself with nearly ten thousand men—not the army he wished for,
but one that was at least capable of asserting itself.*
  *During the critical months leading to this point, the Americans
were puzzled by the attitude of the British. The danger that the
British would attack the besiegers seemed very real, but nothing
happened. The Americans had reason to be especially alert for
a change in the enemy's policy as early as October, when Thomas
Gage was recalled to England and his command fell to Sir William
Howe. One of the officers in Washington's camp who gave some careful thought to the enemy's attitude and its effect was young Captain
James Wilkinson:*
  It is difficult to account for Sir William Howe's extreme caution
after he succeeded General Gage in command. . . . But whatever
may have been the cause, whether motives of personal policy, or
views to ulterior operations on a more favorable theatre, or the
desire to spare his troops until he should receive reinforcements;
or whether . . . he waited for instructions from his government, his
conduct operated favourably for the revolution. The free use of his
artillery familiarised our men to danger; and by suffering himself
to be shut up in the town of Boston, he enabled General Washington

Portrait of Sir William Howe published in England in 1778.
(Library of Congress)

to make a selection of officers, to levy a new army, to organize his corps, to assimilate, partially, their modes of duty and exercise, to cherish the confidence of his troops, and to infuse among them some sense of the *esprit de corps*. Nor did he imitate the example of his antagonist; for, however puny his force, however circumscribed his means, [Washington] omitted no enterprise calculated to straiten the quarters of the enemy.

One such enterprise was described in a letter written by a British officer in Boston:

On the 8th [of January], between eight and nine o'clock at night, we were alarmed by some of the enemy, who came over a small neck of land by a mill upon Charlestown side and came into some houses that were not destroyed [during the Battle of Bunker Hill], where they surprised and took one sergeant and three private men prisoners, who belonged to a wooding party; after which they set fire to the houses and retreated under a heavy fire of cannon and musketry from one of our redoubts.

Among the rest, they had got a stout fellow of ours (a grenadier) . . . who pretended to be lame and [that he] could walk but slowly . . . and the rebel captain who commanded the party told his men to retreat [on the run], saying, "I swear I will take this serpent of a regular under my charge." But upon his going over the neck of land, the grenadier struck the captain a severe blow on his face with his fist, took him up in his arms, pitched him headlong into the mud, and then ran off.

But what is most extraordinary, a new farce was that night to have been acted at Boston, called the Blockade of Boston [said to have ·been written by General Burgoyne]. The [preliminary] play was just ended and the curtain going to be drawn up for the farce when the actors heard [a report] from without that an attack was made on the heights of Charlestown; upon which one of them [went on the stage] dressed in the character of a Yankee sergeant (which character he was to play), desired silence and informed the audience . . . that the rebels had attacked . . . and were at it tooth and nail over at Charlestown.

The audience, thinking this was the opening of the new piece, clapped prodigiously. But soon finding their mistake, a general scene of confusion ensued. They immediately hurried out of the house to their alarm posts, some skipping over the orchestra, trampling on the fiddles, and everyone making his most speedy retreat. The actors (who were all officers) calling out for water to wash the smut and paint from off their faces; women fainting; and, in short, the whole house was nothing but one scene of confusion, terror and tumult.

I was on guard at the advance lines before the town of Roxbury, and we expected a general attack that night; but the rebels were not so forward, for in a few hours everything was quiet.

On January 18, General William Heath noted in his journal: "Col. Knox, of the artillery, came to camp. He brought from Ticonderoga a fine train of artillery which had been taken from the British, both cannon and mortars. . . ." Henry Knox, a huge, amiable man who had been a bookseller in Boston before the war, had performed a remarkable feat and a valuable service. He had brought about sixty heavy weapons almost two hundred miles over snowy mountains and ice-covered waterways. His conveyances were sleds drawn by oxen and horses.

Gaining this ordnance raised Washington's spirits and increased his confidence. While the weapons were being set up in well-chosen places along the lines, he made plans to bring the long siege to a climax. In General Heath's words:

The heights round Boston [and Charlestown], except those at Dorchester, having been taken possession of, it was now determined that these also should be occupied; and great previous preparation was made for the purpose. It was imagined that so near an approach to the British would induce them to make a sally. . . .

Writing on March 1, Major Samuel Webb of Connecticut added:

This is what we wish for. . . . This would be a means of rescuing from their hands our Capital and many of our friends who are now confined there. . . . Should they not sally on us, we have a prospect of making them to take to their ships and flee. In this case we fear the loss of the Town by their setting fire to it—but this is trifling in comparison to the loss of our Invaluable Privileges. . . .

On the following day, Webb wrote:

'Tis intended this night to convince the enemy we have it in our power to disturb their camp by shells [from our present positions] and to keep them under arms. . . .

According to a British colonel named Charles Stuart:

. . . at nine o'clock . . . they began a pretty hot cannonade and bombardment. Their shells . . . took effect near the centre of the town and tore several houses to pieces. . . . One shot killed 8 men of the 22nd Regt. . . .

Major Webb took no part in the night's action:
    I am unhappily confined to my room, but from my window have a most pleasing and yet dismal view of the firey Ministers of Death flying thro the air. Poor inhabitants, our friends, we pity most sincerely. . . .

The British returned the fire, but with poor results. At dawn the exchange became sporadic, and it remained so throughout the day. But darkness saw it stepped up again, to the fascination of England's Colonel Charles Stuart:
    . . . a nobler scene it was impossible to behold: sheets of fire seemed to come from our batteries. Some of the shells crossed one another in the air, and then bursting, looked beautiful.

Again, with the coming of daylight the firing diminished. On the third evening (March 4) the Americans moved to occupy Dorchester Heights. Dr. Thacher penned in his journal:
    We are favored with a full bright moon, and the night is remarkably mild and pleasant. The preparations are immense. More than three hundred loaded carts are in motion. By the great exertions of General [Thomas] Mifflin, our quarter-master-general, the requisite number of teams has been procured. The covering party of eight hundred men advance in front. Then follow the carts with the intrenching tools; after which, the working party of twelve hundred, commanded by General [John] Thomas. . . . Next in the martial procession are a train of carts loaded with fascines [tightly bound bundles of sticks] and hay screwed into large bundles of seven or eight hundred weight [materials to be used for erecting defenses]. The whole procession moved on in solemn silence. . . .

However, writes General Heath, noise existed elsewhere: "There was an almost incessant roar of cannon and mortars during the night, on both sides." Connecticut's Major Webb says of this:
    . . . we had one lieut. and one private killed, and two privates slightly wounded. . . . Our shell raked the houses [in Boston] terri-

bly, and the crys of poor women and children frequently reached our ears.

Few, if any, civilians actually were harmed by this fire; nor were there many military casualties. General Heath goes on:

The Americans took possession of Dorchester Heights and nearly completed their works . . . by morning. Perhaps there was never so much work done in so short a space of time. The adjoining orchards were cut down to make the abatis; and a very curious and novel mode of defence was added to these works. The hills on which they were erected were steep, and clear of trees and bushes. Rows of barrels, filled with earth, were placed round the works. They presented only the appearance of strengthening the works; but the real design was, in case the enemy made an attack, to have rolled them down the hill. They would have descended with such increasing velocity as must have thrown the assailants into the utmost confusion, and have killed and wounded great numbers.

Says Charles Stuart, the British colonel:

. . . at daybreak . . . we perceived two posts upon the highest hills of Dorchester peninsula that appeared more like majick than the work of human beings.

Another redcoat commented that the defenses "were raised with an expedition equal to that of the Genii belonging to Aladdin's lamp." Returning to Dr. Thacher's journal:

The enemy having discovered our works . . . commenced a tremendous cannonade from the forts in Boston and from their shipping in the harbor. Cannon shot are continually rolling and rebounding over the hill; and it is astonishing to observe how little our soldiers are terrified by them.

During the forenoon we were in momentary expectation of witnessing an awful scene. Nothing less than the carnage of Breed's Hill battle was expected. . . . The hills and elevations in this vicinity are covered with spectators to witness deeds of horror in the expected conflict. His Excellency General Washington is present, animating and encouraging the soldiers, and they in return manifest their joy and express a warm desire for the approach of the enemy.

Washington's desire for the enemy's approach doubtless exceeded that of his men. He intended to hurl a second force against Boston as soon as it should be left weakened. But not until late in the day, he explains, did the British make a move:

. . . a considerable number of their troops embarked on board of their transports and fell down to [Castle Island], where part of them landed before dark. One or two of the vessels got aground and were fired at by our people with a field-piece, but without any damage. . . . It would seem as if they meant an attack. . . . If such was their design, a violent storm that night, and which lasted till eight o'clock the next day, rendered the execution of it impracticable.

Washington had guessed right. General Howe later reported to England that he had indeed planned to land troops on the Dorchester peninsula during the night but was frustrated by the storm. He added:

The weather continuing boisterous the next day and night, gave the enemy time to improve their works, to bring up their cannon and to put themselves into such a state of defence that I could promise myself little success by attacking them under all the disadvantages I had to encounter. . . .

Howe's position was now untenable. The Dorchester cannon overlooked Boston's wharves, and not a ship in the harbor was safe. On March 8, Dr. Thacher wrote:

A flag of truce has come out of Boston . . . acquainting General Washington that General Howe has come to the determination to evacuate the town; and that he would leave it standing, provided his army should be permitted to retire without being molested; at the same time intimating . . . that in case he should be attacked by our army the town should be set on fire in different places in order to secure his retreat.

Sir William describes his preparations for departure:

A thousand difficulties arose on account of the disproportion of transports for the conveyance of the troops, the well-affected inhabitants [the Loyalists], their most valuable property, and the quantity of military stores to be carried away. However, as the enemy gave no interruption but during the nights, and that inconsiderable . . . this operation was effected on the 17th. . . .

As reported by an American newspaperman:

This morning the British army in Boston . . . consisting of up-wards of seven thousand men, after suffering an ignominious block-ade for many months past, disgracefully quitted all their strong-holds in Boston and Charlestown, fled from before the army of the United Colonies, and took refuge on board their ships. . . .

The joy of our friends in Boston, on seeing the victorious and gallant troops of their country enter the town almost at the heels of their barbarous oppressors, was inexpressibly great. The mutual congratulations and tender embraces, which soon afterwards took place, between those of the nearest connections in life, for a long time cruelly rent asunder by the tyranny of our implacable enemies, surpasses description.

From such a set of beings, the preservation of property was not expected. And it was found that a great part of the evacuated houses had been pillaged, the furniture broken and destroyed, and many of the buildings greatly damaged. It is worthy of notice, how-ever, that the buildings belonging to the honorable John Hancock, Esq., particularly his elegant mansion house, are left in good order. . . .

All their forts, batteries, redoubts, and breastworks remain en-tire and complete. They have left many of their heaviest cannon mounted on carriages, and several of them charged, all of which are either spiked or have a trunnion beaten off. They have also left several of their largest mortars. Quantities of cannon shot, shells, numbers of small arms and other instruments of war have been found, thrown off the wharves, concealed in vaults, or broken in pieces. In the fort on Bunker's Hill several hundred good blankets were found. It is said about fifteen or twenty of the king's horses have also been taken up in the town; and it is thought that about the same number of Tories remain behind.

We are told that the Tories were thunder-struck when orders were issued for evacuating the town, after being many hundred times assured that such reinforcements would be sent as to enable the king's troops to ravage the country at pleasure. Thus are many of those deluded creatures, those vile traitors to their country, obliged at last, in their turn, to abandon their once delightful habi-tations, and go they know not where.

Washington felt that Howe would move quickly to occupy the port of New York. By gaining command of the Hudson River, which extended northward toward Lake Champlain, the British could isolate New England from the rest of the colonies and strive for control of the inland water route to Canada. Howe did intend to occupy New York, but he sailed first for Halifax, Nova Scotia, in order to revitalize his troops and await a promised reinforcement from England. According to Captain James Wilkinson, of Washington's command:

For the safety of New York, General Lee [some weeks earlier] had been ordered to that city, and the rifle regiment and other corps had been detached to support him. The commander-in-chief now put in motion for the same place the main body of his inlisted yeomanry, who were engaged to the end of the year.

During the brief time that Washington himself lingered in Boston, Wilkinson says, he was treated as a hero.

. . . General Washington enjoyed his triumph and the merited honours conferred on him by the voice of Massachusetts with characteristic dignity and reserve. . . .

Washington's rewards for his victory—which was considered a great one—included an honorary degree from Harvard College. Later, when he was in New York, the general received a letter from the Continental Congress voting him its thanks and telling him that he was to be given a specially struck gold medal. A prophetic passage included these words:

Those pages in the annals of America will record your title to a conspicuous place in the temple of fame, which shall inform posterity that, under your direction, an undisciplined band of husbandmen, in the course of a few months, became soldiers. . . .

10

CARLETON TAKES THE OFFENSIVE

A T QUEBEC, *according to Dr. Isaac Senter's journal, the winter had passed without major incident:*
We were, however, alarmed often by their coming out into the suburbs, pillaging after fire-wood, etc. They took down any building they could come at for that purpose. This occasioned the Colonel [Benedict Arnold] to give orders to our troops to burn and destroy as many of the houses as they would be likely to obtain, in order to distress them, in hopes they would be obliged to capitulate for want of fire-wood, etc. We, however, came short in our expectations to reduce them in this way, notwithstanding every house was burnt in the city suburbs where our troops could come nigh enough.

. . . to the 18th of March [1776] nothing extraordinary happening. Burning the houses to prevent the enemy's getting them often occasioned slight skirmishing, with various success, but nothing capital. About this time arrived troops from Montreal to our assistance. Several deserters coming out [to us], but never able to obtain a true state of their army. From this to April the 3d, no occurrences of moment. Troops [from the colonies] coming up to our relief. A battery opened from Point Levi upon the city, but being scanty of ammunition were allowanced only a few rounds per day, just to keep the enemy in continual alarm. . . . Arnold had some time since received a brigadier's commission, but being a younger officer than General Wooster, then commanding at Montreal, [he] was superseded. . . .

General Arnold had so far recovered of his wound ere General Wooster's arrival [at Quebec] as to be able to ride a horseback. This aspiring genius, so much disgusted at being superseded at a time when he had not only nearly recovered of his wound but was in daily expectation of the enemy's surrendering for lack of necessaries. His tarry after this was short. He repaired to Montreal and took the command there.

The 22d of this month [April] a battery [of ours] opened from the bank of Charles River. . . . From this was discharged red hot shot, in hopes of firing the town. They returned the fire exceeding heavy, but no considerable harm from either side. Two of our artillery men were wounded very much by the cartridges taking fire while ramming them home, but recovered again. The enemy continued their cannonade and bombardment excessive heavy, while we were restricted to a certain number per day in consequence of very little ammunition. . . .

The reign of Wooster was but short, and about the 5th of May he was superseded by Gen. [John] Thomas [from Massachusetts]. About this time a plot was formed to burn the shipping in the harbour. A fire ship was completed in charge of Adjutant Anderson, a very brave officer, but proved abortive by reason of the tide ebbing before he could get up to the shipping. The combustibles took fire before he intended, by which accident he was much burnt. He was, however, got on shore, and no lives lost.

The small-pox still continued in the army. Numbers of the soldiers inoculated themselves, and indeed several officers, tho' contrary to orders at this time. Scarce any of the New England recruits had ever had the disorder, and coming into the army when it was very [rife] gave apprehensions of taking it in the natural way, which many did.

. . . to the sixth of May, no momentous occurrence from either side, except a report from down the river [toward the sea], brought us by some of the honest peasants, that a fleet was coming up. To this there was not sufficient credit given, imagining it impossible for any arrival so early in the spring.

General Wooster being superseded gave him great distress, and General Thomas being an utter stranger in the country, and much terrified [of] the small-pox. Strongly neglecting the reports of the approach of the enemy's fleet, tho' repeatedly attested to by several of the good inhabitants, till the morning of the sixth, when we were alarmed by the discharge of cannon down the river. These [salutes] were immediately answered from the city, and at half an hour by sun, four ships arrived in the harbour. Immediately upon landing their marines, soldiers, etc., they rushed out in parties, the one for [our] Head Quarters upon the Plains of Abraham, and the other for [our] Hospital General.

The army was in such a scattered condition as rendered it impossible to collect them either for a regular retreat or to bring them into action. In this dilemma, orders were given to as many of the troops to retreat as the time would permit; and in the most irregular, helter skelter manner we raised the siege, leaving every thing: all the camp equipment, ammunition, and even our clothing, except what little we happened to have on us.

Among the Americans in outlying areas who received the news somewhat late was Private Lemuel Roberts, a Massachusetts man who had just recently come north:

. . . we observed a man running towards us. On coming up he enquired for head quarters and informed [us] that our army were on the retreat. . . . The occurrences which ensued shocked me exceedingly. A groupe of exceeding pale faces appeared around me. . . . The symptoms of the small pox, or some other symptoms, operated too extensively to suit my feelings. One cried, "I cannot carry my pack!", another, "I must leave my clothes!", etc. In short, all was bustle and confusion. And, according to my conception, the *pale symptoms* were rather more evident in the officers than among the men. . . .

Though I was something weakened by dieting, etc., for the small pox, my pack was too valuable for me to abandon. And while I was preparing to swing it, our ensign offered me two good shirts if I would carry a third for him, and I packed them up. Our captain, too, wanted me to take a pair of his shoes, and a pair of his son's, who waited on him; and I obliged him—and kept receiving from one and another till my pack weighed about seventy pounds. And using much persuasion to induce others to follow my example, so far at least as to save their own clothes, and laughing some out of their plea of inability, I swung my pack and started with them on our march for the bank of the river St. Lawrence to join our retreating army. On reaching the bank of the river, we perceived two British vessels had passed us and lay at anchor some distance from the shore, on the line of our projected march. On our coming opposite to them, a great part of our men crept along up the bank among the bushes, and [only] a few kept the road on the flats, in sight of the enemy.

Setting down in this place with one of my comrades, on a pile of rails which lay in the road, and looking at these vessels, I humorously observed to him that as long as I had been a soldier I never yet had an opportunity to fire at the enemy, and was thinking to improve it now. On this, levelling my piece about topmast high and discharging it in fun—at that very instant the vessels gave us one or two broadsides each. And it became laughable to see the skulkers scamper out of the bushes into the road as the balls made tearing work among the brush, while they entirely overshot the flats [which the skulkers had been avoiding]. From this firing of the enemy I believe no injury was received.

Dr. Senter's narrative resumes:

They . . . kept in chase of us up the river, both by land and water; and in the most disorderly manner we were obliged to escape as we could. . . . The most of our sick fell into their hands, with all hospital stores, etc. The first stand we endeavoured to make was at Point De Shombo [Deschambault], 45 miles from Quebec. But, not being able to collect provisions sufficient, were obliged to abandon it and proceed up along [the river]. The poor inhabitants, seeing we were abandoning their country, were in the utmost dilemma, expecting as many as had been aiding us . . . to be sacrificed to the barbarity of those whose severity they had long felt. . . .

No provisions could be obtained but by the force of arms. No conveniences for ferrying our troops over the rivers emptying in upon either side of the St. Lawrence, except a canoe or two, and these were rare. By reason of the spring flood, which in this country is amazing in many low places, the army were obliged to travel a great distance round them, as the river had overflowed its banks in many places to the distance of several miles. In this perplexed situation we, however, arrived at Sorel, about forty miles [from] Montreal, where we made a stand and collected our whole force, which was not very formidable, notwithstanding several [bodies of] new recruits had by this time arrived.

Temporarily, the pursuit had slacked off. The British were pausing to enable their reinforcements to catch up. Dr. Senter goes on:

The small-pox still very rife. . . . I was ordered by Gen. Thomas . . . to repair to Montreal and erect an hospital for their reception—

as well by the natural way as inoculation. I accordingly [went there], made application to General Arnold, then commanding in the city, and obtained a fine capacious house belonging to the East India Company. It was convenient for nigh six hundred. I generally inoculated a regiment at a class. . . . About this time an action happened up above Montreal, at the Cedars . . . between [an American party led by] Major [Henry] Sherburne . . . and a number of savages with one company of regular troops. Sherburne and the chief [portion] of his party were taken, some few killed, etc.

Senter fails to mention that the major and his men had been marching to the aid of several hundred Americans at a post that an enemy force, including many Indians, had surrounded. The post surrendered just before Sherburne's troops arrived; and as a result, after a short fight, they, too, were overcome. Benedict Arnold advanced on the enemy with seven hundred men, but his attack plans were frustrated by the threat the Indians posed to the prisoners; and he reluctantly agreed to negotiations for an exchange (the Americans having taken numerous prisoners at Chambly and St. John's the preceding autumn).

Dr. Senter says that discouragement was now strong in the American ranks:

Fortune and the country seemed jointly against us. . . . Our prospect was . . . gloomy. A committee from Congress had been in Montreal for some time . . . but it answered no purpose. Gen. Thomas [as he had feared] caught the natural small-pox, sickened . . . and died. Soon after this, General [John] Sullivan [of New Hampshire] arrived and took the command. Wooster went to Montreal, and Arnold to Chambly.

Early in June, General Sullivan decided to send a large detachment from Sorel (in newly acquired batteaux) to attack the British, who were then consolidating their forces at Three Rivers, a village about thirty miles back along the St. Lawrence. One of the redcoats at Three Rivers was Sergeant Roger Lamb, who wrote on June 8:

At three o'clock this morning our drums beat to arms, and we soon marched out of the village to meet our foe. This being the first skirmish I ever was engaged in, it really appeared to me to be a very serious matter. . . . This was a very bold enterprise indeed of the Americans to attack our troops. Two thousand of them [had] crossed over from Sorel in fifty boats, landed at the Point du Lac

. . . with an intention to surprise us. . . . General [Simon] Fraser, who commanded the British van, was not to be taken by surprise.

The Americans soon found that they were greatly mistaken in their intelligence concerning our position. When they discovered their mistake they were greatly alarmed, particularly when they found that Brigadier-General Nesbit, who had landed the troops from the transports, had got behind them. After some time they gave up offensive measures and retreated to the woods. Our troops . . . pushed forward in hopes of taking their boats and cutting off their retreat. Two boats only were taken; the rest escaped. The number of the Americans killed and wounded were considerable. About two hundred surrendered or were taken prisoners in the woods.

There were more Americans in the woods; but Sir Guy Carleton was on the scene, and he soon put an end to the hunt. He asked one of his officers, "What would you do with them? Have you spare provisions for them? Or would you send them to Quebec to starve? No, let the poor creatures go home and carry with them a tale which will serve his majesty more effectually than their capture."

Carleton, whose command had increased to nearly ten thousand men since the first reinforcements had reached Quebec, was now ready to resume his pressure on the whole body of the Americans. Dr. Senter describes the result:

Enemy drawing upon us from every quarter, assimilating the savages. Our army, weakened by the small-pox, and . . . every movement against the enemy unsuccessful, a retreat was ordered to St. John's.

Some of the troops fled by water, and others by land. Lemuel Roberts was among the marchers:

On the day this retreat commenced I was taken exceeding severely with the dissentery, and being on the rear guard I was obliged to drop behind . . . and was most severely put to it to regain my place. Endeavoring to do it . . . I came up to an imperious young officer stationed in the rear. This man, feeling the importance of his commission, used me with very rough language for straggling behind with intention, as he suggested, to be taken by the enemy.

I resented this insult with spirit; and he, furnishing himself

with a heavy club, threatened me with loud sounding words, and
told me how he would serve me if I did not run. I told him I was
unable to run, and he came at me with apparent fury. But having
a tomahawk in my hand, with a long handle, which I had used as a
staff, I stood my ground; and he was careful not to come within my
reach. There were in company with this choleric young officer one or
two others, who earnestly requested him to desist, and he readily
complying with their request . . . we soon parted company. My
necessary stops were so frequent as to render it impossible for me
to overtake the guard till the regiment halted. . . .

A large British force reached Sorel by water on June 14. Among
its officers was General John Burgoyne, lately of Boston. Its enlisted
men included Sergeant Roger Lamb, who shared the general ex-
citement caused by the discovery of burning campfires, which indi-
cated that the last American units had just left:
Our troops began to march in three columns. . . . Continued
our march day and night, expecting every hour to come up with
them. . . . It must be confessed that their distresses at this time
were very great. A British army close on their rear and threatening
them with destruction; their men obliged to drag their loaded
batteaux up the rapids by mere strength, often to their middle in
water. They were likewise encumbered with great numbers la-
bouring under that dreadful disease, the small pox, which is so fatal
in America. It was said that two regiments at one time had not a
single man in health; another had only six, and a fourth only forty;
and two more were nearly in the same condition.
While the Americans were retreating, they were daily annoyed
by the remonstrances of the inhabitants of Canada, who had either
joined or befriended them. Many of the Canadians had . . . in-
curred the heavy penalties annexed to the crime of supporting
rebellion. . . . The retreating army recommended them to cast
themselves on the mercy of that government against which they had
offended. . . . They did indeed receive mercy, for I never saw any
of them either imprisoned or otherwise punished . . . and I was in
Canada for twelve months after this.

The hard-pressed Americans did not linger long at St. John's. They
began crowding into their boats and leaving for Isle aux Noix, at
the northern end of Lake Champlain. Benedict Arnold refused to

hurry his own departure. He watched the embarkations in the company of a new aide-de-camp, Captain James Wilkinson, lately of the army at Cambridge:

After the last boat but Arnold's had put off, at his instance we mounted our horses and proceeded two miles down the direct road to Chambly, where we met the advance of the British division under Lieutenant-General Burgoyne. We reconnoitred it a few minutes, then galloped back to St. John's; and, stripping our horses, Arnold shot his own [to keep it out of the enemy's hands] and ordered me to follow his example, which I did with reluctance.

The sun was now down, and the enemy's front in view, and we took an affectionate leave of Colonel Louis, the faithful chief of the Cachnawaga tribe, and the only Canadian [resident] who accompanied the army in its retreat from Canada. He cast a sorrowful look at our boat and retired precipitately into the adjacent forest. . . . General Arnold then ordered all hands on board, and resisting my proffers of service, pushed off the boat with his own hands, and thus indulged the vanity of being the last man who embarked from the shores of the enemy. We followed the army twelve miles to the Isle aux Noix, where we arrived after dark. . . .

When these last scenes are reviewed, if the escape of our army from Canada was not countenanced by Sir Guy Carleton, it must appear miraculous. . . .

The British came no farther south than St. John's. But the problems of the Americans did not end with their arrival on Isle aux Noix. In the words of one of the Massachusetts men:

Here, what boats could be spared were sent [southward on Lake Champlain] to Crown Point with sick and stores, as a great part of the army were sick. . . . Here we were obliged to wait for boats eight days, where we could get nothing but pork and flour. The island being small, not more than one mile in length and a quarter of a mile in width, the land low, the days hot, and at night great dews; and such a number of men on so small a spot, and many of them sick—the place stunk enough to breed an infection. . . .

During our stay . . . there went a number of officers about a mile below to a house to drink spruce beer; but unfortunately were beset by a party of Indians, who killed and scalped one ensign, one captain and two privates, and took several prisoners. We heard the guns and saw the fire. A party was immediately sent to their assistance; but the enemy were gone and had left the dead stripped all to their shirts. They were brought to the Isle-aux-Noix and decently buried.

"From the Isle aux Noix," says Lemuel Roberts, "we retreated to Crown Point without meeting with any thing worthy of notice." But by this time men were dying of smallpox and other diseases in great numbers. A chaplain who visited Crown Point lamented, "I did not look into a tent or hut in which I did not find either a dead or dying man." One of the camp's doctors wrote: "I wept till I had no more power to weep."

Dr. Isaac Senter, who had left Cambridge with Benedict Arnold's small, robust detachment the preceding autumn and had ended up at Crown Point amid the wreckage of a substantial army, closed his journal with these thoughts about the venture:

. . . it seemed, upon reflection, a strange series of unaccountable misfortunes, the product of various causes; but from none more than an unpardonable neglect either in our commanders in not giving Congress a true representation of the state of the army from time to time; or, if so represented by them, the fault may be sought for in the non-attention of the latter.

Thus ended an expedition of nine months continuance, the ill success of which, in any other cause, would have induced us to have renounced the principles. A heterogeneal concatenation of the most peculiar and unparalleled rebuffs and sufferings that are perhaps to be found in the annals of any nation. . . .

11

THE SOUTH IS THREATENED

ENGLAND's *next move against the rebellion was aimed at the colonies in the South. Plans for this step had been under consideration since the war's beginning. It was believed that the South held firm-hearted Loyalists in numbers so great that, given the backing of a few thousand British troops, they would have little trouble defeating the local rebels.*

In January, 1776, when the British still occupied Boston, Sir Henry Clinton had been put in charge of a detachment aboard a few ships with orders to make his way southward and begin recruiting Loyalist support while he awaited help from England in the form of a larger force under Admiral Sir Peter Parker and General Charles, Lord Cornwallis. The British expected to make their first move in cooperation with Josiah Martin, royal governor of North Carolina. Unfortunately for the British, Martin sent word for his colony's Loyalists to assemble before the regulars were on hand to back him. As a result, on February 27 the Loyalists suffered a shattering defeat in a brief fight with the colony's Patriots at Moore's Creek Bridge, near Wilmington.

This was a severe blow to England's grand design. But with spring's arrival, when Clinton got together with the force under Parker and Cornwallis off Cape Fear, North Carolina, an alternate beginning was decided upon. The combined expedition, with Clinton commanding, would attack and occupy Charleston, South Carolina. As the South's chief city and principal seaport, Charleston naturally was a haven for the privateers that vexed the British so greatly. Furthermore, the port would serve as an excellent base for the development of operations against all parts of the South.

General Charles Lee, Washington's erudite but blunt and "wretchedly profane" second-in-command, had kept pace on land as Clinton made his way down from the North. At first Lee was uncertain of the enemy's intentions and reported himself to be in "a damned whimsical situation . . . like a dog in a dancing school." But there seemed good reason to believe that Charleston was in danger, and Lee headed General John Armstrong in that direction with orders to assume command of South Carolina's troops in the name of the Continental Congress.

By this time South Carolina's revolutionary government was already bolstering Charleston's defenses. Directing the measures were the government's president, John Rutledge, and a veteran Indian fighter named William Moultrie. In Colonel Moultrie's words:

All the mechanics and laborers about the town were employed, and a great number of negroes brought down from the country and put upon the works. Every one seemed to be busy and every thing went on with spirit. . . . At this time it was the general opinion . . . that two frigates would be a sufficient force to knock the town about our ears. . . .

April. General Armstrong arrived from the northward. . . . He was a brave man and a good officer, but not much acquainted with our manner of defence, which was principally forts and batteries. . . . We had at that time at least 100 pieces of cannon mounted in different parts of our harbor.

May 31. Expresses were sent to the President . . . informing him that a large fleet of British vessels were seen off Dewee's Island, about twenty miles to the northward of [our] bar. And on the first of June they displayed about fifty sail before the town, and on the outside of our bar. The sight of these [men-of-war and troop transports] alarmed us very much. All was hurry and confusion; the President with his council busy in sending expresses to every part of the country to hasten down the militia; men running about the town looking for horses, carriages and boats to send their families into the country; and as they were going out through the town gates . . . they met the militia from the country marching into town. . . . Military works going on everywhere; the lead [being taken] from the windows of the churches and dwelling houses to cast into musket balls; and every preparation to receive an attack, which was expected in a few days.

Colonel Moultrie's chief hope was a fort, still in the process of construction, on Sullivan's Island, which lay on the north side of the harbor entrance. Only a few square miles in area, the island was covered with live oaks, palmettos, and myrtle bushes. Fort Sullivan, with its twenty-five or thirty guns, would be the first point to come under attack from the sea. Moultrie resumes:

[Early in June] General Lee arrived from the northward and took the command of the troops. His presence gave us great spirits, as he was known to be an able, brave and experienced officer, though hasty and rough in his manners, which the officers could not reconcile themselves to at first. . . . After Gen. Lee had waited upon the President and talked with him upon his plan of defence, he hurried about to view the different works and gave orders for such things to be done as he thought necessary. He was every day and every hour of the day on horseback, or in boats viewing our situation and directing small works to be thrown up at different places.

When he came to Sullivan's Island, he did not like that post at all. He said there was no way to retreat, that the garrison would be sacrificed. Nay, he called it a "slaughter pen," and wished to withdraw the garrison and give up the post. But President Rutledge insisted that it should not be given up. Then Gen. Lee said it was absolutely necessary to have a bridge of boats for a retreat. . . .

By this time the British commanders had begun to send troops in small boats to Long Island, which lay northeast of Sullivan's, across a narrow breach. It was Sir Henry Clinton's intention to lead an attack across this breach and against the fort which in the meantime would be bombarded from the sea. But stationed in earthworks facing the breach, commanded by Colonel William Thompson, were two pieces of artillery and eight hundred troops, about half of them riflemen—a force quite adequate, Colonel Moultrie believed, to ward off the threat from Long Island. Adverse winds kept the sea force virtually paralyzed for a time. According to an unnamed British surgeon:

All our motions were so languid and so innervate that it was the 9th of June before the *Bristol* and *Pigot* passed [over] the bar of Charlestown. The *Bristol* in passing struck, which alarmed us all

William Moultrie.

exceedingly; but, as it wanted two hours of high water, she soon floated again. The *Prince of Piedmont,* a victualling ship, was totally lost on the north breakers of the bar. General Clinton and Lord Cornwallis were both on board when she struck, but as the weather was very fine, they were not in the least danger.

By our delays we gave the people every opportunity they could have asked for to extend their lines, etc. They were not idle—every hour gave us astonishing proofs of their industry. As we anchored at one league distance from Sullivan's Island, we could see all that was going on with the help of our glasses.

Returning to Colonel Moultrie's account:

Gen. Lee one day on a visit to the fort took me aside and said, "Col. Moultrie, do you think you can maintain this post?"

I answered him, "Yes, I think I can."

That was all that passed on the subject between us.

Another time, Capt. Lamperer, a brave and experienced seaman . . . visited me at the fort. . . . While we were walking on the [gun] platform, looking at the fleet, he said to me, "Well, Colonel, what do you think of it now?"

I replied that we should beat them.

"Sir," said he, "when those ships . . . come to lay alongside of your fort they will knock it down in half an hour." . . .

"Then," I said, "we will lay behind the ruins and prevent their men from landing."

. . . Our fort at this time was not nearly finished. The mechanics and negro laborers were taken from all the works about the town and sent down to the island to complete our fort. We worked very hard, but could not get it nearly finished [on its inland sides] before the action.

On the morning of June 28, Moultrie paid a horseback visit to Colonel Thompson at the breach, which lay about three miles northeastward of the fort:

While I was there, I saw a number of the enemy's [small] boats in motion at the back of Long Island, as if they intended a descent upon our advanced post [at the breach]. At the same time, I saw the men-of-war loose their top-sails. I hurried back to the fort as fast as possible. When I got there the ships were already under sail. I immediately ordered the long roll to beat, and officers and men to their posts. We had scarcely manned our guns when . . .

[eight] ships of war came sailing up, as if in confidence of victory. As soon as they came within the reach of our guns we began to fire. They were soon abreast of the fort, let go their anchors, with springs upon their cables [to keep the vessels broadside to the fort], and begun their attack most furiously about 10 o'clock. . . .

The assault from Long Island, where General Clinton was in personal command, failed to develop. The water of the breach was found to be too deep for wading, and an attempt to start boats across was stopped by American fire. As one redcoat noted, Colonel Thompson's men were entrenched up to their eyes. "They would have killed half of us before we could have made our landing good."

Supporting the sea attack from a distance was the Thunder, *a vessel equipped with mortars that sent heavy shells in a high arc toward the fort. Overcharges of powder soon disabled the beds of the mortars, but at first, says Moultrie, the* Thunder

. . . threw her shells in a very good direction. Most of them fell within the fort. But we had a morass in the middle that swallowed them up instantly, and those that fell in the sand, in and about the fort, were immediately buried, so that very few of them bursted amongst us.

At one time the Commodore's ship swung round with her stern to the fort, which drew the fire of all the guns that could bear upon her. . . . The words that passed along the platform, by officers and men, were, "Mind the Commodore! Mind the two fifty-gun ships!" Most all the attention was paid to the two fifty-gun ships, especially the Commodore, who, I dare say, was not at all obliged to us for our particular attention to him.

In truth, Moultrie's cannon inflicted terrible damage on the Commodore, or flagship, and her crew. Sir Peter Parker himself narrowly escaped a grievous and somewhat embarrassing injury. As one of the fleet's sailors later explained, "In the hottest of the action, a [cannon] ball passed so near Sir Peter's coat tail as to tear it off, together with his clothes, clear to the buff. . . ." Colonel Moultrie continues:

During the action, Gen. Lee paid us a visit through a heavy line of fire and pointed two or three guns himself; then said to me, "Colonel, I see you are doing very well here. You have no occasion for me. I will go up to town again," and then left us. . . . Never

did men fight more bravely, and never were men more cool. Several
of the officers, as well as myself, were smoking our pipes and giving
orders. . . . [The men's] only distress was the want of powder. We
had not more than 28 rounds [each] for 26 guns . . . when we
begun the action; and a little after, 500 pounds from town and 200
pounds from Captain Tufft's schooner lying at the back of the
fort. . . .

They could not make any impression on our fort, built of
palmetto logs and filled in with earth. Our merlons [protective
walls] were 16 feet thick. . . . The men that we had killed and
wounded received their shots mostly through the embrasures.

According to a South Carolina officer named Barnard Elliott:
The expression of a Sergeant McDaniel [Moultrie calls him
"M'Donald"], after a cannon ball had taken off his shoulder and
scooped out his stomach, is worth recording in the annals of America: "Fight on, my brave boys! Don't let liberty expire with me
today!"

Moultrie goes on to tell about a British mishap:
. . . three of the men-of-war, in going round to our west curtain,
got entangled together, by which the *Acteon* frigate went on shore
on the middle ground; the *Sphinx* lost her bow-sprit; and the *Syren*
cleared herself without any damage. Had these three ships effected
their purpose, they would have enfiladed us in such a manner as to
have driven us from our guns.

It being a very hot day, we were served along the platform with
grog [a mixture of liquor and water] in fire-buckets, which we
partook of very heartily. I never had a more agreeable draught. . . .
It may be very easily conceived what heat and thirst a man must feel
in this climate . . . amidst 20 or 30 heavy pieces of cannon in one
continual blaze and roar, and clouds of smoke curling over his head,
for hours together. It was a very honorable situation, but a very
unpleasant one.

During the action, thousands of our fellow citizens were looking
on with anxious hopes and fears (at about six miles distance), some
of whom had their fathers, brothers and husbands in the battle;
whose hearts must have been pierced at every broadside. After some
time, our flag was shot away. Their hopes were then gone, and they
gave up all for lost, supposing that we had struck our flag and had
given up the fort. Sergeant [William] Jasper, perceiving that

the flag . . . had fallen [outside] the fort, jumped from one of the embrasures and brought it up through a heavy fire, fixed it upon a . . . staff and planted it upon the ramparts again.

Our flag once more waving in the air revived the drooping spirits of our friends; and they continued looking on till night . . . hid us from their view [and they saw] only the appearance of a heavy storm, with continual flashes and peals like thunder.

At night when we came to our slow firing (the ammunition being nearly quite gone) we could hear the shot very distinctly strike the ships.

At length the British gave up the conflict. The ships . . . dropped down with the tide and out of the reach of our guns. When the firing had ceased, our friends, for a time, were again in an unhappy suspense, not knowing our fate; till they received an account by a dispatch boat which I sent up to town to acquaint them that . . . we were victorious.

The British were stunned by the amount of damage they had received. In the words of the unnamed surgeon:

The *Bristol* and *Experiment* have suffered most incredibly. The former . . . lost upwards of one hundred men killed and wounded. . . . Twice the quarter-deck was cleared of every person except Sir Peter. . . . Captain Scott, of the *Experiment,* lost his right arm, and the ship suffered exceedingly. She had much the same number killed and wounded as the *Bristol.* . . .

This will not be believed when it is first reported in England. I can scarcely believe what I myself saw on that day—a day to me one of the most distressing of my life.

On the American side, there were only twelve killed and twenty-four wounded. The victory, which was joyously applauded in all parts of the country and which gained William Moultrie special honor in his home colony, was as important as it was spectacular. England's plan to make a quick conquest of the South had been quashed. And it would be two and a half years before she made a major effort in that region again.

12

HOWE SPRINGS A SURPRISE

Dᴜʀɪɴɢ *the months of mobilization leading to the Charleston victory, similar work went on in New York to prepare for the expected British visit there. Hardly a city then, New York had a population of about twenty-five thousand, and occupied only the southern tip of Manhattan Island. The Americans had doubts about their ability to keep the British out, but believed they could at least make the attack costly by fortifying strategic spots around the city and its harbor. The Long Island village of Brooklyn, just across the East River from Manhattan, was one of the points chosen for special attention.*

An urgent appeal for more troops from the various colonies had gone out from New York in March, 1776, and all through the spring months fresh units kept arriving. Among the men sent by Connecticut was a Yale graduate named Benjamin Tallmadge, who had just entered the service as a lieutenant:

I obtained permission to visit my father . . . on my way to New York, and I shall not soon forget his surprise at seeing me dressed in military uniform, with epaulets on my shoulders and a sword by my side. Although he was a firm and decided Whig . . . yet he seemed very reluctant to have me enter the army. However, the die was cast, and I soon left the paternal abode and entered the tented field. . . . We arrived at the city of New York in the month of June . . . and my place of regimental parade was assigned in Wall Street. . . .

This was a time of rising tension in the city, and there was military activity everywhere. Nonetheless, on June 18 half the day was set aside for a major social event. In the words of Captain Caleb Gibbs, of Washington's personal guard:

This afternoon the Provincial Congress of New York gave an elegant entertainment to General Washington and his suite, the general and staff officers, and the commanding officers of the different regiments in and near the city. Many patriotic toasts were offered and drank with the greatest pleasure and decency. After the toasts, little Phil of the Guard was brought in to sing H——'s new campaign song, and was joined by all the under officers, who seemed much animated by the accompanying of Clute's drumsticks and Aaron's fife. Our good General Putnam got sick and went to his quarters before dinner was over, and we missed him a marvel, as there is not a chap in the camp who can lead him in the Maggie Lauder song.

Though Washington's enlisted men were never feted by the Provincial Congress, they found their own entertainments during the hours when they weren't sweating over fortifications or attending to other duties. Many of the men caused the general grief. They swam in the nude under the eyes of sensitive female citizens, they drank too much, fought too much, swore with such abandon that Washington began to fear that these insults to Heaven might affect the army's luck, and spent entirely too much time at the Holy Ground, once a church property but now the resort of "bitchfoxly jades, jills, haggs, strums [and] prostitutes" whose business was "very lucrative."

A soldier in Washington's guard named Thomas Hickey lost more than his money to New York's loose women. Bewitched by their arts, he was persuaded to involve himself in a Tory plot to sabotage the Patriot army and, if rumors of the time can be credited, to assassinate Washington. The plot apparently never got much beyond the planning stage, but when it was discovered, Hickey went to the gallows; a number of people, including the city's Tory mayor, were jailed; and the area's other Loyalists, who had earlier been disarmed by the Patriots and were assembled chiefly in the Long Island county of Queens (which was then Nassau), became the target of the repressive expedition. Says Loyalist Judge Thomas Jones, himself a resident of Long Island:

The rebel colonel, having established his headquarters at Hempstead, converted the Episcopal Church into a store house, forbid the parson to pray for the King or any of the Royal family, and made use of the communion table . . . for his Yankees to eat their pork and molasses upon. A universal hunt after Loyalists took place. Parties . . . were sent into every quarter of the county. . . . The Loyalists were pursued like wolves and bears, from swamp to swamp, from one hill to another, from dale to dale, and from one copse of wood to another. In consequence . . . numbers were taken, some were wounded, and a few murdered. The prisoners were conducted, with infamy, under a guard of rebels to New York, insulted and abused upon the road, and without a hearing ordered by a board of officers . . . to be transported into different parts of New England. The inland parts of Connecticut became filled with loyal prisoners.

Judge Jones, who refers to himself as "a man of property [with] great influence," adds a personal note: "On the 27th of June . . . while peaceably living upon my own estate . . . I was taken by . . . a party of rebels . . . and carried to New York. . . ." The judge was lucky: "On the 30th of June I was discharged . . . upon giving . . . parole. . . ." However, because of his unflinching loyalty to the Crown, Jones was to be harried all through the war. He was to be "treated by the rebels with the utmost severity, indignity and contempt," to suffer "a captivity of nearly a year in Connecticut," and, at different times, to be "robbed, plundered and pillaged." In the end, he was "attainted by the Legislature of New York of high treason, and his estate confiscated. . . ." Through all of his tribulations, however, the judge would remain an alert observer of the general scene. He may be forgiven for his bias, and he will continue to be heard from.

On the morning of June 29, two days after Judge Jones's arrest, a party of Americans at an observation post on the high grounds of Staten Island reacted with astonishment as they looked out over the waters of Lower New York Bay toward Sandy Hook. There was a great white cloud of British sails in sight. In the evening, Connecticut's Samuel Webb, now a colonel and one of Washington's aides, wrote in his journal:

This is the fleet which we forced to evacuate Boston and [which] went to Halifax last March, where they have been waiting for reinforcements, and have now arrived here with a view of putting their cursed plans into execution.

Judge Thomas Jones, a prominent New York Loyalist.

The Halifax fleet was only the beginning. Other squadrons kept arriving for weeks, until the bay bristled with hostile masts. Some of the vessels came from England, under Admiral Richard, Lord Howe, the general's brother. One squadron—not a very proud one— came up along the American coast from South Carolina. Some of the last vessels to arrive from overseas brought thousands of Hessians: German troops, hired by George the Third, and especially resented by the Americans. By mid-August, when it was entirely assembled, the force contained about thirty-four thousand fighting men. The vanguard from Halifax under General Howe met with no opposition and began to set up a camp on Staten Island on July 2.

That same day, something of great moment happened in Philadelphia, where the Continental Congress was in session. A majority of the delegates voted in favor of a formal declaration of independence from England. John Adams, unaware that history would choose to immortalize July 4 because it was then that Thomas Jefferson's composition became America's official declaration, enthused in a letter to his wife:

The second day of July, 1776, will be the most memorable epocha in the history of America. I am apt to believe that it will be celebrated by succeeding generations as the great anniversary festival. It ought to be commemorated, as the day of deliverance, by solemn acts of devotion to God Almighty. It ought to be solemnized with pomp and parade, with shows, games, sports, guns, bells, bonfires and illuminations, from one end of this continent to the other, from this time forward forevermore. . . . I am well aware of the toil and blood and treasure that it will cost us to maintain this declaration and support and defend these states. Yet, through all the gloom, I can see the rays of ravishing light and glory.

A copy of the momentous document was promptly sent to Washington in New York, and July 9 became a special day. As reported in the Pennsylvania Journal:

This afternoon the Declaration of Independence was read at the head of each brigade of the Continental Army. . . . It was received everywhere with loud huzzas and the utmost demonstrations of joy. And tonight the equestrian statue of George III [on the city's bowling green] . . . has, by the Sons of Freedom, been laid prostrate in the dirt—the just desert of an ungrateful tyrant! The lead wherewith the monument was made is to be run into bullets to assimilate with the brains of our infatuated adversaries. . . .

America's Loyalists, of course, were dismayed by the new development. Judge Jones laments:

The Declaration of Independence . . . was the first act that put an end to . . . the administration of justice under the British Crown within the Thirteen Colonies. The revolt was now complete. Upon this event the law, the courts, and justice itself ceased; all was anarchy, all was confusion. A usurped kind of government took place, a medley of military law, convention ordinances, Congress recommendations and committee resolutions.

Less concerned about the state of civil justice than men like Judge Jones, ardent Patriots all through the colonies marked the formal move toward freedom with special ceremonies. A New Jersey orator declared that "a new era in politics has commenced. . . . No people under heaven were ever favored with a fairer opportunity of laying a sure foundation for future grandeur and happiness than we." In his journal, Dr. James Thacher expressed a great admiration for the Declaration's signers:

When we reflect on the deranged condition of our army, the great deficiency of our resources, and the little prospect of foreign assistance, and at the same time contemplate the prodigious powers and resources of our enemy, we may view this measure of Congress as a prodigy. The history of the world cannot furnish an instance of fortitude and heroic magnanimity parallel to that displayed by the members whose signatures are affixed to the Declaration of American Independence. Their venerated names will ornament the brightest pages of American history, and be transmitted to the latest generations.

The two Howe brothers, the general and the admiral, were disturbed by the Declaration. They had been instructed by their government to approach New York with an olive branch, proposing a peace before resorting to the sword. In spite of the Declaration, they made their bid. Washington and Congress were unreceptive, since England was still thinking of peace largely in terms of pardons for rebels who renewed their allegiance to the Crown. The rebuff left the Howes, who as members of England's Whig faction believed that America's grievances were real, with no choice but to proceed with their plans for attack.

Washington was concerned about the enemy's numbers. On August 8 he reported to Congress that the men on duty in his own lines numbered only about 10,500:

Our posts, too, are much divided, having waters between many of them, and some distant from others many miles. These circumstances . . . are much aggravated by the sickness that prevails throughout the army. . . . Under every disadvantage, my utmost exertions shall be employed to bring about the great end we have in view; and so far as I can judge from the professions and apparent disposition of my troops, I shall have their support. The superiority of the enemy, and the expected attack, do not seem to have repressed their spirits.

Shortly after this report was written, Washington began receiving reinforcements in substantial numbers, some from New England and others from the middle colonies. But as the army grew, so did its sick list. At the same time, the British troops in their camp on Staten Island were being described as "riotous as satyrs" as a result of being fed fresh meat instead of salt provisions. It was reported that the young women of the island could not "step into the bushes to pluck a rose without running the most imminent risk of being ravished." The Howe brothers decided to employ this virile army first against the Americans at Brooklyn. The plan called for about twenty thousand men to be landed on Long Island so as to approach the village through the farmlands and woods on its south and east.

The night before the operation was to begin, the New York area was hit by a violent thunderstorm. As described by one of the city's occupants:

It lasted from seven to ten o'clock. Several claps struck in and about New York. Many houses were damaged, and several lives lost. Three officers . . . were struck instantly dead. The points of their swords, for several inches, were melted, [along] with a few silver dollars they had in their pockets. They . . . were seemingly roasted. A dog in the same tent was also killed, and a soldier near it struck blind, deaf and dumb. One in the main street was killed, as likewise ten on Long Island. Two or three were much burnt and greatly hurt. When God speaks, who can but fear?

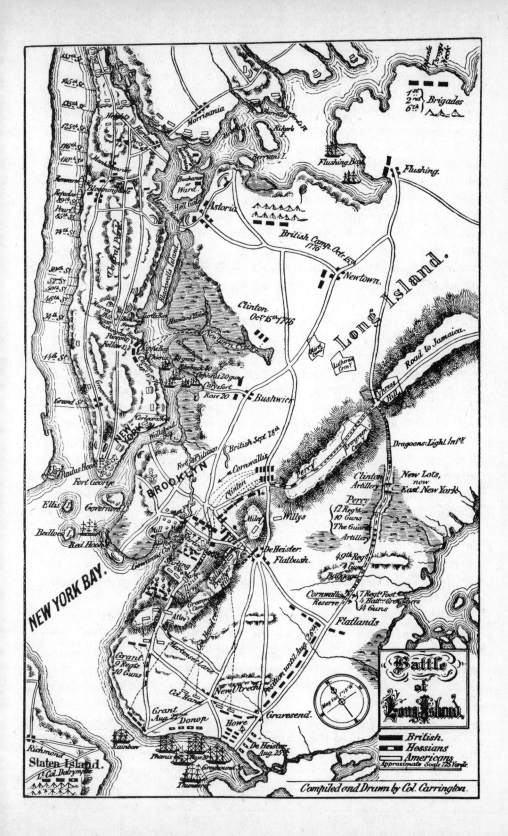

Battle of Long Island

Compiled and Drawn by Col. Carrington.

On the morning of August 22, according to the journal being kept by America's General William Heath:

. . . [The British] landed near Gravesend Bay on Long Island . . . Col. [Edward] Hand with his rifle corps retreating moderately before them and destroying some wheat which would fall into their hands. The British advanced as far as Flatbush, where they halted. Six American regiments were sent over [to Brooklyn] as a rein-forcement. . . . 24th: There were some skirmishes on Long Island, but nothing very material. 25th: A number of the enemy's ships fell down towards the Narrows, it was supposed with intent to land more troops on Long Island. 26th: In the morning a brisk cannonade on Long Island for some time. The British had thrown up some works at Flatbush, from which they fired at the Americans.

By this time Brooklyn's defenders, less than eight thousand in num-ber, had established a series of posts on a broken ridge nearly two miles in front of the main fortifications at the village. About five miles in extent, the posts faced the British van at the hamlet of Flatbush; the main enemy encampment was set up on the plains to the south. The defense plan called for several thousand men to make a stand in these outworks. Since the posts loomed above the enemy, the outnumbered Americans had a tactical advantage. But the situation gave General Howe a fine opportunity to try a surprise maneuver. The first stage, as he planned it, would require the cover of darkness. With half of his force poised in front of the American outworks, he himself, accompanied by Generals Clinton, Cornwallis, and Percy, would quietly march the other half in a great loop to the right. As the first half began a noisy but somewhat restrained attack, the second half would attempt to sweep in behind the Americans and cut them off from their base at Brooklyn.

The British began the operation during the night of August 26. They created their first stir on the American right, the flank op-posite the one Howe was moving to encircle. At this time many of the Americans who were to be involved in the action were still in the works at Brooklyn, sleeping soundly. One of these men later wrote:

. . . we were alarmed by the return of some of our scouting parties, who advised us that the English were in motion and coming up the island with several field pieces.

The sleepy men of several battalions, responding to the roll of the drums, grabbed their weapons and other equipment, formed ranks, and hurried out into the chilly darkness. The unnamed soldier continues:

About sunrise . . . we came up with a very large body of them. [We men of] the Delaware and Maryland battalions made one party. Colonel [Samuel] Atlee with his battalion [of Pennsylvanians] a little before us had taken post in an orchard and behind a barn; and on the approach of the enemy he gave them a very severe fire, which he bravely kept up for a considerable time, until they were near surrounding him, when he retreated to the woods.

The enemy then advanced to us, upon which Lord Stirling [General William Alexander of New Jersey, whose claim to a Scots earldom was accepted by a Scottish jury though not by the House of Lords] . . . drew us up in a line and offered them battle in the true English taste. The British army then advanced within about three hundred yards of us and began a very heavy fire from their cannon and mortars, for both the balls and shells flew very fast, now and then taking off a head. Our men stood it amazingly well. . . . Our orders were not to fire until the enemy came within fifty yards of us; but when they perceived we stood their fire so coolly and resolutely they declined coming any nearer, although treble our number.

The hesitation of British General James Grant's troops was actually part of the plan to give General Howe the time he needed to complete his stealthy encirclement. Too much aggressiveness at this time might have turned the Americans back toward Brooklyn. Restraint was practiced all along the line. The American center, where General John Sullivan commanded, received only long-range artillery fire, this from General Philip von Heister's Hessians. On the American left, where only a small patrol was on duty because the threat from that direction seemed remote, all was still quiet. To many of the Americans on the right, General Grant's attack seemed considerably more than a demonstration. Colonel Samuel Atlee, who had been among the first to undergo fire and had been obliged to hurry his Pennsylvanians toward the cover of a woods, relates:

In this affair I lost but one soldier, shot with a grapeshot through his throat. I had not taken post in the . . . wood but a few minutes when I received a reinforcement of two companies of the Delawares, under Captain Stedman, with orders from Lord Stirling to file off further to the left and prevent, if possible, a body of the enemy observed advancing to flank the brigade. . . . I espied at the distance of about three hundred yards a hill of clear ground which . . . I determined, if possible, to gain before them. At the foot of this hill a few of Huntington's Connecticut Regiment . . . joined me. . . . I ordered the troops to wheel to the right and march up the hill abreast. When within about forty yards of the summit we very unexpectedly received a very heavy fire from the enemy taken post there before us, notwithstanding the forced march I made. . . .

Upon receiving the . . . fire . . . a small halt was made, and the detachment fell back a few paces. Here Capt. Stedman, with all the Delawares except the Lieutenants Stewart and Harney with about sixteen privates, left me and drew after them some of my own. The remainder, after recovering a little from . . . their first shock, I ordered to advance, at the same time desiring them to preserve their fire and aim aright. They . . . with the resolution of veteran soldiers, obeyed the order. The enemy . . . fled with precipitation, leaving behind them twelve killed upon the spot and a lieutenant and four privates wounded. In this engagement I lost my worthy friend and lieutenant-colonel (Parry), shot through the head, who fell without a groan. . . .

This kind of skirmishing continued until midmorning, when General Howe's flanking force reached its planned position between the outworks and Brooklyn. The Americans along the jagged ridge were startled to hear cannons begin thundering in their rear. Immediately afterward the enemy along their front, for whom the cannon fire served as a signal, began to cheer and press up the slopes in large numbers, their bayonets gleaming. Artillerymen, with the aid of horses, began wheeling their heavy weapons through the passes that divided the sections of the ridge. Many of the trapped Americans, completely confused, first ran toward the rear, then turned and ran back to the front, only to be thrown again toward the rear. Some of the troops, however, maintained enough order to meet the emergency with spirit. Says the anonymous man with the Delaware and Maryland forces:

. . . we were ordered to attempt a retreat by fighting our way through the enemy, who had . . . nearly filled every field and road between us and our lines [at Brooklyn]. We had not retreated a quarter of a mile before we were fired upon by an advanced part of the enemy, and those upon our rear were playing upon us with their artillery. Our men fought with more than Roman virtue. . . . Most of our generals were on a high hill in our lines [at Brooklyn] viewing us with glasses. When we began our retreat, they could see the enemy we had to pass through, though we could not. Many of them thought we would surrender in a body, without firing. When we began the attack, General Washington wrung his hands and cried out, "Good God, what brave fellows I must this day lose!"

The encirclement was most effective on the American left and center. Some of the men managed to break through the British lines to Brooklyn, but many were killed, wounded, or captured. According to one redcoat, some of the Hessians and Scotch Highlanders showed no mercy:

. . . it was a fine sight to see with what alacrity they despatched the Rebels with their bayonets after we had surrounded them so that they could not resist. . . . We took care to tell the Hessians that the Rebels had resolved to give no quarters to them in particular, which made them fight desperately and put all to death that fell into their hands. . . . [A]ll stratagems are lawful in war, especially against such vile enemies to their King and country.

The Americans on the extreme right were not altogether surrounded, and as they fell back to a point near the Brooklyn works, a few reinforcements who had just crossed the river from New York began marching to their support. With these new troops was a Connecticut youth, Joseph Plumb Martin, whose account reveals that the advance was made so slowly as to be of little service:

We marched a short distance, when we halted to refresh ourselves. . . . While resting here . . . the Americans [under Stirling] and British [under Cornwallis] were warmly engaged within sight of us. . . . I saw a lieutenant who appeared to have feelings not very enviable. . . . I thought it fear . . . for he ran round among the men of his company, sniveling and blubbering, praying each one if he had aught against him, or if *he* had injured anyone, that they would forgive him, declaring at the same time that he, from his heart, forgave them if they had offended him. . . . A fine soldier you are, I thought; a fine officer, an exemplary man for young soldiers! I would have then suffered anything short of death rather than have made such an exhibition of myself. . . .

After an interval of about twenty minutes, Martin and his comrades were ordered to fall in and proceed. In a short time:

We overtook a small party of the artillery . . . dragging a heavy twelve-pounder [forward] upon a field carriage, sinking halfway to the naves in the sandy soil. They plead hard for some of us to assist them. . . . Our officers, however, paid no attention to their entreaties, but pressed forward towards a creek where a large party of Americans and British were engaged. By the time we arrived, the enemy had driven our men into the creek, or rather millpond (the tide being up), where such as could swim got across. Those that could not swim, and could not procure anything to buoy them up, sunk.

The British, having several field-pieces stationed by a brick house, were pouring the canister and grape upon the Americans like a shower of hail. They would doubtless have done them much more damage than they did, but for the twelve-pounder mentioned above. The men, having gotten it within sufficient distance to reach them, and opening a fire upon them, soon obliged them to shift their quarters. There was in this action a regiment of Maryland troops (volunteers), all young gentlemen. When they came out of the water and mud to us, looking like water rats, it was a truly pitiful sight. Many of them were killed in the pond and more were drowned.

The time was now early afternoon, and the battle was ending. Writes America's General Heath:

Those who escaped retreated to the American works. The British sustained a considerable loss in killed and wounded [about four hundred], and a subaltern and 23 men were taken prisoners. But the American loss was far greater in killed, wounded and prisoners [about fifteen hundred].

Both General Sullivan and Lord Stirling were among the captured. As for the thousands now huddled in the Brooklyn works, they enjoyed no feeling of security. Among them was Connecticut's Benjamin Tallmadge:

. . . the British army took their position, in full array, directly in front of our position. Our intrenchment was so weak that it is most wonderful the British general did not attempt to storm it soon after the battle. . . . Gen. Washington was so fully aware of the perilous situation of this division of his army that he immediately convened a council of war, at which the propriety of retiring to New York was decided on.

After sustaining incessant fatigue and constant watchfulness for two days and nights, attended by heavy rain, exposed every moment to [the danger of] an attack from a vastly superior force in front, and [expecting] to be cut off from the possibility of a retreat to New York by the fleet, which might enter the East River— on the night of the 29th of August Gen. Washington commenced recrossing his troops from Brooklyn to New York [in boats manned by a regiment of Massachusetts fishermen under Colonel John Glover].

To move so large a body of troops, with all their necessary appendages, across a river full a mile wide, with a rapid current, in face of . . . [the before-mentioned enemy threat] seemed to present most formidable obstacles. But . . . the Commander-in-Chief so aranged his business that . . . by 10 o'clock the troops began to retire from the lines in such a manner that no chasm was made . . . but as one regiment left their station . . . the remaining troops moved to the right and left and filled up the vacancies, while Gen. Washington took his station at the ferry and superintended the embarkation. . . .

As the dawn of the next day approached, those of us who remained in the trenches became very anxious for our own safety, and when the dawn appeared there were several regiments still on duty. At this time a very dense fog began to rise, and it seemed to settle in a peculiar manner over both encampments. . . . When the sun rose we had just received orders to leave the lines, but before we reached the ferry the Commander-in-Chief sent one of his aids to order the regiment to repair again to their former station . . . where we tarried until the sun had risen. . . . [T]he fog remained as dense as ever.

Finally, the second order arrived for the regiment to retire, and we very joyfully bid those trenches . . . adieu. When we reached Brooklyn ferry, the boats had not returned from their last trip, but they very soon appeared. . . . I think I saw Gen. Washington on the ferry stairs when I stepped into one of the last boats that received the troops. I left my horse tied to a post at the ferry.

The troops having now all safely reached New York, and the fog continuing as thick as ever, I began to think of my . . . horse, and requested leave to return and bring him off. Having obtained permission, I called for a crew of volunteers to go with me, and, guiding the boat myself, I obtained my horse and got off some distance into the river before the enemy appeared in Brooklyn. As soon as they reached the ferry we were saluted merrily from their musketry, and finally by their field pieces; but we returned in safety.

In the history of warfare I do not recollect a more fortunate retreat.

"General Howe," averred Israel Putnam, "is either our friend or no general. He had our whole army in his power . . . and yet suffered us to escape without the least interruption. . . . Had he instantly followed up his victory, the consequence to the cause of liberty must have been dreadful." A similar view was held by an objective and fair-minded British officer named Charles Stedman, who saw much service in America and published a history of the war in 1794. Stedman has little to say about his own role in the events he describes, but he makes many sound observations. He calls the retreat "particularly glorious to the Americans," but adds:

It cannot be denied but that the American army lay almost entirely at the will of the English. That they were therefore suffered to retire in safety has by some been attributed to the reluctance of the commander in chief to shed the blood of a people so nearly allied to that source from whence he derived all his authority and power. We are rather inclined to adopt this idea. . . . He might possibly have conceived that the late victory would produce a revolution in [American] sentiment capable of terminating the war without the extremity [of action] which it appeared to be, beyond all possibility of doubt, in his power to enforce.

Stedman's view may or may not be correct. The evidence regarding Howe's motivations on this occasion, as on many other occasions during his stay in America, is uncertain. He admitted later that he could have overrun the Brooklyn defenses, but added: ". . . the lines must have been ours at a very cheap rate by regular [siege] approaches, [and] I would not risk the loss that might have been sustained in the assault."

13

A FOX CHASE ON MANHATTAN

T HE SUCCESS *of the retreat to New York gave Washington only a momentary feeling of relief. In a letter to Congress dated September 2, 1776, he complained:*

Our situation is truly distressing. The check our detachment sustained on the 27th ultimo has dispirited too great a proportion of our troops and filled their minds with apprehension and despair. The militia, instead of calling forth their utmost efforts to a brave and manly opposition in order to repair our losses, are dismayed, intractible and impatient to return [home]. Great numbers of them have gone off; in some instances almost by whole regiments, by half ones and by companies at a time.

According to a captain from Pennsylvania named Alexander Graydon:

A greater loss than themselves was that of the arms and ammunition they took away with them. . . . It was found necessary to post a guard . . . to stop the fugitives; and . . . upon one of them being arrested with a number of *notions* in a bag, there was found among them a cannon ball which, he said, he was taking home to his mother for the purpose of pounding mustard.

The only immediate action taken by the Howe brothers after their victory and the retreat was to order the American defenses bom-

barded from Long Island and from ships sent up the East River. This left the majority of the British forces relatively idle; and, says Judge Jones:

. . . a little plunder was connived at, and rather encouraged than discouraged by some principal officers in the army. The Hessians bore the blame at first, but the British were equally alert.

American troops on Manhattan offended in the same way. Abandoned homes (and not only those owned by Tories) were joyfully looted and vandalized, and orchards and vegetable gardens stripped bare. Washington urged his unit commanders to try to keep their men under closer observation by having the roll called three times a day.

Militarily, Washington's problems revolved around the vulnerability of his posts to attack by the enemy fleet. The warships not only dominated New York Bay but could sail almost at will up the rivers on both sides of narrow, elongated Manhattan Island. Washington could oppose these ships only with shore batteries. All Congress had managed to provide him in the way of a navy were a few vessels suited to minor missions, a fleet whose captains, understandably, found much of their satisfaction in their ability to dodge showdowns with the Royal Navy and thus stay afloat.

It was at this point that Washington gave permission to an ingenious New Englander named David Bushnell to make a unique experiment. Bushnell had managed to build a workable submarine, and he was eager to see it tried against the enemy's shipping. The American Turtle *wasn't much bigger than a good-sized barrel. She was made of wood, encircled with iron bands, coated with tar, and provided with several tiny glass windows. The submarine held about a half hour's supply of air for her lone occupant, who was kept busy, hand and foot. He had to operate the valves and pumps of tanks that admitted water when he wanted to submerge, and expelled it when he wanted to surface; and in order to travel underwater he had to manage a rudder and turn cranks that spun propellers, one in front for propulsion and one overhead for ascent and descent. In piggyback style, the* Turtle *carried a heavy waterproofed charge of powder (called a magazine), which was equipped with a timing device and was designed to be screwed to the underside of her target. Says the* Turtle's *inventor:*

After various attempts to find an operator to my wish, I sent one who appeared more expert than the rest from New York [on a calm night] to a fifty-gun ship lying near Governor's Island. He went under the ship [after a long fight with the tide] and attempted to fasten the wood-screw into her bottom, but struck, as he supposes, a bar of iron. Not being well skilled in the management of the vessel, in attempting to move to another place he lost the ship, and after seeking her in vain for some time he rowed [by propeller, underwater] some distance and rose to the surface . . . but found daylight had advanced so far that he durst not renew the attempt. On his return from the ship to New York he passed near Governor's Island and thought he was discovered by the enemy. He cast off the magazine, as he imagined it retarded him in the swell, which was very considerable. After it had been cast off one hour (the time the internal apparatus was set to run) it blew up with great violence.

Afterwards, there were two attempts made in Hudson's River, above the city, but they effected nothing. Soon after this the enemy went up the river and pursued the vessel which had the submarine boat on board, and sunk it with their shot. Though I afterwards recovered the vessel, I found it impossible to prosecute the design any further. I had been in a bad state of health from the beginning of my undertaking, and was now very ill. The situation of public affairs was such that I despaired of obtaining the public attention and assistance necessary. I therefore gave over the pursuit for that time and waited for a more favorable opportunity, which never arrived.

On September 11, in another effort to talk peace, Admiral Howe met with Benjamin Franklin, John Adams, and Edward Rutledge on Staten Island. There was great politeness shown on both sides, but nothing was accomplished. When the admiral declared that he should hate to see America defeated, Franklin assured him that America would do everything in her power to save him that mortification. It became clear to Howe that in spite of Washington's predicament, the Americans planned to continue striving for independence. The admiral and his brother decided that another British attack had become necessary. According to Connecticut's Benjamin Tallmadge,

. . . they began to make preparations for crossing the East River [to Manhattan]. Gen. Washington immediately put his army in motion to leave the city, the stores, etc., etc., having been previously removed. Both rivers . . . were now filled with British shipping. . . .

On the morning of September 15, covered by a squadron of warships, a great number of small boats filled with troops crossed from Long Island to Kip's Bay, two and a half miles north of New York City. Washington had stationed a sizable force behind earthworks along the shores of the bay, but at the time of the invasion he himself was directing the fortification of Harlem Heights, about five miles farther to the north. A tremendous cannonade from the British warships drew his attention southward:

. . . I rode with all possible dispatch towards the place of landing, when to my surprise and mortification I found the troops that had been posted in the lines retreating with the utmost precipitation, and those ordered to support them . . . flying in every direction and in the utmost confusion, notwithstanding the efforts of their generals to form them. I used every means in my power to rally and get them in order, but my attempts were fruitless and ineffectual. . . .

Washington galloped back and forth, indifferent to his own safety, sometimes flourishing his sword and sometimes a pistol as a threat to the troops. At last he drew up, threw his hat to the ground, and exclaimed, "Are these the men with which I am to defend America?" Then he turned his horse back toward Harlem Heights, hoping to be able to rally the army there.

Among the men fleeing from Kip's Bay at this time was Joseph Plumb Martin, the Connecticut youth who'd had his baptism of fire as a reinforcement at Brooklyn:

. . . we had to cross a level clear spot of ground . . . exposed to the whole of the enemy's fire . . . which served to quicken our motions. When I had gotten a little out of the reach of their combustibles, I found myself in company with one who was a neighbor of mine when at home, and one other man belonging to our regiment. Where the rest of them were, I knew not. We went into a house by the highway, in which were two women and some small children, all crying most bitterly. We asked the women if they had any spirits in the house. They placed a case bottle of rum upon the table and bid us help ourselves. We each of us drank a glass, and bidding them goodbye, betook ourselves to the highway again.

The enemy also paused for refreshment, according to Dr. Thacher:

. . . Major-General Putnam, at the head of three thousand five hundred continental troops, was . . . the last that left the city. In order to avoid any of the enemy that might be advancing in the direct road to the city [from Kip's Bay], he made choice of a road parallel with and contiguous to the [Hudson] River, till he could arrive at a certain angle, whence another road would conduct him in such a direction as that he might form a junction with our army [to the northward].

It so happened that a body of . . . British and Hessians were at the same moment advancing [across the island] on the road which would have brought them in immediate contact with General Putnam before he could have reached the turn into the other road. Most fortunately, the British generals, seeing no prospect of engaging our troops, halted their own and repaired to the house of a Mr. Robert Murray, a Quaker and friend of our cause. Mrs. Murray treated them with cake and wine, and they were induced to tarry two hours or more. . . . By this happy incident General Putnam, by continuing his march, escaped. . . .

Actually, the British generals did their tarrying at the Murray house not because of the cake and wine, but because a good part of their force was late in landing and joining them. Though Washington lost over 350 men (most of them captured), he was able to deploy the rest of the army in a seemingly defensible position on Harlem Heights. However, the general had been left with doubts about his men's will to fight. The first test came the next day, when the British sent a small force northward to probe the American lines. As the redcoats approached, now supremely confident, they "sounded their bugle horns as is usual after a fox chase." Washington hurried his mount toward the American advanced post:

When I arrived I heard a firing, which I was informed was between a party of our rangers . . . and an advance party of the enemy. . . . I immediately ordered three companies of Colonel Weedon's Virginia regiment under Major Leitch and Colonel Knowlton with his rangers to try and get in the rear, while a disposition was making as if to attack them in front and thereby draw their attention that way. This took effect as I wished on . . . the enemy. On the appearance of our party in front, they immediately ran down hill, took possession of some fences and bushes; and a smart firing began, but at too great a distance to do much execution on either side.

The parties under Colonel Knowlton and Major Leitch unluckily began their attack too soon, as it was rather in flank than in rear. In a short time Major Leitch was brought off wounded, having received three balls in his side; and in a short time Colonel Knowlton got a wound which proved mortal. The men continued the engagement with the greatest resolution. Finding that they wanted a support, I advanced part of Colonel Griffith's and Colonel Richardson's Maryland regiments, who were nearest the scene of action. These troops charged the enemy with great intrepidity and drove them from the wood into the plain, and were pushing them from thence, having silenced their fire in a great measure, when I judged it prudent to order a retreat, fearing the enemy . . . were sending a large body to support their party.

Such a body did come up, but nothing more happened. One of the Americans who had taken part in the skirmish was Joseph Plumb Martin, whose regiment was kept on the alert until late in the day:

When we came off the field we brought away a man [of our forces] who had been shot dead. . . . Having provided a grave, which was near a gentleman's country seat (at that time [also] occupied by the Commander-in-Chief), we proceeded, just in the dusk of evening, to commit the poor man, then far from friends and relatives, to the bosom of his Mother Earth.

Just as we had laid him in the grave in as decent a posture as existing circumstances would admit, there came from the house towards the grave two young ladies who appeared to be sisters. . . . Upon arriving at the head of the grave, they stopped and, with their arms around each other's neck, stooped forward and looked into it, and with a sweet pensiveness of countenance . . . asked if we were going to put the earth upon his naked face. Being answered in the affirmative, one of them took a fine white gauze handkerchief from her neck and desired that it might be spread upon his face, tears at the same time flowing down their cheeks. After the grave was filled up, they retired to the house in the same manner they came. . . . Such a sight as those ladies afforded . . . was worthy and doubtless received the attention of angels.

Washington's feelings toward his men had improved; they were not just a lot of frightened foxes after all. They had routed the hunters, inflicting about a hundred casualties while suffering little more than half that number themselves. The next day Washington issued the following announcement:

The General most heartily thanks the troops . . . who first advanced upon the enemy, and the others who so resolutely supported them. The behavior yesterday was such a contrast to that of some of the troops the day before, as must show what may be done where officers and soldiers will exert themselves. Once more, therefore, the General calls upon officers and men to act up to the noble cause in which they are engaged. . . .

New York City's fall to the British had been quick and complete. But even while the troops were still settling in, their tenancy was drastically threatened—but not in a military way. The story is told by John Joseph Henry, of Pennsylvania, who had been captured by Sir Guy Carleton's troops during the attack on Quebec and was now aboard a British ship anchored in New York Bay, about four miles southwest of the city. He was with a group of Americans who had been paroled by Carleton and were waiting to be set ashore in New Jersey. During the night of September 20, Henry's slumber below decks was interrupted by a deck sentry's cry that there was a fire in New York:

Running upon deck, we could perceive a light which at the distance we were from it . . . was apparently of the size of the flame of a candle. . . . The wind was southwardly and . . . the flames at this place . . . increased rapidly. In a moment we saw another light at a great distance from the first. . . . The latter light seemed to be an original, distinct and new-formed fire. . . . Our anxiety for the fate of so fine a city caused much solicitude, as we harbored suspicions that the enemy had fired it. The flames were fanned by the briskness of the breeze and drove the destructive effects of the element on all sides. When the fire reached the spire of a large steeple . . . which was attached to a large church, the effect upon the eye was astonishingly grand. . . . The deck of our ship for many hours was lighted as at noon day.

In the commencement of the conflagration we observed many boats putting off from the fleet, rowing speedily towards the city. Our [ship's] boat was of the number. This circumstance repelled the idea that our enemies were the incendiaries. . . . The boat [from our ship] returned about daylight, and from the relation of the officer and the crew we clearly discerned that the burning of New York was the act of some mad-cap Americans. The sailors told us . . . that they had seen one American hanging by the heels dead, having a bayonet wound through his breast. . . . They averred he was caught in the fact of firing the houses. They told us also that they had seen one person who was taken in the fact tossed into the fire, and that several who were stealing and suspected as incendiaries were bayonetted. Summary justice is at no time laudable, but in this instance it may have been correct.

In a prompt report to England, Sir William Howe stated:
    . . . a most horrid attempt was made by a number of wretches to burn the town of New York, in which they succeeded too well. . . . And had it not been for the exertions of Major-General [Archibald] Robertson, the officers under his command in the town, and the brigade of guards detached from the camp, the whole must infallibly have been consumed, as the night was extremely windy. The destruction is computed to be about one-quarter of the town. . . .

General Washington had nothing to do with this sabotage, but he wasn't unhappy about it: "Providence or some good honest fellow has done more for us than we were disposed to do for ourselves."
    On September 21, while the city was still smoldering, a young American spy named Nathan Hale (formerly a Connecticut schoolmaster) was arrested on Long Island. Since the fire had put the British in an especially vengeful mood, Hale, brought to New York for interrogation by General Howe, was ordered to be hanged the next morning. He accepted his fate "with great composure and resolution," and while the noose was being readied he made "a sensible and spirited speech." Upholding the sacredness of duty and the rightness of the American cause, he closed with the words, "I only regret that I have but one life to lose for my country."

14

THE BATTLE OF LAKE CHAMPLAIN

D URING *these early autumn days of 1776, a new fuse sputtered in the war's northernmost theater. Ever since driving the Americans from Canada, Sir Guy Carleton had been preparing for an attempt to retake Crown Point and Ticonderoga and make himself master of Lake Champlain. This would enable him to extend his forces southward along the Hudson River for an expected meeting with an expedition sent northward from New York City. British control of the lake and the river would interrupt all land communication between New England and the rest of the colonies. In effect, the rebellion's head would be cut off. The Americans, fully aware of Lake Champlain's importance, had been making every effort to rally from their drastic defeat at Carleton's hands and to strengthen their fortifications, particularly those of Ticonderoga.*

Both armies had been building fleets, the British in river waters just north of the lake, and the Americans at the lake's southern end. Since this was frontier country, the task was a prodigious one for both sides, requiring great ingenuity as well as strenuous exertion. However, by the first week in October the British had twenty-five or thirty warships ready, and the Americans had about fifteen. Both fleets were composed of small vessels such as schooners, rowgalleys, gondolas, and gunboats, with the exception of one three-masted ship of eighteen guns possessed by the British—a ship from England that had been brought up Canada's St. Lawrence River, dissembled, and transported in pieces to the frontier shipyard.

In spite of their difference in size, the fleets were about evenly matched in their number of guns, though the British had more guns of the heavier weights. In general, the British were much better equipped. Captain Thomas Pringle was Sir Guy's naval commander, while the American fleet was commanded by General Benedict Arnold. Whereas Pringle had full confidence in his men, Arnold complained: "We have a wretched, motley crew. . . . The marines are the refuse of every regiment, and the seamen, few of them were ever wet with salt water."

No American in the northern theater showed a greater interest in the new developments than James Wilkinson, now a major but no longer on Arnold's personal staff. Fate was to deny Wilkinson a part in the showdown, but he would record its events in detail:

Whilst actively engaged in the duties of my station—while every hand was employed in preparing for the reception of the enemy, and every heart panted for the rencontre, I was suddenly struck down by a typhus fever which prevailed with great violence. . . . Being forced from the scene of operations by the hand of Heaven, what I shall say of the subsequent events of the campaign of 1776 in the northern department is founded on information derived from correct sources [a sergeant on Arnold's flagship, Arnold's official reports, the *British Annual Register*] and my own knowledge of the topography of the country.

Wilkinson goes on to explain that Arnold, in spite of his fleet's inferiority, sailed fifty miles north of Crown Point and on October 9 "determined to risk a battle against any force the enemy could produce":

On this day he formed a line . . . in the narrow pass between . . . Valcour Island and the main[land] and came to anchor, his flanks being secured by the opposite shores. . . . Valcour Island . . . is . . . in the widest part of Lake Champlain but lies . . . close in with the western shore. . . . Looking towards Canada, Arnold had withdrawn himself behind this island, and so near to the main, that he could not be discovered by the enemy before they had turned the southern point of it. . . . Early on the morning of the 11th . . . Arnold's guard boats warned him of the approach of the enemy under a press of sail with a fresh breeze from the northwest. He had before shifted his flag from the *Royal Savage* [a schooner] to the *Congress* galley. . . .

In Arnold's words:

We immediately prepared to receive them. The galleys and *Royal Savage* were ordered under way. The rest of our fleet lay at an anchor. At eleven o'clock [the enemy] ran under the lee of Valcour and began the attack. The [*Royal Savage*], by some bad management, fell to leeward and was first attacked. One of her masts was wounded and her rigging shot away. The captain thought prudent to run her on the point of Valcour, where all the men were saved.

England's Captain Pringle found that, because of the direction of the wind, "for a considerable time nothing could be brought into action . . . but the gunboats. The Carleton *schooner . . . by much perseverance at last got to their assistance." Arnold says: "At half-past twelve the engagement became general and very warm. Some of the enemy's ships and all her gondolas beat and rowed up within musket shot of us." At this range, the cannon fire of both sides was devastating. There was a sustained roar, and a myriad patches of smoke were tumbled across the water by the wind. Shouted orders, cheers, and oaths mingled with the cries of the wounded.*

"During the action," relates James Wilkinson, "the enemy landed large bodies of Indians on the island and the main. . . . He also embarked 1000 men on board of batteaux to be ready to cut us up, should we be driven on shore." The Indians added their war whoops to the general din. An English officer named James Hadden noted that the Indians "had the effect of now and then obliging the rebels to turn a gun that way, which danger the savages avoided by getting behind trees."

One of the English gunboats was commanded by a German artillery captain named Georg Pausch, who tells how, in the hottest part of the action, he turned to give aid to some distressed Germans in another gunboat. Pausch refers to the gunboats as batteaux:

Lieut. Dufais came very near perishing with all his men; for a cannon ball from the enemy's guns going through his powder magazine, it blew up. . . . The sergeant who served the cannon on my batteau was the first one who saw the explosion and called my attention to it as I was taking aim with my cannon. At first I could not tell what men were on board; but, directly, a chest went up into the air, and after the smoke had cleared away I recognized the men by the cords around their hats.

Dufais's batteau [approached] burning; and I hurried toward it to save, if possible, the lieutenant and his men; for, as an additional misfortune, the batteau was full of water. All who could, jumped on board my batteau, which, being thus overloaded, came near sinking. At this moment a lieutenant of artillery by the name of Smith came with his batteau to the rescue, and took on board the lieutenant, Bombardier Engell and one cannonier. The remainder of Dufais's men . . . remained with me; and these, added to my own force . . . in all 48 persons, came near upsetting my little boat, which was so overloaded that it could hardly move. In what a predicament was I! Every moment I was in danger of drowning with all on board. . . . It being by this time nearly evening, the batteaux retired.

Benedict Arnold says: "We suffered much for want of seamen and gunners. I was obliged myself to point most of the guns on board the Congress, *which I believe did good execution." He explains how the battle ended, and tells of the damage done his fleet:*

They continued a very hot fire with round and grape shot until five o'clock, when they thought proper to retire to about six or seven hundred yards distance, and continued the fire until dark. The *Congress* and *Washington* have suffered greatly; the latter lost her first-lieutenant killed, captain and master wounded. The *New York* lost all her officers except her captain. The *Philadelphia* was hulled in so many places that she sunk in about one hour after the engagement was over. The whole killed and wounded amounts to about sixty.

"It was a desperate conflict on our part," writes Wilkinson, "and the wind and our proximity to the shore saved us from capture or destruction." But Sir Guy Carleton's forces were well aware they'd been in a real fight, having lost two vessels and forty men killed or wounded. Captain Pausch admits: "The cannon of the rebels were well served, for, as I saw afterwards, our ships were pretty well mended and patched up with boards and stoppers."

England's James Hadden says that the Royal Savage, *which had been disabled and run ashore on Valcour Island at the fight's beginning, was destroyed that evening: "This . . . was an unnecessary measure, as she might at a more leisure moment have been got off, or at all events her stores saved. . . ." Captain Pausch noted that "her ammunition blowing up, caused a fine fire. . . ." Returning to Wilkinson:*

At nightfall the wind, which had been high throughout the day, subsided into a gentle breeze, still from the northwest. General Arnold convened his captains on board the *Congress,* and after a consultation it was determined to attempt a retreat. Some of the council were for hauling round the island, through the narrow pass, but Arnold decided on attempting a passage directly through the enemy's line as the only practicable means of escape. . . . The night was profoundly dark and the atmosphere was charged with a heavy fog. Strict silence and stillness was enjoined, and we passed the enemy's line without seeing one of his vessels or being ourselves perceived.

"This retreat," writes James Hadden, "did great honor to Gen. Arnold." But the Englishman adds that the fugitives were soon retarded by a change in the wind:

. . . making but little way in the night, they were scarcely out of sight when their retreat was discovered at daybreak. The British fleet stood after them and gained ground considerably till the violence of the wind and a great swell obliged both fleets to anchor. Towards evening the weather was more moderate and the [British] fleet proceeded, the boats using their oars to make head against the wind.

Benedict Arnold was at this time sitting in the battered Congress, *occupied with pen and paper. Around him were shrouded corpses, wounded men with drawn faces, and working parties busy with repairs. Arnold was adding the final lines to the battle report quoted earlier:*

The enemy's fleet is under way to leeward and beating up. As soon as our leaks are stopped, the whole fleet will make the utmost despatch to Crown Point. . . . On the whole, I think we have had a very fortunate escape and have great reason to return our humble and hearty thanks to Almighty God for preserving and delivering so many of us from our more than savage enemies.

But the conflict wasn't over. The wind, which rose again during the night, was still from the southwest, and the Americans made little progress toward Crown Point. In fact, says Wilkinson, "two or three [vessels] were forced on the eastern shore, where they were abandoned and destroyed." He goes on:

At sunrise the next morning the fog was so thick that a vessel could not be discerned a cable's length [away]. But between eight and nine o'clock it cleared off, and the enemy's squadron was discovered getting under way with a fresh breeze from the northwest, which brought up their leading vessels within five miles of us before we felt its influence. . . .

Unhappily for the Americans, Captain Pringle's principal vessels— the Inflexible, *the* Maria, *and the* Carleton—*were also his fastest sailers. By noon they were in a position to begin firing. Benedict Arnold made a valiant attempt to fight back, but the opposition was overwhelming. The* Washington, *one of the stronger American vessels, soon surrendered. Wilkinson relates that Arnold in the* Congress *now came under a tremendous fire:*

. . . beset by dreadful odds, he passed the narrows at Split Rock, continuing the action until he found his vessel [taking on] water fast, that others were almost sinking, and that no chance for escape [from the gunfire] remained. He then ran his own galley and four gunboats ashore in a cove on the eastern coast of the lake and set them on fire, but ordered the colours not to be struck. . . . [T]he marines were directed to jump overboard, with their arms and accoutrements, to ascend a bank about twenty-five feet elevation and form a line for the defence of their vessels and flags against the enemy, Arnold being the last man who debarked.

The enemy did not venture into the cove, but kept up a distant cannonade until our vessels were burnt to the water's edge; after which Arnold commenced his march for Crown Point, about fifteen miles distant, by a bridle way through an unsettled wilderness; crossed the lake at that place and proceeded to Ticonderoga, where he had been preceded by Colonel Wigglesworth in the *Trumbull*, with two schooners, the sloop and one gondola, being all of our squadron which escaped. When the action commenced on the 11th, Arnold's galley mustered seventy-three hands including himself, of whom twenty-seven were killed or wounded; and of the last, three only survived, and these with the loss of limbs. . . .

Having demolished our flotilla, Sir Guy Carleton landed at Crown Point [which had been burned and abandoned by the Americans], where he awaited the arrival of his army, the rear of which got up a few days after, being retarded by adverse winds. . . .

The delays incident to such weather and the lateness of the season in that inhospitable clime discouraged Sir Guy's designs against Ticonderoga. . . .

Carleton went so far as to reconnoiter the American works. But then he ordered all of his troops back to Canada to begin establishing themselves in winter quarters. Benedict Arnold's fleet, then, hadn't been sacrificed in vain. If Carleton hadn't been delayed by the need to build warships to contend with those of the Americans, he would doubtless have arrived before Ticonderoga early enough to besiege and take it and then move down the Hudson to meet with a detachment from New York City, and the American cause must have tottered. General Arnold (doubling as an admiral), with his fifteen makeshift vessels and "a wretched, motley crew," had performed a great service. No one would ever say it better than the naval historian Admiral Alfred Thayer Mahan: "Never had any force, big or small, lived to better purpose or died more gloriously. . . ."

15

A FORT BECOMES A TRAP

I N THE *Manhattan Island area, the three weeks following the
devastating fire of September 21, 1776, were relatively quiet. At
Harlem Heights, Washington spent the time struggling with problems related to organization, training, equipment, and rations,
while in New York City Sir William Howe consolidated his position
and planned his next move. The British offensive was resumed
on October 12. Enveloped by an early-morning fog, eighty or
ninety vessels of all types, many of them filled with land forces,
ascended the East River, which divides Manhattan and Long Island. Turning eastward through the treacherous waters of Hell
Gate, the flotilla passed Flushing Bay and discharged its troops on
Throg's Neck (or Frog's Neck), a small peninsula jutting from
what is now the Bronx. Howe intended to make a northwesterly
march toward the Hudson for the purpose of encircling the American army's rear and cutting off its escape route northward by land.*

*But the operation developed too slowly. Howe was held up by
American parties sent to skirmish with his van, and by the need
to await reinforcements and supplies. Washington had ample time
to plan a course of action. In council on October 16 it was decided that the main body of the army must leave Manhattan. On
the eighteenth, while a detached force under Colonel John Glover
clashed with the British, the army crossed the Harlem River at
King's Bridge, at the island's northern end. The only spot on Manhattan left garrisoned (under a colonel named Robert Magaw) was*

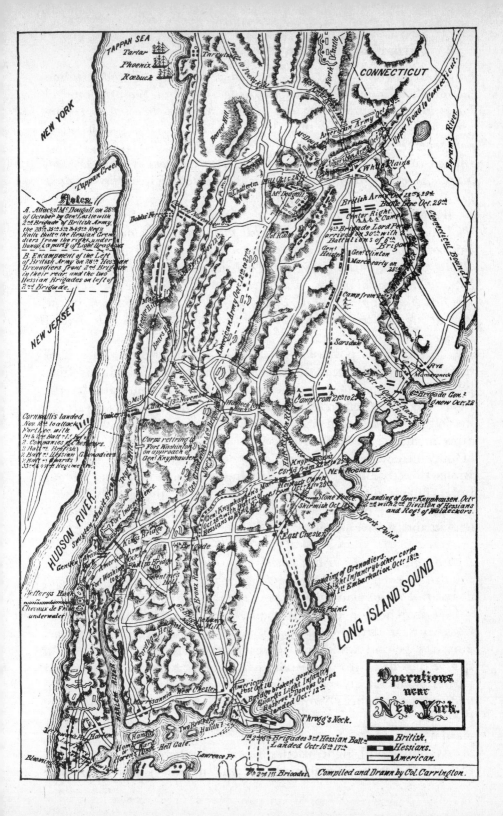

Operations near New York.

TAPPAN SEA
Tartar
Phoenix
Roebuck

CONNECTICUT

NEW YORK

Tappan Creek

Notes.

A. Attack of McDougall on 28th
of October by Genl Leslie with
2nd Brigade of British Army,
the 28th 35th 5th & 49th Regts
Ralls Battn the Hessian Gren-
diers from the right under
Donop & a party of Light Dragoons.

B. Encampment of the Left
of British Army on 28th Hessian
Grenadiers front 2nd Brigade
in their rear and the two
Hessian Brigades on left of
2nd Brigade.

NEW JERSEY

White Plains

British Army Oct 28th & 29th
Battle Line Oct. 29th
Center Right
4th Brigade Lord Percy
arrived on 30th with
Battalions of 6th
Genl Hessian

Genl Clinton
March early on
28th

Camp from Oct 21st

Sursdale

RYE
Mamaroneck

6th Brigade Genl
Knew Oct 22

Camp from 21st to 25

Hudson River

Cornwallis landed
Nov 18th to attack
Fort Lee, with
1st & 2nd Battn 1st Lt
2. Companies of Chasseurs.
2 Battn British.
2 Battn Hessian Grenadiers
2 Battn Guards
33rd & 42d Regiments.

Yonkers

Corps retiring to
Fort Washington
on approach of
Genl Knyphausen.

Fort Independence

Jefferys Hook
Chevaux de Frise
underwater.

Fort Washington

Kings Bridge

Phillips Bridge

Valentines Hill

Bronx River

Portland Heights

New Chester

Morrisania

Harlem

Randalls
Horns Hook
or Morris Rock Hell Gate

Lawrence Pt

Knyphausen's

NEW ROCHELLE

Landing of Genl Knyphausen. Octr
22 with a 2nd Division of Hessians
and Regt of Waldeckers.

Stone Fence
Skirmish Oct 18th

Myers Point.

East Chester

Landing of Grenadiers, other corps
Light Infantry & other corps.
1st Embarkation. Oct 18th

LONG ISLAND SOUND

American
Post Oct 18
Bridge broken down
Guards Light Infantry
Reserve & Donops Corps
landed Oct. 12th

Throgg's Neck.

1st 2nd 4th Brigades 3rd Hessian Battn
Landed Octr 16th 17th

6th 2nd 1st Brigades

Operations near New York.

British.
Hessians.
American.

Compiled and Drawn by Col. Carrington.

Fort Washington, a set of earthworks overlooking the Hudson two or three miles below King's Bridge. General Washington had some doubts about leaving Magaw and his men behind, but Congress had recommended that the fort be held as long as possible, and several of Washington's generals believed that it was strong enough to withstand a lengthy siege. In an emergency, they argued, Magaw's force probably could be evacuated across the Hudson to Fort Lee on the New Jersey shore.

Washington now established a series of small defensive posts in the woods and farmlands stretching northward along the west bank of the modest Bronx River toward the village of White Plains, about a dozen miles from King's Bridge. Howe reacted by beginning a parallel move east of the Bronx. Washington next assembled his troops at White Plains in order to deploy them in the way of the British advance. According to America's Lieutenant Benjamin Tallmadge:

. . . [He took] possession of the high ground north and east of the town. Here he seemed determined to take a stand, his lines [ran southwest to northeast] extending from a mountain on the right called Chatterton's Hill to a lake or large pond of water on his left. An intrenchment was thrown up . . . behind which our army formed. . . . Chatterton's Hill was separated from the right of our intrenchment by a valley of some extent, with the river Bronx directly before it. . . . [B]eing within cannon shot of our intrenchment on the right, Gen. Washington thought it best to occupy it, and ordered Gen. [Alexander] McDougall . . . to defend it, and if driven from it, to retire upon the right of the line.

Approaching the American position on the morning of October 28, the British encountered a large advance party under General Joseph Spencer. An anonymous American describes the action:

We marched on to a hill about one mile and a half from our lines with an artillery company and two field-pieces, and placed ourselves behind walls and fences in the best manner we could to give the enemy trouble. About half after nine o'clock . . . the light parties of the enemy, with their advanced guard . . . came in sight and marched on briskly towards us, keeping the high grounds; and the light horse pranced on a little in the rear, making a very martial appearance. . . .

As our [own] light parties . . . [revealed] where we were, the enemy began to cannonade us, and to fling shells from their hobits [howitzers] and small mortars. Their light parties soon came on, and we fired upon them from the walls and fences, broke and scattered them at once. But they would run from our front and get round upon our wings to flank us; and as soon as our fire [revealed] where we were, the enemy's artillery would at once begin to play upon us in the most furious manner. We kept the walls until the enemy were just ready to surround us, and then we would retreat from one wall and hill to another and maintain our ground there in the same manner, till numbers were [again] just ready to surround us.

Once the Hessian grenadiers came up in front of Colonel [William] Douglas's regiment, and we fired a general volley upon them . . . and scattered them like leaves in a whirlwind; and they ran off so far that some of the regiment ran out to the ground where they were when we fired upon them, and brought off their arms and accoutrements and rum (that the men who fell had with them), which we had time to drink round with before they came on again.

Benjamin Tallmadge, another of General Spencer's men, agrees that the units fought well:

It, however, became necessary to retreat wholly before such an overwhelming force. To gain Chatterton's Hill, it became necessary to cross the Bronx, which was fordable at that place. The troops immediately entered the river and ascended the hill, while I, being in the rear and mounted on horseback, endeavored to hasten the last of our troops, the Hessians being then within musket shot. When I reached the bank of the river and was about to enter it, our chaplain, the Rev. Dr. Trumbull, sprang up behind me on my horse and came with such force to carry me with my accoutrements, together with himself, headlong into the river. This so entirely disconcerted me that by the time I reached the opposite bank of the river [still unmounted] the Hessian troops were about to enter it. . . . As we ascended the hill I filed off to the right, expecting our troops on the hill would soon give them a volley. When they had advanced within a few yards of a stone wall behind which Gen. McDougall had placed them, our troops poured upon the Hessian column . . . such a destructive fire that they retreated down the hill in disorder, leaving a considerable number of the corps on the field. This relieved me from my perilous situation. . . .

The main body of the enemy, covered by cannon fire that "echoed terribly" among the hills, was now coming on the scene in two long columns, marching abreast. A little ahead of the right column (the one farthest from Chatterton's Hill) galloped a small band of horsemen, shouting confidently and brandishing swords that flashed in the sun as they advanced. Their impetuosity carried them too far—right up to some concealed Americans of the main line. General William Heath, who commanded in this area, observed what happened:

The light-horse leaped the fence of a wheat field at the foot of the hill on which Col. [William] Malcolm's regiment was posted —of which the light-horse were not aware until a shot from Lieut. [Ephraim] Fenno's field-piece gave them notice by striking in the midst of them, and a horseman pitching from his horse. They then wheeled short about, galloped out of the field as fast as they came in, rode behind a little hill in the road and faced about, the tops of their caps only being visible. . . .

The two columns of the main body halted when their leading units were abreast of Chatterton's Hill. General Heath had a good view of a large number of these men: "The sun shone bright, their arms glittered, and perhaps troops never were shewn to more advantage than these now appeared." Sir William Howe made no move to deploy the columns for an attack on the main line. Instead, he turned a furious cannonade against Chatterton's Hill and then sent a strong detachment wading across the Bronx to renew the attack begun by his vanguard. General Heath goes on:

As the troops . . . ascended the hill, the cannonade on the side of the British ceased; as their own men became exposed to their fire, if continued. The fire of small arms was now very heavy. . . . This led some American officers, who were looking on, to observe that the British were worsted, as their cannon had ceased firing; but a few minutes evinced that the Americans were giving way. They moved off the hill [toward the right of the main line] in a great body, neither running nor observing the best order. The British ascended the hill very slowly; and when arrived at its summit formed and dressed their line, without the least attempt to pursue the Americans.

Having suffered this setback, Washington, who had no great confidence in the strength of his main position, was much relieved when Howe did nothing more that day than fire some cannon shots *and set his men to digging in. This work continued the next day, while Washington prepared to draw back, sending off his sick and wounded and a part of his baggage. On the thirtieth, writes General Heath, "the British remained upon the ground they had taken." On the thirty-first, which dawned stormily, they "continued as before." That night the Americans evacuated their works. Says the anonymous American quoted earlier:*

We carried off all our stores, and planted our artillery on the hills about a mile and a half back of the centre of the town. The enemy advanced [on November 1] on to the ground we left, but as soon as they came over the hill we saluted them with our cannon and field-pieces, and they advanced no further.

General Heath observes: "A shot from the American cannon . . . took off the head of a Hessian artilleryman. They also left one of the artillery horses dead on the field." Sir William, having failed in his original aim to encircle the American rear, now decided to give up the game. The news of this decision was to amaze Judge Jones: ". . . the British General thought it needless (as he expressed it himself) to pursue a flying enemy. Most people differ with the General upon this . . . and think a flying enemy the only enemy that can be pursued. . . ." Actually, the "flying enemy" had taken up a strong position. Had Howe attacked, another Bunker Hill might have resulted. The general had been given his chance on October 28 but had declined to take it.

The caustic Judge Jones was later to make the acquaintance of General Gold Silliman, an American of the White Plains army:

In one of our conversations the subject turned upon the situation . . . at the White Plains . . . when the General (who is rather enthusiastic) thus expressed himself: "Providence there favoured us in a most remarkable manner. A mist was cast before the British General's eyes. It was no doubt an act of the Almighty, who favoured our righteous cause. General Howe had our whole army in his power, and had he not been blinded by the directions of Providence, every soul of us must have been prisoners, and our cannon, baggage and stores either taken or destroyed."

I asked the General what would have been the consequence of such [a] defeat? He lifted up his eyes and exclaimed, "The Lord befriended us! Had we been then defeated . . . another army could never have been raised. The Colonies must have submitted and accepted such terms as Great Britain would have offered." Then, again lifting up his eyes, [he] sighed and with great emphasis uttered, "The Lord was our protector!" The rebel army, I fancy, were much more obliged to a factious opposition in England, of which the General was a member, than they were to the Lord of Hosts.

Like many other Loyalists, the judge refused even to consider the possibility that Howe's cautious way of proceeding might have been based on military reasoning he believed quite sound.

General Heath tells of the days immediately following the halfhearted British advance of November 1:

The two armies lay looking at each other, and within long cannon shot. In the night time the British lighted up a vast number of fires, the weather growing pretty cold. These fires, some on the level ground, some at the foot of the hills and at all distances to their brows, some of which were lofty, seemed to the eye to mix with the stars and to be of different magnitudes. The American side doubtless exhibited to them a similar appearance. . . .

3d: The centinels reported that, during the preceding night, they heard the rumblings of carriages to the southeastward; and it was apprehended that the British were changing their position. 5th: The British centinels were withdrawn from their advanced posts. . . . The American army was immediately ordered under arms. At 2 o'clock p.m. the enemy appeared, formed on Chatterton's Hill and on several hills to the westward of it. Several [American] reconnoitring parties who were sent out reported that the enemy were withdrawing. About 12 o'clock this night a party of the Americans wantonly set fire to the court house, Dr. Graham's house, and several other private houses which stood between the two armies. This gave great disgust to the whole American army. . . .

The leader of this pack of vandals was shortly court-martialed and dismissed from the army in disgrace. As for General Howe, he first took his columns westward toward the Hudson and then south-ward toward King's Bridge. Washington now suspected that Sir William had designs on America's twin forts on the lower Hudson —Fort Washington on Manhattan, and Fort Lee, directly across the river in New Jersey. But Washington had no way of being sure of Howe's intentions, so he split his army. Leaving General Charles Lee, his second-in-command, with a large body in the White Plains region (for the protection of New England), he marched to Peeks-

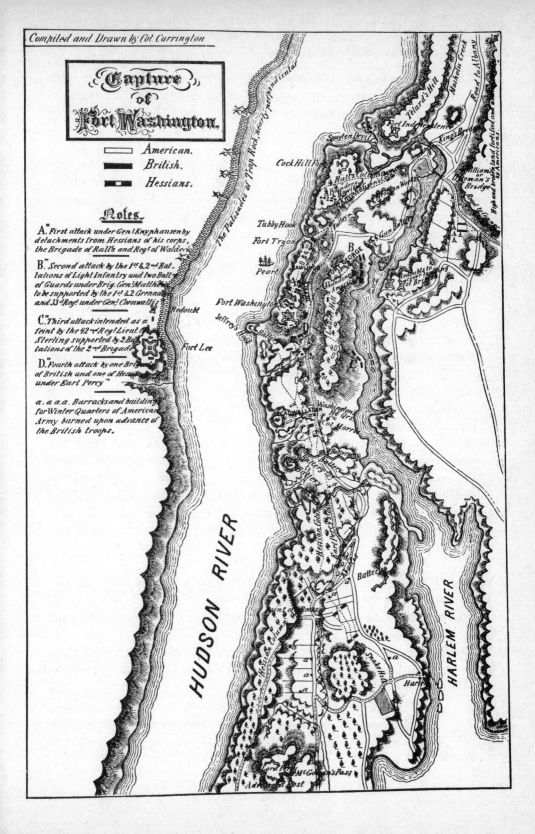

Compiled and Drawn by Col. Carrington.

Capture
of
Fort Washington.

☐ American.
■ British.
▣ Hessians.

Notes.

A." First attack under Gen¹ Knyphausen by detachments from Hessians of his corps, the Brigade of Rall's and Reg¹ of Walderk.

B." Second attack by the 1ˢᵗ & 2ⁿᵈ Battalions of Light Infantry and two Batt of Guards under Brig. Gen¹ Matthews to be supported by the 1ˢᵗ & 2 Grenadiers and 33ʳᵈ Reg¹ under Gen¹ Cornwallis.

C." Third attack intended as a feint by the 42ⁿᵈ Reg¹ Lieut. Col. Sterling supported by 2 Battalions of the 2ⁿᵈ Brigade.

D." Fourth attack by one Brigade of British and one of Hessians under Earl Percy."

a. a. a. a. Barracks and buildings for Winter Quarters of American Army burned upon advance of the British troops.

HUDSON RIVER

HARLEM RIVER

kill on the Hudson. There he posted another body to guard the Highlands, the gateway to the upper Hudson and Lake Champlain. With the remainder of his army, about two thousand men, he crossed the Hudson and moved down the river into New Jersey to be near Fort Lee, where General Nathanael Greene of Rhode Island commanded.

General Howe moved first against the post on his side of the river, launching his assault on Fort Washington, the last American post on Manhattan, during the early morning hours of November 16. The plan called for troops to advance against the fort on all of its landward sides. General Heath explains that the attackers were opposed first by Americans in the fort's outworks:

General [Wilhelm von] Knyphausen, with a heavy column of Hessians, advanced [southward from] King's Bridge. They were discovered by the Americans from the high grounds north of Fort Washington as the day broke, and cannonaded from the field-pieces placed at this advanced post. The Hessian column divided into two. . . . The first obtained the ground without much difficulty; but the Americans made a most noble opposition against the latter, and for a considerable time kept them from ascending the hill, making a terrible slaughter among them. But the great superiority of the assailants, with an unabating firmness, finally prevailed. Their loss was greater here than at any other place. Meanwhile the British crossed Harlem Creek [east of the fort] in two different places, charged and finally routed the Americans on that side . . . Lord Percy at the same time advancing . . . towards the fort . . . [from the south]. The Americans, now generally driven from their outworks, retired to the fort. . . .

Not all of them made it. Scores were cut off and captured. Captain Alexander Graydon of Pennsylvania, along with some others, ended up in the custody of a party commanded by a Scottish sergeant. Graydon relates:

The sergeant was a decent looking man who . . . bestowed upon us in broad Scotch the friendly admonition of, "Young men, ye should never fight against your king!"

The little bustle produced by our surrender was scarcely over when a British officer on horseback . . . rode up at full gallop exclaiming, "What? Taking prisoners? Kill them! Kill every man of them!"

My back was towards him when he spoke . . . and turning to him I took off my hat, saying, *"Sir, I put myself under your protection."*

No man was ever more effectually rebuked. His manner was instantly softened. He met my salutation with an inclination of his body; and after a civil question or two, as if to make amends for his sanguinary mandate, he rode off. . . .

By this time Fort Washington had become a trap. It was greatly overcrowded, and the British were placing their cannon in such a way as to bring it under heavy fire. Heath's account continues:

Gen. Washington was now a spectator of this distressing scene from the high bank at Fort Lee on the opposite side of the Hudson. And having a wish to communicate something to Col. Magaw, the commanding officer at Fort Washington [that he try to hold out until nightfall, when an escape across the river might be attempted], Capt. [John] Gooch of Boston, a brave and daring man, offered to be the bearer of it. He ran down to the river, jumped into a small boat, pushed over the river, landed under the bank, ran up to the fort and delivered the message—came out, ran and jumped over the broken ground, dodging the Hessians, some of whom struck at him with their pieces, and others attempted to thrust him with their bayonets. Escaping through them, he got to his boat and returned to Fort Lee.

The British had summoned Col. Magaw to surrender and were preparing their batteries to play on the fort, when Col. Magaw thought it best to surrender the post; which he did accordingly, between two and three thousand men becoming prisoners. The loss in killed and wounded on the American side was inconsiderable; but the loss in prisoners was a serious blow indeed.

16

WASHINGTON RALLIES THE CAUSE

T HE FALL *of Fort Washington left the Americans stunned; and Sir William Howe, for a change, decided to press his advantage. He quickly ordered a strike against New Jersey's Fort Lee. About four thousand men under Lord Cornwallis and General John Vaughan crossed the Hudson during the cold and rainy night of November 19, 1776, landing at the foot of the Palisades a few miles north of the fort. By dawn of the twentieth the force had mounted the height through a rocky gorge and was marching southward to the attack.*

Says one of these men: "On the appearance of our troops the rebels fled like scared rabbits, and in a few moments after we reached the hill near their intrenchments not a rascal of them could be seen." According to the way Judge Jones heard it, they left "their artillery, stores, baggage and everything else behind them; they left their very pots boiling upon the fire."

Some gunpowder had been saved, but that was about all. The fort's commander, General Nathanael Greene, took his demoralized troops northwestward to Hackensack, where the army under Washington was camped. The commander in chief decided on an immediate retreat southward through New Jersey. Judge Jones writes that the American troops were at this time nothing more than "half-starved, half-clothed, half-armed, discontented, ungovernable, undisciplined wretches." He goes on:

Lord Cornwallis and General Vaughan . . . differing in opinion from the Commander-in-Chief [Howe], *pursued the flying enemy.*

The British invading New Jersey. From a water color attributed to Francis, Lord Rawdon.

. . . The rebels fled towards New Brunswick upon the Raritan. . . . Whenever a British detachment . . . fell in with a rebel detachment, the latter was instantly dispersed. So great was the panic at this time among the rebels that a captain of theirs with above 50 men . . . took to their heels upon the approach of six waggoners dressed in red coats.

The pursuit wasn't as rapid as the judge makes it seem; but it was, for a time at least, sustained. On December 2, one of Washington's men recorded in his diary:

Yesterday, on the appearance of the enemy at Brunswick, General Washington ordered a retreat to Princeton, where we arrived early this morning. We are in a terrible situation, with the enemy close upon us and whole regiments of Marylanders and Jerseymen leaving us. Tomorrow we go to Trenton. . . . A Tory . . . was brought in here today by a party of the Pennsylvania boys. . . . This afternoon, after taking off his breeches and giving him an absolution by setting him on the ice (to cool his loyalty) they set him to work bringing in fagots. He seems pleased with his new office, knowing that he got off easy.

"At Brunswick," Judge Jones complains, "Lord Cornwallis halted. . . ." Howe had given him orders "to proceed no further." The commander in chief was at this time in New York City, having just finished some business of a different nature. He had sent a large amphibious force under Sir Peter Parker and Sir Henry Clinton to occupy the Newport area of Rhode Island. The judge says of this:

The conquest of this island was of no service to Great Britain or to the general cause. It divided the army, New York and Rhode Island being 200 miles apart. Common report . . . asserted that the expedition was planned in order . . . to wipe off some aspersions that had been cast upon the naval and land commanders for their conduct . . . in South Carolina the preceding summer. . . .

Newport was an especially fine place to shelter sailing vessels, but the chief effect of the occupation was to tie up a good part of the British forces for the next three years.

On December 6, General Howe, leading a reinforcement, joined Cornwallis at New Brunswick and assumed personal command of the pursuit of Washington. By this time the Americans were beginning to cross the Delaware River at Trenton. According to a participant, the last boats had scarcely reached the Pennsylvania bank on December 8 when Sir William's vanguard approached the river:

. . . the enemy came marching down with all the pomp of war, in great expectation of getting boats and immediately pursuing; but of this we [had taken] proper care by destroying every boat, shallop, etc., we could lay our hands on. They made forced marches up and down the river in pursuit of boats, but in vain.

Feeling secure at least for the moment, Washington deployed his troops along the Delaware's bank. He was now in the most urgent

*need of reinforcements. During his flight through New Jersey he
had several times sent word to his second-in-command, General
Charles Lee, whom he had left east of the Hudson after the affair
at White Plains, to join him as soon as possible. But Lee had
become very unhappy with the way Washington was running the
war and seemed to be pondering the feasibility of moving against
the British on his own. He had crossed the Hudson on December 4
but was tarrying on his way through New Jersey. He wasn't too
worried about being attacked, for he was keeping to the west of
the enemy's main routes.*

*Washington, of course, found Lee's conduct extremely frustrating.
On December 11 he sent still another messenger to entreat Lee to
hurry southward with all the help he could manage to bring.
At this same time, a messenger from the north also was approaching
Lee, somewhat by chance. He was young Major James Wilkinson,
now recovered from the fever he'd been stricken with just before
the Battle of Lake Champlain. General Horatio Gates was bringing
a force down from Ticonderoga to assist Washington, and he had
sent Wilkinson ahead for specific orders. The major had planned
to go to Washington; but on learning that the general's second-
in-command was closer, decided to go to him instead. Wilkinson
found Lee's troops encamped near Morristown. Lee himself was
lodging at a tavern about three miles away. On December 13,
relates Wilkinson:*

I arose at the dawn, but could not see the General . . . before
eight o'clock. After some inquiries respecting the campaign on the
northern frontier he gave me a brief account of the operations of
the grand army, which he condemned in strong terms. He observed . . . that the attempt to defend islands against a superior land
and naval force was madness; that Sir William Howe could have
given us check-mate at his discretion; and that we owed our salvation to his indolence or disinclination to terminate the war. . . .

. . . we did not sit down to breakfast before 10 o'clock. General
Lee was engaged in answering General Gates's letter, and I had
risen from the table and was looking out of an end window, down a
lane about one hundred yards in length, which led to the house
from the main road, when I discovered a party of British dragoons
turn a corner . . . at a full charge. Startled at this unexpected spectacle, I exclaimed, "Here, Sir, are the British cavalry!"

"*Where?*" replied the General, who had signed his letter in the
instant.

"Around the house." For they had opened files and encompassed the building.

General Lee appeared alarmed, yet collected. . . . "Where is the guard? Damn the guard! Why don't they fire?" And after a momentary pause he turned to me and said, "Do, Sir, see what has become of the guard."

The women of the house at this moment entered the room and proposed to him to conceal himself in a bed, which he rejected with evident disgust. I caught up my pistols, which lay on the table, thrust the letter he had been writing into my pocket, and passed into a room at the opposite end of the house, where I had seen the guard in the morning. . . . [T]he men were absent. I stepped out of the door and perceived the dragoons chasing them in different directions; and, receiving a very uncivil salutation, I returned into the house. . . . I . . . sought a position where I could not be approached by more than one person at a time, and with a pistol in each hand I awaited the expected search. . . .

I did not remain long in this unpleasant situation, but was apprised of the object of the incursion by the very audible declaration, *"If the General does not surrender in five minutes, I will set fire to the house;"* which after a short pause was repeated with a solemn oath; and within two minutes I heard it proclaimed, *"Here is the General; he has surrendered."* A general shout ensued; the trumpet sounded the assembly; and the unfortunate Lee, mounted on my horse which stood ready at the door, was hurried off in triumph, bareheaded, in his slippers and blanket coat, his collar open and his shirt very much soiled from several days' use.

It was careless of Lee to be caught unaware like this, several miles from his command. Ironically, Lee's letter to Gates (which James Wilkinson would deliver safely) included the opinion that "a certain great man is most damnably deficient." Lee, of course, was speaking of Washington. The ink of the slur was barely dry before Lee was revealed as being more than a little deficient himself. The British patrol moved swiftly to spirit Lee from American-occupied territory. Says a Patriot newspaper called the Freeman's Journal:

The enemy showed an ungenerous—nay, boyish triumph—after they had got him secure at Brunswick, by making his horse drunk while they toasted their king till they were in the same condition. A band or two of music played all night to proclaim their joy for this important acquisition.

Dr. Thacher lamented in his journal that Lee's capture was "another disaster of much importance":

The loss of this favorite general officer, it is feared, will be attended with very serious consequences as respects the American cause. . . . Such is now the gloomy aspect of our affairs that the whole country has taken the alarm. Strong apprehensions are entertained that the British will soon have it in their power to vanquish the whole of the remains of the Continental Army. The term of service of a considerable part of our troops has nearly expired, and new recruits do not arrive in sufficient numbers to supply their places. His Excellency General Washington is continually making every possible effort to produce a change of circumstances more auspicious to our country. The critical and distressing situation in which he is placed is sufficient to overwhelm the powers of any man of less wisdom and magnanimity than our commander-in-chief. . . .

The king's commissioners, flushed with the success of the royal army, have . . . put forth another proclamation, granting pardons to all those who shall within sixty days subscribe a declaration to remain peaceable, not to take up arms, nor encourage others to act against the king's authority. And at the same time they charge and command all who are assembled in arms against his majesty to disband, and all . . . general and provincial congress committees, etc., to desist from their *treasonable* practices and relinquish their usurped power. . . .

The [Continental] Congress resolved on the 12th [of December] that it be recommended to all the United States as soon as possible to appoint a day of fasting and humiliation. This is according to the custom of our pious ancestors in times of imminent dangers and difficulties.

Considering the rapid movements of the enemy, and knowing it to be their intention to possess themselves of the city of Philadelphia, the Congress have resolved to retire to Baltimore in Maryland. They have also ordered that hand-bills be circulated through the states with the view of rousing the whole people to a sense of the impending danger and the calamities that will ensue should the enemy succeed in the attempt to get possession of the capital.

Another step taken by the worried delegates just before their flight from the endangered city concerned the commander in chief:

Resolved, that until Congress shall otherwise order, General

Washington be possessed of full power to order and direct all things relative to the department and to the operations of war.

American prospects seemed bleak indeed, but some stout hearts remained. Among the volunteers who retreated through New Jersey with Washington was Thomas Paine, the author of Common Sense. *December 19 saw the publication of a new pamphlet by Paine, one dealing with* The American Crisis. *This was the start of a series he would continue through the war. The first essay began:*

These are the times that try men's souls. The summer soldier and the sunshine patriot will, in this crisis, shrink from the service of their country; but he that stands it *now* deserves the love and thanks of man and woman. Tyranny, like hell, is not easily conquered; yet we have this consolation with us, that the harder the conflict, the more glorious the triumph. What we obtain too cheap, we esteem too lightly: it is dearness only that gives everything its value. Heaven knows how to put a proper price upon its goods; and it would be strange indeed if so celestial an article as FREEDOM should not be highly rated.

This was a period of great suffering in the occupied parts of New Jersey. Judge Jones admits:

. . . a licentious army was suffered to plunder and to commit every kind of rapine, injustice and violence indiscriminately upon the inhabitants, the consequence of which became dismal.

Dr. Thacher complained in his journal:

. . . hundreds of inhabitants, both male and female, have been deprived of their dwellings and sustenance, stripped of their clothing and exposed to the inclemency of the winter and to personal insult and abuse of almost every description.

The ease with which his troops had pushed through New Jersey after being eminently successful on Long Island and Manhattan had convinced Sir William Howe that the rebellion was well under control; and, averse to keeping the field in cold weather, he decided to delay his move toward Philadelphia. Judge Jones carps:

Washington's army, at crossing the Delaware, were reduced to less than 4,000 men. Had the pursuit been continued, the rebel chief . . . would scarcely have stopped short of Maryland, and perhaps gone even into Virginia. . . . The only reason I ever heard given

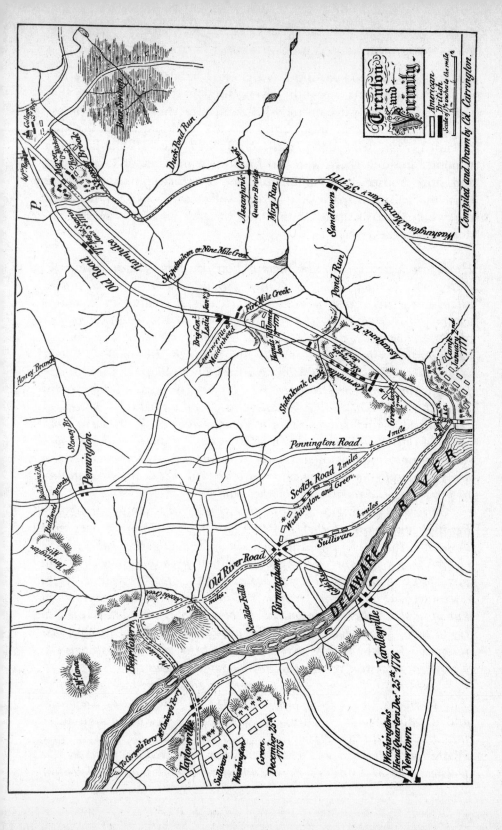

Trenton and Vicinity.

American
British
Scale of ¾ inches to a mile

Compiled and Drawn by Col. Carrington.

for the General not passing the Delaware was that the rebels had carried all the boats across the river. But I have been told . . . that there was a board yard, entirely full, and directly back of the house in which the Commander-in-Chief had his headquarters, and which he must have seen every time he looked out of his bedroom window. Besides, there were in Trenton a number of large barns and store houses, built of boards, out of which rafts might have been made in the space of two days sufficient to have transported the whole British army, with their baggage, artillery and provisions across the river. . . .

Howe, in fact, didn't even remain long in New Jersey. After deciding not to continue the winter pursuit, he had issued orders establishing his army in a series of towns stretching in a southwesterly direction from the lower Hudson to the Trenton region of the Delaware—a deployment that spanned much of the country the Americans had fled through—and then, on December 13, had returned to the comforts and pleasures of New York City. Judge Jones claims that something about Howe's disposal of the troops "was thought remarkable." Posted at Trenton was "a parcel of Hessians who understood not a word of English." They were commanded by a Colonel Johann Rall, who "though a brave man [was] a notorious drunkard." So contemptuous of the American army was Rall that he neglected to take "the necessary precaution" of providing the town with fortifications.

General Washington, whose lines were still strung along the Pennsylvania bank of the Delaware across from Trenton, was now desperate for a victory; and the enemy's negligence gave him a chance to try for one. Having been joined by about two thousand men lately commanded by Charles Lee, a few regiments from Ticonderoga, and some fresh militiamen from Pennsylvania (and knowing that others were on call in New Jersey), he determined to try to take the Hessians by surprise during the early morning hours following Christmas Day, when they would doubtless be sluggish as a result of excessive celebrating in the Savior's honor.

Washington believed that Trenton might be turned into a trap. The town lay in a corner formed by the junction of the Delaware and a tributary, the Assunpink Creek. The creek, though often fordable, was presently swollen as a consequence of winter rains. Washington decided to boat twenty-five hundred men across the Delaware at McConkey's Ferry, about nine miles above Trenton, march them down, and have them approach the town in two col-umns in such a way as to pin the Hessians in their corner. While this major march was in progress, two smaller forces from the American camp were to cross the Delaware below the Assunpink, one to block a bridge over the creek at Trenton, and the other to divert the attention of a Hessian post commanded by Colonel Carl von Donop at nearby Bordentown.

By late afternoon on Christmas Day the main American force was assembling at McConkey's Ferry in preparation for the crossing. The scene was pathetic. Many of the men wore only ragged summer clothing. Some had wrapped themselves in blankets. Shoes and boots with worn-out soles and split sides were everywhere in evi-dence, and a few of the men had nothing on their feet but knotted rags. A light snow lay on the ground, tinged here and there with blood left by feet too long abused. But these tattered soldiers gave a young officer named Alexander Hamilton the impression that they were "ready, every devil of them . . . to storm hell's battlements in the night."

Major James Wilkinson was one of the last men to join the expedition. He came bearing a letter from General Gates for the commander in chief. Washington complained, "What a time is this to hand me letters!" Wilkinson says:

. . . boats were in readiness, and the troops began to cross about sunset; but the force of the current, the sharpness of the frost, the darkness of the night, the ice . . . and a high wind, rendered the passage of the river extremely difficult.

At the oars were Colonel John Glover's Massachusetts fishermen, the heroes of the retreat from Long Island. The task, which re-quired many of the boats to make several trips, was soon made even harder by a storm of sleet and snow that began to sweep the river. In addition to the troops, there were horses and equipment to be transported. Included were eighteen pieces of artillery. Col-onel Henry Knox of Boston, writes Wilkinson, was the spirit of the enterprise, employing "stentorian lungs and extraordinary ex-ertions." The burly Knox himself says that "perseverance accom-plished what at first seemed impossible."

But it was nearly four o'clock in the morning before the ex-pedition was formed and set marching. Most of the men were silent now, and the artillery pieces rolled along stiffly behind plodding horses. Affixed to the pieces, according to a Connecticut man named

Elisha Bostwick, were torches that "sparkled and blazed in the storm."

About halfway to Trenton, the troops halted in the bitter dawn to divide for the double approach. Washington, with his cloak drawn about him, rode along the lines and (writes Elisha Bostwick) "in a deep and solemn voice" cautioned the soldiers to stay close to their officers. Bostwick adds:

While passing a slanting, slippery bank, His Excellency's horse's hind feet both slipped from under him, and he seized his horse's mane and the horse recovered.

Washington attached himself to the left column, which was commanded by General Nathanael Greene. The right column was commanded by General John Sullivan, who had been exchanged very soon after his capture on Long Island. "The storm," says Henry Knox, "continued with great violence, but was in our backs. . . ." Though Major Wilkinson was with the right column, he learned later that Washington took up a position near an artillery captain named Thomas Forrest, which placed him close to the left column's front:

As he approached the village, he inquired of an inhabitant who was chopping wood by the roadside, "Which way is the Hessian picket?"

"I don't know," replied the citizen, waiving an answer.

"You may speak," said Captain Forrest, "for that is General Washington."

The astonished man raised his hands to heaven and exclaimed, "God bless and prosper you, Sir! The picket is in that house, and the sentry stands near that tree."

The men of the picket were promptly dislodged. Two or three were captured, while the rest retreated through the lashing snow and sleet toward the town. Washington's men pursued. At the same time, Wilkinson relates, the right column was also nearing the objective:

The attack . . . on the left . . . was immediately answered by Colonel [John] Stark in our front, who forced the enemy's picket and pressed it into the town, our column being close at his heels. The enemy made a momentary shew of resistance by a wild and undirected fire from the windows of their quarters, which they abandoned as we advanced, and made an attempt to form in the main

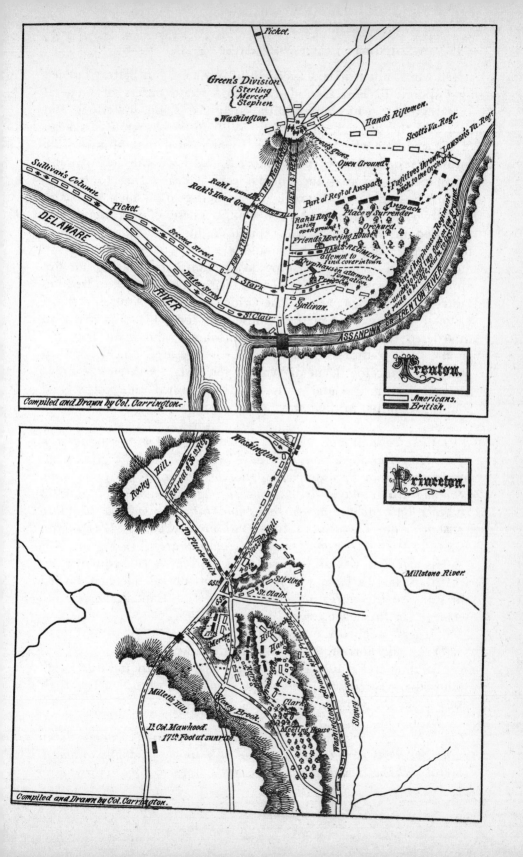

Trenton.

Green's Division
Sterling
Mercer
Stephen

• Washington.

Hand's Riflemen.

Scott's Va. Regt.

Forrest's Guns

Open Ground

Fugitives thrown
back to the orchard

Rahl wounded

Rahl's Head Qrs.

Part of Regt of Anspach

Place of Surrender

Anspach

Rahl's Regt.
taking
open ground

Orchard.

Friend's Meeting House.

RAHL'S REGIMENT
attempt to
find cover in town

Knyphausen attempts
formation

Preston

Sullivan

Fire of Knyphausen Regiment,
unable to haul two guns on the ground,
on route to bridge, then retrograde.

Sullivan's Column

Picket.

DELAWARE

Second Street

Water Street

King Street

Stark

St. Clair

RIVER

ASSANPINK

TRENTON RIVER

Americans.

British.

Compiled and Drawn by Col. Carrington.

Princeton.

Rocky Hill.

Retreat of 55 & Regt.

Washington.

Millstone River.

To Pluckemin.

Nassau Hall.

40th

55th

Stirling

St. Clair

Mercer

Hitchcock

Hand

Millett's Hill.

Stony Brook.

Clark

Stony Brook.

Stony Brook.

Frog Hollow Stonybrook

Meeting House.

Lt. Col. Mawhood.
17th Foot at sunrise.

Compiled and Drawn by Col. Carrington.

street, which might have succeeded but for a six-gun battery opened by Captain T. Forrest under the immediate orders of General Washington . . . which annoyed the enemy in various directions; and [but for] the decision of Captain William Washington [a cousin of the general] who, seconded by Lieutenant James Monroe [the future President], led the advanced guard of the left column [and], perceiving that the enemy were endeavouring to form a battery, rushed forward, drove the artillerists from their guns and took two pieces in the act of firing. These officers were both wounded in this charge, the captain in his wrist, the lieutenant through the fleshy part of his shoulder. . . .

Pressed in front [by Washington's column] and hearing our fire approach . . . a troop of dragoons, with about five hundred infantry, took to flight across [the bridge over] the Assunpink. . . . Colonel Rall, while exerting himself to form his dismayed and disordered corps, being shot from his horse, the main body retired . . . up the Assunpink, with the apparent inclination to escape to Princeton. General Washington instantly threw the brave Colonel [Edward] Hand with his distinguished rifle corps [and some other units] in their way. . . .

The right column now sealed off the bridge. There was no sign of the American force that, according to Washington's original plan, was supposed to be approaching the bridge from the other side. Nor had any sound of firing come through the screen of snow to indicate that the fleeing dragoons and infantrymen had run into resistance. On the attack's left, Wilkinson explains, Washington had returned to directing the fire of Captain Forrest's guns:

His position was an exposed one, and he was frequently intreated to fall back, of which he took no notice. He had turned the guns on the retreating enemy, when . . . Captain Forrest observed, "Sir, they have struck."

"Struck?" replied the General.

"Yes," said Forrest, "their colours are down."

"So they are," observed the chief, and galloped towards them, followed by Forrest and his whole command, who . . . left their guns to see the show.

The Hessians, in the end, after having suffered several dozen casualties, had been trying to form in a snowy field and orchard. As they threw down their arms, their ragged conquerors, with triumphant shouts, surrounded them and made them prisoners. Washington was as jubilant as his men. Later, however, the general took the time to pay a sympathetic visit to the fatally wounded Colonel Rall. James Wilkinson continues:

In this affair we lost no officer; and those [two] before mentioned, with four men only, were wounded. Two were killed and one frozen to death. Our trophies were four stand of colours, twelve drums, six brass field pieces, a thousand stand of arms and accoutrements; and our prisoners twenty-three officers and almost 1,000 noncommissioned officers and privates. . . .

The execution of this enterprize reflected high honour on General Washington, but his triumph was abridged by the failure of two simultaneous attacks . . . under General [John] Cadwalader and . . . General [James Ewing], which made a part of his plan. These officers employed every exertion to cross the river, but were baffled by the ice; and in consequence the [troops who had crossed the bridge] escaped from Trenton, and Count Donop, with the detachments below, was enabled to make good his retreat. . . . This [attack of ours] was a desperate undertaking, justified by the deplorable state of our affairs and worthy [of] the chief who projected it. I have never doubted that he had resolved to stake his life on the issue.

On the same day as the battle, Washington and his men, with their prisoners and their trophies, made the return trip to the Pennsylvania side of the Delaware—this in spite of the continued severity of the weather. Says a newspaper writer who reported the affair: "Luckily they found some hogsheads of rum at Trenton, large draughts of which alone preserved the lives of many." According to Judge Jones:

The prisoners were sent to Philadelphia and treated with insult. They were paraded about the city as a spectacle to the people. The officers, though some of them field ones and connected with some of the best families in Germany, were not exempt from this parade. Officers and privates all fared alike.

A brighter word is added by Dr. Thacher:

General Washington allowed the Hessian prisoners to retain their baggage and sent them into the interior of Pennsylvania, ordering that they be treated with favor and humanity. This conduct, so contrary to their expectations, excited their gratitude and veneration for their amiable conqueror, whom they styled "a very good rebel."

The victory at Trenton had the effect that Washington hoped for. In Wilkinson's words:

The joy diffused throughout the union . . . reanimated the timid friends of the revolution and invigorated the confidence of the resolute. . . . Success had triumphed over despondency. . . .

17

DELIVERANCE FOR NEW JERSEY

IMMEDIATELY *after the downfall of the Hessian garrison under Johann Rall, the enemy troops of the other Delaware outposts flew to the safety of posts to the north, the first of which was at Princeton, about twelve miles from Trenton. It seemed almost certain that this disruption of his lines would stir General Howe to strong countermeasures; but Washington, in spite of his relative weakness, decided to continue on the offensive. Only three days after the Battle of Trenton he ordered his men to ready themselves for another move into New Jersey. James Wilkinson was among those who regarded the order with surprise:*

. . . the masterly judgment of General Washington seems to have been beguiled by his good fortune, or the panic of the enemy . . . for we find him again preparing to cross the Delaware to "pursue the enemy in his retreat; try to break up more of their quarters; and in a word, in every instance adopt such measures as the exigency of our affairs require and our situation will justify."

. . . Pursuant to his resolution, General Washington on Monday morning the 30th of December, 1776 . . . crossed the Delaware and took post at Trenton; but owing to the drifting ice, the passage of the river had become extremely difficult and fatiguing, and the rear of the troops did not join him before the next evening.

In the course of that day, Colonel Joseph Reed, with a reconnoitring party of twelve dragoons, was sent out to inquire for the enemy, of whom General Washington had no certain advice; and

. . . he surprised a commissary and foraging party . . . whom he charged and made prisoners. . . . The information received from the prisoners . . . left no doubt of the enemy's superiority and his intention to advance upon us, which . . . put General Washington in a critical situation. To make a safe retreat was impracticable, should the enemy act with energy; and if it could be effected at all it would depreciate the influence of antecedent successes and check the rising spirit of the community. On the other hand, to give battle . . . would be to hazard the annihilation of the grand army. . . .

In this awful conjuncture the resolution adopted was the most acceptable to the feelings of a soldier. . . . [H]e determined to procrastinate the combat . . . but to take post . . . behind the Assunpink . . . to wait the enemy's advance and avail himself of circumstances; that is, to fight and die if he could not conquer or extricate himself with honour.

To "procrastinate the combat," Washington sent some picked units along the road toward Princeton, where the British were assembling. The Americans had orders to do all they could to impede the columns when they began their march. In addition, Washington placed two artillery pieces on a hill overlooking the Princeton road just outside Trenton. Wilkinson resumes:

Such was the position of the two armies on the night of the 1st of January, 1777. Great exertions had been made the preceding evening to induce the Continental troops, whose term of service expired at 12 o'clock p.m. to remain with the General and stick by the cause of the country. The men were addressed by companies, regiments, brigades and divisions; and finally after all the persuasive arts were exhausted, 1,200 or 1,400 consented to engage for an additional six weeks on the receipt of ten dollars bounty. This was, of necessity, conceded by the General, whose whole force then consisted of this number of Continental troops . . . and 3,500 or [3],600 Pennsylvania volunteer militia. That of the enemy was estimated at 8,000. . . . How dreadful the odds. . . .

It rained during the night of January 1. About the middle of the next morning the attention of the Americans in the muddy lines at Trenton was arrested by the rattle of gunfire that came, under the lingering clouds, from the direction of Princeton. Throughout the day the noise grew louder as the British columns, commanded by Lord Cornwallis, drove the American harassers before them. At last

*the two artillery pieces on the hill near Trenton began booming.
The* Pennsylvania Journal *was later to report that they*

. . . were managed with great advantage and did considerable
execution for some time; after which they were ordered to retire
to the station occupied by our forces on the south side of the
bridge. . . .

*As the conflict reached the edge of town the chaplain of a Pennsyl-
vania unit who was lagging behind had the misfortune to fall into
the hands of some rancorous Hessians. According to the* Pennsylvania Evening Post:

. . . one of them struck him on the head with a sword or cutlass
and then stabbed him several times with a bayonet. . . . After he
was thus massacred he was stripped naked and . . . left lying in
an open field. . . .

"In their way through the town," states the Journal, *"the enemy
suffered much by an incessant fire of musketry from behind the
houses and barns." James Wilkinson writes:*

I had a fair . . . view of this little combat from the opposite side
of the Assunpink. . . . [T]he sun had set and the evening was so
far advanced that I could distinguish the flame from the muzzles of
our muskets.

*The weary Americans shortly gave up the fight and crowded over
the bridge to take refuge with the main body. Wilkinson goes on:*

A cannonade ensued between the two armies with little effect,
during which Lord Cornwallis displayed his columns and extended
his lines . . . on the heights above the town. If there ever was a
crisis in the affairs of the revolution, this was the moment. Thirty
minutes would have sufficed to bring the two armies into contact, and thirty more would have decided the combat; and . . .
Columbia might have wept the loss of her beloved chief and most
valorous sons.

In this awful moment the guardian angel of our country ad-
monished Lord Cornwallis that his own troops were fatigued and
that the Americans were without retreat; and . . . he addressed his
general officers, "the men had been under arms the whole day;
they were languid and required rest; he had the enemy safe enough
and could dispose of them the next morning; for these reasons he
proposed that the troops should make fires, refresh themselves and

take repose." General [James] Grant, his second, acquiesced, and others followed, but Sir William Erskine [his quartermaster general] exclaimed, "My Lord, if you trust those people tonight, you will see nothing of them in the morning!" This admonition was not regarded, and the enemy made their fires and went to supper, as we did also, our advanced sentries being posted [the creek between them] within 150 yards of each other.

Immediately after dark, General Washington called a council of war in the house he was using as his headquarters. The hearth was bright, and there was wine and tobacco, but all of the leaders were solemn. Some believed that the army should stand and fight in spite of the odds, while others favored trying to retreat down along the Delaware toward Philadelphia. Then someone (probably General Arthur St. Clair) came up with a daring suggestion. It was based on the assumption that, with a great part of the enemy's New Jersey army lying across the Assunpink, the posts to the north had only light garrisons. Why not steal quietly away in the night, circle around the enemy's rear, and make a quick strike at Princeton? Perhaps the attack could even be carried farther north to New Brunswick, a major supply base. James Wilkinson says that Washington liked the idea:

. . . and the more effectually to mask the movement, he ordered the guards [along the creek] to be doubled, a strong fatigue party to be set to work on an intrenchment . . . within distinct hearing of the sentinels of the enemy, the baggage [being temporarily dispensable] to be sent [down along the river] to Burlington, the troops to be silently filed off by detachments, and the neighbouring fences to be used for fuel [by] our guards to keep up blazing fires until toward day, when they had orders to retire. The night, although cloudless, was exceedingly dark, and though calm, most severely cold. . . . [T]he movement was so cautiously conducted as to elude the vigilance of the enemy.

At dawn, the cold-numbed British sentries were startled into animation when they looked across the frosty Assunpink and saw nothing but diminishing campfires and trailing smoke. There wasn't an American soldier in sight. The news was rushed to Lord Cornwallis, who had expected to bag Washington as a hunter bags a fox. While the British general and his staff were still trying to figure out what had happened, there came a thunder-like rumble from the north. Now realizing that he had been outgeneraled, Corn-

wallis put his army on a fast march for Princeton. He had left Colonel Charles Mawhood there with about two thousand men, but had later sent back word for him to move closer to Trenton. The colonel was supposed to be starting his march at the very time Cornwallis heard that ominous rumble.

The Americans had approached the village, noting that "an hoar frost . . . bespangled every object," on two roads not far apart. Washington with the main body was on the right, while General Hugh Mercer with about four hundred men was on the left and a little ahead. It was Mercer who ran into the first units of the enemy leaving town. James Wilkinson, who was with the main body, explains that Mercer and his men aligned themselves along a rail fence:

The first fire was delivered by General Mercer, which the enemy returned with a volley, and instantly charged; and many of our men . . . were forced after the third round to abandon the fence, and fled in disorder. . . . The time from the discharge of the first musket until I perceived our troops retreating did not exceed five minutes; and . . . the smoke from the discharge of the two lines mingled as it rose, and went up in one beautiful cloud.

General Mercer was mortally wounded at this time. On foot and trying to rally his men, he was surrounded by several of the enemy, struck down from behind by a gun butt, and repeatedly bayonetted. Meanwhile, fresh files of redcoats approached the combat area at a trot. Their leader (presumably Colonel Mawhood) was mounted, and in front of his horse ran a pair of springer spaniels who barked merrily at the sport. Wilkinson continues:

On hearing the fire, General Washington directed the Pennsylvania militia to support General Mercer, and in person led them on with two pieces of artillery. . . . The enemy [had] pursued the detachment of General Mercer as far as the brow of [a] declivity . . . when discovering our whole army instead of a partisan corps, they halted and brought up their artillery. . . .

In the cannon duel that followed, one of the first casualties was a civilian in one of the town's outlying houses. According to an eighty-five-year-old Princeton man: " . . . a womans leg was shot off at her ancle. . . . It was thought to be done by one of Genl. Washingtons field pieces." The old man adds:

The battle was plainly seen from our door . . . and the guns went off so quick and many together that they could not be numbered. We presently went down into the cellar to keep out of the way of the shot. There was a neighbour woman down in the cellar with us that was so affrighted that she imagined that the field was covered with blood. . . .

To Washington's chagrin, some of the Pennsylvanians he had led forward began to give way before a second British surge. Astride his white horse, the general made a conspicuous target as he rallied these troops and strengthened the line with others. An aide in a slightly safer spot once covered his eyes, being certain that his chief was about to fall. But, as always in situations like this, Washington remained untouched. His valor inspired his men, and smoke swirled about him as their muskets began to volley.

The outnumbered redcoats fought with extraordinary courage; but at last, subjected to a withering fire and threatened with encirclement, they broke and scattered. The Americans cheered as they swarmed in pursuit, and Washington cried joyously, "It is a fine fox chase, my boys!" In the end, the snow-patched fields were scattered with dead and wounded redcoats. A large party of the fugitives took refuge in Princeton's Nassau Hall, but were quickly dislodged. A number resumed their flight, while the rest surrendered. In all, some two hundred prisoners were taken.

The group of civilians that included the eighty-five-year-old man now came up from their cellar. Taking a look outdoors, the "affrighted" woman suffered an hallucination. What she had imagined before now seemed real. The field really was covered with blood, she cried out. In the old man's words:

This I mention only to show into what strange mistakes sudden frights with the fear of Death may put into us. Almost as soon as the firing was over, our house was filled and surrounded with Genl. Washington's men, and himself on horseback at the door. They brought in with them on their shoulders two wounded regulars. One of them was shot in at his hip and the bullet lodged in his groin, and the other was shot through his body just below his short ribs. He was in very great pain and bled much out of both sides, and often desired to be removed from one place to another, which was done accordingly. . . . The other also bled much and they put a cloth dipt in vinegar to the wound to stop it. . . . [The man hit below the ribs was dying, but the other would recover.]

. . . Though [the Americans] were both hungry and thirsty, some of them [were] laughing out right, others smileing, and not a man among them but showed joy in his countenance. It really animated my old blood with love to those men that but a few minutes before had been couragiously looking Death in the face in releiveing a part of their country from the barbarous insults and ravages of a bold and dareing enemy.

James Wilkinson continues:

We found in the town some shoes and blankets, which were very opportune; and for my own part, I made a most seasonable acquisition in a breakfast at the provost's house, which had been prepared for a mess of the 40th Regiment, who the steward informed me were sitting down as the fire commenced.

Before we got clear of the town, our rear guard . . . was exchanging shot with the enemy from Trenton, and Captain Forrest with his artillery was . . . engaged in covering our retreat. Pressed as we were for time, it was the desire of the Commander-in-Chief and the inclination of every officer to make a stroke at Brunswick, which had been left with a small garrison . . . but our physical force could not bear us out. The men had been under arms eighteen hours and had suffered much from cold and hunger.

Lord Cornwallis, whose own troops were fatigued from their forced march, showed no interest in pressing the pursuit beyond Princeton. His main concern was the vulnerable supplies at New Brunswick. Washington was soon able to rest his army, though many of the men, because the baggage had been sent to Burlington, had to lie on the cold ground without blankets. The American commander next decided to head northward toward Morristown, where he planned to establish his winter quarters. He had no intention of turning idle, however. His successes had given him confidence. There seemed now a chance—if he could assemble enough troops—for him to reconquer New Jersey. General Howe's failure to bestir his forces to countermeasures left Judge Jones astonished:

. . . [He] fixed their quarters at New Brunswick and Amboy, thus giving up and abandoning the whole province to the rebels (the two last-mentioned towns excepted). There were not less than 5,000 troops in each of these towns. . . . Both . . . lay upon the Raritan. Everything, of course, necessary for the garrison could be transported from New York by water. The troops in these towns were fairly cooped up by the rebels during the remainder of the winter. Their numbers were sufficient to have driven Washington out of Jersey. . . . But orders were wanting. Cornwallis commanded at Brunswick, Vaughan at Amboy, both generals of spirit. Nothing could be done without the directions of the Commander-in-Chief, who was diverting himself in New York in feasting, gunning, banqueting, and in the arms of Mrs. Loring.

Sir William had gained his mistress in a novel manner. During 1776 the British had accumulated thousands of American prisoners, both land troops and sailors (the latter mostly privateersmen). A commissary of prisoners had to be appointed. As Judge Jones tells it:

 . . . one Joshua Loring, a Bostonian, was commissioned to the office, with a guinea a day and rations of all kinds for himself and family. In this appointment there was reciprocity. Joshua had a handsome wife. The General . . . was fond of her. Joshua made no objections. He fingered the cash; the General enjoyed madam.

Jones adds this about the New Jersey situation:

Not a stick of wood, a spear of grass, or a kernel of corn could the [British] troops . . . procure without fighting for it, unless sent from New York. Every foraging party was attacked in some way or another.

General Washington's prestige was high during this period. Many Americans believed, according to Dr. Thacher's journal, that he "was born for the salvation of his country, and that he is endowed with all the talents and abilities necessary to qualify him for the great undertaking." The general was pleased with his standing, but his winter was hardly one of total triumph. In its earliest days, for example, several thousand New England militiamen east of the Hudson who were ordered to distract General Howe's attention from New Jersey by demonstrating down toward Manhattan failed in their purpose as the result of excessive caution.

In New Jersey, Washington's number of Continental troops dwindled alarmingly, and winter was a poor season for enlisting new men. Fortunately, New Jersey's militiamen were feeling particularly bitter toward the enemy and needed little urging to keep the field. The problems at the Morristown encampment included a smallpox epidemic.

As for provisions and equipment, they continued to be hard to procure. Though the Congressional delegates (now back in Philadelphia) applauded Washington and urged him to maintain his pres-

sure, they were unable to provide him the kind of financial support he needed. Fortunately, he knew how to make the very most of his meager resources.

In March and April, 1777, there were brushes between larger detachments of the two New Jersey armies, but the British made no determined attempt to contest Washington's domination of the area. However, the British did launch two vigorous raids northward from New York City. One was directed at a magazine, or supply depot, at Peekskill on the Hudson. The Americans, before retreating, set some fires, and with particular sadness staved in "a great number of hogsheads of rum." The British destroyed almost everything else they found.

The second place raided was Danbury, Connecticut, another supply base. In the process of the destruction a number of buildings were put to the torch, and a few citizens who resisted too strenuously were slain and thrown into the flames. General Benedict Arnold happened to be in Connecticut at this time; and he, along with Generals David Wooster and Gold Silliman, led some militia units against the retiring raiders. Wooster was fatally wounded, and Arnold had a narrow escape. As reported by the Connecticut Journal:

The general had his horse shot under him when the enemy were within about ten yards of him, but luckily received no hurt. Recovering himself, he drew his pistol and shot the soldier who was advancing with his fixed bayonet.

The British escaped across Long Island Sound. Connecticut's Joseph Plumb Martin, who was a part of this action, shortly afterward viewed the devastation at Danbury:

I saw the inhabitants, after the fire was out, endeavoring to find the burnt bones of their relatives amongst the rubbish of their demolished houses.

As the warmer weather set in, Washington's New Jersey army increased in numbers. By mid-May he had eight or nine thousand Continentals who had enlisted, under an emergency provision of Congress, for long terms: some for three years and some for the war's duration. If the army's equipment wasn't first-rate, it was passable. Arms and ammunition, at least, now were in good supply. England's old enemy, France, had seen to this, though unofficially and quietly. By the end of May, Washington felt strong enough *to move closer to the enemy. He set up his lines on some high ground at Middlebrook, only a few miles from New Brunswick. The position was a strong one.*

According to the British soldier-historian Charles Stedman, General Howe had been delaying his move against Washington because he was awaiting supplies and reinforcements:

The tents and other necessaries, together with a fresh supply of troops, being at length arrived from England, in the beginning of June [on the twelfth] the Commander-in-Chief left New York and crossed over to the Jerseys with an intention of opening the campaign immediately. The British troops were, as usual, greatly superior in point of number to the Americans. . . . Sir William Howe was thoroughly sensible of the impracticability of making an attack on General Washington in his present situation. He therefore made use of every possible effort to induce him to quit his position and to hazard an engagement. . . .

But the British maneuvering had little effect other than to place Washington in a state of uncertainty. Toward the end of June, General Howe, by suddenly retreating toward the Jersey coast, drew the Americans a few miles out of their strong position; but as the British swung about to attack, the Americans fell back to safety with only one part of the army being hit, and with moderate casualties. "Sir William Howe," writes Charles Stedman, "being now sensible that every scheme of bringing the Americans to an engagement would be unattended with success, resolved to retire from the Jerseys." On June 30 the entire British army crossed over to Staten Island.

This exodus left New Jersey altogether free of the ravaging redcoats and Hessians for the first time in more than seven months, and the citizens rejoiced. Washington's satisfaction, however, was qualified. He seemed to have saved Philadelphia and to have reconquered New Jersey, as was his aim; but he was left perplexed as to Howe's intentions. This perplexity was to be prolonged for some weeks.

18

BURGOYNE INVADES FROM CANADA

T HE SAME *period that saw the expiration of strife in New Jersey saw the birth of a major campaign in the Lake Champlain theater. In mid-June, 1777, Dr. Thacher, then stationed at Ticonderoga, explained in his journal:*

Congress have appointed Major-General [Philip] Schuyler to command in the northern department, including Albany [on the Hudson], Ticonderoga, Fort Stanwix [at the source of the Mohawk River, a little over a hundred miles northwest of Albany] and their dependencies; and Major-General [Arthur] St. Clair has the immediate command of the posts of Ticonderoga and [nearby] Mount Independence.

It is also understood that the British government have appointed Lieutenant-General Burgoyne commander-in-chief of their army in Canada, consisting, it is said, of eight or ten thousand men. According to authentic reports, the plan of the British government for the present campaign is that General Burgoyne's army shall take possession of Ticonderoga and force his way [southward] through the country to Albany. To facilitate this event, Colonel [Barry] St. Leger is to march [from Canada by a western route] with a party of British, Germans, Canadians and Indians to the Mohawk River and make a diversion in that quarter. The royal army at New York, under command of General Howe, is to pass up the Hudson River; and, calculating on success in all quarters, the three armies are to form a junction at Albany. Here, probably, the three com-

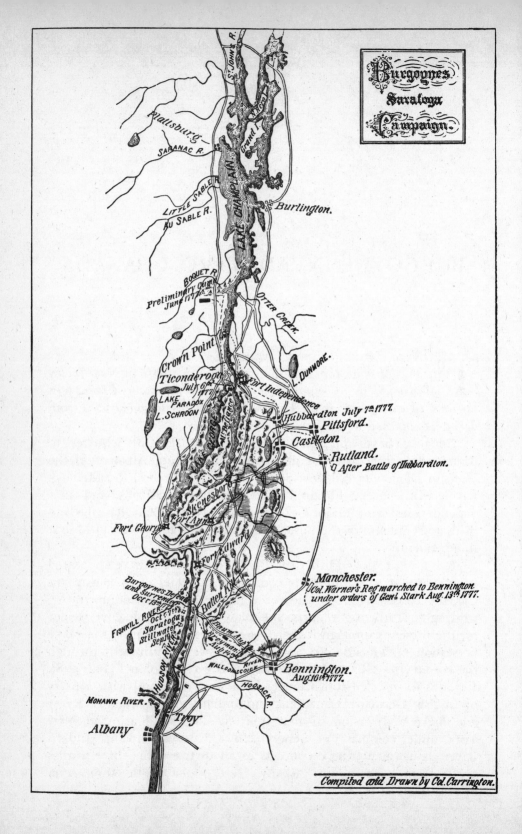

manders are to congratulate each other on their mighty achieve-
ments and the flattering prospect of crushing the rebellion. . . .
[T]he communication between the southern and eastern states
will be interrupted, and New England, as they suppose, may become an easy prey.

*This is the way the plan had been conceived in England, and the
way the Americans believed it would be pursued. But Sir William
Howe's part was not so clearly defined. He was indeed expected to ascend the Hudson, but had no explicit orders to do so.
He had wide discretionary powers as commander in chief, since he
was on the spot and was presumed by the planners in England to have a better knowledge of the situation than they. Dr.
Thacher goes on:*

Judging from the foregoing detail, a very active campaign is to
be expected, and events of the greatest magnitude are undoubtedly
to be unfolded. The utmost exertions are now making to strengthen
our works at Ticonderoga. . . . Mount Independence, directly
opposite to Ticonderoga [on the lake's Vermont shore] is strongly
fortified and well supplied with artillery. . . . The communication
between these two places is maintained by a floating bridge. . . .

*General Burgoyne's invasion fleet came southward on Lake Cham-
plain in latter June. The vessels were of various sizes and types, with
the bulk of the fighting men occupying batteaux. According to British Lieutenant Thomas Anburey, whose published journal, though
replete with plagarisms from contemporaries, provides a valuable
record of the Burgoyne campaign:*

When we were in the widest part of the lake . . . the whole
army appeared at one view in . . . perfect regularity. . . . In the
front the Indians went with their birch canoes, containing twenty
or thirty in each; then the advanced corps in a regular line, with
the gunboats; then followed the *Royal George* and *Inflexible* . . .
with the other brigs and sloops following; after them the first
brigade in a regular line; then the Generals Burgoyne, [William]
Phillips and [Friedrich Adolph von] Riedesel in their pinnaces;
next to them were the second brigade, followed by the German
brigades; and the rear was brought up with the sutlers and followers
of the army.

Among the British enlisted men was Sergeant Roger Lamb, who

writes that the entire expedition was assembled at Crown Point,
about twelve miles north of Ticonderoga, by June 30:

In the evening the following orders were given: "The army
embarks tomorrow to approach the enemy. The services required
on this expedition are critical and conspicuous. During our progress
occasions may occur in which, nor difficulty, nor labour, nor life
are to be regarded. This army must not retreat."

Returning to Dr. Thacher's journal:

July 1st: We are now assailed by a proclamation of a very extraordinary nature from General Burgoyne, enumerating a
string of titles which he has doubtless received from his royal
master as a reward for his merit. From the pompous manner in
which he has arrayed his titles we are led to suppose that he con-
siders them as more than a match for all the military force which
we can bring against him. . . . This sanguinary proclamation is to
be viewed as the forerunner of his formidable army, and all the
opposers of his authority are menaced with his avenging power.

"I have," says the proclamation, "but to give stretch to the Indian forces under my direction . . . to overtake the hardened enemies
of Great Britain and America. I consider them the same wherever
they may lurk." The British ministry, not satisfied with the disgraceful expedient of hiring foreign mercenaries, resort also to the
savages of the wilderness for aid in the glorious cause of tyranny
and of spreading the horrors of war by fire and sword throughout
our country.

The militia of New England are daily coming in to increase our
strength. . . . One fact, however, is notorious—that when the troops
are directed to man the lines there is not a sufficient number to
occupy their whole extent. . . .

July 2d: The British army is now approaching. Some of their
savage allies have been seen in the vicinity of our outworks. . . . On
the 3d and 4th, the enemy are making their approaches and
gaining, as is supposed, some advantages. They have taken possession of Mount Hope [which held an outwork], our batteries
are now opened, and a cannonading has commenced. General St.
Clair endeavors to animate the troops. . . . 5th: It is with astonishment that we find the enemy have taken possession of an eminence
called Sugarloaf Hill or Mount Defiance, which, from its height
and proximity completely overlooks and commands all our works
at Ticonderoga and Mount Independence. This mount, it is said,
ought long since to have been fortified by our army; but its

General John Burgoyne.

extreme difficulty of access and the want of a sufficient number of men are the reasons assigned for its being neglected.

The mount had scarcely been occupied before a few cannon shot came hurtling down. General St. Clair, in the company of James Wilkinson (now holding the rank of colonel and serving as deputy adjutant general to the northern army), made anxious use of his spyglass. Wilkinson relates:

After reconnoitring [the enemy's] position attentively, the General turned to me . . . and observed, "We must away from this, for our situation has become a desperate one." A council of war . . . unanimously decided on an immediate evacuation [southward], which was effected during the night as well as the hurried preparation would permit, with troops the best of whom were but half formed. . . . Our baggage, sick and convalescents, our ordnance, hospital and other stores, with a quantity of provisions, were despatched by the lake for Skenesborough [now Whitehall] . . . and the main body of the troops [under St. Clair] retired by an unfinished road through the wilderness [of Vermont] . . . to Hubbardton. . . .

Dr. Thacher was with the party that fled by way of the lake. He writes that the fleet consisted of five armed galleys and two hundred batteaux, all heavily laden. His description of the fleet's cargo agrees with Wilkinson's, but he adds that the army's women were also on board:

The night was moonlight and pleasant. The sun burst forth in the morning with uncommon lustre. . . . The shore on each side exhibited a variegated view of huge rocks, caverns and clefts, and the whole was bounded by a thick impenetrable wilderness. . . . The occasion was peculiarly interesting, and we could but look back with regret, and forward with apprehension. We availed ourselves, however, of the means of enlivening our spirits. The drum and fife afforded us a favorite music. Among the hospital stores we found many dozen bottles of choice wine; and, breaking off their necks, we cheered our hearts with the nectareous contents.

At three o'clock in the afternoon we reached our destined port at Skenesborough. . . . Here we were unsuspicious of danger. But, behold! Burgoyne himself was at our heels. In less than two hours [after landing] we were struck with surprise and consternation by a discharge of cannon from the enemy's fleet on our gallies and batteaux lying at the wharf. . . . It was not long before it was perceived that a number of their troops and savages had landed and were rapidly advancing towards our little party. . . . We took the route [southward] to Fort Anne through a narrow defile in the woods and were so closely pressed by the pursuing enemy that we frequently heard calls from the rear to "march on; the Indians are at our heels." Having marched all night [and the enemy having dropped behind], we reached Fort Anne at five o'clock in the morning, where we found provisions for our refreshment.

A small rivulet called Wood Creek is navigable for boats from Skenesborough to Fort Anne, by which means some of our invalids and baggage made their escape; but all our cannon, provisions, and the bulk of our baggage, with several invalids, fell into the enemy's hands.

On the 7th instant we received a small reinforcement from Fort Edward [about a dozen miles to the south, on the Hudson] . . . and on discovering that a detachment of the enemy . . . had arrived in our vicinity, a party from our fort was ordered to attack them. . . . The two parties were soon engaged in a smart skirmish, which continued for several hours. . . . The enemy, being almost surrounded, were on the point of surrendering when, our ammunition being expended and a party of Indians arriving and setting up the war-whoop, this being followed by three cheers from their [nearly beaten] friends the English, the Americans were induced to give way and retreat. . . .

England's Roger Lamb was in the thick of this skirmish. Two men were killed near him. One was shot through the heart, and the other received a ball in the forehead that tore off the roof of his skull: "He reeled round, turned up his eyes, muttered some words, and fell dead at my feet." Lamb says that the British had three officers and nineteen men killed or wounded:

It was a distressing sight to see the wounded men bleeding on the ground, and what made it more so, the rain came pouring down like a deluge upon us. . . . The poor fellows earnestly entreated me to tie up their wounds. Immediately I took off my shirt, tore it up, and with the help of a soldier's wife (the only woman that was with us, and who kept close by her husband's side during the engagement) made some bandages, stopped the bleeding of their wounds and conveyed them in blankets to a small hut about two miles in our rear.

"Fort Anne," writes Dr. Thacher, "being a small picket fort of no importance, orders were given to set it on fire, and on the 8th we departed [unpursued] for Fort Edward. . . ."

As for the Americans under General St. Clair, who had hurried southeastward from Ticonderoga along the moonlit Hubbardton road: They were almost immediately followed by an enemy force under General Simon Fraser and the Baron von Riedesel. Among the pursuers was Lieutenant Thomas Anburey:

We marched [from four in the morning] till one o'clock, in a very hot and sultry day, over a continued succession of steep and woody hills. . . . On our march we picked up several stragglers, from whom General Fraser learnt that the rear guard of the enemy was composed of chosen men commanded by a Colonel Francis, who was reckoned one of their best officers. During the time [our] advanced corps halted to refresh, General Riedesel came up, and after consulting with General Fraser and making arrangements for continuing the pursuit, we marched forward again three miles nearer the enemy . . . where we lay that night on our arms.

At three in the morning our march was renewed, and about five we came up with the enemy, who were busily employed in cooking their provisions. Major Grant, of [our] 24th Regiment, who had the advanced guard, attacked their picquets, which were soon driven in to the main body [of their rear guard]. From this attack we lament the death of this very gallant and brave officer. . . . Upon his coming up with the enemy, he got upon the stump of a tree to reconnoitre, and had hardly given the men orders to fire when he was struck by a rifle ball, fell off the tree, and never uttered another syllable.

The light infantry then formed, as well as the 24th Regiment, the former of which suffered very much from the enemy's fire. . . . The grenadiers were ordered to form to prevent the enemy's getting to the road that leads to Castleton [six miles to the south] . . . and were repulsed, upon which they . . . scrambled up an ascent which appeared almost inaccessible. . . . Although the grenadiers . . . gained the summit of this mountain, and the Americans . . . lost great numbers of their men [including] their brave commander Col. Francis . . . the contest remained doubtful till the arrival of the Germans, when the Americans fled on all sides. . . .

This action cost the Americans between three and four hundred men killed, wounded, and captured, while the British lost about two hundred. Only the American rear guard was involved. General St. Clair now began a maneuver that was to take his army out of the enemy's reach. He marched eastward through Vermont for a few miles and then made a long southwesterly loop toward Fort Edward on the Hudson.

The party that included Dr. Thacher, having made a direct march from the burning Fort Anne, reached Fort Edward first. Soon Thacher was writing:

On the 12th, General St. Clair arrived here with the remains of his army, greatly distressed and worn down by fatigue. General Schuyler [the northern department's top commander] is . . . at this post. He has a small army of Continentals and militia and is [sending parties out and is] making every possible exertion, by taking up bridges, throwing obstructions in the roads and passes, by fallen trees, etc., to impede the march of Burgoyne's army . . . [now reorganizing at Skenesborough].

The abandonment of Ticonderoga and Mount Independence has occasioned the greatest surprise and alarm. No event could be more unexpected, nor more severely felt throughout our army and country. This disaster has given to our cause a dark and gloomy aspect. . . . The conduct of General St. Clair . . . has rendered him very unpopular. . . . General Schuyler is not altogether free from public reprehension, alleging that he ought, in duty, to have been present at Ticonderoga during the critical period.

It is predicted by some of our well-informed and respectable characters that this event, apparently so calamitous, will ultimately prove advantageous by drawing the British army into the heart of our country and thereby place them more immediately within our power.

19

THE CAMPAIGN FALTERS

THOUGH *the distance between Skenesborough and Fort Edward was only about twenty-five miles, General Burgoyne's army spent many days getting there. Lieutenant Thomas Anburey explains:*

The country . . . was a continuation of woods and creeks, interspersed with deep morasses; and to add to these natural impediments the enemy had very industriously augmented them by felling immense trees, and various other modes, that it was with the utmost pains and fatigue we could work our way through them. Exclusive of these, the watery grounds and marshes were so numerous that we were under the necessity of constructing no less than forty bridges to pass them, and over one morass there was a bridge of near two miles in length.

As the British made their approach to Fort Edward late in July, 1777, Philip Schuyler withdrew his forces southward along the Hudson toward the west-bank town of Saratoga (now Schuylerville, about ten miles from present-day Saratoga Springs). Just before the British arrived at the fort, their Indian allies committed an atrocity that was to attract widespread attention. The victim was a young woman named Jane McCrea, who lived in one of the houses in the fort's environs. Dr. Thacher writes:

The father of Miss McCrea was friendly towards the royalists, and the young lady was engaged to marry a refugee officer [an

American] in Burgoyne's army by the name of Jones. . . . When our army retreated from Fort Edward, Miss McCrea had the indiscretion to remain behind, probably with the expectation of meeting her lover. The Indians, however, soon made her their prisoner; and on their return towards Burgoyne's camp a quarrel arose to decide who should hold possession of the fair prize. During the controversy one of the monsters struck his tomahawk into her skull and immediately stripped off her scalp.

In spite of Jane McCrea's royalist sympathies, her murder angered not only the troops with Schuyler but Patriot residents of all parts of New York and New England. Many able-bodied men who had been hesitating at home now took up their muskets and tramped through the wilderness to join Schuyler's army. When the news of this turnout reached Washington down in New Jersey, he found it heartening, since the need for additional troops in the north was weakening his own army.

General Burgoyne was obliged to linger at Fort Edward to await the arrival of some delayed artillery pieces, ammunition, and provisions. But British activity continued elsewhere. Colonel Barry St. Leger, having reached New York from Canada by way of the St. Lawrence River and Lake Ontario, was now marching eastward toward New York's Mohawk Valley. He had a force of more than fifteen hundred men, about two thirds of them Indians. In James Wilkinson's words:

Colonel St. Leger invested Fort Schuyler [also called Fort Stanwix] . . . at the head of the Mohawk River and 110 miles from Albany on the 3d of August. The intelligence of his approach . . . had roused the militia of the upper settlements of that river; and General [Nicholas] Herkimer marched the same day with about 800 men to succour the garrison. . . . This body of citizens . . . was led on without the ordinary precautions of front or flank guards, and in the morning of the 6th, about five miles from the fort, fell into an ambuscade of Indians and royalists under the direction of Sir John Johnson, who had been detached by St. Leger to meet them. A fierce and obstinate action ensued, in which the militia, although surprised and fighting under manifest disadvantages, maintained their ground with great resolution. Herkimer was mortally wounded in the onset, yet refused to be carried off the field, and continued to animate his men, who . . . when the enemy ceased their fire and drew off . . . retreated with such deliberation as to carry off their wounded.

Many of the New Yorkers had been killed, however, while others were soon to die. The number of fatal wounds inflicted by the enemy's guns, tomahawks, and knives exceeded 150, a circumstance that would "spread sorrow over an extensive American settlement." But the ambushers did not depart unhurt. The Indians, in fact, found their losses disheartening. Wilkinson says that "thirty . . . were killed, and the same number wounded, among whom there were several of their favourite chiefs and . . . warriors."

About the time this action was ending, another began closer to the fort. Colonel Peter Gansevoort, the fort's commander, had hoped to provide some diversionary assistance for Herkimer by sending out 250 men under Colonel Marinus Willett to make a hit-and-run attack on St. Leger's siege lines. Colonel Willett was too late to divert any attention from Herkimer, but, with the siege lines only thinly manned in the absence of the ambushers, the attack was effective. Colonel Willett relates:

Nothing could be more fortunate than this enterprise. We totally routed two of the enemy's encampments, destroyed all the provisions that were in them, brought off upwards of 50 brass kettles and more than 100 blankets (two articles which were much needed), with a quantity of muskets, tomahawks, spears, ammunition, clothing, deerskins, a variety of Indian affairs, and five [flags]. . . .

The Indians took chiefly to the woods, the rest of the troops then at their posts to the river. The number of men lost by the enemy is uncertain. Six lay dead in their encampments, two of which were Indians; several [lay] scattered about in the woods; but their greatest loss appeared to be in crossing the river, and an inconsiderable number on the opposite shore. I was happy in preventing [my] men from scalping even the Indians. . . .

We were out so long that a number of British regulars, accompanied by what Indians, etc., could be rallied, had marched down to a thicket on the other side of the river, about 50 yards from the road we were to pass on our return. Near this place I had ordered [a] field-piece. The ambush was not quite formed when we discovered them and gave them a well-directed fire. . . . Here also the enemy were annoyed by the fire of several cannon from the fort, as they marched round to form the ambuscade. The enemy's fire was

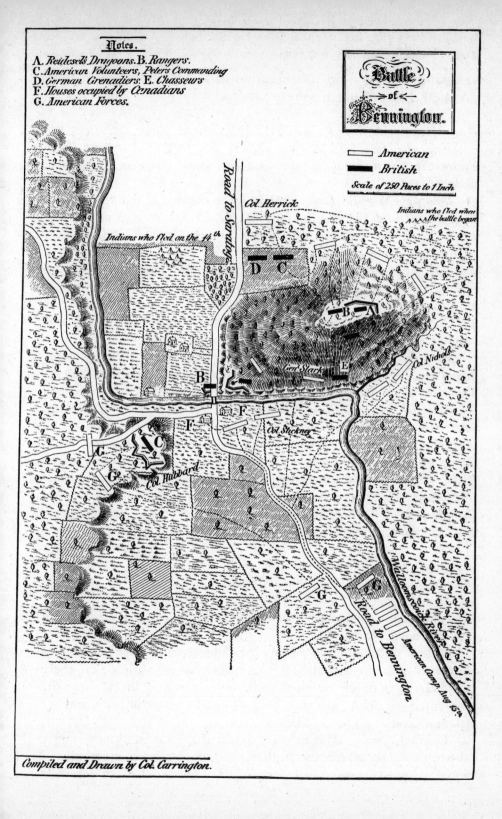

Notes.
A. *Reidesel's Dragoons.* B. *Rangers.*
C. *American Volunteers, Peters Commanding*
D. *German Grenadiers.* E. *Chasseurs*
F. *Houses occupied by Grenadians*
G. *American Forces.*

Battle
← of →
Bennington.

☐ *American*
■ *British*
Scale of 250 Paces to 1 Inch.

Indians who fled when the battle began.

Col. Herrick

Road to Saratoga

Indians who fled on the 14th

D C

B A

Gen Stark E *Col Nichols*

B

F *Col Stickney*

F

G C

G *Col Hubbard*

G *Walloomsac River*

American Camp Aug 15th

Road to Bennington

Compiled and Drawn by Col. Carrington.

very wild and . . . did no execution at all. We brought in four prisoners, three of which were wounded.

One of the first things that Willett's jubilant party did upon re-entering the fort was to run up the five captured enemy flags under the Continental banner; and the whole garrison gave three cheers.

Two days later St. Leger sent word to the fort that unless it was quickly surrendered the Indians in the British service would advance upon the civilian inhabitants of the Mohawk Valley. The threat was disregarded and the refusal to surrender was defiantly worded; but the garrison's numbers were only half those of the enemy; consequently that night Colonel Willett and a companion slipped out of the fort, maneuvered their way through the shadows past the British sentinels and the Indians and their dogs, and hurried eastward through the forest to seek reinforcements.

By this time General Schuyler had retreated through Saratoga (the site of his own estate) and had continued southward along the west bank of the Hudson another dozen miles to Stillwater. The British were beginning to extend their lines down along the east bank opposite Saratoga. Burgoyne had been informed of St. Leger's investment of Fort Stanwix and was aware that the main army ought to cooperate with the colonel by making a vigorous push in its own area. But Burgoyne was still having supply problems. He needed such things as horses, ox teams, wagons, and food stores. Knowing that Bennington, Vermont, about twenty-five miles southeast of Saratoga, was a major American supply station, he determined to send a party to raid it. Picked for the task were some six hundred men, a large part of them Hessians, led by Colonel Friedrich Baum. A New Hampshire brigade under John Stark, now a brigadier general, was in Bennington at this time. Stark writes that at first he received word that only a party of Indians was heading for the town:

I sent Colonel Greg of my brigade to stop them with two hundred men. In the night I was informed by express that there was a large body of the enemy on their march in the rear of the Indians. I rallied all my brigade and what militia was at [Bennington]. . . . I likewise sent to Manchester [Vermont] to Colonel [Seth] Warner's regiment that was stationed there; also sent expresses for the militia to come in [from other places] with all speed to our assistance. . . . I then marched in company with . . . all the men that were present. About five miles from [Bennington] I met Colonel Greg on his retreat and the enemy in close pursuit after him.

I drew up my little army in order of battle. But when the enemy hove in sight they halted [and began entrenching] on a very advantageous hill. . . . I sent out small parties in their front to skirmish with them, which scheme had a good effect . . . but the ground that I was upon did not suit for a general action. I marched back about one mile and encamped, called a council, and it was agreed that we should send two detachments in their rear, while the other attacked them in front. But the 15th [of August] it rained all day; therefore . . . could do nothing but skirmish with them. On the 16th, in the morning, was joined by . . . some militia from Berkshire County [Massachusetts]. I pursued my plan . . . and about three o'clock we got all ready for the attack.

At this time, it is reputed, General Stark pointed his sword at the enemy's breastworks and said, "There, my lads, are the Hessians! Tonight our flag floats over yonder hill, or Molly Stark is a widow!" Three cheers were raised as the men moved out. They had a considerable numerical advantage, and the terrain provided them good cover, including trees and brush, as they approached the enemy from several directions. Shortly the position was about two-thirds surrounded, and the action began. Says General Stark: "It lasted two hours, the hottest I ever saw in my life. It represented one continued clap of thunder." An anonymous American participant writes that the attack was made "with irresistible impetuosity" and that the enemy finally "deserted their covers and ran." According to a Tory participant:

I saw all my companions were going over the wall on the other side, and I went too. We had open fields before us and scattered in all directions, some followed by our enemies. I ran some distance with another man, and looking around saw several . . . soldiers who were coming after us level their muskets to fire. We had just reached a rail fence, and both of us gave a jump at the same instant to go over it. While I was in the air, I heard the guns go off. We reached the ground together, but my companion fell and lay dead by the fence, while I ran on with all my might. . . .

The anonymous American exults:

. . . in about five minutes their whole camp was in the utmost confusion and disorder. All their battalions were broken in pieces and fled most precipitately; at which instant our whole army pressed after with redoubled ardor, pursued them for a mile, made considerable slaughter amongst them and took many prisoners. . . . At this time our men stopped the pursuit to gain breath. . . .

General Stark takes up:

I then gave orders to rally again in order to secure the victory, but in a few minutes was informed that there was a large reinforcement [sent by General Burgoyne] on their march within two miles. Lucky for us, that moment Colonel Warner's regiment came up fresh, who marched on and began the attack afresh. I pushed forward as many of the men as I could to their assistance. The battle continued obstinate on both sides till sunset. The enemy was obliged to retreat. We pursued them till dark. . . . [H]ad day lasted an hour longer we should have taken the whole body of them. We [took] . . . about 700 prisoners, 207 dead on the spot. . . . That part of the enemy that made their escape marched all night, and we returned to our camp. . . . Our loss was inconsiderable: about forty wounded and thirty killed.

This victory was an important one, the British having been divested of about a tenth of their total forces. Though in a report to England on August 20 Burgoyne claimed that "the consequences of this affair . . . have little effect upon the strength or spirits of the army," he admitted that the prospects of the campaign as a whole were "far less prosperous" than they were in the beginning:

In spite of St. Leger's victory [over Herkimer], Fort Stanwix holds out obstinately. . . . On this side I find daily reason to doubt the sincerity of the resolution of the professing loyalists. . . . The great bulk of the country is undoubtedly with the Congress in principle and zeal. . . . Wherever the King's forces point, militia . . . assemble in twenty-four hours . . . and, the alarm over, they return to their farms. . . .

Another most embarrassing circumstance is the want of communication with Sir William Howe. Of the messengers I have sent, I know of two being hanged and am ignorant whether any of the rest arrived. The same fate has probably attended those dispatched by Sir William Howe; for only one letter is come to hand, informing me that his attention is for Pennsylvania. . . .

General Howe, who believed that Burgoyne's forces were self-sufficient (even as Burgoyne himself had believed before he left Canada), was convinced that his own first concern ought to be the capture of Philadelphia, the rebellion's capital. A move from New York City in that direction, he felt, would aid Burgoyne's advance by drawing Washington's attention from the north. With preparations made to approach Philadelphia by sea, Howe had sailed from Sandy Hook with a large part of his New York forces on July 23.

General Burgoyne goes on to explain that Howe's letter also informed him:

That, after my arrival at Albany, the movements of the enemy must guide mine; but that he wished the enemy might be driven out of the province [of New York] before any operation took place against . . . Connecticut; that Sir Henry Clinton remained in the command in the neighbourhood of New York [City] and would act as occurrences might direct. No operation . . . has yet been undertaken in my favour. The Highlands [of the Hudson] have not even been threatened. . . .

Had I a latitude in my orders, I should think it my duty to wait in this position, or perhaps as far back as Fort Edward . . . till some event happened to assist my movement forward; but my orders being positive to "force a junction with Sir William Howe," I apprehend I am not at liberty to remain inactive longer than shall be necessary to collect twenty-five days provision, and to receive the reinforcement of the additional companies . . . now . . . on Lake Champlain. . . .

When I wrote more confidently, I little foresaw that I was to be left to pursue my way through such a tract of country, and hosts of foes, without any co-operation from New York; nor did I then think the garrison[ing] of Ticonderoga would fall to my share alone [when there were extra troops in Canada under Sir Guy Carleton]. . . .

I yet do not despond. Should I succeed in forcing my way to Albany, and find that country in a state to subsist my army, I shall think no more of a retreat, but, at the worst, fortify there and await Sir W. Howe's operations.

Even while Burgoyne was writing this letter, something was happening that would further complicate his problems. Help from the main American army was on the way to Fort Stanwix. The force was only a small one—but its leader was the remarkably talented General Benedict Arnold. To improve his chances against St. Leger, Arnold decided to employ a ruse. Obtaining custody of a Tory named Hon Yost Schuyler who had been sentenced to death for activities against the New York Patriots, he promised the man his life and the freedom to return home if he went on ahead of the American detachment and saw to it that certain false information reached St. Leger's Indians (who comprised the bulk of his force). Hon Yost, who was considered to be a half-wit but had his own brand of shrewdness and could speak the Indian language, was only too glad to make the bargain.

The first information that St. Leger's scouts brought in was the truth—that only about a thousand Americans were approaching. But even this news, St. Leger writes, was enough to cause trouble:

The same zeal no longer animated the Indians. They complained of our thinness of troops and their former losses. I immediately called a council of the chiefs, encouraged them as much as I could, promised to lead them on myself [when the Americans arrived] and bring into the field 300 of the best troops. They listened to this and promised to follow me, and agreed that I should reconnoitre the ground properest for the field of battle the next morning, accompanied by some of their chief warriors, to settle the plan of operations.

When upon the ground appointed for the field of battle, scouts came in with the account of the first number swelled to 2,000. Immediately after, a third [account claimed] that General Burgoyne's army was cut to pieces, and that Arnold was advancing by rapid and forced marches with 3,000 men. . . . A council, according to their custom, was called . . . before the breaking up of which I learned that 200 were already decamped. In about an hour they insisted that I should retreat, or they would be obliged to abandon me. I had no other [course] to take. . . .

When General Arnold reached Fort Stanwix on August 24, the besiegers were gone. They were fleeing in a disorderly manner, cursing the Americans and quarreling among themselves, along the same wilderness route by which they had come. "And thus," Dr. Thacher was soon rejoicing in his journal, "have we clipped the right wing of General Burgoyne." Arnold returned to the main army, which hadn't stopped retreating at Stillwater but was now encamped at the junction of the Mohawk and the Hudson. There was a new commander: Congress had replaced Philip Schuyler with

Portrait of General Horatio Gates published in England in
1778. (*Library of Congress*)

General Horatio Gates. Arriving at a time when the army's pros-
pects looked very promising, Gates soon decided to move forward.
According to his deputy adjutant general, Colonel James Wilkinson:

The American army, about six thousand strong, began to retrace its steps towards the enemy on the 8th of September and
reached Stillwater the next day. The march was made in good order,
and the character of the corps seemed renovated—courage and confidence having taken place of timidity and distrust. . . . [T]he
following order was issued on the 10th—"Whether it may be immediately necessary to engage the enemy on this ground, or push
them into Canada, the General has the firmest opinion that both
officers and soldiers will be ready, at a moment's notice, to execute
his commands."

The struggle between Gates and Burgoyne was soon to begin.
But first there would be another meeting of the armies under
Washington and Howe.

20

THE BATTLE OF BRANDYWINE

D
URING *the last week in July, 1777, while Sir William Howe's
troops, having just left New York, jostled one another aboard
Admiral Richard Howe's ships, and while Washington wondered
anxiously about the fleet's destination, a nineteen-year-old French
nobleman completed a long and arduous trip, by sea and land,
from France to America's capital city. He was the rich and per-
sonable Marie Joseph Paul Yves Roch Gilbert du Motier, the
Marquis de Lafayette, who had interrupted a life of luxury and had
parted from a lovely young wife to aid the American cause. The
youth had been a captain of dragoons in France and was seeking
military glory, as he readily admitted, but he also believed
very sincerely that "the welfare of America is closely bound up
with the welfare of mankind." Speaking of himself in the third person, Lafayette tells of his journey and his reception:*

After having encountered for seven weeks various perils and
chances [at sea], he arrived at Georgetown, in [South] Carolina.
Ascending the river in a canoe, his foot touched at length the
American soil; and he swore that he would conquer or perish in
that cause. . . . To repair to the Congress of the United States,
M. de Lafayette rode nearly 900 miles on horseback. . . . After a
fatiguing journey of one month he beheld at length . . . Philadelphia. . . .

. . . the moment . . . was peculiarly unfavorable to strangers. The
Americans were displeased with the pretensions and disgusted with
the conduct of many Frenchmen. . . . The coldness with which M.

de Lafayette was received might have been taken as a dismissal; but without appearing disconcerted by the manner in which the deputies addressed him, he entreated them to return to Congress and read the following note: "After the sacrifices I have made, I have the right to exact two favors. One is to serve at my own expense; the other is to serve at first as a volunteer." The style . . . awakened their attention . . . and . . . the rank of major-general was granted to M. de Lafayette. . . .

The two Howes having appeared before the capes of the Delaware, General Washington came to Philadelphia; and M. de Lafayette beheld for the first time that great man. . . . M. de Lafayette accompanied him in his examination of the fortifications [on the Delaware]. . . . With . . . perfect ease and simplicity was formed the tie that united two friends whose confidence and attachments were to be cemented by the strongest interests of humanity.

The American army, stationed some miles from Philadelphia, was waiting until the movements of the hostile army should be decided. . . . About 11,000 men, ill armed and still worse clothed, presented a strange spectacle to the eye of the young Frenchman. Their clothes were parti-colored, and many of them were almost naked. The best clad wore hunting shirts. . . .

After having menaced the Delaware, the English fleet again disappeared, and during some days the Americans amused themselves by making jokes at its expense. These jokes, however, ceased when it reappeared in the Chesapeake; and in order to approach it more closely . . . the patriot army crossed through [Philadelphia on August 24]. Their heads covered with green branches [i.e., twigs stuck in their hats, to give them a semblance of uniformity] and marching to the sound of drums and fifes, these soldiers, in spite of their state of nudity, offered an agreeable spectacle to the eyes of all the citizens. General Washington was marching at their head, and M. de Lafayette was by his side.

The army stationed itself upon the heights of Wilmington [Delaware], and . . . the enemy landed in the Elk River [in Maryland]. . . . During that time Howe was only thinking of Philadelphia, and it was at the expense of the northern expedition [under Burgoyne] that he was repairing thither by an enormous circuit.

According to Benjamin Tallmadge, of the American army:
As the enemy advanced, Gen. Washington took his station [at Chadds Ford, Pennsylvania] on the . . . north[east] side of the

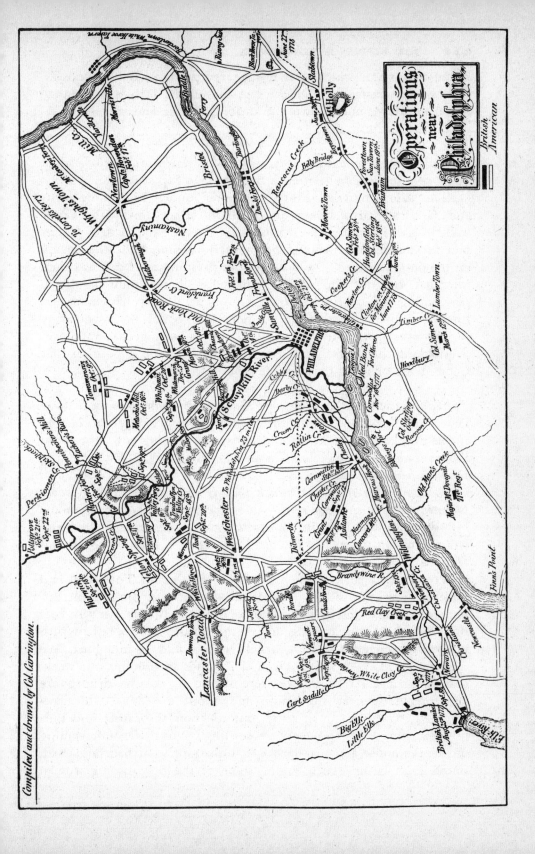

Operations near Philadelphia

British
American

Compiled and drawn by Col. Carrington.

Brandywine, near which river it appeared probable that the hostile armies must engage. . . . On the morning of the 11th of September . . . Gen. Howe put his army in order of battle and moved on towards the Brandywine.

One of Howe's officers was young John André (later to play a tragic role in Benedict Arnold's treason). He explains:

The army marched in two columns under Lord Cornwallis and General Knyphausen. Sir William Howe was with [Cornwallis]. . . . The design . . . was that General Knyphausen, taking post at Chadds Ford, should begin early to cannonade the enemy on the opposite side . . . and make him presume an attack was then intended with the whole army, whilst the other column should be performing [an upriver] detour. . . . General Knyphausen posted himself early in the day on the heights opposite the rebel army [which] was distributed on all the most advantageous eminences overlooking the ford. . . . It was not without some opposition that General Knyphausen took up his ground. . . .

This opposition was provided by General William Maxwell. "Unfortunately," says Washington, "the intelligence received of the enemy's advancing up the Brandywine and crossing at a ford about six miles above us was uncertain and contradictory, notwithstanding all my pains to get the best." Thus the American army was not prepared for the flank attack that Howe and Cornwallis were planning. A British move upriver, however, was anticipated by many of the people who lived in the country above the exposed American wing. One of these was Joseph Townsend, a twenty-one-year-old Quaker:

Possessed of curiosity . . . my brother William Townsend and myself, with some others, rode alongside of the Brandywine for some distance to discover the approach of the British army in case they should attempt to cross any of the fords. . . . We fell in with many like ourselves, but no intelligence could be obtained. We then returned . . . to assemble with Friends in holding our weekday meeting. . . . While we were sitting . . . some disturbance was discovered near the house and about the door, which occasioned some individuals to go out to know the cause; and they not returning . . . the meeting accordingly closed. On our coming out of the house and making some inquiry of what had happened, found it to be an alarm among some of the neighboring women

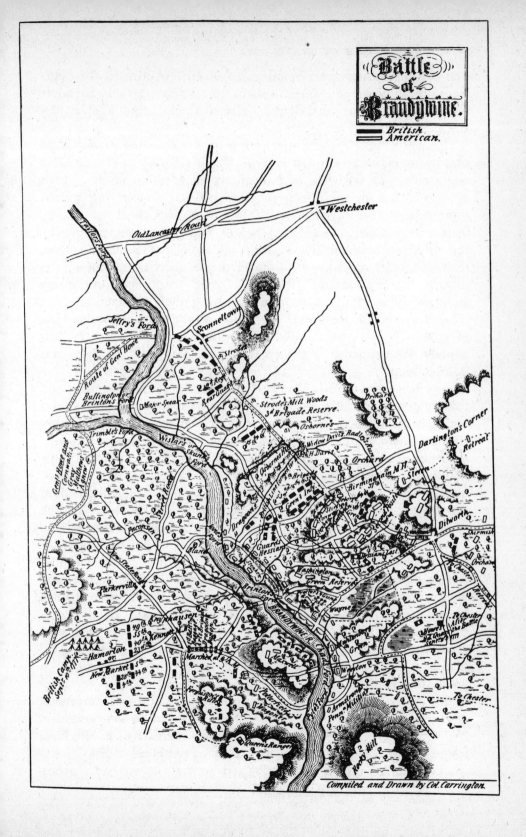

that the English army was coming. . . . In a few minutes the fields were literally covered over with them. . . . Their arms and bayonets being raised, shone as bright as silver, there being a clear sky and the day exceedingly warm.

Recollecting that there was no one at our dwelling except some of our sisters, we concluded it advisable to return home. . . . After our arrival . . . we were in momentary expectation of the army's approach; but in this we were disappointed; and having waited some time, we ventured down the roads towards them. . . . Being disposed to have a better and nearer view . . . and passing by the dwelling of Abel Boake, we soon after met Sarah, his wife, who had been as curious as ourselves and had been among the soldiers as they marched along. . . . She encouraged our going amongst them, at the same time admiring their appearance. . . . Thus encouraged, we walked on until we approached the flanking party, when a soldier under arms called out, "Where are you going?" We replied "we wished to see the army, etc., if there was no objection."

. . . leave was readily obtained, and in a few minutes we found ourselves in the midst of . . . a continued march of soldiers, and occasionally a troop of horse passing. Great numbers of baggage wagons began to make their appearance. . . . We passed through them until we reached [and entered] one of the most eligible houses in [Sconneltown]; and soon after, divers of the principal officers came in, who manifested an uncommon social disposition. They were full of their inquiries respecting the rebels. . . . The officers . . . were replied to by brother William Townsend, who modestly and spiritedly told them that if they would have patience a short time, he expected they would meet with General Washington and his forces, who were not far distant. . . . They inquired what sort of a man Mr. Washington was. My brother had a knowledge of him . . . and replied that he was a stately, well-proportioned, fine-looking man of great ability, active, firm and resolute, of a social disposition, and was considered to be a good man . . . to which one of them answered "that he might be a good man, but he was most damnably misled to take up arms against his sovereign." During the interview, while I was conversing with one of the officers . . . he . . . observed to me in some rapture, "You have got a hell of a fine country here, which we have found to be the case ever since we landed at the Head of Elk."

The house we were in was elevated, so that . . . we had a pretty full view of the army as they progressed along; and while we were conversing together, my brother called on me to step to the door to see General Lord Cornwallis, who was passing by. He was on horseback, appeared tall, and sat very erect. His rich scarlet clothing, loaded with gold lace, epaulets, etc., occasioned him to make a brilliant and martial appearance.

The advanced part of the army made a halt at this place and refreshed their horses by hastily cleaning off some of the corn patches. . . . It may be observed that most or all of the officers who conversed with us were of first rank, and were rather short, portly men, were well dressed and of genteel appearance, and did not look as if they had ever been exposed to any hardship, their skins being . . . white and delicate. . . .

Having by this time become familiar with them . . . my curiosity . . . was increased. . . . I invited James Johnson, an acquaintance . . . to accompany me, and we proceeded through the crowd on the public road until we reached the advanced guard, who were of the German troops. Many of them wore their beards on their upper lips. . . . On turning our faces back, we had a grand view of the [main] army as they advanced over and down the south side of Osborne's Hill and the lands of James Carter. . . . While we were amusing ourselves . . . to our great astonishment and surprise the firing of . . . musketry took place. The advanced guard . . . were fired upon by a company of the Americans [in the wing of the army commanded by General John Sullivan]. . . . The attack was immediately returned. . . .

Townsend now "concluded it best to retire." Soon he reached Osborne's Hill, which held some British officers on horseback and a gathering of his acquaintances:

I joined in with them. . . . The battle had commenced in earnest. Little was to be heard but the firing of the musketry and the roaring of cannon. . . . It appeared that those on horseback were some of the principal officers of the British army with their aids. . . . Among them was General Howe. He was mounted on a large English horse much reduced in flesh, I suppose from their being so long confined aboard the fleet between New York and the . . . Chesapeake Bay. . . . The General was a large portly man of coarse features. He appeared to have lost his teeth, as his mouth had fallen in. . . .

While the officers were in consultation . . . we heard a tremendous roaring of cannon and saw the volume of smoke arising therefrom at Chadds Ford. General Knyphausen having discovered that the engagement was on . . . immediately forced the troops under his command across the Brandywine, and the whole of General Washington's army in that station were routed from their breastworks and the different positions which they had taken to impede the march of the British. From these circumstances General Washington concluded it prudent to effect a retreat. . . .

. . . we had the opportunity of making many observations— the engagement of both armies, the fields in front of us containing great heaps of blankets and baggage, thrown together to relieve the men for action, the regular march of the British army, consisting of horse and foot, artillery, baggage and provision wagons, arms and ammunition, together with a host of plunderers and rabble that accompanied the army. . . .

. . . when the engagement appeared to be nearly over . . . and the day being on the decline . . . I proposed to some of my companions that we should go over to the field of battle and take a view of the dead and wounded, as we might never have such another opportunity. . . . We hastened thither, and awful was the scene to behold—such a number of fellow beings lying together severely wounded, and some mortally—a few dead, but a small proportion of them considering the immense quantity of powder and ball that had been discharged.

It was now time for the surgeons to exert themselves. . . . Some of the doors of the meeting house were torn off and the wounded carried thereon into the house to be occupied for an hospital. . . . After assisting in carrying two of them into the house, I was disposed to see an operation performed by one of the surgeons, who was preparing to amputate a limb by having a brass clamp or screw fitted thereon, a little above the knee joint. He had his knife in his hand . . . and was about to make the incision when he recollected that it might be necessary for the wounded man to take something to support him during the operation. He mentioned to some of his attendants to give him a little wine or brandy to keep up his spirits, to which he replied, "No, doctor . . . my spirits are up enough without it."

. . . As I was listening to the conversation . . . one of my companions caught me by the arm and mentioned that it was necessary to go out immediately, as they were fixing the picquet guards, and if we did not get away in a few minutes we should have to remain within the lines . . . during the night. I instantly complied. . . .

The American withdrawal, which was covered by General Nathan-
ael Greene, is described by the Marquis de Lafayette, who had been
in the fore of the action and had received a musket ball through the
leg:
    . . . the Chester road became the common retreat of the whole army. In the midst of that dreadful confusion, and during the darkness of the night, it was impossible to recover. But at Chester, 12 miles from the field of battle, [the army] met with a bridge which it was necessary to cross. M. de Lafayette occupied himself in arresting the fugitives. Some degree of order was re-established; the generals and the commander-in-chief arrived; and [Lafayette] had leisure to have his wound dressed.

The Americans drew up between Chester and Darby, near the
corner formed by the meeting of the Schuylkill with the Delaware.
Lafayette goes on:
    The inhabitants [of Philadelphia] had heard every cannon that was fired. . . . The two parties [Whigs and Tories], assembled in two distinct bands in all the squares and public places, had awaited the event in silence. The last courier at length arrived, and the friends of liberty were thrown into consternation. The Americans had lost from 1,000 to 1,200 men. . . . M. de Lafayette, having been conveyed by water to Philadelphia, was carefully attended to by the citizens, who were all interested in his situation and extreme youth. That same evening the Congress determined [that it would be necessary] to quit the city. A vast number of the inhabitants deserted their own hearths. Whole families, abandoning their possessions, and uncertain of the future, took refuge in the mountains.

But Philadelphia was not immediately molested. This was another
occasion when Sir William Howe followed a victory with a period
of hesitation.

21

FURY AT FREEMAN'S FARM

It was *mid-September, 1777, and the trees along the Hudson were showing their first tinges of color when General Burgoyne used a bridge of boats to cross from the east bank to Saratoga. He planned to move down the west bank, confront General Gates, and try forcing his way to Albany. One of the officers with the first units to cross the bridge was Lieutenant Thomas Anburey:*

. . . we . . . encamped in the plains of Saratoga, at which place there is a handsome and commodious dwelling house, with out-houses, an exceeding fine saw and grist mill, and, at a small distance, a very neat church with several houses round it, all of which are the property of General Schuyler. This beautiful spot was quite deserted, not a living creature on it. On the grounds were great quantities of fine wheat, as also Indian corn. The former was instantly cut down, threshed, carried to the mill to be ground, and delivered to the men to save our provisions. The latter was cut for forage for the horses. Thus a plantation with large crops of several sorts of grain, thriving and beautiful in the morning, was before night reduced to a scene of distress and poverty! What havoc and devastation is attendant on war!

. . . On the 15th the whole army made a movement forward and encamped at a place called Dovacote [*sic*]. . . . On the 17th the army renewed their march, repairing a great number of bridges, and encamped on a very advantageous ground at the distance of about four miles from the enemy . . . strongly posted at Stillwater.

At our last encampment a circumstance occurred, which though trifling in itself, marks how provident Nature has been to the younger part of the brute creation. It is the custom in camp to picket the horses in the rear of the tents. In the night I was awakened [by] a great rustling of my tent cords and a squeaking noise. On getting up I found it was a little colt that my mare had foaled. When we resumed our march the next day I was much embarrassed what to do with the colt, fearful it would weaken my mare and render her unable to convey my baggage; but I would not have it destroyed. And, believe me, this little creature, only dropped the night before, though in a journey of such a distance as seventeen miles, through thick woods and bad roads, was as gay and cheerful when we arrived at our encampment as if it had been in a meadow. . . .

On the 18th the enemy appeared in force to obstruct the men who were repairing the bridges. . . . A small loss was sustained in skirmishing; and the repair of the bridges was effected. At this encampment a number of men got into a potato field, and whilst gathering them a scouting party of the enemy came across and fired on them, killing and wounding near thirty, when they might with ease have surrounded the whole party and taken them prisoners.

General Burgoyne chose the morning of September 19 to launch an attack against the American lines at Stillwater. Writes General Gates:

. . . I was informed by my reconnoitring parties that the enemy had struck their camp and were removing towards our left. I immediately detached Colonel [Daniel] Morgan's corps, consisting of the rifle regiment and the light infantry of the army, to observe their direction and harass their advance.

Young Deputy Adjutant General James Wilkinson takes up:

About half after twelve o'clock a report of small arms announced Morgan's Corps to be engaged in front of our left. . . . I asked leave [of Gates] to repair to the scene of action, but was refused with this observation: "It is your duty, sir, to wait my orders."

This firing was of short duration, but was soon recommenced

Battle of Freemans Farm.

Burgoyne's Camp from the 17th to the 19th Septr. 1777.

(Rentz.)
(Specht.)
Hanau
Breidese
6 Cos. of 47.

Sword House.
Thassel
Grenadiers
Rentz

R. Artz.
24th Grenadiers
R. Artz.
9th
21st
Royal Artz.
62nd
20th
Jagers

Indians
Cannadian
Rangers

British Light Infy.

Route of British to Freeman's Farm

Route of

Route of Hessian Colm.

Route of Hessian Column

Am Vols.
German Gren.
1st Inft.
62nd

British Gren.
Cannadians 21th
Rangers

21st
62nd

Farm
20th
Jagers
Specht
Reidesel

Cannadian driven back

MILL

British.
American.
400 800 1200 Yards

American Works and Main Camp

Flanking
Works begun
but not needed

Gates Hd Quar's
Hospital

Fell's
Church

Bemis
Tavern

South Ranging

Compiled and Drawn by Col. Carington.

HUDSON RIVER

Road to Saratoga

with redoubled vivacity. I then made an excuse to visit the picket
on the left for intelligence, put spurs to my horse and, directed
by the sound, had entered the wood about an hundred rods when
the fire suddenly ceased. I however pursued my course. . . .

*Wilkinson soon began to come upon small, disorganized parties of
Americans. He says that among the officers he met was a Major
Morris:*

From him I learnt that the corps was advancing by files in two
lines when they unexpectedly fell upon a picket of the enemy,
which they almost instantly forced; and, pursuing the fugitives,
their front had as unexpectedly fallen in with the British line;
that several [American] officers and men had been made
prisoners. . . .

*By the time Wilkinson learned this, one of the captured officers was
already undergoing interrogation. Redcoat Thomas Anburey explains:*

. . . General Fraser . . . could obtain no other answer than that
their army was commanded by Generals Gates and Arnold. General
Fraser, exceedingly provoked . . . told him if he did not immediately inform him as to the exact situation of the enemy he
would hang him up directly. The officer, with the most undaunted
firmness, replied, "You may, if you please." The General, perceiving he could make nothing of him, rode off. . . .

*During his reconnoitering, James Wilkinson was twice warned to be
on his guard against enemy sharpshooters, since his being on horseback made him an especially good target:*

I then turned about to regain the camp and report to the General, when my ears were saluted by an uncommon noise, which I
approached, and perceived Colonel Morgan, attended by two men
only, who with a *turkey call* was collecting his dispersed troops. . . .
Having reported to the General, he ordered out [Colonel Joseph]
Cilley's and [Colonel Alexander] Scammell's regiments, of New
Hampshire. . . . These regiments advanced through the woods,
took ground on the left of Morgan; and the action was renewed
about one o'clock. . . . [Several other regiments] were successively
led to the field. . . . About three o'clock the action became
general. . . .

The British line was formed on an eminence in a thin pine

wood having before it Freeman's farm . . . which was bordered on the opposite side by a [thick] wood. . . . The fire of our marksmen from this wood was too deadly to be withstood by the enemy [advancing across the cleared ground] in line; and when they gave way and broke, our men rushing from their covert pursued them to the eminence, where . . . they rallied; and, charging in turn, drove us back into the wood—from whence a dreadful fire would again force them to fall back. And in this manner did the battle fluctuate, like waves of a stormy sea. . . .

Curiously, the record is at odds concerning Benedict Arnold's part in the conflict. Wilkinson claims that Gates kept him off the field because he disapproved of his rashness. But General Enoch Poor, though he did not see Arnold himself, writes that a participant named "S" (probably Colonel Scammell) told him that "Arnold rushed into the thickest of the fight with his usual recklessness, and at times acted like a madman." Captain Ebenezer Wakefield puts it this way: "Nothing could exceed the bravery of Arnold on this day. He seemed the very genius of war."

On the English side, according to Sergeant Roger Lamb, no officer showed more courage than the commander in chief:

General Burgoyne . . . shunned no danger. His presence and conduct animated the troops (for they greatly loved the general). He delivered his orders with precision and coolness; and in the heat, fury and danger of the fight maintained those true characteristics of the soldier—serenity, fortitude and undaunted intrepidity.

Roger Lamb, like James Wilkinson, writes that the battle was an uncommonly fierce one:

. . . a constant blaze of fire was kept up, and both armies seemed to be determined on death or victory. . . . Men, and particularly officers, dropped every moment on each side. Several of the Americans placed themselves in high trees, and as often as they could distinguish a British officer's uniform, took him off by deliberately aiming at his person. . . .

Burgoyne adds:

It will naturally be supposed that the Indians would be of great use against this mode of fighting. The example of those that remained after the great desertion [following the first British setbacks] proved the contrary, for not a man of them was to be brought within the sound of a rifle shot. The Canadians were formerly very expert in service of this nature; but, besides the change in their military character which I noticed before, their best officer was killed early in the action, which event cast a general damp upon the corps. A few of the [Tory] provincials were serviceable; but the best men I had to oppose [the] marksmen were the German chasseurs, though their number was so small as not to be one to twenty of the enemy.

Roger Lamb resumes:

The 20th, 21st and 62nd regiments greatly distinguished themselves. The stress of the action lay chiefly on these regiments. . . . Most of the other corps of the army bore a good share in this desperate conflict. . . . Major General Phillips . . . made his way through a difficult part of the wood to the scene of action and brought up with him . . . four pieces of artillery. This reinforcement animated our troops. . . . Major General Riedesel [the German baron] then brought forward part of the left wing and arrived in time to charge the enemy with regularity and bravery.

Huddling in a house not far behind the British lines were the Baron von Riedesel's wife and three small daughters, who had been traveling with the army. The baroness was sick with worry about her husband:

. . . I . . . shivered at every shot, for I could hear everything. I saw a great number of wounded; and what was still more harrowing, they even brought three of them into the house where I was. One of these was Major Harnage, the husband of a lady of our company. . . . He had received a shot through the lower part of the bowels, from which he suffered exceedingly.

Thomas Anburey tells of another British casualty:

. . . Lieutenant Hervey . . . a youth of sixteen and nephew to the adjutant-general of the same name, received several wounds and was repeatedly ordered off the field. . . . But his heroic ardor would not allow him to quit the battle while he could stand and see his brave lads fighting beside him. A ball striking one of his legs, his removal became absolutely necessary; and while they were conveying him away, another wounded him mortally. In this situation the surgeon recommended him to take a powerful dose of opium. . . . This he immediately consented to. . . . [H]e had one request, which he had just life enough to utter: "Tell my uncle I died like a soldier!"

According to Wilkinson, the battle lasted for four hours:

It was truly a gallant conflict . . . and certainly a drawn battle, as night alone terminated it, the British army keeping its ground in [the] rear of the field of action, and our corps, when they could no longer distinguish objects, retiring to their own camp. Yet General Burgoyne claimed a victory. . . .

Our whole loss was reported at 65 killed, 218 wounded and 38 missing—but of the last, fifteen were killed. . . . I learned [later] . . . that the British loss was 600 killed and wounded. . . .

22

PAOLI AND GERMANTOWN

A**FTER** regrouping his defeated army near Chester, Pennsylvania, on September 12, 1777, Washington had hurried across the Schuylkill River and through Philadelphia to nearby Germantown, where he allowed the troops a day of rest. Then he marched them about ten miles westward on the Schuylkill's north side, took them splashing southward across a fording place, and headed them toward the loitering Howe with the intention of provoking another engagement. "The arrangements were made," writes American Major Benjamin Tallmadge, "and the advance parties had already commenced firing, when there came on a violent shower of rain which unfitted both armies for action."

Howe's follow-up maneuvering prompted Washington to make a return to the north side of the river; but he left behind fifteen hundred men under General Anthony Wayne with orders to circle quietly to the rear of Howe's troops for the purpose of harassing them, especially if they attempted to cross the river for a march to Philadelphia. Wayne secreted his men in a woods near the Paoli Tavern. But the area's Tories quickly got the word to Howe. Wayne was unaware of this. England's John André relates that on September 20:

. . . a plan was concerted for surprising him, and the execution entrusted to Major General [Sir Charles] Grey. The troops for this service were [in two detachments]. . . . General Grey's detachment marched at 10 o'clock at night; that under Colonel

[Thomas] Musgrave at 11. No soldier of either was suffered to load [as the attack was to be made with bayonets and swords]. . . . General Grey's detachment marched by the road leading to White Horse and took every inhabitant with them as they passed along [to prevent the raising of an alarm]. About three miles from [the British] camp they turned to the left and proceeded to the Admiral Warren [Tavern], where, having forced intelligence from a blacksmith, they came in upon the out-sentries, piquet and camp of the rebels. The sentries fired and ran off. . . . The piquet was surprised and most of them killed in endeavoring to retreat.

On approaching the right of the camp we perceived the line of [camp]fires; and the light infantry being ordered to form to the front, rushed along the line, putting to the bayonet all they came up with; and, overtaking the main herd of the fugitives, stabbed great numbers and pressed on their rear till it was thought prudent to order them to desist. . . . Seventy-one prisoners were brought off. Forty of them, badly wounded, were left at different houses on the road. . . . We lost Captain Wolfe killed, and one or two private men. Four or five were wounded, one an officer. . . . Colonel Musgrave [had] marched a different way . . . and his detachment saw nothing of them. . . . We took eight wagons and teams with flour, biscuit and baggage. Their guns we could not overtake. The detachment returned to camp by daybreak. . . .

American losses in killed, wounded, and captured were about one hundred and fifty. Though General Wayne led the great majority of his men to safety, the incident was to become known among the Patriots as the "Paoli Massacre."

Washington and the main army were at this time encamped facing the north bank of the Schuylkill at a point about twenty miles from Philadelphia. On September 21 Washington got word that the British were in motion along the river's south side, but in a direction away from the city. On the twenty-third the general wrote:

This induced me to believe that they had two objects in view, one to get round the right of the army, the other, perhaps, to detach parties to Reading, where we had considerable quantities of military stores. To frustrate those intentions I moved the army up . . . the river . . . determined to keep pace with them; but early this morning I received intelligence that they had crossed the fords [behind us].

This maneuver put the British, unimpeded, on the road down-river toward Philadelphia. They had got a good start, and the Americans made no attempt to pursue. The men were tired from their several forced marches since Brandywine. Moreover, at least a thousand of them were without shoes. General Howe stopped at Germantown and set up his main camp. In an item dated September 26, a Loyalist newspaper reported:

This morning a large detachment under the command of the Right Honorable the Earl Cornwallis entered Philadelphia, marched through Second Street and, after placing the proper guards, encamped to the southward of the town. The fine appearance of the soldiery, the strictness of their discipline, the politeness of the officers, and the orderly behavior of the whole body immediately dispelled every apprehension of the inhabitants, kindled joy in the countenances of the well-affected, and has given the most convincing refutation of the scandalous falsehoods which evil and designing men [Whigs] have been long spreading to terrify the peaceable and innocent. A perfect tranquillity now prevails in the city. Numbers who have been obliged to hide themselves from the former tyranny, and to avoid being forced into measures against their conscience, have [re]appeared to share the general satisfaction and to welcome the dawn of returning liberty.

Philadelphia's fall had been expected by many of the Patriots, so the gloom over the incident was not as deep as it might have been. Benjamin Franklin, the city's first citizen, was at this time in Paris seeking French aid for the cause. When he heard that Howe had captured Philadelphia, he exclaimed, "No, Philadelphia has captured Howe!" Washington reacted to the occupation by posting his army at Skippack Creek, about sixteen miles from Germantown. Up to this time, Washington's military methods had been largely Fabian; that is, he had avoided decisive contests when he could, yet had done his best to keep the enemy harassed. Now, chagrined at having lost America's capital, he became aggressive. Major Benjamin Tallmadge explains:

Efforts were . . . made to draw in all detachments of the army and to collect a force that might enable Gen. Washington to cope with the adversary. Although defeated at the Brandywine and foiled in several smaller encounters, our American Fabius retained his full determination to give these hostile invaders no

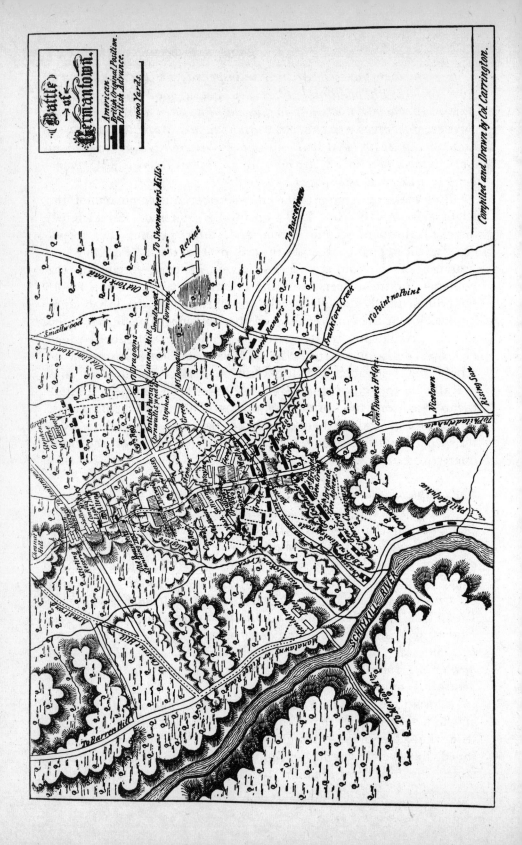

respose. . . . [He] determined to attack them [at Germantown].
. . . Such was the order of battle that the front, the flanks, and
even the rear of the British encampment were to have been attacked at the same time. My own position was at the head of
Gen. Sullivan's division. . . .

*This division had been picked for one of the central positions. It
would attack directly in the enemy's front. Major Tallmadge
continues:*

Having marched from our camp on the evening of the 3rd of
October . . . by 3 o'clock the next morning we found ourselves
[halted] close in upon the scene of action. Just before the dawn of
day, the troops were put in motion, and in a few moments the
firing commenced [in the attack's center]. The outposts and advanced guards of the enemy were driven in with great precipitation. . . .

*One of the men marching with the main attack's left, under Gen-
eral Nathanael Greene, was young Joseph Plumb Martin of
Connecticut:*

. . . there was a low vapor lying on the land, which made it
very difficult to distinguish objects at any considerable distance.
About daybreak our advanced guard and the British outposts came
in contact. The curs began to bark. . . . Our brigade moved off to the
right into the fields. We saw a body of the enemy drawn up behind
a rail fence on our right flank. We immediately formed in line and
advanced upon them. Our orders were not to fire till we could see
the buttons upon their clothes; but they were so coy that they would
not give us an opportunity to be so curious, for they hid their
clothes in fire and smoke before we had either time or leisure to
examine their buttons. They soon fell back, and we advanced. . . .

*The attack jarred Sir William out of a sound sleep. His persistent
critic, Judge Jones, claims that he had "just returned from the
faro table, not having been in bed above an hour." Upon riding
forward through the heavy fog, Howe got the impression that the
attack was being made by nothing more than a scouting party;
but he changed his mind when grapeshot began to rattle about his
ears. Turning his horse, he galloped toward the rear to organize his
defense.*

By nine o'clock, according to Major Tallmadge, Washington's central columns were almost in the heart of Germantown:

At this critical moment, Col. Musgrave of the British army threw his regiment into a large stone house [owned by Benjamin Chew] directly in front of our division in the centre, from which he poured a heavy and galling fire upon our troops. All attempts to dislodge them were ineffectual; and although they would have been harmless . . . if we had passed them by, yet through the importunity of Gen. [Henry] Knox (which I distinctly heard), Gen. Washington permitted him to bring his field artillery to bear upon it, but without effect.

By this time, units of the attack's left wing were also entering the town. In Joseph Plumb Martin's words:

The enemy were driven quite through their camp. They left their kettles, in which they were cooking their breakfasts, on the fires; and some of their garments were lying on the ground, which the owners had not time to put on. Affairs went on well for some time. The enemy were retreating before us, until the first division that was engaged had expended their ammunition. Some of the men unadvisedly calling out that their ammunition was spent, the enemy were so near that they overheard them, when they first made a stand and then returned upon our people. . . .

Among the Americans in the center who had passed the Chew House were the survivors of the "Paoli Massacre" under Anthony Wayne. So zealous was Wayne in his efforts to avenge his defeat that he was heedless of danger. He writes:

The fog together with the smoke occasioned by our cannon and musketry made it almost as dark as night. . . . [M]y roan horse was killed under me within a few yards of the enemy's front, and my left foot a little bruised by one of their cannon shot. . . . My poor horse received one musket ball in the breast and one in the flank at the same instant that I had a slight touch [by a ball] on my left hand. . . .

As for the divisions of the attack that, in accord with the original plan, had circled around the flanks of the town: They had been delayed at its outer defenses and had accomplished very little. The fog, Washington explains, was everywhere an extreme annoyance:

This circumstance, by concealing from us the true situation of the enemy, obliged us to act with more caution and less expedition than we could have wished; and gave the enemy time to recover from the effects of our first impression; and, which was still more unfortunate, it served to keep our different parties in ignorance of each other's movements, and hinder their acting in concert. It also occasioned them to mistake one another for the enemy. . . .

There were units that exchanged volleys of fire with each other and thus added to the extensive damage the rallying redcoats had begun to inflict. The redcoats themselves, however, were still taking punishment. Washington says that he had been anticipating "a decisive and glorious" victory:

But Providence designed it otherwise; for, after we had driven the enemy a mile or two; after they were in the utmost confusion and flying before us in most places; after we were upon the point, as it appeared to everybody, of grasping a complete victory, our own troops took flight and fled with precipitation and disorder. How to account for this I know not, unless . . . the fog represented their own friends to them [as] a reinforcement of the enemy, as we [had] attacked in different quarters at the same time and were about closing the wings of our army when this happened.

Mourns Major Tallmadge:

. . . notwithstanding all our attempts to rally the retiring troops, it seemed impossible to effect it, even by the presence of the Commander-in-Chief. I threw my squadron of horse across the road, by order of Gen. Washington, repeatedly to prevent the retreat of the infantry; but it was ineffectual. In addition to this, after our attack had commenced, Lord Cornwallis had commenced his march from Philadelphia with the grenadiers and light troops and had reached Germantown. This relieved the enemy greatly. But they pursued us very cautiously. After our army had passed Chestnut Hill, the enemy halted, as did also our troops. . . . Gen. Washington [then] fell back to his old quarters at Skippack, where the dispersed troops assembled, and the enemy retired to [Germantown and] Philadelphia.

John André says of the Americans:

Their disposition for the attack . . . seems to have been too complicated. Nor do their troops appear to have been sufficiently animated for the execution of it in every part, although the power of strong liquor had been employed. Several, not only of their soldiers but officers, were intoxicated when they fell into our hands.

The number of killed, wounded, and missing was high on both sides. Howe lost between five and six hundred. Washington sums up:

Our loss . . . was . . . about one thousand men; but of the missing, many, I dare say, took advantage of the time and deserted. General [Francis] Nash of North Carolina was [fatally] wounded. . . . Many [other] valuable officers . . . were also wounded, and some killed. In a word, it was a bloody day. Would to heaven I could add that it had been a more fortunate one for us.

23

CLIMAX AT SARATOGA

For two and a half weeks after the Battle of Freeman's Farm the armies of Gates and Burgoyne held their positions. According to James Wilkinson: "The weather in the autumn of 1777 on the Hudson's River was charming, and the time glided away without any notable occurrence." At night the American camp was the scene of much drunken revelry around great fires. A spirited optimism prevailed as fresh militiamen kept trooping in and increasing the camp's size. Wilkinson says that a band of Oneida Indians also came to lend their services:

These sons of the forest almost daily presented scalps and prisoners at headquarters, and their shocking death halloo resounded through our lines. This was turning upon the enemy the vengeance which they had prepared to inflict upon us; but it was an inhuman resort against which my feelings revolted.

During the preparations for further action, a dispute developed between Gates and Arnold, who had small regard for one another. Gates had given Arnold no official credit for his work on September 19, and a few days after the battle had cut the size of his command. Dr. Thacher explains:

A conscious superiority on one side and an arrogant temper on the other sufficed to render the contention almost irreconcilable. The consequence was that Arnold in a rage requested to be discharged from under the command of General Gates, and the latter immediately gave him a passport to repair to General Washington's headquarters. . . . He postponed his departure, however. . . .

For General Burgoyne, these were days of rising concern. His only solace was a letter from Sir Henry Clinton, commanding at New York City, which stated that a move up the Hudson was in preparation. Burgoyne wrote back that Clinton should hurry, explaining that the Americans had moved to disrupt his communications with Canada and that his provisions were running low. He followed the appeal with other messages of a similar nature, but most were intercepted.

Under the date October 6, British Lieutenant Thomas Anburey's journal relates:

Our present situation is far from being an inactive one, the armies being so near that not a night passes but there is firing and continual attacks upon the advanced picquets. . . . We are now become so habituated to fire that the soldiers seem to be indifferent to it, and eat and sleep when it is very near them. The officers rest in their cloaths, and the field officers are up frequently in the night. The enemy . . . within hearing, are cutting trees and making works. . . .

We have, within these few evenings—exclusive of other alarms —been under arms most of the night, as there has been a great noise, like the howling of dogs, upon the right of our encampment. It was imagined the enemy set it up to deceive us while they were meditating some attack. The two first nights this noise was heard, General Fraser thought it to have been the dogs belonging to the [British] officers, and an order was given for the dogs to be confined within the tents. . . . The next night the noise was much greater; [therefore] a detachment of Canadians and Provincials were sent out to reconnoitre; and it proved to have arisen from large droves of wolves that came after the [hastily buried] dead bodies. They were similar to a pack of hounds; for, one setting up a cry, they all joined; and when they approached a corpse their noise was hideous till they had scratched it up.

On the morning of October 7 the Baroness von Riedesel had her breakfast in the house occupied by General Burgoyne:

I observed considerable movement among the troops. My husband thereupon informed me that there was to be a reconnoissance, which . . . did not surprise me, as this often happened. On my way homeward I met many savages in their war dress, armed with guns. To my question where they were going, they cried out to me, "War! War!", which meant that they were going to fight. This completely overwhelmed me. . . .

The day before, unknown to Burgoyne, Sir Henry Clinton had captured two Hudson River forts, Montgomery and Clinton, about a hundred miles below Albany. But the action was intended only as a diversion in Burgoyne's favor and not as the beginning of a large-scale rescue attempt. Clinton sent a small force probing farther northward but was unwilling to risk endangering New York City by withdrawing enough troops for a bold move toward Gates's rear. Nor would such a move have been approved by Supreme Commander Sir William Howe. Burgoyne writes:

. . . no intelligence having been received of the expected cooperation . . . it was judged adviseable to make a movement to the enemy's left, not only to discover whether there were any possible means of forcing a passage, should it be necessary to advance, or of dislodging him for the convenience of a retreat, but also to cover a forage [mission] of the army, which was in the greatest distress on account of the scarcity. A detachment of fifteen hundred regular troops, with two twelve-pounders, two howitzers, and six six-pounders, were ordered to move, and were commanded by myself, having with me Major-General Phillips, Major-General Riedesel and Brigadier-General Fraser. . . . I formed the troops within three-quarters of a mile of the enemy's left. . . .

Burgoyne had set the stage for the Battle of Bemis Heights. It was now early afternoon. On the American side, says James Wilkinson, the advance guard of the army's center beat to arms:

The alarm was repeated throughout the line, and the troops repaired to their alarm posts. I was at headquarters when this happened, and with the approbation of the General mounted my horse to inquire the cause. But on reaching the guard where the beat commenced I could obtain no other satisfaction but that some person had reported the enemy to be advancing against our left. I proceeded over open ground, and ascending a gentle acclivity in front of the guard, I perceived, about half a mile from the line of our encampment, several columns of the enemy . . . entering a wheat field. . . . After entering the field, they . . . sat down in double ranks. . . . Foragers then proceeded to cut the wheat . . . and I soon

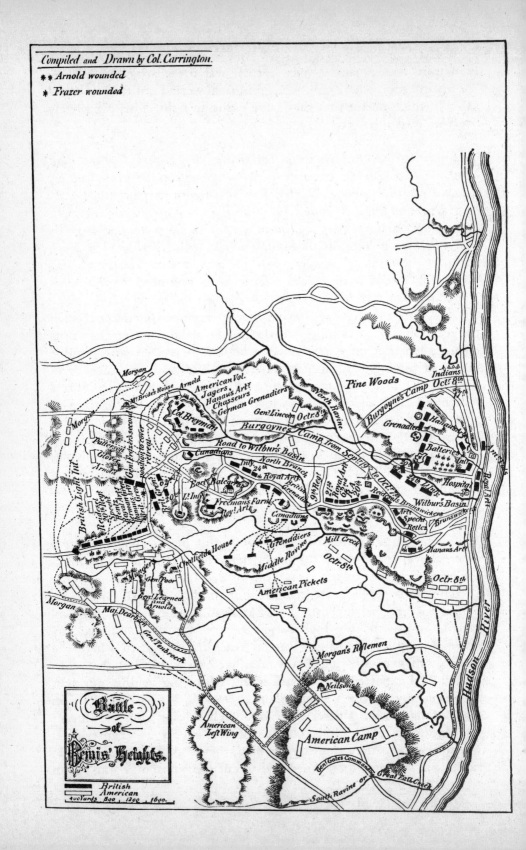

after observed several officers . . . on the top of a cabin, from whence with their glasses they were endeavouring to reconnoitre our left. . . . I returned and reported to the General, who asked me what appeared to be the intentions of the enemy.

"They are foraging and endeavouring to reconnoitre your left; and I think, sir, they offer you battle."

"What is the nature of the ground, and what your opinion?"

"Their front is open and their flanks rest on woods, under cover of which they may be attacked. Their right is skirted by a lofty height. I would indulge them."

"Well, then, order on Morgan to begin the game."

I waited on the Colonel, whose corps was formed in front of our centre, and delivered the order. He knew the ground, and inquired the position of the enemy. . . . Colonel Morgan, with his usual sagacity, proposed to make a circuit with his corps . . . under cover of the wood, to gain the height on the right of the enemy, and from thence commence his attack so soon as our fire should be opened against their left. . . . This proposition was approved by the General, and it was concerted that time should be allowed the Colonel to make the proposed circuit and gain his station on the enemy's right before the attack should be made on their left. Poor's Brigade was ordered for this service, and the attack was commenced in due season. . . .

True to his purpose, Morgan at this critical moment poured down like a torrent from the hill and attacked the right of the enemy in front and flank. [Major Henry] Dearborn, at the moment when the enemy's light infantry were attempting to charge front, pressed forward with ardour and delivered a close fire, then leapt the fence, shouted, charged and gallantly forced them to retire in disorder. Yet headed by that intrepid soldier the Earl of Balcarres, they were immediately rallied and reformed behind a fence in rear of their first position.

During this opening strife, one of the ablest leaders on the American side was still back in camp. Benedict Arnold, Wilkinson explains, was without command as the result of his disagreement with General Gates:

. . . it was very natural that an officer of his ambition should, on the commencement of the action, feel irritated by the humiliating situation in which he found himself. It was remarked that . . . he rode about the camp betraying great agitation and wrath, and it

was said that he was observed to drink freely. At length he was
found on the field of battle exercising command [of some newly
committed regiments], but not by the order or permission of General Gates.

Arnold arrived just as Burgoyne's force, under the pressure of over-
whelming numbers, was beginning to fall back toward the fortifi-
cations that ringed the British camp. Arnold's conduct, Wilkinson
states, "was exceedingly rash and intemperate, and he exposed
himself with great folly and temerity." But the enlisted men broke
into cheers, and, following Arnold's example, lunged headlong after
the retreating enemy. One of the British officers hit at this time
was the brave and much-admired General Simon Fraser. Mourns
redcoat Roger Lamb:

After he was wounded, he was supported by two officers, one on
each side of his horse. When he arrived in camp the officers all
anxiously enquired as to his wound. The downcast look and melancholy [on his face] that were visible to everyone too plainly spoke
his situation, and all the answer he could make to the many inquiries was a shake of his head, expressive that all was over with
him.

Wilkinson describes the section of the battlefield that came under
his observation as the enemy reeled back:

The ground which had been occupied by the British grenadiers
presented a scene of complicated horror and exultation. In the
square space of twelve or fifteen yards lay eighteen grenadiers in the
agonies of death, and three officers propped up against stumps of
trees, two of them mortally wounded, bleeding, and almost
speechless. . . . I found the courageous [American] Colonel Cilley
astraddle on a brass twelve-pounder and exulting in the capture—
whilst a surgeon . . . who was dressing one of the [enemy] officers,
raising his blood-besmeared hands in a frenzy of patriotism, exclaimed, "Wilkinson, I have dipt my hands in British blood!" He
received a sharp rebuke for his brutality, and with the troops I
pursued the hard-pressed flying enemy, passing over killed and
wounded. . . .

The incredible Benedict Arnold, who had begun the day without
a whit of authority, was now in chief command of the attack. First
he drove the enemy entirely within their camp's defenses. Then

*he led a charge against the camp's center, but was hurled back.
Undismayed, he galloped leftward, alone, between the American
and British lines, exposed to both fires, to take command of an
assault on the camp's extreme right. According to Wilkinson:*

The roar of cannon and small arms at this juncture was sublime.
. . . This right-flank defence of the enemy, occupied by the German
corps of [Lieutenant Colonel Heinrich von] Breymann, consisted of
a breastwork of rails . . . and extended about 250 yards across an
open field. . . .

*During this attack, made near the day's end, Arnold's horse was
killed under him and he himself was badly wounded—in the same
leg that had been hit during the assault on Quebec. As Arnold
went down, he cried out: "Rush on, my brave boys!" Wilkinson
writes that the Germans were quickly bested:*

They . . . retreated in disorder, leaving their gallant commander,
Lieutenant-Colonel Breymann, dead on the field. By dislodging this
corps, the whole British encampment was laid open to us; but the
extreme darkness of the [ensuing] night, the fatigue of the men,
and the disorder incident to undisciplined troops after so desultory
an action put it out of our power to improve the advantage. . . .

*The Baroness von Riedesel had spent the afternoon in her quarters,
shuddering at the frightful sounds from the battlefield, worrying
about her husband, and helping to comfort the dying General
Fraser, who had been brought to her on a litter:*

The ball had gone through his bowels. . . . I heard him often,
amidst his groans, exclaim: "Oh, fatal ambition! Poor General
Burgoyne! My poor wife!" Prayers were read to him. He then sent a
message to General Burgoyne, begging that he would have him
buried the following day at six o'clock in the evening, on the top
of a hill which was a sort of a redoubt. I knew no longer which way
to turn. The whole entry and the other rooms were filled with the
sick, who were suffering with . . . a kind of dysentery.

Finally, toward evening, I saw my husband coming, upon which
I forgot all my sufferings and thanked God that He had spared him
to me. He ate in great haste with me and his adjutant, behind the
house. We had been told that we had gained an advantage over
the enemy, but the sorrowful and downcast faces which I beheld
bore witness to the contrary; and before my husband again went
away he drew me [to] one side and told me that everything might

go very badly and that I must keep myself in constant readiness for departure. . . .

My Lady [Harriet Acland] occupied a tent not far from our house. . . . Suddenly one came to tell her that her husband was mortally wounded and had been taken prisoner. At this she became very wretched. We comforted her by saying that it was only a slight wound [which happened to be closer to the truth], but as no one could nurse him as well as herself, we counseled her to go at once to him, to do which she could certainly obtain permission. She loved him very much, although he was a plain, rough man, and was almost daily intoxicated. With this exception, however, he was an excellent officer. She was the loveliest of women.

I spent the night in this manner—at one time comforting her, and at another looking after my children, whom I had put to bed. As for myself, I could not go to sleep, as I had General Fraser and all the other gentlemen in my room, and was constantly afraid that my children would wake up and cry, and thus disturb the poor dying man, who often sent to beg my pardon for making me so much trouble. . . . Early in the morning . . . he expired. After they had washed the corpse, they wrapped it in a sheet and laid it on a bedstead. We . . . had this sad sight before us the whole day. At every instant, also, wounded officers of my acquaintance arrived, and the cannonade again began. A retreat was spoken of, but there was not the least movement made toward it. . . . We learned that General Burgoyne intended to fulfill the last wish of General Fraser, and to have him buried at six o'clock in the place designated by him. This occasioned an unnecessary delay. . . .

Precisely at six o'clock the corpse was brought out, and we saw the entire body of generals with their retinues on the hill assisting at the obsequies. The English chaplain, Mr. Brudenel, performed the funeral services. The cannon balls flew continually around and over the party. The American general, Gates, afterward said that if he had known that it was a burial he would not have allowed any firing in that direction. Many cannon balls also flew not far from me, but I had my eyes fixed upon the hill, where I distinctly saw my husband in the midst of the enemy's fire, and therefore I could not think of my own danger.

The order had gone forth that the army should break up [camp] after the burial, and the horses were already harnessed to our calashes. . . . The greatest silence had been enjoined. Fires had been kindled in every direction, and many tents left standing to

The Baroness von Riedesel
and, below, Lady Harriet
Acland and children.

make the enemy believe that the camp was still there. We traveled continually [northward along the Hudson] the whole night. Little Frederica was afraid and would often begin to cry. I was therefore obliged to hold a pocket handkerchief over her mouth, lest our whereabouts should be discovered.

At six o'clock in the morning a halt was made [to rest the troops and to allow some provision-laden batteaux on the river to catch up]. . . . My husband was completely exhausted, and seated himself, during this delay, in my calash, where my maid-servants were obliged to make room for him, and where he slept nearly three hours with his head upon my shoulder. . . . At last the army again began its march, but scarcely had we proceeded an hour on the way when a fresh halt was made, in consequence of the enemy being in sight. They were about two hundred men who came [only] to reconnoitre. . . . It rained in torrents. My Lady [Acland] had her tent set up. I advised her once more to betake herself to her husband. . . . Finally she yielded to my solicitations, and sent a message to General Burgoyne . . . begging permission to leave the camp. I told her that she should insist on it, which she did, and finally obtained his consent. The English chaplain, Mr. Brudenel, accompanied her; and, bearing a flag of truce, they went together in a boat [downriver] to the enemy. . . .

It was dark when the pair reached one of the American outposts on the river bank. According to Dr. Thacher's journal:

The sentinel, faithful to his duty, detained them in the boat till Major Dearborn, the officer of the guard, could arrive. He permitted them to land, and afforded Lady [Acland] the best accommodations in his power, and treated her with a cup of tea in his guard-house. When General Gates, in the morning, was informed of the unhappy situation of Lady [Acland] he immediately ordered her a safe escort and treated her himself with the tenderness of a parent. . . . She was soon conveyed to Albany, where she found her wounded husband.

The Baroness Riedesel resumes:

On the 9th we spent the whole day in a pouring rain, ready to march at a moment's warning. The savages had lost their courage, and they were seen in all directions going home. The slightest reverse of fortune discouraged them, especially if there was nothing to plunder. . . . Toward evening we at last came to Saratoga, which was only half an hour's march from the place where

we had spent the whole day. I was wet through and through . . .
and was obliged to remain in this condition the entire night,
as I had no place whatever where I could change my linen. I therefore seated myself before a good fire and undressed my children;
after which we laid ourselves down together upon some straw. I
asked General Phillips, who came up to where we were, why we did
not continue our retreat while there was yet time, as my husband
had pledged himself to cover it and bring the army through.

"Poor woman," answered he, "I am amazed at you! Completely
wet through, have you still the courage to wish to go further in this
weather? Would that you were only our commanding general! He
halts because he is tired and intends to spend the night here and
give us a supper."

In this latter achievement, especially, General Burgoyne was
very fond of indulging. He spent half the nights in singing and
drinking and amusing himself with the wife of a commissary, who
was his mistress, and who, as well as he, loved champagne.

On the 10th, at seven o'clock in the morning, I drank some tea
by way of refreshment; and we now hoped . . . that at last we
would again get under way. General Burgoyne, in order to cover
our retreat, caused the beautiful houses and mills at Saratoga,
belonging to General Schuyler, to be burned. . . . Thereupon we
set out upon our march, but only as far as another place not far
from where we had started. The greatest misery and the utmost
disorder prevailed in the army. . . . The whole army clamored for a
retreat [to Ticonderoga], and my husband promised to make it
possible, provided only that no time was lost. But General
Burgoyne, to whom [membership in] an order had been promised
if he brought about a junction with the army of General Howe,
could not determine upon this course. . . .

About two o'clock in the afternoon the firing of cannon and small
arms was again heard, and all was alarm and confusion. My husband sent me a message telling me to betake myself forthwith into
a house which was not far from there. I seated myself in the calash
with my children and had scarcely driven up to the house when I
saw on the opposite side of the Hudson River five or six men with
guns which were aimed at us. Almost involuntarily I threw the
children on the bottom of the calash and myself over them. At the
same instant, the churls fired and shattered the arm of a poor
English soldier behind us, who was already wounded and was also
on the point of retreating into the house.

Immediately after our arrival a frightful cannonade began,

principally directed against the house in which we had sought
shelter, probably because the enemy believed, from seeing so many
people flocking around it, that all the generals made it their headquarters. Alas! It harbored none but wounded soldiers or women!
We were finally obliged to take refuge in a cellar, in which I
laid myself down in a corner not far from the door. My children
laid down on the earth with their heads upon my lap, and in this
manner we passed the entire night. . . . On the following morning
the cannonade again began, but from a different side.

I advised all to go out of the cellar for a little while, during
which time I would have it cleaned, as otherwise we would all
be sick. They followed my suggestion, and I at once set many hands
to work, which was in the highest degree necessary, for the women
and children being afraid to venture forth, had 'soiled the whole
cellar. . . . I for the first time surveyed our place of refuge. It consisted of three beautiful cellars, splendidly arched. I proposed that
the most dangerously wounded of the officers should be brought
into one of them; that the women should remain in another; and
that all the rest should stay in the third. . . .

I had just given the cellars a good sweeping and had fumigated
them by sprinkling vinegar on burning coals, and each one had
found his place . . . when a fresh and terrible cannonade threw us
all once more into alarm. . . . Eleven cannon balls went through the
house, and we could plainly hear them rolling over our heads. One
poor soldier, whose leg they were about to amputate, having been
laid upon a table for this purpose, had the other leg taken off . . .
in the very middle of the operation. His comrades all ran off, and
when they again came back they found him in one corner of the
room, where he had rolled in his anguish, scarcely breathing.

I was more dead than alive, though not so much on account of
our own danger as for that which enveloped my husband, who,
however, frequently sent to see how I was getting along and to tell
me that he was still safe. . . . Often my husband wished to withdraw
me from danger by sending me to the Americans, but I remonstrated with him. . . . He promised me, therefore, that I should
henceforward follow the army. Nevertheless, I was often in the
night filled with anxiety lest he should march away. At such times I
. . . crept out of my cellar to reassure myself; and if I saw the
troops lying around the fires (for the nights were already cold)
I would return and sleep quietly. . . .

Our cook saw to our meals, but we were in want of water;

and . . . I was often obliged to drink wine, and give it also to the children. . . . As the great scarcity of water continued, we at last found a soldier's wife who had the courage to bring water from the river; for no one else would undertake it, as the enemy shot at the head of every man who approached the river. This woman, however, they never molested. . . .

In this horrible situation we remained six days. Finally, they spoke of capitulating, as by temporizing for so long a time our retreat had been cut off. A cessation of hostilities took place; and my husband, who was thoroughly worn out, was able, for the first time in a long while, to lie down upon a bed. . . . But about one o'clock in the night someone came and asked to speak to him. . . . Soon after this, General Burgoyne requested the presence of all the generals and staff officers at a council of war, which was to be held early the next morning—in which he proposed to break the capitulation already made with the enemy, in consequence of some false information just received.

(Word had at last reached Burgoyne of Sir Henry Clinton's expedition up the Hudson from New York City, and there seemed a possibility that it would be extended into the kind of operation Burgoyne had been hoping for.) The Baroness concludes:

It was, however, finally decided that [breaking the capitulation] was neither practicable nor advisable. And this was fortunate for us, as the Americans said to us afterwards that had the capitulation been broken we all would have been massacred, which they could have done. . . . On the 17th of October the capitulation was consummated.

Young James Wilkinson, as one of Gates's representatives, had taken an active part in the negotiations:

A youth in a plain blue frock, without other military insignia than a cockade and sword, I stood in the presence of three experienced European generals [Burgoyne, Phillips, and Riedesel], soldiers before my birth.

On the day of the surrender, Wilkinson was sent to Burgoyne's headquarters to escort him, along with a number of subordinates, toward a beginning of the ceremonies:

. . . I . . . accompanied him to the ground where his army was to lay down their arms, from whence we rode to the bank of the

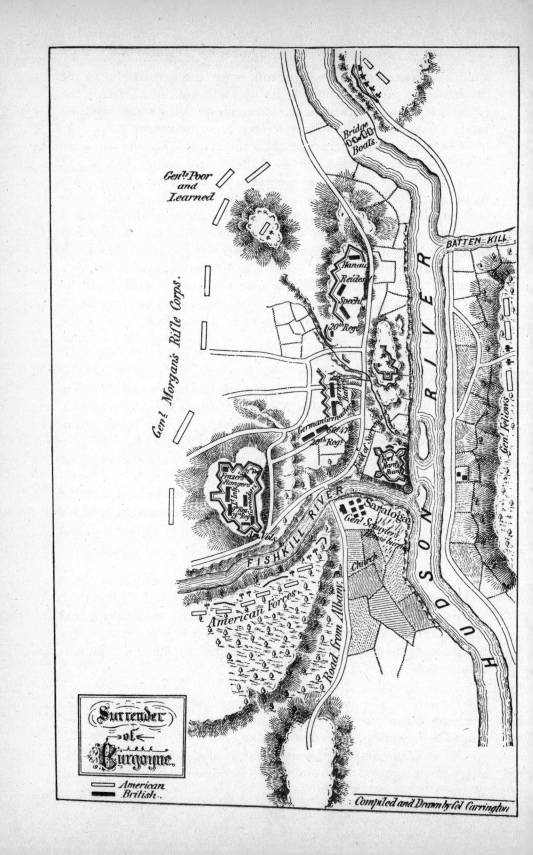

Gen^{ls} Poor and Learned

Genl Morgan's Rifle Corps.

Bridge of Boats.

BATTEN KILL

Hanau Reides Specht.

20th Reg^t

German Grenadiers Col 47.
20th Reg^t

Fort Hardy Ruins

HUDSON RIVER

Genl Fellows

Frazers Rangers
Brit Grenadier
47th Reg^t

Field of Surrender

Saratoga.
Genl Schuylers House burnt.

Vol^s

FISHKILL RIVER

Church.

American Forces

Road from Albany.

Surrender of Burgoyne.

☐ American
◼ British.

Compiled and Drawn by Col Carrington.

Hudson's River, which he surveyed with attention and asked me whether it was not fordable.

"Certainly, sir; but do you observe the people on the opposite shore?"

"Yes," replied he, "I have seen them too long."

He then proposed to be introduced to General Gates, and we . . . proceeded towards his headquarters. . . . General Gates, advised of Burgoyne's approach, met him at the head of . . . camp, Burgoyne in a rich royal uniform and Gates in a plain blue frock. When they had approached nearly within sword's length, they reined up and halted. . . . General Burgoyne, raising his hat most gracefully, said, "The fortune of war, General Gates, has made me your prisoner;" to which the conqueror, returning a courtly salute, promptly replied, "I shall always be ready to bear testimony that it has not been through any fault of your excellency."

Gates was more exuberant about his great triumph in a letter to his wife, stating proudly that his prisoners included "about a dozen members of Parliament, Scotch lords, etc.," and adding that "if Old England is not by this lesson taught humility, then she is an obstinate old slut, bent upon her ruin." Dr. Thacher observes:

There are perhaps few examples in the annals of warfare of a whole army under a celebrated general and officers of the first character, gentlemen of noble families and military merit, being reduced to the mortifying condition of captives, led through a country which it was designed should have been devoted to their all-conquering power. . . . This event will make one of the most brilliant pages of American history.

Wilkinson says of the victory:

. . . [It] prostrated the power of the enemy in the north, disconcerted a dangerous project, and distracted his future operations. It invigorated the national spirit, retrieved disasters [to] the south, and encouraged the public councils to resist the insidious plans of the British cabinet to disunite the American people and disarm opposition.

The victory had another effect of vital importance. Up to this time France had been aiding the Americans only unofficially. Now she began moving toward an open entry into the war.

24

TURBULENCE ON THE DELAWARE

ONE *Frenchman who had already made a full commitment to the American cause, the charmingly boyish Lafayette, was at this time in Bethlehem, Pennsylvania, recuperating from "what I pompously call my wound in order to give myself airs and make myself interesting." He writes that he had been taken in by a family of Moravians:*

. . . the mild religion of the brotherhood, the community of fortune, education and interests amongst that large and simple family formed a striking contrast to scenes of blood and the convulsions occasioned by a civil war. . . . Provinces, towns and families were divided by the violence of party spirit. Brothers (officers in the two opposing armies), meeting by chance in their father's house . . . [sometimes] seized their arms to fight with each other. Whilst . . . the English committed horrible acts of license and cruelty . . . in that same army were seen regiments of Americans [Loyalists] who, trampling under foot their brethren, assisted in enslaving their wasted country. Each [district] contained a . . . number whose sole object was to injure the friends of liberty and give information to those of despotism. To these inveterate Tories must be added the numbers of those whom fear, private interest or religion rendered adverse to the war. If the Presbyterians . . . detested royalty, the Lutherans, who had sprung from it, were divided among themselves. The Quakers hated slaughter but served willingly as guides to the royal troops.

Insurrections were by no means uncommon. Near the enemy's stations, farmers often shot each other. Robbers were even encouraged. The republican chiefs were exposed to great dangers when they traveled through the country. It was always necessary for them to declare that they should pass the night in one house, then take possession of another, barricade themselves in it, and only sleep with their arms by their side. In the midst of these troubles, M. de Lafayette was no longer considered as a stranger. Never was any adoption more complete than his own. . . .

The young nobleman looked forward to an early return to active duty. In the meantime, the strife between the two armies in the Philadelphia area continued. According to Major Benjamin Tallmadge, of Washington's forces:

. . . Lord Howe had assembled his fleet in the Delaware Bay, and as the obstructions which had been placed in the river below Philadelphia to prevent the [ascent] of the fleet still remained, and the army [occupying Philadelphia] were obliged to depend on the fleet for all their provisions, it became necessary that these obstructions should be removed. The *chevaux-de-frise* [spiked barriers] could not be removed so long as our forts protected them.

The forts were Fort Mifflin, on Port Island (often called "Mud Island" in contemporary accounts), and Fort Mercer, at Red Bank, on the Jersey shore. As reported in the New Jersey Gazette *in the form of a letter written by an unnamed American observer on October 23, 1777:*

Yesterday morning about fifteen hundred Hessians under the command of [Colonel Carl von] Donop came down from Philadelphia to Red Bank in order to take the fort [Mercer] under the command of Colonel [Christopher] Greene. . . . About four o'clock in the afternoon the attack was begun by a most furious cannonade, which held a quarter of an hour. The Hessians then rushed on to storm the fort, and got into the old part of the works, when they thought it was all their own, and gave three cheers, but were soon obliged to retreat out of it in the utmost hurry. The [American] galleys [on the river] at the same time kept up a constant fire on them, which did great execution; and in about three-quarters of an hour's attack they ran off with the greatest precipitation, leaving behind them, dead, about ninety persons. . . . And from a good authority we are assured that the enemy buried one colonel and

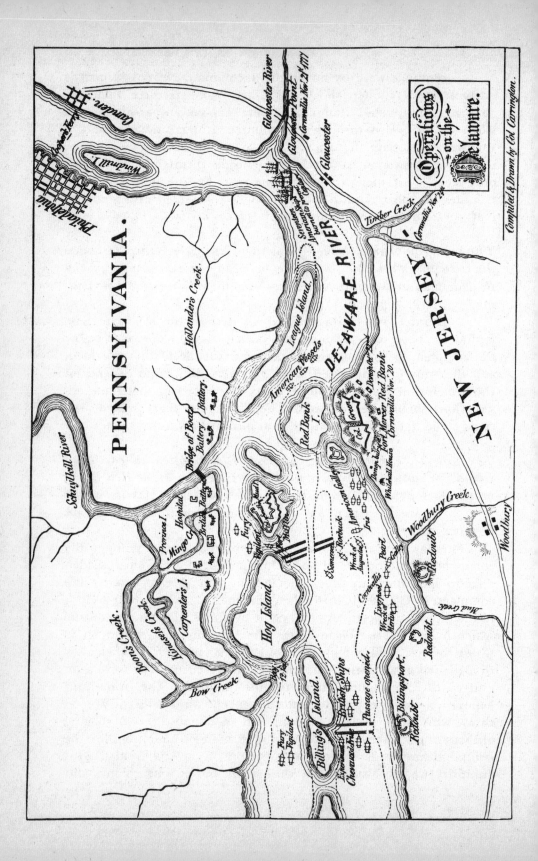

Operations on the Delaware.

Compiled & Drawn by Col. Carrington.

twenty-one privates between the fort and Cooper's Ferry [on the bank opposite Philadelphia], and carried over not less than two hundred wounded. The enemy left on the field, wounded, Count Donop [soon to die], his brigade-major, a lieutenant and about eighty privates. . . .

While the enemy was attacking the fort, the *Augusta*, of sixty-four guns, the *Roebuck*, of forty-four, two frigates of thirty-two, the *Merlin*, of eighteen, and their large galleys came through the lower *cheval-de-frise* and kept up a great firing in order to draw off the galleys from giving any assistance to the fort; but they were mistaken. The *Augusta*, in going down in the evening, got aground. Early this morning all the [American] galleys and floating batteries began the attack, when an incessant fire was kept up on both sides, so that the very elements seemed to be on fire. At eleven o'clock the *Augusta* was set on fire, and at twelve she blew up with an astonishing blast. One of our people was killed in a galley by the fall of a piece of timber, and we were so near that some of our powder-horns took fire and blew up. The engagement still continued; but the *Roebuck* fell lower down, and the *Merlin* . . . ran aground, and at three o'clock the enemy set fire to her, when the engagement ceased, the enemy falling still lower down. Thus ended two glorious days.

But the British persisted, soon laying siege to Fort Mifflin on Port Island and bombarding it from positions on the Pennsylvania shore and from the decks of ships. One of the men in the fort was Connecticut's Joseph Plumb Martin:

We continued here, suffering cold, hunger and other miseries, till the fourteenth day of November. On that day, at the dawn, we discovered [ten vessels menacing the fort]. . . . We immediately opened our batteries upon them, but they appeared to take very little notice. . . . The enemy soon began their firing upon us, and there was music indeed. . . . Some of our officers endeavored to ascertain how many guns were fired in a minute by the enemy, but it was impossible; the fire was incessant. . . . I saw five artillerists belonging to one gun cut down by a single shot, and I saw men who were stooping to be protected by the works, but not stooping low enough, split like fish to be broiled.

About the middle of the day some of our galleys and floating batteries, with a frigate, fell down and engaged the British with their long guns, which in some measure took off the enemy's fire from the fort. . . . Nearly every gun in the fort was silenced by midday. Our men were cut up like cornstalks. . . . The cannonade continued, directed mostly at the fort, till the dusk of the evening. As soon as it was dark we began to make preparations for evacuating the fort. . . .

We left our flag flying when we left the island, and the enemy did not take possession of the fort till late in the morning after we left it.

British officer Charles Stedman was later to record in his History:
. . . the redoubt at Red Bank was also abandoned, upon the approach of Lord Cornwallis with a detachment from camp sent to reduce it; and the [American] water force, being now no longer protected by the works on shore, quitted its station and retired up the river. Some few of the smaller galleys, by keeping close on the Jersey shore, passed Philadelphia in the night and escaped. The rest were abandoned and burnt. And thus a communication by the Delaware was at last opened between the navy and army.

By this time Washington had moved his main army from its post at Skippack Creek to Whitemarsh, about twelve miles from Phila-delphia. Early in December, General Howe marched his own army to Whitemarsh and deployed it as though he intended to fight. Joseph Plumb Martin says that an attack was hourly expected:
We had a commanding position and were very sensible of it. We were kept constantly on the alert, and wished nothing more than to have them engage us, for we were sure of giving them a drubbing, being in excellent fighting trim, as we were starved and as cross and ill-natured as curs. The British, however, thought better of the matter; and, after several days maneuvering . . . very civilly walked off into Philadelphia again.

25

THE MONTHS AT VALLEY FORGE

T HE BRITISH *commander now set about establishing his army in
winter quarters. Less than twenty miles away, at Valley Forge
on the Schuylkill, Washington did the same. Once again the American outlook was dimming. Lafayette, who had returned to duty,
explains:*

Notwithstanding the success in the north, the situation of the
Americans had never been more critical than at the present moment. A paper money without any certain foundation, and un-
mixed with any specie, was both counterfeited by the enemy and
discredited by their partisans. . . . The people, who had risen against
the taxation of England, were astonished at paying still heavier
taxes now; and the government was without any power to [compel]
them. On the other side, [British-held] New York and Philadelphia
were overstocked with gold and various merchandises. The threatened penalty of death could not stop a communication [with the
British] that was but too easy. To refuse the payment of taxes, to
depreciate the paper currency and feed the enemy was a certain
method of attaining wealth. Privations and misery were only experienced by good citizens. . . . The sacred fire of liberty was not
extinguished, it is true, and the majority of the citizens detested
British tyranny; but the triumph of the north and the tranquillity of
the south had lulled to sleep two-thirds of the continent.

. . . the greatest difficulty was that, in order to conceal misfortunes from the enemy, it was necessary to conceal them from the

nation also. . . . At [York, Pennsylvania], behind the Susquehanna, Congress was divided into two factions. . . . The deputies substituted their private intrigues for the wishes of the nation. Several impartial men had retired. Several states had but one representative, and in some cases not even one.

Though the incomparable journal keeper, Dr. James Thacher, spent the winter of 1777 and 1778 in New York and Massachusetts, he nonetheless learned enough about the Valley Forge encampment from friends to pen an excellent summary of the problems that faced the army and its commander:

In the month of December the troops were employed in erecting log huts for winter quarters, when about one-half of the men were destitute of small-clothes, shoes and stockings. Some thousands were without blankets, and were obliged to warm themselves over fires all night, after the fatigues of the day, instead of reposing in comfortable lodgings. At one time nearly three thousand men were [listed] unfit for duty from the want of clothing; and it was not uncommon to track the march of the men over ice and frozen ground by the blood from their naked feet. Several times . . . they experienced little less than a famine in camp; and more than once our general officers were alarmed by the fear of a total dissolution of the army from the want of provisions. . . . It cannot be deemed strange that sickness and mortality were the consequence of such privations in the midst of an inclement season. Under these unexampled sufferings, the soldiers exercised a degree of patience and fortitude which reflects on them the highest honor, and which ought ever to entitle them to the gratitude of their country. The army . . . was not without consolation, for his excellency the commander-in-chief . . . manifested a fatherly concern and fellow-feeling for their sufferings and made every exertion in his power to remedy the evil and to administer the much-desired relief. Being authorized by Congress, he reluctantly resorted to the unpopular expedient of taking provisions from the inhabitants by force, and thus procured a small supply for immediate necessity.

. . . a foreign officer of distinction said to a friend of mine that he despaired of our independence, for while walking with General Washington along the soldiers' huts he heard . . . many voices echoing through the open crevices between the logs, "No pay, no clothes, no provisions, no rum;" and when a miserable being was seen flitting from one hut to another his nakedness was only covered by a dirty blanket. . . .

This was the unhappy condition of that army on whom General Washington had to rely for the defence of everything held most dear by Americans; and this too while situated within sixteen miles of a powerful adversary. . . . But a fact which excites the greatest indignation and astonishment is that, at the critical period above mentioned a party in Congress, in concert with General [Thomas] Conway, was endeavoring to remove General Washington from the supreme command. . . . No man, perhaps, ever had a greater combination of vexatious evils and uncontrollable obstacles to encounter than this incomparable patriot and warrior; and no one surely ever possessed in a more eminent degree the peculiar talents and qualities requisite for the discharge of the important duties assigned him in his elevated station. He has acquired the full confidence of every faithful officer and soldier under his command, and his wisdom and judgment are considered adequate to the most trying exigencies. He rises in the midst of distress, and gains strength by misfortunes.

The Assembly of Pennsylvania and a certain party in our Congress entertain an idea that the royal army was permitted to take possession of Philadelphia by the timidity, or by the extreme caution, of our commander-in-chief. It is well known that from necessity he has evinced himself more the disciple of Fabius Maximus than of Marcellus. He temporizes and acts on the defensive when a superior force and the peculiar circumstances of his army compel him to adopt such conduct. But no one will deny that he has displayed the greatest courage in opposing danger, and the greatest presence of mind in retreating from it. He has perplexed the enemy by his judicious manoeuvres, and braved him frequently in his camp; and it is by his superior generalship and the unfailing resources of his mind that the enemy was not sooner in possession of Philadelphia, and that our feeble, half-starved, naked army has not been entirely destroyed. . . .

It is most unfortunate that Congress appears to be split into factions at this eventful period, when the salvation of our country depends on the harmony and unanimity in our councils. A strong party exists in this body who are exerting every nerve to effect their favorite scheme of elevating General Gates to the supreme command. This gentleman is made the object of their applause and caresses. . . . These unhappy dissensions and jealousies occasion the greatest solicitude in our army, and consequences of a fatal tendency are seriously apprehended.

*Horatio Gates, indeed, was highly esteemed at this time, though the credit for the Saratoga victory probably belonged as much to Benedict Arnold and Daniel Morgan as to him. Thomas Conway was a French citizen of Irish birth who was in America courting military fortune and had won the favor of Congress. The "Conway Cabal," which wasn't really as strongly organized as Dr. Thacher makes it seem, came to light through James Wilkinson, Gates's aide and friend. Getting a look at a letter from Conway to Gates in which Washington was called "a weak general," Wilkinson repeated the line as a choice bit of news among drinking companions, some of whom were devoted to Washington, and the discord began. Washington, according to Lafayette, preserved "the noble composure which belongs to a strong and virtuous mind" and declared: "I have not sought for this place. If I am displeasing to the nation, I will retire. But until then I will oppose all intrigues." He op-*posed this one by letter, and the principal soon began retreating *before his stern accusations. The campaign, however, occupied a place among his many other concerns for several months.*

The general and his deprived troops were provided a welcome moment of amusement by some news they heard at the outset of the new year. The affair began with an experiment made by David Bushnell, who had earlier built America's first submarine and was now working with floating explosives:

. . . I fixed several kegs under water charged with powder, to explode upon touching anything as they floated along with the tide. I set them afloat in the Delaware, above the English shipping at Philadelphia. . . . I was unacquainted with the river and obliged to depend upon a gentleman very imperfectly acquainted with that part of it, as I afterwards found. We went as near the shipping as we durst venture. I believe the darkness of the night greatly deceived him, as it did me. We set them adrift, to fall with the ebb upon the shipping. Had we been within sixty rods, I believe they must have fallen in with them immediately, as I designed; but as I afterwards found, they were set adrift much too far distant, and did not arrive until after being detained some time by the frost. They advanced in the daytime in a dispersed situation and under great disadvantages. One of them blew up a boat with several persons in it, who imprudently handled it too freely, and thus gave the British that alarm which brought on the "Battle of the Kegs."

An account of this "battle" in the New Jersey Gazette *gave rise to much Patriot laughter. According to the item, dated January 6, 1778:*

Philadelphia has been entertained with a most astonishing instance of the activity, bravery and military skill of the royal navy of Great Britain. The affair is somewhat particular, and deserves notice. Sometime last week, two boys observed a keg of a singular construction floating in the river opposite to the city. They got into a small boat, and attempting to take up the keg, it burst with a great explosion and blew up the unfortunate boys.

Yesterday, several kegs of a like construction made their appearance. An alarm was immediately spread through the city. Various reports prevailed, filling the city and the royal troops with consternation. Some reported that the kegs were filled with armed rebels who were to issue forth in the dead of night, as the Grecians did of old from their wooden horse at the siege of Troy, and take the city by surprise; asserting that they had seen the points of their bayonets through the bungholes of the kegs. Others said they were charged with the most inveterate combustibles, to be kindled by secret machinery, and setting the whole Delaware in flames, were to consume all the shipping in the harbor; whilst others asserted that they were constructed by art magic, would of themselves ascend the wharves in the nighttime and roll all flaming through the streets of the city, destroying everything in their way.

Be this as it may, certain it is that the shipping in the harbor and all the wharves in the city were fully manned. The battle began, and it was surprising to behold the incessant blaze that was kept up against the enemy, the kegs. Both officers and men exhibited the most unparalleled skill and bravery on the occasion; whilst the citizens stood gazing as solemn witnesses of their prowess. From the *Roebuck* and other ships of war, whole broadsides were poured into the Delaware. In short, not a wandering ship, stick or drift log but felt the vigor of the British arms.

The action began about sunrise and would have been completed with great success by noon, had not an old market woman coming down the river with provisions unfortunately let a small keg of butter fall overboard, which . . . floated down to the scene of action. At sight of this unexpected reinforcement of the enemy, the battle was renewed with fresh fury, and the firing was incessant till the evening closed the affair. The kegs were either totally demolished or obliged to fly, as none of them have shown their heads since. It is said His Excellency Lord Howe has despatched a swift sailing packet with an account of this victory to the court of London. In a word, Monday the fifth of January, 1778, must ever be distinguished in history for the memorable Battle of the Kegs.

This furious action was further satirized in a long ballad by Francis Hopkinson, one of the signers of the Declaration of Independence. No stanza delighted America more than one that told of General Howe's whereabouts during the night hours preceding the first alarm:

> *Sir William, he, snug as a flea,*
> *lay all this time a-snoring;*
> *Nor dreamed of harm as he lay warm*
> *in bed with Mrs. Loring.*

Though the winter of 1777–1778 was miserable enough, the snows were not excessive, and Washington tried to keep his camp on something of a training schedule. He got some unexpected help in this area from a native of Prussia, Friedrich Wilhelm Ludolf Gerhard Augustin, Baron von Steuben. In Dr. Thacher's words:

He . . . presented himself with his credentials to Congress, proffering his services in our army without any claim to rank, and requested permission only to render such assistance as might be in his power in the character of a volunteer. . . . Congress voted him their thanks for his zeal and the disinterested tender of his services, and he joined the main army under General Washington at Valley Forge. His qualifications for a teacher of the system of military tactics were soon manifested, having for many years practised on the system which the King of Prussia had introduced into his own army. . . . He exerted all his powers for the establishment of a regular system of discipline, economy and uniformity among our heterogeneous bodies of soldiers.

Joseph Plumb Martin says: "I was kept constantly, when off other duty, engaged in learning the Baron de Steuben's new Prussian exercise. It was a continual drill." The baron, though a hard driver, was well liked by both officers and men. He was fair-minded and generous and was usually aglow with amiability. Though he was given to fits of rage on the drill field, they seemed more theatrical than real. Since he spoke German and French but not much English, the Americans found his outbursts more amusing than offensive. He sometimes called to his aides in French: "Come and swear for me in English. These fellows won't do what I bid them." Steuben proved a godsend to Washington and was soon made a major general. His brand of training and discipline was exactly what the young army needed. Not only was there a great improvement in efficiency, but the soldiers found a new pride in themselves that helped them to emerge from the winter at Valley Forge in a fair state of morale.

Early in April the army took part in a ceremony of special note. Since December, 1776, America's General Charles Lee had been a prisoner of the British. They had now agreed to exchange him for General Richard Prescott, who had been kidnapped by the Americans in a daring night raid on British headquarters near Newport, Rhode Island, in July, 1777. The arrangements for Lee's return were made by Washington's commissary general of prisoners, Elias Boudinot:

When the day arrived, the greatest preparations were made for his reception. All the principal officers of the army were drawn up in two lines, advanced of the camp about 2 miles towards the enemy. Then the troops, with the inferior officers, formed a line quite to headquarters. All the music of the army attended. The General [Washington] with a great number of principal officers and their suites, rode about four miles on the road towards Philadelphia and waited till Genl. Lee appeared. Gen. Washington dismounted and received Gen. Lee as if he had been his brother. He passed through the lines of officers and the army, who all paid him the highest military honors, to headquarters, where Mrs. Washington was, and there he was entertained with an elegant dinner, and the music playing the whole time.

A room was assigned him, back of Mrs. Washington's sitting room, and all his baggage was stowed in it. The next morning he lay very late, and breakfast was detained for him. When he came out he looked as dirty as if he had been in the street all night. Soon after, I discovered that he had brought a miserable dirty hussy with him from Philadelphia (a British sergeant's wife) and had actually taken her into his room by a back door, and she had slept with him that night.

Lee was very appreciative of Boudinot's work on his behalf, but he hadn't changed his opinion of Washington's leadership; privately, he told Boudinot that he didn't think Washington fit to command a sergeant's guard. Writes Boudinot: "This mortified me greatly after all the kindness shown him by Genl. Washington."

As for Washington's troubles related to the Conway Cabal, they were now entirely over. Dr. Thacher was relieved to be able to record:

The brigadiers and a number of colonels have remonstrated in strong terms to Congress respecting . . . General Conway. The machinations of this insolent foreigner have at length recoiled on his own head. Having, by his vile intrigue and insufferable effrontery, rendered himself an object of disgust in his station, he has been induced to resign his commission and has withdrawn himself from the army. On this serious occasion the character of Washington was found unassailable, and it shines with redoubled lustre.

On May 1, Washington received the joyous news that France had recognized American independence and that the two governments had signed a treaty of alliance against England. A celebration was set for May 6, and the troops, now somewhat better equipped than they had been at the winter's beginning, got the chance to show the public some of the things they had learned under the dedicated Steuben. As reported by an unknown eyewitness:

After the chaplains had finished their discourses and the second cannon was fired, the troops began their march. . . . Major-General Lord Stirling commanded on the right, the Marquis de Lafayette on the left, and the Baron [Johann] de Kalb the second line. But this arrangement can convey no adequate idea of their movements to their several posts, of the appearance of his excellency during his circuit round the lines, of the air of our soldiers, the cleanliness of their dress, the brilliancy and good order of their arms, and the remarkable animation with which they performed the necessary salute as the General passed along. Indeed, during the whole of the review the utmost military decorum was preserved. . . .

The commander-in-chief, his suite, the Marquis de Lafayette, his train, Lord Stirling, General Greene, and the other principal officers . . . having finished the review, retired to the centre of the encampment. . . . On firing of the third signal gun, the *feu de joie* [the formal firing in token of joy] commenced. It was conducted with great judgment and regularity. The gradual progression of the sound from the discharge of cannon and musketry, swelling and rebounding from the neighboring hills and gently sweeping along the Schuylkill, with the intermingled huzzas . . . "Long live the King of France!", "Long live the friendly European powers!", and "Long live the American States!" composed a military music more agreeable to a soldier's ear than the most finished pieces of your favorite Handel.

The *feu de joie* being over and the troops marched back to their different quarters, the officers came forward to the entertainment provided by his excellency. . . . The officers approached the place of entertainment in different columns, thirteen abreast and closely linked together in each other's arms. . . . The number of officers composing each line signified the Thirteen American States, and the interweaving of arms a complete union and most perfect confederation.

The amphitheatre looked elegant. The outer seats for the officers were covered with tent canvas stretched out upon poles, and the tables in the centre shaded by elegant markees raised high and arranged in a very striking and agreeable style. An excellent band of music attended during the entertainment; but the feast was still more animating by the discourse and behavior of his excellency. . . . Mrs. Washington, the Countess of Stirling [and] Lady Kitty (her daughter), Mrs. Greene and a number of other ladies favored the feast with their company. . . . The wine circulated in the most genial manner. . . . The French gentlemen of rank and distinction seemed peculiarly pleased with this public approbation of our alliance with their nation.

Another eyewitness adds:

The entertainment was concluded with a number of patriotic toasts, attended with huzzas. When the General took his leave, there was a universal clap, with loud huzzas, which continued till he had proceeded a quarter of a mile, during which time there were a thousand hats tossed in the air. His Excellency turned round with his retinue and huzzaed several times.

In Philadelphia, less than two weeks later, there was a celebration of a different kind. Sir William Howe had asked to be recalled to England, and had been instructed to turn his command over to Sir Henry Clinton. A group of Howe's younger officers, led by the popular, bright, and artistic John André, decided to give him a grand send-off. The fete they arranged was called the Mischianza (Italian for "medley"). "This entertainment," says England's Charles Stedman in his History, *"not only far exceeded anything that had ever been seen in America, but rivalled the magnificent exhibitions of that vain-glorious monarch and conqueror, Louis XIV of France." Stedman thus describes the Mischianza's main feature:*

All the colours of the army were placed in a grand avenue three hundred feet in length, lined with the King's troops, between two triumphal arches, for the two brothers, the Admiral, Lord Howe, and the General, Sir William Howe, to march along in pompous procession followed by a numerous train of attendants, with seven silken knights of the blended rose and seven more of the burning mountain, and fourteen damsels dressed in the Turkish fashion, to an area of one hundred and fifty yards square, lined also with the King's troops, for the exhibition of a tilt and tournament, or mock fight of old chivalry, in honour of those two heroes. On the top of each triumphal arch was a figure of Fame bespangled with stars, blowing from her trumpet in letters of light, *Tes lauriers sont immortels* (Thy laurels are immortal). This romantic triumph, after so many disgraces and disappointments, did not escape the severest satire, both in private conversation and in printed papers. . . .

The affair was considered "a most ridiculous farce" by Judge Jones:

It is really surprising that men of sense could be regaled with such nonsense. Yet it seems to have given great satisfaction to the brothers. . . . It tickled their vanity. It pleased their ambition. The exhibition of this triumphal Mischianza will be handed down to posterity, in the annals of Great Britain and America, as one of the most ridiculous, undeserved and unmerited triumphs ever yet performed. Had the General been properly rewarded for his conduct while Commander-in-Chief in America, an execution and not a Mischianza would have been the consequence.

The reasons behind Howe's manner of prosecuting the war would never be fully explained. Some of his own statements seemed to indicate that his experience at Bunker Hill had left him overly re-

spectful of American arms. At other times, he asserted that the king's ministers had never made his orders definite, and that he had pro- ceeded as he thought best, and that his decisions had been the right ones.

Although some persons [he argued] condemn me for having endeavoured to conciliate His Majesty's rebellious subjects by taking every means to prevent the destruction of the country instead of irritating them by a contrary mode of proceeding, yet am I . . . satisfied in my own mind that I acted . . . for the benefit of the King's service. Ministers themselves . . . did at one time entertain a similar doctrine, and . . . it is certain that I should have had little reason to hope for support from them if I had been disposed to acts of great severity.

This argument had some merit, for even during Howe's last months in command the British government had been working on another bid to placate the Americans. As explained in Dr. Thacher's journal:

It appears that in consequence of the capture of General Burgoyne and his army, the Parliament had manifested great mortification and alarm, and have been induced to pass some acts, with a view of reconciliation, more consistent with the just claims of America than those formerly declared. The royal commissioners have presented to our Congress their proposals for a mutual ad- justment of existing difficulties. . . . There is, however, a very im- portant and radical defect in the terms proposed by the commis- sioners: they are not authorized to treat with Congress on the prin- ciples of independency, but still adhere to the idea of a reunion of the states, as colonies, under the government of Great Britain. Firm in their determination never to relinquish this fundamental prin- ciple, the Congress unanimously rejected the proferred conditions; and it is morally certain that no terms short of an explicit acknowl- edgment of our independence will ever be accepted.

26

PURSUIT TO MONMOUTH

Angered *by the rejection of their proposals, which they considered very generous, England's leaders now decided to adopt a harsher policy toward the rebellion. But the entry of France into the war made it necessary for them to revise their strategy. In Charles Stedman's words:*

. . . the command of the sea was about to be disputed by the contending parties. Hence, greater circumspection became necessary in the choice of posts for the British army. It was uncertain where the French might attempt to strike a blow; whether upon the continent of America or in the West Indies. It was therefore proper that the army should occupy a station from which reinforcements might be most easily and expeditiously sent wherever they should be required. But of all the stations hitherto occupied . . . Philadelphia was the least adapted to such a purpose. It was distant from the sea . . . and communicated with it only by a winding river.

Philadelphia was also especially vulnerable to naval blockade. Sir Henry Clinton effected the city's evacuation in mid-June of 1778. According to Judge Jones, who learned the details from participants:

The [Loyalist] inhabitants who thought it advisable to leave . . . embarked with their movable property on board [Admiral Howe's] transports. The artillery, stores, baggage and provisions not wanted for the army [on its march] were also embarked. This done, Sir Henry crossed the Delaware with his whole army . . .

Sir Henry Clinton.

and entered New Jersey on his way by land to New York. This being effected, Lord Howe with the men-of-war, armed ships, transports and merchantmen, also left Philadelphia, and sailed for New York. . . . The General proceeded in his march with caution. The number of wagons employed to carry the baggage, stores and provisions were amazing. The wagons only, in the line of march, extended 12 miles in length. The movements were of course slow. The rebels had taken care to break down all the bridges, blow up the causeways and fill up the wells in the route which it was supposed the British army would take. This put them to great difficulties.

The work of disruption was done by Americans in small, fast-moving parties. At the same time, Washington marched in pursuit of the British with the main army. On June 28, General Charles Lee was several miles in the lead with a large body of picked men, having been ordered to attack the enemy's rear. The plan called for Washington to move quickly to his support. Among the men with Lee was Colonel John Laurens, son of the South Carolina statesman, Henry Laurens, and one of Washington's favorite aides:

The situation of the two armies . . . was as follows: Gen. Washington, with the main body of our army, was at 4 miles distance from Englishtown. Gen. Lee . . . was *at* that town. . . . The enemy's rear was preparing to leave Monmouth village . . . 6 miles . . . [beyond Englishtown]. . . . [O]ur advanced corps was marching towards them. The militia of the country kept up a random running fire with the Hessian Jagers. No mischief was done on either side. I was with a small party of horse, reconnoitering the enemy in an open space before Monmouth, when I perceived two parties of the enemy [who had doubled back] advancing by files in the woods on our right and left, with a view, as I imagined, of enveloping our small party or preparing a way for a skirmish of their horse. I immediately wrote an account of what I had seen to [Washington] and expressed my anxiety on account of the languid appearance of the Continental troops under Gen. Lee.

Some person in the meantime reported to Gen. Lee that the enemy were advancing upon us in two columns, and I was informed that he had, in consequence, ordered [General James] Varnum's Brigade, which was in front, to [fall back]. . . . I went myself and assured him of the real state of the case [that the "columns" were merely small parties]. His reply to me was that his accounts had been so contradictory that he was utterly at a loss what part to take. I repeated my account to him in positive distinct terms and returned

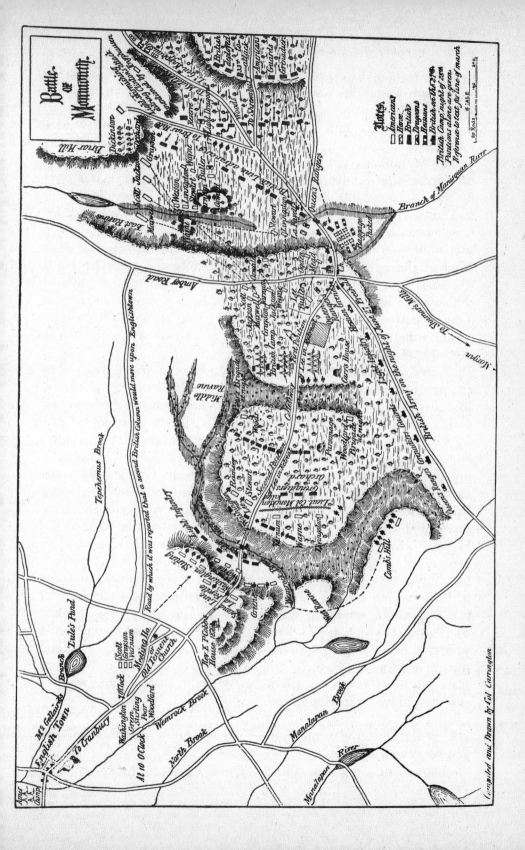

to make farther discoveries. I found that the two parties had been withdrawn from the wood. . . . I wrote a second time to Gen. Washington.

Gen. Lee at length gave orders to advance. The enemy were forming themselves on the Middletown road [beyond and to the left of Monmouth village], with their light infantry in front and cavalry on the left flank, while a scattering, distant fire was commenced between our flanking parties and theirs. I was impatient and uneasy at seeing that no disposition was made [by Lee]. . . . Two pieces of artillery were posted on our right without a single foot soldier to support them. Our men were formed piecemeal in front of the enemy, and there appeared to be no general plan or disposition. . . . The enemy began a cannonade from two parts of their line. Their whole body of horse made a furious charge upon a small party of our cavalry . . . and drove them till the [sight] of our infantry and a judicious discharge or two of artillery made them retire precipitately.

Three regiments of ours that had advanced in a plain open country towards the enemy's left flank were ordered by Gen. Lee to retire and occupy the village of Monmouth. They were no sooner formed there than they were ordered to quit that post and [retire to] the woods. One order succeeded another with a rapidity and indecision calculated to ruin us. The enemy . . . were advancing in full march towards us. Our men were fatigued with the excessive heat. The artillery horses were not in condition to make a brisk retreat. A new position was ordered but not generally communicated, for part of the troops were forming on the right of the ground, while others were marching away, and all the artillery driving off. The enemy, after a short halt, resumed their pursuit. No cannon was left to check their progress. A regiment was ordered to form behind a fence, and as speedily commanded to retire. All this disgraceful retreating passed without the firing of a musket, over ground which might have been disputed inch by inch. We passed a defile and arrived at an eminence beyond. . . . Here, fortunately for the honour of the army and the welfare of America, Gen. Washington met the troops retreating in disorder and without any plan to make an opposition.

One of the men who got a close look at Washington at this time was Joseph Plumb Martin:
I heard him ask our officers "by whose order the troops were

retreating," and being answered, "by General Lee's," he said something, but as he was moving forward all the time . . . he was too far off for me to hear it distinctly. Those that were nearer to him said that his words were "Damn him!" . . . [H]e seemed at the instant to be in a great passion; his looks . . . seemed to indicate as much. After passing us he rode on to the plain field and took an observation of the advancing enemy. He remained there some time upon his old English charger, while the shot from the British artillery were rending up the earth all around him.

John Laurens was greatly relieved to see Washington take firm charge:

He ordered some pieces of artillery to be brought up to defend the pass, and some troops to form and defend the pieces. . . . A few shot . . . and a little skirmishing in the wood checked the enemy's career. The General expressed his astonishment at this unaccountable retreat. Mr. Lee indecently replied that the attack was contrary to his advice and opinion in council.

Some witnesses say that Washington reacted to Lee's words with a controlled reprimand. Others say he lost his temper, which seems more likely. Virginia's General Charles Scott, who considered himself a connoisseur of profanity, says that "he swore . . . till the leaves shook on the trees—charming, delightful!" Laurens resumes:

We were obliged to retire to a position which, though hastily reconnoitered, proved an excellent one. Two regiments were formed behind a fence in front of the position. The enemy's horse advanced in full charge with admirable bravery to the distance of forty paces, when a general discharge from these two regiments did great execution among them and made them fly with the greatest precipitation. The [British] grenadiers succeeded to the attack. At this time my horse was killed under me. In this spot the action was hottest, and there was considerable slaughter of British grenadiers. The General ordered [General William] Woodford's Brigade with some artillery to take possession of an eminence on the enemy's left, and cannonade from thence. This produced an excellent effect. The enemy were prevented from advancing on us, and confined themselves to cannonade, with a show of turning our left flank. Our artillery answered theirs with the greatest vigour.

During these moments Joseph Plumb Martin got a glimpse of Mary

Ludwig Hays, the woman who was to go down in history as "Molly Pitcher" because, on this scorching day, she carried pitcher after pitcher of cool water for the artillerymen and the wounded. Martin noted that she also helped to serve one of the cannon:

While in the act of reaching a cartridge and having one of her feet as far before the other as she could step, a cannon shot from the enemy passed directly between her legs without doing any other damage than carrying away all the lower part of her petticoat. Looking at it with apparent unconcern, she observed that it was lucky it did not pass a little higher, for in that case it might have carried away something else, and continued her occupation.

Laurens goes on:

The cannonade was incessant, and the General ordered parties to advance from time to time and engage the British grenadiers and guards. The horse shewed themselves no more. The grenadiers showed their backs and retreated everywhere with precipitation. They returned, however, again to the charge, and were again repulsed.

Among the grenadiers slain during this fighting was the popular Colonel Henry Monckton. Charles Stedman says that the colonel "had been selected for the hazardous duty to which he was this day appointed on account of the cool intrepidity of his character" and that his fall was "greatly and deservedly lamented." Laurens tells how the battle ended:

They finally retreated and got over the strong pass where . . . Gen. Washington first rallied the troops. We advanced in force and continued masters of the ground. The standards of liberty were planted in triumph on the field of battle. We remained looking at each other, with the defile between us, till dark. . . .

A French volunteer, the Chevalier de Pontgibaud, adds:

We slept on the field of battle amongst the dead, whom we had no time to bury. The day had been so hot, in both senses, that everyone had need of rest. The British army retreated, about midnight, in silence, and we entered the village at six o'clock in the morning. The enemy had left behind some of his baggage; and . . . his wounded . . . were to be found in every house and in the church. Every possible care was taken of them.

Though the Americans claimed a victory, the Battle of Monmouth gained them little but plaudits for valor. The British, not seriously hurt, continued on their way to New York. Washington started his own troops, in easy stages under a punishing sun, northward through New Jersey for a crossing of the Hudson River to White Plains.

"General Lee, I think," wrote John Laurens, "must be tried for misconduct." Lee insisted that his retreat had saved his corps—and even Sir Henry Clinton felt that Lee had been wise to fall back upon the main army. But Lee was charged with "disobedience of orders . . . of misbehavior before the enemy . . . and of disrespect to the commander-in-chief. . . ." A general court-martial found him guilty, and he was sentenced to suspension from command for a year. Thus was ruined the "odd genius" who at first had the confidence of all America but whose service was marred by periods of inexplicable conduct and an unremitting jealousy of Washington, whom he considered an amateur soldier. Lee would never return to duty.

27

THE FRENCH ARRIVE

Eᴀʀʟʏ *in July, 1778, a powerful French squadron commanded by Charles Hector, Count d'Estaing, appeared off the coast of Virginia. America's Patriots were elated, while the Loyalists were dismayed. Judge Jones, of course, viewed this development bitterly:*

In this fleet the King of France sent a plenipotentiary to the rebel Congress. . . . He also wrote a letter to his new friends and allies, and the letter is directed thus: "To our very dear, great friends the President and Members of the General Congress of North America." Thus did the grand monarch ally himself with, countenance and flatter a set of the most ungrateful rebels the world has ever produced.

About the middle of July D'Estaing arrived upon the coast of New York and anchored off Sandy Hook. Had he been a month sooner, or had he fallen in with the latter coast on his arrival, instead of that of Virginia, the consequence to the British fleet and army, then returning from Philadelphia to New York, must have been dreadful. But making Virginia at first and sailing slowly on to the northward before he arrived off the Hook, the whole fleet of transports had entered the harbour of New York. The British fleet under Lord Howe was moored within the Hook, and the army under General Clinton were . . . . quartered upon Staten Island, York Island and Long Island. This was not completed more than 12 days before D'Estaing's arrival off the Hook.

An attack upon New York was now expected. The French fleet was greatly superior to the English. . . . D'Estaing captured every vessel that was bound to New York. Lord Howe was in possession of the Hook and took every necessary step to repel the enemy should an entrance be attempted. Batteries, redoubts and other fortifications were erected on the shore and garrisoned by skilful artillerymen. The ships were put into a proper and most judicious position. They were well-manned by experienced sailors, a number of them volunteers from the transports in New York. The whole body of the light infantry and all the grenadiers belonging to the British army were, at their own request, permitted to serve on board the British fleet. These were headed by some of the first blood in England. . . .

Towards the end of July, D'Estaing's fleet weighed anchor, and, as everybody then supposed, with an intention to attack Lord Howe, and, if successful, then New York—the capture of which would have terminated the American war. . . . D'Estaing, however, instead of attempting the Hook, stood out to sea and was soon out of sight. Soon after this, Lord Howe was joined by . . . [four ships from overseas]. They all arrived singly, and had D'Estaing continued off Sandy Hook, each must have been taken. Lord Howe was now superior in number of ships to the French; the latter, however, superior in weight of metal and largeness of ships. Each fleet was equally well manned.

The French having failed in the grand object of their expedition, "the reduction of New York, the destruction of the navy there, and the capture of the British army," an attack upon [Newport] Rhode Island became the favourite plan.

In the words of one of the American army's French volunteers, the Chevalier de Pontgibaud:

A combined attack was to be made. The French fleet was to blockade [the island that held] Newport . . . whilst a part of the [American] army, under the command of General Sullivan and [including] the division of the Marquis de Lafayette, was to besiege [Newport] by land. We effected our landing on this beautiful island [at its northern end] in the most orderly manner . . . under the protection of . . . Comte d'Estaing. Hardly had the troops disembarked before the [American] militia . . . horse and foot arrived [led by General John Hancock]. I have never seen a more laughable spectacle. All the tailors and apothecaries in the country

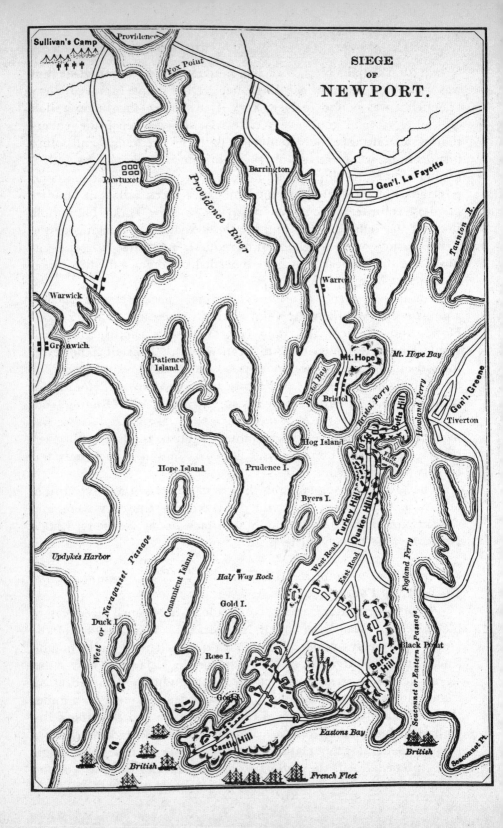

must have been called out, I should think. One could recognize them by their round wigs. They were mounted on bad nags and looked like a flock of ducks in cross-belts. The infantry was no better than the cavalry, and appeared to be cut after the same pattern. I guessed that these warriors were more anxious to eat up our supplies than to make a close acquaintance with the enemy. . . .

While Sullivan and D'Estaing were maturing their attack plans, Lord Howe's fleet hove in sight. Pontgibaud goes on:

Comte d'Estaing at once gave orders to sail. There was little wind, but what there was was favourable. Our fleet defiled majestically in front of the enemy's earthworks [in the south, where Newport was located]. Each vessel as she passed gave a broadside of half her guns . . . to which the forts replied. . . . Our fleet gave chase to the British [vessels], who made all sail. Both fleets were soon lost to sight. We awaited the news of a victory, but our fleet was dispersed by a terrible storm, and the Admiral's vessel, the *Languedoc*, dismasted by the gale, was very nearly captured by the enemy. The *Caesar* . . . [while] separated from the rest of the squadron, had a very severe engagement with some of the enemy's vessels. The captain lost his right arm but managed to save his ship. . . .

The siege [which, following a march southward, had been launched against Newport] still went on; but when M. d'Estaing reappeared before Newport he told us he must withdraw the three frigates he had left to protect us, and we must raise the siege. D'Estaing took all the fleet to Boston for repairs. General Sullivan, angry at finding himself no longer supported by the French fleet, went so far as to insult our nation and call the French traitors. Our two generals [Sullivan and Lafayette] were almost on the point of fighting a duel.

Judge Jones, who was finding the news from the trouble zone of great interest, soon learned the following:

The leaving of Rhode Island was lucky for the Count. Lord Howe had [again] sailed for Rhode Island, his fleet in complete repair; and a continuance of two days longer would, in all probability, have been fatal to the French fleet. His Lordship, getting intelligence that D'Estaing had left Rhode Island . . . pushed for Boston Bay, hoping to arrive there before the French. But when he entered the bay he found the Comte at anchor in Nantasket roads and in such a situation as rendered an attack upon his fleet impracticable. He therefore left the bay, returned to New York, delivered the fleet up to Admiral [James] Gambier, and sailed for England. Here ended His Lordship's command in America. Sullivan, upon D'Estaing leaving Rhode Island . . . took the necessary steps to raise the siege and secure his retreat.

On August 29, according to a British newspaper printed at Newport:
 . . . it being discovered that the rebels had dismantled their redoubts opposite to our lines, Sir Robert Pigot gave orders for the grenadiers and light infantry, with the Hessian chasseurs, to advance; which they did with their usual alacrity, being supported by the 22d, 43d, Brown's and Fanning's regiments, with the regiment De Huyne and two regiments of Anspach. It was discovered as they advanced that the rebels had been for several days removing their stores and heavy cannon to the north end of the island. The troops met with little opposition till they had advanced some miles, when they were fired upon behind stone walls by large parties of the rebels posted to annoy them. But these obstacles were soon removed by the ardor of the troops, who rushed on with such impetuosity that the rebels were soon obliged to betake themselves to their last post. . . .

An artillery duel followed, after which the British again pressed forward. As reported in the New York Journal, *a Patriot publication:*
They were twice driven back in much confusion, when a third effort was made with greater numbers. General Sullivan now ordered the right to be reinforced, and a sharp conflict of near an hour succeeded, in which the artillery of both armies played briskly from the hills. The enemy were at length routed, and fled in great confusion to a hill where they had cannon and works to cover them, leaving their dead and wounded on the field. We took about sixty prisoners. . . . Immediately after the repulse of the enemy on the right, they appeared advancing on the left, in consequence of which [General John] Glover's Brigade and General [John] Tyler's Militia, supported by Titcomb's Brigade, were ordered to advance and form in a crossroad within half a mile of the enemy. They accordingly took post, and a cannonade, with skirmishing, ensued and continued till dark.

Total losses on each side came to between two and three hundred men. The next day's action was limited to artillery exchanges and a

*few skirmishes; and when night came Sullivan slipped his army, with
all of its equipage, across to the mainland. Judge Jones concedes
that Sullivan's retreat gained him honor:*

The British allow it was well conducted, admirable, and scarcely
to be equalled by the most experienced military character. This
retreat was . . . made in good time, for scarcely had Sullivan got
footing on the main than General Clinton arrived from New York
[by sea] with such a body of troops as would most effectually have
prevented his leaving the island. . . . In a word, Sullivan was born
under a lucky planet. General Clinton, finding nothing to be done,
returned to New York, but dispatched General [Sir Charles] Grey
with about 4,000 men, under the convoy of some frigates, to the
eastward to exterminate the nests of some rebel privateers which
abounded in the harbours, rivers and creeks about Buzzard's Bay
in the old colony of Plymouth. This business was effectually performed. At Fairhaven [and nearby places] 70 sail of shipping were
destroyed, with small craft in abundance. The magazines, wharfs,
stores, warehouses, rope-walks and vessels on the stocks were all
burnt. . . .

From Fairhaven the General proceeded to Martha's Vineyard,
the Elizabeth Isles, Nantucket and Block Island, and disarmed the
inhabitants (who had never interfered in the contest), laid them
under contribution, plundered their houses and brought with them
to New York . . . sheep . . . fat cattle . . . hogs and . . . horses [in large
numbers]. . . . The sheep, cattle and hogs were, at New York,
delivered to the commissaries, killed and distributed in rations to
the army; and though they cost the commissary nothing . . . yet
he had the conscience to charge the Crown 2 shillings sterling for
every pound. He besides sold the heads, skins and hides, and put
the money into his own pocket. The horses were delivered to the
quarter-master, and the Crown [was] charged £20 sterling for
each. No wonder that commissaries, barrack-masters and quarter-
masters [amassed] such amazing estates. . . .

*The touchy situation that had developed between the Americans
and their French allies is analyzed by England's Charles Stedman:*

The total failure of the expedition against Rhode Island occasioned great murmuring throughout the American continent,
particularly amongst the inhabitants of the northern states, who
were most interested and had in a more especial manner exerted
themselves to promote its success. In these states the clamours of

the people were loud against the Count d'Estaing for deserting them in the midst of an expedition which he knew was undertaken only in consequence of his promise of co-operation.

These murmurings the governing powers prudently endeavoured to suppress, that they might not give offence to their new allies. But they were nevertheless, in part, the cause of a dangerous riot that happened at Boston between the American and French seamen, in which several of the latter were severely wounded [one fatally]. Nearly about the same time, too, a similar riot happened at Charleston in South Carolina between the same classes of people, but more fatal in the effects, as some lives on both sides were lost.

Indeed, the manners of the people were yet so little assimilated that a cordial agreement could scarcely be expected. At both those places, however, means were fallen upon to appease the tumults, and great pains were taken to give satisfaction to the French, whom, at this early stage of the connexion, it would have been highly imprudent to disgust.

A Boston social note dated October 29 reveals one of the methods used to placate the ruffled Frenchmen:

This evening a superb ball was given at the Concert Hall in Boston by General Hancock, at which were present His Excellency Count d'Estaing and a number of officers belonging to the French fleet. There were upwards of a hundred of the principal ladies of the town present, who, being richly and elegantly dressed, added a most enchanting brilliancy to the evening and . . . gave no bad specimen of American female grace and beauty.

A few days later, D'Estaing headed his fleet toward the West Indies to join the French forces that were threatening England's interests there. At the same time, Sir Henry Clinton sent a squadron and five thousand men from New York to help meet the threat. Thus the first solid benefit America derived from France's entry into the war (other than an increase in supplies) was that it drew a substantial number of the enemy from American shores.

28

TOMAHAWKS ON THE FRONTIER

Nearly the whole time since Lexington and Concord, while the rival armies maneuvered and clashed in the Atlantic coastal corridor, another kind of strife convulsed the frontier that stretched in a great westerly arc from the back country of Maine to the border of West Florida. Many of the Indians of these vast forest lands were naturally hostile toward the intruding American pioneers; and England, with forts in the wilds below the Great Lakes, and having access to the west also from stations in East Florida, quickly took advantage of this antagonism after the eruption on the coast. Small parties of redcoats and Tories circulated among the Indians, offering gifts and professing friendship, and urged them to go on the warpath. A long series of cruel and deadly encounters had resulted; and the combat was to continue in much the same way to the war's end.

Frontiersman Daniel Boone had already established a reputation for himself in Kentucky by mid-1778. And soon a young Virginian named George Rogers Clark was to win great glory for his exploits, with a small number of followers, against the redcoats, Tories, and Indians of the Old Northwest, between the Ohio River and the Great Lakes. But, by and large, the wilderness campaigns—the long marches, the sieges and skirmishes at the log forts, the raids and counter-raids among the white and Indian settlements, the massacres and the other incidents that made up this part of the Revolution— had little effect on the war's outcome. They did, however, in-

fluence (to America's advantage) the western boundaries set by the peace treaty of 1783. And they added profusely to America's pioneer lore.

Much of the time, the war in the west seemed remote to the Americans in the Atlantic settlements; but on occasion it came uncomfortably close to them. In the summer of 1778 a large band of Indians, accompanied by a number of redcoats and Tories, made a raid at Wilkes-Barre, Pennsylvania. As reported in the New York Journal *on July 20:*

During the past week many of the distressed refugees from the Wyoming settlement on the Susquehanna who escaped the general massacre of the inhabitants have passed through Poughkeepsie, in New York. From them we have collected the following account. . . . Previous to the narrative, it may be necessary to inform some of our readers that this settlement was made by the people of Connecticut on a grant of lands purchased . . . of the Indian proprietors; and that these lands, falling within the limits of the Pennsylvania claim, a dispute . . . [arose] between the two governments and proceeded to frequent acts of hostility. When it was at a height that threatened the disturbance of the other governments, Congress interposed . . . and . . . the decision of the dispute was suspended till that with Great Britain . . . was concluded. . . . On this footing the dispute has lain dormant for two or three years.

The inhabitants lived happily and the settlement increased, consisting of eight townships . . . Lackawanna, Exeter, Kingston, Wilkes-Barre, Plymouth, Nanticoke, Huntington and Salem, each containing five square miles. . . . The lands are exceeding good, beautifully situated along both sides of the Susquehanna . . . and produced immense quantities of grain of all sorts, roots, fruits, hemp, flax, etc., and stock of all kinds in abundance. The settlement had lately supplied the Continental Army with three thousand bushels of grain, and the ground was loaded with the most promising crops of every kind. The settlement included upwards of a thousand families, which had furnished our army with a thousand soldiers besides the garrisons of four forts in the townships of Lackawanna, Exeter, Kingston and Wilkes-Barre. One of these forts was garrisoned by upwards of four hundred soldiers, chiefly of the militia, the principal officers in which were Colonels [Nathan] Dennison and Zebulon Butler.

The Tories and Indians had given some disturbance to these settlements last year before General Herkimer's battle . . .

near Fort Stanwix; and our skirmishes soon after with parties of the enemy at and near Schoharie [west of Albany] . . . dispersed [them]; and the Tories concealed themselves among our different settlements. The people here remained undisturbed during the rest of the year. About this time, the inhabitants having discovered that many of these villainous Tories who had stirred up the Indians and been with them in fighting against us were within the settlements, twenty-seven of them were, in January last, taken up and secured. Of these, eighteen were sent to Connecticut; the rest, after being detained some time and examined were, for want of sufficient evidence, set at liberty. They immediately joined the enemy and became active in raising in the Indians a spirit of hostility against us. This disposition soon after began to appear in the behavior of the Tories and Indians, which gave the people apprehensions of danger and occasioned some preparations for defence.

The people had frequent intimations that the Indians had some mischievous design against them, but their fears were somewhat abated by the seeming solicitude of the Indians to preserve peace. They sent down at different times several parties with declarations of their peaceable disposition toward us, and to request the like on our part towards them. They were always dismissed with assurances that there was no design to disturb them. But one of these Indians getting drunk, said he and the other messengers were only sent to amuse the people in the settlement, but that the Indians intended, as soon as they were in order, to attack them. On this the Indian men were confined, and the women sent back [under] a flag [of truce].

In March, appearances became more alarming, and the scattered families settled for thirty miles up the river were collected and brought into the more populous parts. In April and May, strolling parties of Indians and Tories . . . made frequent incursions into the settlement, robbing and plundering the inhabitants of provision, grain and livestock. In June, several persons . . . at work on a farm . . . were attacked, and one man of them killed. Soon after, a woman . . . was killed, with her five children, by a party of these Tories and Indians, who plundered the house of everything they could take away, and destroyed the rest.

On the first instant (July) the whole body of the enemy . . . (about three hundred of whom were thought to be Indians . . . the rest Tories painted like them, except their officers, who were dressed like regulars), the whole under the command of Colonel

John Butler (a Connecticut Tory . . .), came down [the west bank of the Susquehanna] near the upper fort [at Exeter], but concealed the greatest part of their number. Here they had a skirmish with the inhabitants, who took and killed two Indians, and lost ten of their own men, three of whom they afterwards found killed, scalped and mangled in the most inhuman manner.

Thursday, July 2: The enemy appeared on the mountains back of Kingston, when the women and children then fled into the fort [Forty Fort, on the river's west bank, across from Wilkes-Barre]. Most of the garrison of Exeter Fort were Tories who treacherously gave it up to the enemy. The same night . . . they took Lackawanna Fort. . . . A small number only escaped.

Friday, July 3: This morning Colonel Zebulon Butler [of the Patriot forces], leaving a small number to guard the fort (Wilkes-Barre), crossed the river with about four hundred men and marched into [Forty Fort]. The enemy sent in a flag, demanding a surrender of the fort in two hours. Colonel Butler answered he should not surrender. . . . They sent in a second flag, demanding an immediate surrender, otherwise that the fort should be stormed, plundered and burnt. . . .

Zebulon Butler, even though his force consisted mainly of elderly men and boys (most of the area's ablest men being with Washington's army), now decided to leave the fort and march toward the concealed besiegers. One of the hidden men was later to write (as quoted by Commager and Morris) that the party came on shouting, "Come out, ye villainous Tories! Come out, if ye dare, and show your heads, if ye durst, to the brave Continental Sons of Liberty!" The newspaper account goes on to say that the Patriot leader was tricked into marching his force into an ambush:

He and his men bravely stood and returned the fire for three-quarters of an hour with such briskness and resolution that the enemy began to give way . . . when one of . . . [the] men, either through treachery or cowardice, cried out that the Colonel ordered a retreat. This caused a cessation of their fire, threw them into confusion, and a total rout ensued. The greatest part fled to the river, which they endeavored to pass to Fort Wilkes-Barre. The enemy pursued them with the fury of devils. Many were lost or killed in the river, and no more than about seventy, some of whom were wounded, escaped. . . .

This victory gained the Indians numerous prisoners whom they spent the early part of the night torturing to death. In the morning about two hundred bloody scalps were held up for the view of the people in Forty Fort. But John Butler, the enemy leader, offered humane terms if Forty Fort and Wilkes-Barre were surrendered. Both garrisons accepted the offer. But now, with the raiders still in a wild mood, a systematic destruction of property was begun. First the two forts were burned. Then, says the Journal:

. . . they proceeded to the destruction of every building and improvement (except what belonged to some Tories) that came within their reach [throughout] all these flourishing settlements, which they have rendered a scene of desolation and horror almost beyond description, parallel or credibility; and were not the facts attested by numbers of the unhappy sufferers from different quarters of the settlement, and unconnected with each other, it would be impossible to believe that human nature could be capable of such prodigious enormity. When these miscreants had destroyed the other improvements, they proceeded to destroy the crops . . . letting in the cattle and horses to the corn, and cutting up as much as they could of what was left. Great numbers of the cattle they shot and destroyed. . . .

It is reported that these wretches, after completing their horrid business at Wyoming, are going . . . to Cherry Valley [New York] and the parts adjacent.

This report proved to be correct. According to a New Jersey Gazette *item dated November 11:*

This day a party of Tories, Indians and regulars . . . made a descent on the fort at Cherry Valley. An officer who was in the fort gives the following account of the affair:

. . . The enemy . . . surrounded the fort, excluding several officers who were quartered out of the garrison and had gone to dinner. They commenced a very heavy fire upon the fort, which [lasted] three and a half hours and was as briskly returned. They were so near as to call to the fort and bid the "damned rebels" to surrender, which was answered with three cheers and a discharge of cannon and musketry. At four p.m. the enemy withdrew. Captain Ballard sallied out with a party, which the enemy endeavored to cut off, but were prevented by a reinforcement.

The next day they made it their whole business to collect

horses, cattle and sheep, which they effected, and at sunset left the place. The enemy killed, scalped and most barbarously murdered thirty-two inhabitants, chiefly women and children; also Colonel Alden and . . . [ten] soldiers of his regiment. . . . [Five] officers were taken prisoners . . . [as were] thirteen privates. [They] burnt twenty-four houses with all the grain, etc.; took above sixty inhabitants prisoners, part of whom they released on going off. They committed the most inhuman barbarities on most of the dead. Robert Henderson's head was cut off; his skull bone was cut out with the scalp. Mr. Willis' sister was ripped up; a child of Mr. Willis', two months old, scalped and arm cut off; the clergyman's wife's leg and arm cut off, and many others as cruelly treated.

Many of the inhabitants and soldiers shut out from the fort lay all night in the rain with the children, who suffered very much. The cattle that were not easy to drive they shot. We were informed by the prisoners they sent back that . . . all the officers and continental soldiers [whom they took along] were stripped and drove naked before them.

The fort was commanded by the brave Major Whiting, of Dedham in Massachusetts, and the two cannon under the direction of the brave Captain Hickling of Boston, who was chief engineer in building the fort, and whose assistance contributed in saving it.

Greatly alarmed by the Wyoming and Cherry Valley massacres, the people of the Pennsylvania and New York borderlands clamored for an expedition against the Indians by Washington's troops. The general agreed that such an expedition was necessary, but it would be six months before one could be launched.

29

NEW TROUBLE FOR THE SOUTH

*I*n the *autumn of 1778, after the failure of the Rhode Island operation, Washington deployed the major part of his army in a great semicircle about New York City. The lines extended from western Connecticut, through the West Point area of New York, and down through northern New Jersey. Sir Henry Clinton made no significant response. He had other plans. Since all of England's efforts in the North had failed to crush the rebellion, she had decided to make another attempt in the lightly defended South. If Georgia and the Carolinas and Virginia could be subdued, the war planners believed, the surrender of the North would have to follow.*

Clinton's first move was to order the assembling of a special squadron at New York. The command of its landing force (about thirty-five hundred men) was given to Colonel Archibald Campbell. Charles Stedman, who learned what ensued from British reports, says in his History:

The squadron . . . arrived off the island of Tybee, at the mouth of the Savannah River, on the twenty-third of December. It seems evident that the people of South Carolina and Georgia, apprehending themselves secure against an invasion ever since the unfortunate attempt upon Charleston made by Sir Peter Parker and Sir Henry Clinton in the year 1776, were rather occupied in planning and making preparations for the conquest of [British-owned] East Florida than in providing for their own defence. Between the inhabitants of East Florida and those of Georgia a kind of predatory war had been carried on. . . .

Savannah, the capital of Georgia, lies on the south side of the river of that name, about fifteen miles from the sea. In the vicinity of this place, Major General Robert Howe, with a force consisting of some regiments of American regular troops and the militia of the province, in the whole about fifteen hundred men, was encamped for its protection. . . . The country between Savannah and the sea being low and marshy and intersected by creeks and cuts of water, the first practicable landing place was at the plantation of one Gerridoe, about twelve miles up the river; and there a descent was proposed to be made without delay. In pursuance of this determination, the fleet, on the twenty-eighth of December, in the morning, proceeded up the river . . . with the design of landing the troops at Gerridoe's plantation that evening; but several of the transports having got aground from the difficulty of the navigation, the descent was necessarily postponed till the following morning. With the rising of the tide, the transports being floated off, moved up to their station; and at daybreak of the twenty-ninth the debarkation began.

Colonel Archibald Campbell describes the landing:

The light infantry, under Captain Cameron, having first reached the shore, were formed and led briskly forward to the bluff, where a body of fifty rebels were posted, and from whom they received a smart fire of musketry. But the Highlanders, rushing on with their usual impetuosity, gave them no time to repeat it. They drove them instantly to the woods and happily secured a landing for the rest of the army. Captain Cameron, a spirited and most valuable officer, with two Highlanders, were killed on this occasion, and five Highlanders wounded.

Colonel Campbell, upon reconnoitering, discovered that General Robert Howe's troops were drawn up in battle formation about a half mile east of Savannah. Campbell also learned, from a Negro he met, of a concealed path that circled to the American rear. While a part of his force was deployed along Howe's front, a strong detachment was sent quietly around in back. Caught between two fires, Savannah's defenders were quickly shattered. Campbell states with pride:

Thirty-eight officers . . . and four hundred and fifteen noncommissioned officers and privates, one stand of colors, forty-eight pieces of cannon, twenty-three mortars, ninety-four barrels of powder, the fort with all its stores . . . and, in short, the capital of Georgia, the shipping in the harbor, with a large quantity of provisions, fell into our possession before it was dark, without any other loss on our side than that of Captain Peter Campbell, a gallant officer of Skinner's light infantry, and two privates killed, one sergeant and nine privates wounded. Eighty-three of the enemy were found dead on the common, and eleven wounded. By the accounts received from their prisoners, thirty lost their lives in the swamp, endeavoring to make their escape.

This news astonished Patriots throughout America. In the words of Henry "Light-Horse Harry" Lee (father of the more famous Robert E. Lee): "Never was a victory of such magnitude so completely gained with so little loss. . . ."

By this time, General Augustine Prevost, commander of the British forces in East Florida, was on his way northward to cooperate in Georgia's reduction. After taking Sunbury, some miles below Savannah, the general joined Campbell. The time was mid-January, 1779. Prevost assumed command of the combined forces, established his headquarters at Savannah, and sent Campbell up the Savannah River to take Augusta. This was accomplished with little trouble. Georgia's Patriot forces were now dispersed, and the state was wholly in British hands.

The Savannah River was the border between Georgia and her northeastern neighbor, South Carolina. With British troops posted along a great stretch of the river, South Carolina's citizens were thoroughly alarmed. One of these citizens was Eliza Wilkinson, a young widow who lived on her father's plantation in the coastal country southwest of Charleston:

. . . I heard they had got possession of the Georgia State and used the inhabitants cruelly, paying no respect to age or sex. But then again I heard to the contrary, that their behavior to the ladies was unexceptionable. I did not know what to think, much less what to do, should they invade our state, which was daily expected. Thousands would I have given to have been in any part of the globe where I might not see them, or to have been secure from the impending evils which were ready to burst over our heads. I was in Charleston when we heard that a large party of them had landed somewhere near Beaufort [on Port Royal Island, about fifty miles down the coast from Charleston]. I saw several detachments of our southern troops leave town to oppose the invaders of their country. They marched with the greatest alacrity imaginable, not regarding the weather, though the rain poured down incessantly upon them. I cannot describe my feelings upon the sight—gratitude, affection and pity for my countrymen filled my heart and my eyes, which pursued them until out of sight. . . .

The attack on the British detachment at Beaufort, made on February 3, was led by General William Moultrie, victor over Sir Peter Parker and Sir Henry Clinton in 1776. Moultrie relates:

This action was reversed from the usual way of fighting between the British and Americans, they taking to the bushes and we remaining upon the open ground. After some little time, finding our men too much exposed to the enemy's fire, I ordered them to take trees. About three quarters of an hour after the action began, I heard a general cry through the line of "no more cartridges" and was also informed . . . that the ammunition for the field-pieces was almost expended. . . . Upon this I ordered the field-pieces to be drawn off very slowly, and [the] right and left wings to keep pace with the artillery to cover their flanks, which was done in tolerable order for undisciplined troops. The enemy had beat their retreat before we began to move, but we had little or no ammunition and could not . . . pursue. They retreated so hastily as to leave an officer, one sergeant and three privates wounded, in a house near the action, and their dead lying on the field.

"It was not long," writes Eliza Wilkinson, "before our little band of patriots returned to their homes in triumph, excepting a few, who had sealed the cause with their blood." Soon afterward, Colonel Andrew Pickens of South Carolina defeated a band of Tories at Kettle Creek, Georgia (northwest of Augusta). The British now decided that they had extended their lines too far, and the garrison at Augusta was withdrawn, in easy marches, down the river. A large party of Americans under General John Ashe crossed the river at Augusta and pressed after. The result was the Battle of Briar Creek (March 3). For a second time the redcoats made use of a stealthy encircling maneuver, and again the maneuver proved disastrous to their opponents. According to an account by an unnamed British participant:

The enemy began a scattering fire of musketry and fired some

cannon, but . . . could not stand the spirited attack of Sir James
Baird's light infantry . . . and from that instant the success of the
day was decided. They were pursued to the creek, into which, after
throwing away their arms, the most active plunged and escaped
by swimming. Their right had no means of escaping but over a
lagoon very deep and broad, and then to cross the River Savannah.
In that place numbers . . . drowned and perished. Many were killed
in the pursuit, and about one hundred taken prisoners. . . . [S]even
pieces of cannon, several stand of colors, their baggage, arms,
ammunition, and everything, in short, fell into the hands of the
brave, victorious troops. Not a whole platoon of the rebel army escaped together, on our right or left. The panic occasioned by the
terror of the bayonet left them no alternative but that of plunging
into the water, many of which, we are since informed, have been
[seen] without any other clothes but a shirt and breeches, and
without arms, numbers of them badly wounded. Few would have
escaped if night had not come on so soon. The loss on our side was
one officer wounded, five privates killed and ten wounded. . . .

The British supreme commander, General Prevost, reacted to Amer-
ican moves against Georgia by making a demonstration up along the
coast toward Charleston. For a number of weeks the area between
the Savannah River and the Charleston coast held scattered units of
both armies, and the civilian population was kept constantly alarmed.
Eliza Wilkinson fled her father's house to lodge with a sister at a
plantation believed to be less exposed to danger. But the place was
soon encompassed by military traffic. Eliza's trials reached a climax
on June 3:

In the morning, fifteen or sixteen horsemen rode up to the
house. We were greatly terrified, thinking them the enemy, but . . .
were agreeably deceived and found them friends. They sat a while
on their horses, talking to us, and then rode off, except two, who
tarried a minute or two longer and then followed the rest, who had
nearly reached the gate. One of the said two [chose to] jump a ditch
—to show his activity, I suppose. . . . [H]e might as well, and
better, have gone in the road. . . . [H]e got a sad fall. We . . . sent a
boy to tell him, if he was hurt, to come up to the house. . . . He and
his companion accordingly came up [and entered]. He looked very
pale, and bled much. His gun, somehow in the fall, had given him
a bad wound behind the ear, from whence the blood flowed down
his neck and bosom plentifully. We were greatly alarmed . . . and

had gathered around him, some with one thing, some with another, in order to give him assistance.

We were very busy examining the wound when a Negro girl ran in, exclaiming, "O! The king's people are coming! It must be them, for they are all in red!" Upon this cry, the two men . . . snatched up their guns, [ran out and] mounted their horses and made off, but had not got many yards from the house before the enemy discharged a pistol at them. Terrified almost to death as I was, I was still anxious for my friends' safety. I tremblingly flew to the window. . . . [S]eeing them both safe, "Thank heaven," said I, "they've got off without hurt!" I'd hardly uttered this when I heard the horses of the inhuman Britons coming in such a furious manner that they seemed to tear up the earth, and the riders at the same time bellowing out the most horrid curses imaginable—oaths and imprecations which chilled my whole frame. . . . But I'd no time for thought. They were up to the house—entered with drawn swords and pistols in their hands. Indeed, they rushed in . . . crying out, "Where're these women rebels?"

. . . The moment they espied us, off went our caps. . . . And for what. . . ? Why, only to get a paltry stone and wax pin which kept them on our heads, at the same time uttering the most abusive language imaginable and making as if they'd hew us to pieces with their swords. But it's not in my power to describe the scene. It was terrible to the last degree. . . . They then began to plunder the house of everything they thought valuable or worth taking. Our trunks were split to pieces, and each mean, pitiful wretch crammed his bosom with the contents, which were our apparel, etc., etc., etc. I ventured to speak to the inhuman monster who had my clothes. I represented to him the times were such we could not replace what they'd taken from us, and begged him to spare me only a suit or two. But I got nothing but a hearty curse for my pains. Nay, so far was his callous heart from relenting that, casting his eyes towards my shoes, "I want them buckles," said he, and immediately knelt at my feet to take them out. . . . [W]hile he was busy . . . a brother villain, whose enormous mouth extended from ear to ear, bawled out, "Shares there, I say! Shares!" So they divided my buckles between them.

The other wretches were employed in the same manner. They took my sister's ear-rings from her ears; hers, and Miss Samuells' buckles. They demanded her ring from her finger. She pleaded for it, told them it was her wedding ring . . . but they still demanded it, and, presenting a pistol at her, swore if she did not deliver it immediately, they'd fire. She gave it to them. And, after bundling up all their booty, they [left the house and] mounted their horses. But such despicable figures! Each wretch's bosom stuffed so full, they appeared to be all afflicted with some dropsical disorder. . . . They took care to tell us, when they were going away, that they had favored us a great deal—that we might thank our stars it was no worse. . . . After they were gone, I began to be sensible of the danger I'd been in, and the thoughts of the vile men seemed worse (if possible) than their presence. . . . I trembled so with terror that I could not support myself. I went into the room, threw myself on the bed, and gave way to a violent burst of grief. . . .

A few days later Eliza and her sister were summoned home by their father. But soon the approach of a party of the enemy sent them flying back to the house they'd left. This time their parents were with them. By mid-June the family could at last feel more secure, for the area was dominated by American troops commanded by Benjamin Lincoln, the Continental general in charge of southern operations. Eliza writes that one day a party of officers rode up to the house:

Mother was at the door. She turned to us, "O, girls, General Lincoln!" We flew to the door, joy in our countenances, for we had heard such a character of the General that we wanted to see him much. When he quitted his horse, and I saw him limp along, I can't describe my feelings. The thought that his limping was occasioned by defending his country [at Saratoga] from the invasion of a cruel and unjust enemy, created in me the utmost veneration and tender concern for him. . . . I think he has something exceeding grave, and even solemn, in his aspect; not forbiddingly so, neither; but a something in his countenance that commands respect. . . . He did not stay above an hour or two with us, and then proceeded on to camp.

Lincoln was about to make an attack. The British force under General Prevost that had been threatening Charleston had withdrawn down along the coast about ten miles to John's Island, posting a rear guard at Stono Ferry. Lincoln moved against the rear guard on the morning of June 20. Says Eliza:

While we were at breakfast, we heard cannon towards Stono Ferry roaring in a horrid manner. We immediately quit the table and ran out of doors. . . . With clasped hands I invoked heaven to protect, to shield my friends and countrymen, and was in the greatest anxiety for the event.

The British, according to one of Lincoln's officers, were found well prepared to receive the attack:

They were advantageously posted and covered by three strong redoubts and a well-constructed abatis supported by several pieces of artillery. The picket having been driven in, the attack began on the right, which was instantly continued through the line. A large body of Highlanders sallied out on the left of the Americans but were soon driven into their redoubts with considerable slaughter.

But this was only a temporary gain. Another American account tells of the battle's outcome:

The enemy's works being found much stronger than was expected, the American field-pieces making no impression on them, and intelligence being . . . received that the enemy had drawn in a reinforcement . . . from John's Island, General Lincoln gave orders for retreating, which the troops performed in good order, carrying off their dead and wounded. The light infantry covered the rear and maintained so good a countenance that the enemy did not attempt to follow more than four hundred yards, and at a respectable distance.

As summed up in Charles Stedman's History:

The militia under General Lincoln were disheartened by this unsuccessful attack; and the greatest part of them soon afterwards quitted the army and returned home. The British troops were no farther molested. The post at Stono Ferry was evacuated; and the army, retiring along the seacoast, passed from island to island until it reached Beaufort in the island of Port Royal. At Beaufort General Prevost established a post, the garrison of which he left under the command of Lieutenant-Colonel [John] Maitland, and returned with the rest of the army to Georgia that the troops might rest during the hot and sickly season, which in this southern province prevents the operations of an army as effectually as the rigour of winter does in a more northerly climate. For the same reason the American [regulars] retired to Sheldon [about ten miles northwest of Beaufort]; and nothing of any consequence was attempted by either during the months of July and August.

30

SUNDRY EXPEDITIONS

IN THE *North, the year 1779 had begun quietly. Washington spent several weeks in Philadelphia discussing the war with Congress, making public bows and enjoying the geniality of private hearths. According to a* Pennsylvania Packet *announcement dated February 2:*

This morning, His Excellency General Washington set off from Philadelphia to join the army in New Jersey. During the course of his short stay . . . he has been honored with every mark of esteem which his accomplished fortitude as a soldier and his exalted qualities as a gentleman and a citizen entitle him to. . . . The council of this state being desirous of having his picture in full length, requested his sitting for that purpose, which he politely complied with, and a striking likeness was taken by Mr. [Charles Willson] Peale of Philadelphia. . . . His Excellency's stay was rendered the more agreeable by the company of his lady and the domestic retirement which he enjoyed at the house of the Honorable Henry Laurens, Esquire. . . .

There was little contact between the forces under Washington and Clinton as 1779 advanced. Clinton's strongest efforts were in the form of punitive raids in civilian areas. In May an expedition to the Virginia coast did heavy damage, and early in July a harsh blow was dealt to Connecticut. America's Colonel Samuel Webb, writing at Wethersfield, in the afflicted state, on Sunday, July 11, reported angrily:

. . . the whole country [is] in an uproar. The enemy, about 2,000 under the infamous Governor Tryon [the former royal governor of New York], have been at New Haven. They took possession of the town on Monday last, there being only about 100 of the militia to oppose them. . . . [O]n Tuesday they embarked, after plundering the town and burning a few stores, went over to East Haven and burnt all the buildings next the shore. From this they took [to their] shipping and went for Fairfield, where they landed and took possession. . . . At 12 o'clock Thursday night they sent a flag to the inhabitants, who had collected on the heights out of town, acquainting them if they would come in, give up their arms and swear allegiance to George the Third the town should be preserved. They returned for answer that . . . they should never submit to the government of Britain's tyrant. The enemy went immediately to plundering, and at seven o'clock set fire to the town, which now remains a heap of rubbish. This village was large and as beautiful as any in this state, the buildings large and elegant. To add to the misfortune, the inhabitants had not time to remove any of their property, so that many reputable, worthy families are reduced from a state of affluence to poverty.

Thus are these wretches, the servants and slaves of George the Third, burning defenceless towns and waging war against innocent women and children. A child of three years old was taken from the arms of its mother and thrown into the flames, and the mother, to stop her shrieks, knocked down with a musket. A man who was taken prisoner, being an old countryman, was rolled in a sheet, bound fast, the sheet wet with rum and set fire to. In this situation, just before he expired, our people found him. Several Negro servants who were left to take care of their masters' property were burnt alive for attempting to extinguish the fire. Indeed . . . this . . . excursion . . . has been marked with more savage cruelty than before known. . . .

The raiding party, according to one of Fairfield's plundered citizens, was made up of Britons, Germans, and Tories:

The Britons were the least inveterate. Some of the officers seemed to pity the misfortunes of the country, but in excuse said they had no other way to gain their authority over us. Individuals among the British troop were exceedingly abusive, especially to women. They solicited, they attempted their chastity; and though no rape was committed, yet some were forced to submit to the most indelicate and rough treatment. They exerted their utmost strength in the defence of their virtue. . . .

Shortly after sailing from Fairfield the raiders landed at Norwalk, which they also devastated. They were now appeased. Judge Jones says:

In the course of this expedition all the small privateers in the harbours and creeks along the Connecticut shore were destroyed by the navy. This was an essential piece of service; but to rob, plunder and burn defenceless unfortified towns could answer no purpose. It was not a method of conciliating the deluded. It occasioned rancor and inveteracy, and . . . it widened the breach.

Even as the British raid was ending, Washington was preparing a move of his own. He had asked General Anthony Wayne whether he'd undertake a hazardous attack on a British outpost; "Mad Anthony" had replied that he'd storm hell if Washington made the plans. With about thirteen hundred men, Wayne was sent to surprise the enemy garrison at Stony Point, on the Hudson's west bank about fifty miles above New York City. The British had just recently extended their lines northward along the river and were now in a position to threaten the vital American fortifications at West Point. Wayne advanced to the attack during the night of July 15. As reported in the New York Journal:

The detachment marched in two divisions, and about one o'clock came up to the enemy's pickets, who, by firing their pieces, gave the alarm, and with all possible speed ran to the fort, from every quarter of which, in a short time, they made an incessant fire upon our people. They [the Americans], with fixed bayonets and uncharged pieces, advanced with quick but silent motion through a heavy fire of cannon and musketry, till getting over the abatis and scrambling up the precipices, the enemy called out, "Come on, ye damned rebels! Come on!" Some of our people softly answered, "Don't be in such a hurry, my lads. We will be with you presently."

At this point, according to the New Hampshire Gazette, *General Wayne was dazed by a scalp wound:*

. . . he was a good deal staggered, and fell upon one knee; but the moment he recovered himself he called to his aids . . . and said, "Lead me forward. If I am mortally wounded, let me die in the fort."

Returning to the New York Journal's *account:*

. . . in a little more than twenty minutes from the time the enemy began first to fire, our troops, overcoming all obstructions and resistance, entered the fort. Spurred on by their resentment of the former cruel bayoneting which many of them [at Paoli], and others of our people had experienced, and of the more recent and savage barbarity of plundering and burning unguarded towns, murdering old and unarmed men, abusing and forcing defence-less women, and reducing multitudes of innocent people from comfortable livings to the most distressful want of the means of subsistence—deeply affected by these cruel injuries, our people entered the fort with the resolution of putting every man to the sword. But the cry of "Mercy! Mercy! Dear Americans, mercy! Quarter! Brave Americans, quarter! Quarter!" disarmed their resentment in an instant. . . .

There was no unnecessary slaughter. An hour after the surrender General Wayne, with a blood-tinged bandage about his head, sat down and wrote to Washington: "The fort and garrison . . . are ours. Our officers and men behaved like men who are determined to be free." The British had lost well over a hundred men killed and wounded. More than five hundred were made prisoners. American losses were about fifteen killed and eighty wounded. The Americans shortly abandoned the fort and it was reoccupied by the British, but the brilliance of Wayne's feat was widely applauded by the Patriots. So much was made of Wayne's humanity toward the enemy that a Royalist writer was prompted to reply:

I am willing to believe, for the honor of America, that the rebels on this occasion relaxed in their usual barbarity. As it was the first time, it should be recorded—though it would have lost nothing had it been expressed in less exaggerated terms.

The attention of the Americans was next drawn to the nation's northeastern extremity. In a journal entry made early in August, Dr. Thacher related:

The British, a few weeks since, detached a force from Halifax and established a post on Penobscot River in the Province of Maine. . . . This invasion of our territory has excited the greatest indignation, and all classes of people are burning with an ardent desire of revenge. The General Court of Massachusetts have planned an expedition for the purpose of driving the invading foe from our shores. Such was their zeal and confidence of success that it is said the General Court neither consulted any experienced military character nor desired the assistance of any Continental troops on this important enterprise—thus taking on themselves the undivided responsibility and reserving for their own heads all the laurels to be derived from the anticipated conquest. They drafted one thousand five hundred militia and appointed General [Solomon] Lovell . . . to command the expedition. They obtained of Congress the loan of the United States Frigate *Warren* of thirty-two guns; and with an unprecedented spirit of enterprise and industry, no less than nineteen Continental, state and private ships, and more than twenty transports, were specially equipped and prepared to cooperate with the land forces destined for this service. With a laudable spirit of patriotism, and animated by the flattering prospect of success, thirty masters of merchant vessels in Newburyport honorably volunteered their services as common seamen. Captain [Dudley] Saltonstall was appointed commodore of the fleet and took his station on board the *Warren* frigate. This combined force sailed about the 20th of July on their destined service.

But having some reason to apprehend a failure of their enterprise, the General Court have applied to General Gates for permission for Colonel Jackson's Regiment [presently at Providence, Rhode Island] to [follow and] reinforce General Lovell . . . and we are accordingly under marching orders. . . . Our regiment consists of about four hundred men in complete uniform, well disciplined, and not inferior to any in the Continental Army.

We commenced a forced march from Providence [to Boston for embarkation] on the 10th [of August] and completed the forty miles in twenty-four hours. A severe rain all night did not much impede our march, but the troops were broken down with fatigue. We reached Boston Neck at sun-rising; and near the entrance of the neck is a tavern having for its sign a representation of a globe, with a man in the act of struggling to get through it. His head and shoulders were out, his arms extended, and the rest of his body inclosed in the globe. On a label from his mouth was written, "Oh, how shall I get through this world?" This was read by the [greatly fatigued] soldiers, and one of them exclaimed, "[En]list, damn you! [En]list, and you will soon get through this world! Our regiment will all be through it in an hour or two, if we don't halt [for rest] by the way!"

We are treated by the gentlemen of this town with great attention and respect. They have generously presented to Colonel Jackson and the officers of his regiment a hogshead of Jamaica spirits and a cask of wine. For the soldiers they have collected a liberal sum of money, which is distributed among them. . . .

On the 14th our regiment marched through the town to the Long Wharf . . . receiving as we passed through King Street the cheers of the inhabitants. After the regiment had embarked, the officers, according to previous arrangement, returned to the Bunch of Grapes Tavern, where a liberal and elegant entertainment had been provided, and where we were politely received by a number of respectable gentlemen of the town. Having dined and enjoyed a number of songs over the cheering glass, wishing success to the Penobscot Expedition, we repaired on board our respective transports, awaiting a fair wind for our voyage.

On August 17 the little fleet left the harbor and started for Maine to join the force under Saltonstall and Lovell. Two days later, however, orders came for the reinforcement to abandon its journey and put into Portsmouth, New Hampshire. Dr. Thacher soon afterward learned the following story from "several gentlemen just returned from Penobscot":

. . . on the 28th of July, the militia [under Lovell], with about three hundred [of Saltonstall's] marines, were disembarked, and soon effected a landing under a height which rose almost perpendicularly from the banks of the [Penobscot] River, on the summit of which the enemy's advanced guard was posted under cover of a wood. Our militia were opposed by about an equal number of the enemy, whom they bravely encountered and drove within their works. But we suffered a loss of several officers of merit, and about one hundred of the militia and marines were killed and wounded. It now became a subject of consideration whether it was expedient to storm the enemy's principal works; but in a council it was decided that our force was inadequate to the object. It was at this juncture supposed that by a vigorous cooperation of our navy a complete victory might have been obtained, and the most urgent and pressing entreaties were made to Commodore Saltonstall for the purpose; but he declined. . . .

On the 14th [of August] Sir George Collier, with [a British fleet that included] a sixty-four-gun ship . . . arrived from New York. General Lovell, on receiving this intelligence, ordered all his troops, with the artillery and baggage, to be embarked on board

Henry "Light-Horse Harry" Lee.

the transports, which, with our whole fleet, moved up the Penobscot River, pursued by the British. On the near approach of the enemy, our vessels were abandoned. Two of them fell into the hands of the enemy. The remainder were burned and blown up. General Lovell and General Peleg Wadsworth, the second-in-command, both of whom have the reputation of brave men, now dispensed with all command of the troops, as did Saltonstall of the seamen. The soldiers separated from their officers, and every individual was seeking his own safety, wandering in the wilderness, suffering fatigue, hunger and vexation, till after much difficulty they reached the settlements on the Kennebec. A few of their number indeed actually perished in the wilderness. Thus disgracefully has ended the famous Penobscot Expedition. . . .

America's disappointment over this affair was partly offset by a daring hit-and-run attack, on August 19, by a detachment under Major "Light-Horse Harry" Lee. The raid, made on the British garrison at Paulus Hook, on the Jersey shore across from New York City, was smaller in scale than the attack on Stony Point but was no less skillfully executed. About 150 prisoners were brought off.

Meanwhile, on the Pennsylvania and New York frontiers the Americans had finally launched a full-scale expedition against the Iroquois, and it was now progressing to a climax. Dr. Thacher explains:

The bloody tragedy acted at Wyoming in 1778 had determined the commander-in-chief . . . to employ a large detachment from the Continental Army to operate into the heart of the Indian country to chastise the hostile tribes and their white associates and adherents for their cruel aggressions on the defenceless inhabitants. The command of this expedition was committed to Major-General Sullivan, with express orders to destroy their settlements, to ruin their crops, and make such thorough devastations as to render the country entirely uninhabitable for the present, and thus to compel the savages to remove to a greater distance from our frontiers. General Sullivan had under his command several brigadiers and a well-chosen army, to which were attached a number of friendly Indian warriors. With this force he . . . possessed himself of numerous towns and villages of the savages. During this hazardous expedition, General Sullivan and his army encountered the most complicated obstacles, requiring the greatest fortitude and perseverance to surmount.

Judge Jones takes up:

Sullivan . . . though . . . attacked upon the march by a number of Indians, refugees and Tories under the command of Colonel [John] Butler . . . and the famous Mohawk warrior Captain [Joseph] Brant, no kind of impression could be made by them. . . . I have heard Colonel Butler compare it to the driving of a wedge into a stick of wood. Nothing stopped or disturbed its motion. Upon this expedition, Sullivan burnt forty towns, some of which contained 130 houses, destroyed 160,000 bushels of corn, took away all their poultry, and cut down all their orchards.

Though the Americans complained heavily of the burning and plundering of Fairfield and Norwalk, in the State of Connecticut . . . as an act of inhumanity in the British . . . yet in their annual Thanksgiving . . . their ministers did not forget to return thanks to Almighty God for the success which had attended Sullivan's burning, plundering, cruel, marauding, distressing expedition against these Indians, the allies of Britain. So that, what the New England rebels termed barbarity in the British was deemed a righteous, godly and Christian-like act when perpetrated by themselves.

Years later, the great Seneca chief, Corn Planter, was to tell Washington: "When your army entered the country of the Six Nations, we called you The Town Destroyer; and to this day, when that name is heard, our women look behind them and turn pale, and our children cling close to the necks of their mothers."

31

JOHN PAUL JONES

The TINY *Continental Navy, founded in 1775, had accomplished little to brag about in the first four years of the war. England had no trouble maintaining the upper hand in American waters until strong French squadrons began surging across the Atlantic in 1778. America's "Marine Committee" commissioned about forty ships in all, and their captains enjoyed two or three successes over isolated British men-of-war and captured a considerable number of merchant vessels, but by 1779 the navy had dwindled sadly. Many of the ships had been captured, sunk, or burned. Some had been destroyed by the hard-pressed Americans themselves. But in spite of the Continental Navy's inferior status, a few commanders were assigned the risky task of attacking merchant vessels in England's home waters.*

It was through the raids in English waters that America gained her first great naval hero, John Paul Jones. Born John Paul in Scotland, he was an experienced merchant captain against whom British authorities had placed a murder charge in connection with the death of one of his seamen, and he added "Jones" to his name upon taking secret refuge in America before the war. He had already established a reputation for ability and daring in the Continental Navy by the time he left the French coast on a voyage against England late in the summer of 1779. He commanded a small squadron that he had assembled in France, with some aid from Benjamin Franklin. His crews were made up of seamen of various nationalities besides American, and his flagship, the Bon Homme Richard *(named after the*

John Paul Jones. From the portrait by Charles Willson Peale.
(Library of Congress)

"Poor Richard" of Franklin's famous almanac), was old, unsound, and none too strong in armament. Jones also was handicapped by the jealous, insubordinate, and sometimes irrational conduct of one of his captains, a Frenchman named Pierre Landais, of the frigate Alliance. *Nonetheless, the squadron soon took several merchant vessels and their crews.*

Then, on September 23, while in the vicinity of Flamborough Head on England's eastern coast, Jones sighted a fleet of about forty merchantmen. As he pressed forward, the merchantmen fled for the protection of some shore batteries, while the two naval vessels that had been escorting them, the frigate Serapis *and the sloop-of-war* Countess of Scarborough, *came to challenge the intruders. Pierre Landais ignored Jones's order to prepare for battle. Instead, he took the* Alliance *toward the British ships for a closer look, then swung around and withdrew to a safe distance to observe developments. Night was near when Jones, relying on a heavy thirty-gun vessel named the* Pallas *to subdue the little twenty-gun* Scarborough, *advanced in the seaworn* Richard, *which carried forty guns, to face the* Serapis, *a new frigate of fifty guns, with a determined commander, Richard Pearson. According to Jones's first lieutenant, Richard Dale, it was dark by the time the two vessels were within hailing distance:*

... the *Serapis* demanded, "What ship is that?" He was answered, "I can't hear what you say." Immediately after, the *Serapis* hailed again, "What ship is that? Answer immediately, or I shall be under the necessity of firing into you." At this moment, I received orders from Commodore Jones to commence the action with a broadside, which indeed appeared to be simultaneous on board both ships.

As fifteen or twenty cannons on each ship roared and flashed in the darkness, two of the Richard's *eighteen-pounders blew up, horribly mangling their crews. The ship's other four eighteen-pounders were quickly abandoned. These being the heaviest weapons on board, the loss was crippling. But Jones refused to be discouraged. He relates:*

The battle, thus begun, was continued with unremitting fury. Every method was practiced on both sides to gain an advantage, and rake each other; and I must confess that the enemy's ship, being much more manageable than the *Richard*, gained thereby several times an advantageous situation in spite of my best endeavors to prevent it. As I had to deal with an enemy of greatly superior force, I was under the necessity of [trying to close] with him, to prevent the advantage which he had over me in point of maneuver.

Both vessels had crews with light weapons stationed in the tops—the small platforms surrounding the heads of the lower masts. One of the men with a bird's-eye view of the battle from his position in the Richard's *maintop was Midshipman Nathaniel Fanning, who said of the* Serapis:

. . . she raked us with whole broadsides and showers of musketry. Several of her 18-pound shot having gone through and through our ship . . . she made dreadful havock among our crew. . . . All this time our tops kept up an incessant and well-directed fire into the enemy's tops. . . .

Soon the maneuvering of the vessels resulted in their coming together in a manner that gave little advantage to either: The bow of the Richard *touched up against the stern of the* Serapis. *In Lieutenant Dale's words:*

We had remained in this situation but a few minutes when we were again hailed by the *Serapis,* "Has your ship struck?" [i.e., "Has she surrendered?"] To which Captain Jones answered, "I have not yet begun to fight!" As we were unable to bring a single gun to bear upon the *Serapis,* our topsails were backed, while those of the *Serapis* being filled, and ships separated.

A bright moon had risen, adding to the light of the shipboard lanterns and improving visibility between the opponents. For a brief time they maneuvered on a parallel course, with the Richard *on the left. Then the* Richard *managed to surge ahead and cross in front of the* Serapis. *The British vessel could not avoid a collision; her jib boom (the spar extending from her bowsprit) pushed up on deck near the* Richard's *rearmost mast and became entangled in its ropes. This was precisely the kind of contact that Jones had been hoping for:*

. . . I made both ships fast together in that situation, which by the action of the wind on the enemy's sails, forced her stern close to the *Richard's* bow, so that the ships lay square alongside of each other, the yards [the spars that supported the sails] being all entangled and the cannon of each ship touching the opponent's side.

When this position took place it was eight o'clock, previous to which the *Richard* had received sundry 18-pound shots below the water and leaked very much.

Says Midshipman Fanning:
. . . the fire from our tops having been kept up without intermission, with musketry, blunderbusses, coehorns, swivels and pistols, directed into their tops . . . [they] at this time became silent, except one man in her fore-top, who would once in a while peep out from behind the head of the . . . fore-mast and fire into our tops. . . . I ordered the marines in the main-top to reserve their next fire, and the moment they got sight of him to level their pieces at him and fire; which they did, and we soon saw this skulking tar, or marine, fall out of the top. . . .

The cannon fire was continued at point-blank range, with the Serapis *doing most of the damage. Her lower guns—those firing from the ports nearest her waterline—blew cavernous holes in the* Richard's *hull. Some of the openings extended from side to side, and there were times when balls passed completely through the ship without touching anything en route. One by one, the* Richard's *guns were knocked out until, said Jones:*
I had . . . only two pieces of cannon, 9-pounders on the quarterdeck, that were not silenced, and not one of the heavier cannon was fired during the rest of the action. The purser . . . who commanded the guns on the quarter-deck, being dangerously wounded in the head, I was obliged to fill his place, and with great difficulty rallied a few men and shifted over one of the lee quarter-deck guns, so that we afterward played three pieces of 9-pounders upon the enemy. The tops alone seconded the fire of this little battery. . . . I directed the fire of one of the three cannon against the main-mast, with double-headed shot, while the other two were exceedingly well served with grape and canister shot to silence the enemy's musketry and clear her decks. . . .

According to Fanning, it wasn't long before a new trouble developed:
. . . the enemy's light sails . . . caught fire. This communicated itself to her rigging, and from thence to ours. Thus were both ships on fire at one and the same time; therefore the firing on both sides ceased till it was extinguished by the contending parties, after which the action was renewed again. By this time the top-men

in our tops had taken possession of the enemy's tops, which was done by reason of the *Serapis*'s yards being locked together with ours, that we could with ease go from our main-top into the enemy's fore-top, and . . . from our fore-top into the *Serapis*'s main-top. Having knowledge of this, we transported from our own into the enemy's tops stink-pots, flasks, hand grenadoes, etc., which we threw in among the enemy whenever they made their appearance. . . .

This advantage gave Jones fresh hope. And the hope suddenly be-came a vision of victory when he noted that the unpredictable Pierre Landais was at last approaching with the Alliance:

. . . I now thought the battle at an end; but, to my utter astonish-ment, he discharged a broadside full into the stern of the *Bon Homme Richard!* We called to him: "For God's sake to forbear firing into the *Bon Homme Richard!*" Yet he passed along the off side of the ship and continued firing. There was no possibility of his mistaking the enemy's ship for the *Bon Homme Richard,* there being the most essential difference in their appearance and con-struction. Besides, it was then full moonlight. . . . Every tongue cried that he was firing into the wrong ship, but nothing availed. He passed round, firing into the *Bon Homme Richard's* head, stern and broadside; and by one of his volleys killed several of my best men and mortally wounded a good officer. . . . My situation was really deplorable. The *Bon Homme Richard* received various shots under water from the *Alliance* [which finally desisted and stood off]. The leaks gained on the pumps. . . .

This caused three officers below decks to panic. The carpenter, the master-at-arms, and the gunner, or ordnance officer, decided that the Richard *was lost. First the master-at-arms freed the scores of pris-oners taken earlier in the cruise, telling them to try to save them-selves. Then the trio rushed up to the main deck. Midshipman Fan-ning observed from aloft:*

These three men . . . mounted the quarter-deck and bawled out [toward the *Serapis*] as loud as they could, "Quarters! Quar-ters! For God's sake, quarters! Our ship is a-sinking!" And [they] immediately got upon the ship's poop with a view of hauling down our colours. . . . The three poltroons, finding the ensign . . . gone [the staff had been shot away] . . . proceeded [forward] upon the quarter-deck and were in the act of hauling down our pendant, still bawling for quarters, when I heard our commodore say in a loud voice, "What damned rascals are them? Shoot them! Kill them!" He was upon the fore-castle when these fellows . . . made their appearance upon the quarter-deck . . . [and] he had just discharged his pistols at some of the enemy. The carpenter and the master-at-arms, hearing Jones's voice, skulked below, and the gunner was attempting to do the same when Jones threw both of his pistols at his head, one of which . . . fractured his skull and knocked him down at the foot of the gang-way ladder, where he lay till the battle was over.

The freed prisoners remaining a problem, Jones had Lieutenant Dale assemble them and tell them that it was really the Serapis *that was ready to go down at any minute, and that their lives depended on their helping to keep the* Richard *afloat by taking turns at the pumps. The stratagem was successful. Fanning resumes:*

Both ships now took fire again; and on board of our ship it communicated to . . . our main-top . . . which threw us into the greatest consternation imaginable for some time. . . . The water which we had in a tub in the fore part on the top was expended without extinguishing the fire. We next had recourse to our clothes . . . pulling off our coats and jackets and then throwing them upon the fire and stamping upon them. . . . Both crews were . . . now, as before, busily employed in stopping the progress of the flames, and the firing on both sides ceased. . . . The combat . . . recommenced again with more fury, if possible, than before . . . and continued for a few minutes, when the cry of fire was again heard on board of both ships. The firing ceased, and both crews were once more employed in extinguishing it, which was soon effected, when the battle was renewed again. . . .

Finally, a man from the Richard's *foretop who had worked his way across the interlocked yards to the maintop of the enemy vessel with a leather bucket full of hand grenades managed to drop one of the missiles through her main hatchway, and it struck an exposed supply of gunpowder. In the words of British officer Francis Heddart:*

It was awful! Some twenty of our men were fairly blown to pieces. There were other men who were stripped naked, with nothing on but the collars of their shirts and wristbands. Farther aft there was not so much powder, perhaps, and the men were scorched or burned more than they were wounded. I do not know how I escaped. . . .

This was a demoralizing blow. Fanning writes that "the enemy now in their turn . . . bawled out, 'Quarters! Quarters! Quarters, for God's sake!'" But the men were rallied by Captain Pearson, and the battle continued for nearly an hour longer. Then, with the main-mast of the Serapis *beginning to totter as the result of Jones's cannon fire, Pearson decided to surrender.*

It was, however, some time [Fanning's account continues] before the enemy's colours were struck. The captain of the *Serapis* gave repeated orders for one of his crew to ascend the quarter-deck and haul down the English flag, but no one would stir to do it. They told the captain they were afraid of our riflemen. . . . The captain . . . therefore ascended the quarter-deck and hauled down the very flag which he had nailed to the flag-staff a little before the commencement of the battle; and which flag he had at that time, in the presence of his principal officers, swore he never would strike to that infamous pirate, J. P. Jones.

Captain Pearson, whose courage came close to matching that of the "infamous pirate," was later to explain the Richard's *victory in this manner:*

Long before the close of the action, it became clearly apparent that the American ship was dominated by a command will of the most unalterable resolution, and there could be no doubt that the intention of her commander was, if he could not conquer, to sink alongside.

Jones promptly sent a party commanded by Lieutenant Dale to take possession of the Serapis, *and Captain Pearson and several other officers came on board the* Richard *to make a formal surrender. As he presented his sword to Jones, Pearson alluded to the fact that Jones was considered an outlaw in England, and grumbled at the indignity of having to surrender to a man who had fought "with a halter about his neck." Jones responded by congratulating Pearson on his gallant fight, and the Englishman was moved to accept an invitation to Jones's cabin for "a glass or two of wine."*

The battle had lasted between three and four hours. Exact casualty figures are unknown, but it would appear that at least one hundred and fifty men were killed or wounded on each side. Writes Jones:

. . . a person must have been an eyewitness to form a just idea of the tremendous scene of carnage, wreck and ruin that everywhere appeared. Humanity cannot but recoil from the prospect of such finished horror, and lament that war should produce such fatal consequences.

Fanning was both saddened by the groans of the wounded and dying, and appalled by the mangled corpses, scattered entrails, and great splotches of blood:

Upon the whole, I think this battle and every circumstance attending it minutely considered, may be ranked with propriety the most bloody, the hardest fought, and the greatest scene of carnage on both sides, ever fought between two ships of war of any nation under heaven.

Jones transferred his battered company and his original prisoners to the Serapis, *for the* Richard *was beyond saving. The "infamous pirate" had bested a first-rate warship with one that was not only improvised and second-rate but now was also on her way to the bottom! The feat delighted those nations that were hostile toward England and earned Jones worldwide fame.*

The Continental Navy accomplished little during the rest of the war, becoming virtually extinct. Most of the individual states managed to keep small navies afloat, but their primary function continued to be home defense. Only America's privateers operated persistently in all quarters until the war's close. There were hundreds of these vessels, many with large crews, and they took a high toll of British merchantmen, sometimes diverting their cargoes to the Patriot army. Of course, the British punished America's trade in a similar manner.

All in all, the war at sea probably involved as many Americans as did the land war. And the sea endeavors were at every moment a serious nuisance to the British, an impediment to their freedom of action. America's chances of winning her independence would doubtless have been considerably smaller without her thousands of venturesome seamen.

32

THE SIEGE OF SAVANNAH

I N THE *South, while the two rival armies sat out the hot summer
of 1779 after the American repulse at Stono Ferry, South Carolina, Governor John Rutledge and General Benjamin Lincoln, at
meetings in Charleston, centered their hopes of saving the state and
of regaining Georgia on securing French aid. In the spring, even before Stono Ferry, an appeal had been sent to Charles Hector, Count
d'Estaing, in the West Indies. It was suggested that he come northward late in summer when the danger of hurricanes made operations
in the Indies impracticable. The count had liked the idea, since it
offered him a chance to make up for his failure at Newport, Rhode
Island, the preceding year. He closed his Indies campaign in July
with the capture of the British island of Grenada. This put him in
a confident mood; and in August, even though his fleet needed re-
fitting, he sailed for the Georgia coast. Among those in Charleston
who were putting much reliance on French aid was General William
Moultrie:*

About the 4th of September an officer came to town from Count
d'Estaing's fleet . . . to acquaint Gen. Lincoln that the Count . . . was
ready to co-operate with him in the reduction of Savannah, and at the
same time to urge the necessity of dispatch, as he could not remain
long upon our coast at this season of the year. This information put
us all in high spirits. The legislature adjourned; the governor
and council and the military joined heartily in expediting everything that was necessary. Boats were sent to Count d'Estaing's fleet

to assist in taking the cannon and stores on shore [a dozen miles from Savannah]. Everyone was cheerful, as if we were sure of success; and no one doubted but that we had nothing more to do than to march up to Savannah and demand a surrender. The militia were draughted, and a great number of volunteers joined readily to be present at the surrender, and in hopes to have the pleasure of seeing the British march out and deliver up their arms. . . .

On the 5th of September Gen. Lincoln ordered all officers and soldiers to join their respective regiments; and on the 8th the Continentals were drawn from the [Charleston] forts. . . . Gen. Lincoln goes off to take command of the army at Sheldon [its headquarters since the fight at Stono Ferry] about the 12th . . . leaving myself the command of Charleston with a few Continentals and the militia. . . . The French army lay before Savannah . . . before Gen. Lincoln's army got up, and [D'Estaing] demanded a surrender on the 16th September, and the garrison requested 24 hours to consider. . . . In the meantime, Col. Maitland got into Savannah [from across the river] with a strong reinforcement from Beaufort.

Maitland's redcoats were those who had taken station at Beaufort after the affair at Stono Ferry. Savannah's garrison raised three cheers at Maitland's arrival. British General Augustine Prevost, though his back was toward a blockaded river, was now determined to fight. D'Estaing, with American aid, prepared to lay siege to the city. Trenches were opened and positions were chosen for heavy weapons. According to an unnamed French officer, the British tried to disrupt the work on September 24:

At seven o'clock in the morning, when a thick fog which arose at daylight had disappeared, the enemy . . . made a sortie with six hundred men to attack us. They are repulsed at the point of the bayonet and driven back to their entrenchments. Our imprudence in leaving our trench to pursue them exposed us to the artillery fire of their redoubts and batteries and caused the loss of seventy men killed and wounded. . . .

The British sortie was a bold measure, especially considering that the Savannah garrison was badly outnumbered by the besieging forces. Says England's Charles Stedman in his History:

. . . the disparity in numbers was in some degree compensated by the extraordinary zeal and ardour which animated the besieged, from the commander-in-chief down to the humble African, whose

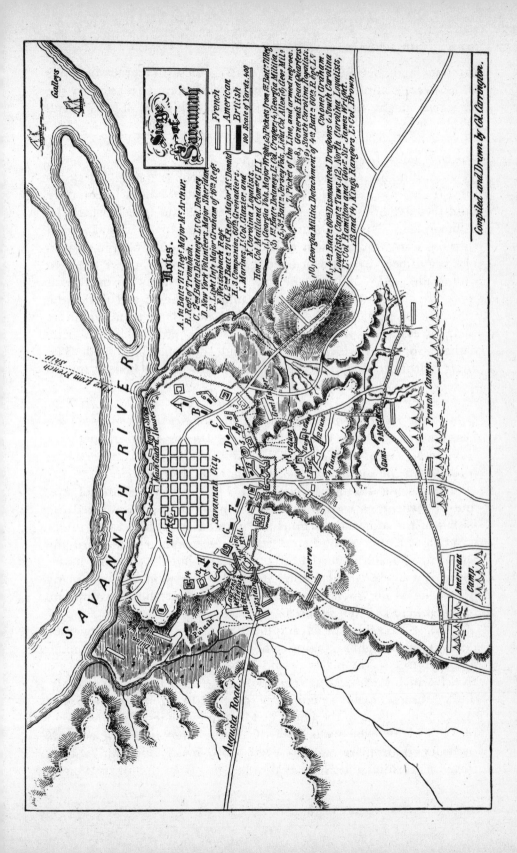

Siege of Savannah

French
American
British

100 Scale of Yards. 400

Notes.

A. 1st Batt. 71st Reg. Major McArthur.
B. Reg. of Trombäch.
C. 2nd Batt. Delanceys. Lt. Col. Delaney.
D. New York Volunteers. Major Sheridan.
E. Light Inf. Major Graham of 16th Reg.
F. Weisenbach Reg.
G. 2nd Batt. 71st Reg. Major McDonald.
H. 3 Companies. 60th Grenadiers.
I. Marines. Lt. Col. Glazier and
N. Carolina Loyalists.
Hon. Col. Maitland Com. G. H. I.

(1) Georgia Vols. Major Wright, (2) Pickets from S.E. Batt. (3) Reg.
(3) Batt. Delaneys. Lt. Col. Cruger, (4) Georgia Militia.
(5) 3rd Batt. Jersey Vol., Lieut. Col. Allen, (6) Geor. Mil.

Picket of the Line, and armed negroes.

(8), General's Head Quarters.
(9), South Carolina
Colonel Graham

(10), Georgia Militia Detachment of 4th Batt. G. South Carolina.

(11), 4th Batt. 60th Dismounted Dragoons. C. South Carolina
Loyalists Cap. Taws. (12), North Carolina Loyalists.
Lt. Col. Hamilton and Gov. Sir James Wright.
13th and 14th Kings Rangers, Lt. Col. Brown.

Compiled and Drawn by Col. Carrington.

incessant and cheerful labours, in rearing those numerous defences which were completed with so much expedition as to astonish the besiegers, ought not to be forgotten in a history of this memorable siege.

On October 3, relates the French officer:

At midnight . . . the bombardment [from the siege lines] begins. It ceases at two o'clock by order of M. de Noailles because the misdirected bombs fell in great numbers in the trench which he commanded. This bad firing was occasioned by a mistake of a ship's steward who had sent to the cannoneers a keg of rum instead of a keg of beer. . . . At four o'clock in the morning . . . we begin to cannonade and bombard the city and the enemy's works with more vivacity than precision. The cannoneers being still under the influence of rum, their excitement did not allow them to direct their pieces with proper care. Besides, our projectiles did little damage to works which were low and constructed of sand. The effect of this very violent fire was fatal only to the houses and to some women who occupied them.

One of the civilians in Savannah at this time was Anthony Stokes, Georgia's chief justice under the Crown. During the third night of the bombardment a shell ignited his quarters; and with other shells falling near, he decided to flee to a safer part of the city:

I had some distance to go before I got out of the line of fire, and . . . whenever I came to the opening of a street I watched the flashes of the mortars and guns and pushed on until I came under cover of a house; and when I got to the common and heard the whistling of a shot or shell I fell on my face. But the stopping under cover of a house was no security, for the shot went through many houses; and Thomson's daughter was killed at the side opposite to that where the shot entered.

At last I reached an encampment made by [Royalist] Governor [Sir James] Wright's Negroes on the common between Savannah and [suburban] Yammacraw; and it being dark I fell down into a trench which they had dug. I proposed to stop at the house of a Mr. Tully, but a soldier . . . advised me to go further from the line of fire and conducted me to the house of Mr. Moses Nones at the west end of Yammacraw, which was quite out of the direction of the enemy's batteries. This place was crowded, both inside and out, with a number of whites and Negroes who had fled from the town. Women and children were constantly flocking there, melting into tears and lamenting their unhappy fate and the destruction of their houses and property. . . .

The appearance of the town afforded a melancholy prospect, for there was hardly a house which had not been shot through, and some of them were almost destroyed. . . . The troops in the lines were much safer from the bombardment than the people in town.

General William Moultrie, who had remained in Charleston, was later to learn from participants:

The batteries continued their fire for 4 or 5 days. . . . Gen. Prevost sent out to request leave to send the women and children without the lines, but it was denied, supposing he only wanted to gain time.

A second nameless French officer adds:

Many women, however, left the city and presented themselves of their own accord at the French camp. It was necessary for us to take good care of them, as they were unwilling to return.

General Moultrie continues:

Count d'Estaing having been now a month with his fleet on our coast and close in shore, his officers remonstrated to him the dangerous situation the fleet was in and the hazards they run of being attacked by the British fleet whilst theirs was in a bad condition and a great many of their officers and men on shore. These representations determined the Count d'Estaing to call a council, in which the opinion of the engineers was that it would require 10 days more to work into the enemy's lines [employing the usual siege methods], upon which it was determined to try to carry them by an assault. . . .

The attack was organized during the night of October 8. It was to be made by a combined force of French and American troops, moving first in one column and then in several, and it was to be supported by a false attack. In the words of the first French officer quoted earlier:

We commence marching by the left to attack the city on its right. . . . The troops [remaining] in the trenches were ordered to make the false attack a quarter of an hour before day . . . prior to the commencement of the true attack. . . . At five o'clock in the morning . . . the head of [our] column was halted and we were ordered to form into platoons. Day begins to dawn, and we grow impatient. . . . At half past five o'clock we hear on our right and on the enemy's left a very lively fire of musketry and of cannon upon our troops from the trenches who had commenced the false attack. A few minutes afterwards we are discovered by the enemy's sentinels, who fire a few shots.

The General [D'Estaing] now orders an advance at double quick, to shout *Vive le Roi* and to beat the charge. The enemy opens upon us a very brisk fire of artillery and musketry, which, however, does not prevent the vanguard from advancing upon the redoubt, and the right column upon the entrenchments. The ardor of our troops and the difficulties offered by the ground do not permit us long to preserve our ranks. Disorder begins to prevail. The head of the column penetrates within the entrenchments, but, having marched too quickly, is not supported by the rest of the column, which, arriving in confusion, is cut down by discharges of grape shot . . . and . . . musketry fire. . . . We are violently repulsed at this point. . . . Count d'Estaing receives a musket shot [in the arm] almost within the redoubt. . . .

The column . . . which moved to the left, while traversing a muddy swamp full of brambles loses its formation and no longer preserves any order. . . . The firing is very lively; and, although this column is here most seriously injured, it crosses the road to Augusta that it may advance to the enemy's right, which it was ordered to attack. On this spot nearly all the volunteers [making up the column's head] are killed. . . .

At this moment everything is in such disorder that the formations are no longer preserved. The road to Augusta is choked up. It here, between two impracticable morasses, consists of an artificial causeway upon which all our soldiers who had disengaged themselves from the swamps collected. We are crowded together and badly pressed. Two eighteen-pounder guns [of the enemy] . . . charged with canister and placed at the head of the road cause terrible slaughter. The musketry fire from the entrenchments is concentrated upon this spot and upon the swamps. Two English galleys and one frigate [on the Savannah River] sweep this point with their broadsides, and the redoubts and batteries use only grape shot, which they shower down upon this locality.

Notwithstanding all this, our officers endeavor to form into columns this mass which does not retreat, and the soldiers themselves strive to regain their ranks. Scarcely have they commenced to do this when the General orders the charge to be beaten. Three times do our troops advance *en masse* up to the entrenchments which cannot be carried. An attempt is made to penetrate through the swamp on our left to gain the enemy's right. More than half of those who enter are either killed or remain stuck fast in the mud.

D'Estaing's army was accompanied, the British noted, by "the Lord knows how many rebels." By this time many of the militiamen had taken to their heels. But the Continental troops, which included a body of horsemen under Polish Count Casimir Pulaski, were heavily engaged. Says the French narrator: ". . . although repulsed with severe loss, [they] return repeatedly to the assault, thus furnishing a brilliant illustration of their valor." One of Pulaski's officers, a Major Rogowski, relates:

Seeing an opening between the enemy's works, Pulaski resolved, with his legion and a small detachment of Georgia cavalry, to charge through. . . . General Lincoln approved the daring plan. Imploring the help of the Almighty, Pulaski shouted to his men, "Forward!" And we, two hundred strong, rode at full speed after him, the earth resounding under the hoofs of our chargers. For the first two minutes all went well. We sped like knights into the peril. Just, however, as we passed the gap between the two batteries, a cross-fire like a pouring shower confused our ranks. I looked around. Oh, sad moment ever to be remembered! Pulaski lies prostrate on the ground. I leaped towards him, thinking possibly his wound was not dangerous, but a canister shot had pierced his thigh, and the blood was also flowing from his breast, probably from a second wound. Falling on my knees, I tried to raise him. He said in a faint voice, "Jesus! Maria! Joseph!" Further I knew not, for at that moment a musket ball grazing my scalp blinded me with blood, and I fell to the ground in a state of insensibility.

Pulaski's death would be one of painful lingering. There was a particular reason for the high casualties being taken by the attackers. "It was evident beyond a doubt," the second French officer complains bitterly, ". . . that the enemy had been informed by an American [deserter] of all our dispositions and of the hour of the attack."

Charleston's General Moultrie was later to learn:

In all this confusion, Lieuts. Hume and Bush planted the

colors of the Second South Carolina Regiment upon the ramparts, but they were soon killed. Lieut. Grey was on the ramparts, near the colors, and received his mortal wound; and the gallant Jasper [who had rescued the fallen flag during the Sullivan's Island fight in 1776] was with them, and supported one of the colors until he received his death wound. However, he brought off one of the colors with him, and died in a little time after.

Returning to the first Frenchman's account:

Standing in the road leading to Augusta, and at a most exposed point, the General [D'Estaing], with perfect self-possession, surveys this slaughter, demands constant renewals of the assault, and . . . determines upon a retreat only when he sees that success is impossible. We beat a retreat which is mainly effected across the swamp lying to the right of the Augusta road, our forces being entirely— and at short range—exposed to the concentrated fire of the entrenchments which constantly increases in vehemence. At this juncture the enemy show themselves openly upon the parapets and deliver their fire with their muskets almost touching our troops. The General here receives a second shot [this one in the leg]. . . . The fragments of the army hastily form in single column behind the reserve corps and begin marching to our camp.

The British, whose casualties were few, were astonished at the amount of damage they had managed to inflict. "I never saw such a dreadful scene," one man states, "as several hundreds lay dead in a space of a few yards; and the cries of many hundreds wounded was still more distressing to a feeling mind." The Frenchman concludes:

Towards eight o'clock in the morning the army was again in camp, and a cessation of hostilities for the purpose of burying the dead and removing the wounded was proposed and allowed. . . . [W]e had lost in killed and wounded: French soldiers, 760 men; French officers, 61 men; Americans, 312 men; total, 1133. . . . From this moment we thought only of retreat.

General Moultrie writes:

Count d'Estaing's marine officers, being very uneasy at the situation of his fleet, pressed his departure. He then ordered all his cannon and stores on board and embarked his troops . . . and left the coast of America. . . . General Lincoln retreated . . . to Charleston.

Moultrie admits that the defeat left the Americans not only woefully disappointed but also pessimistic about the outlook for Georgia and South Carolina.

As for the twice-wounded D'Estaing, he is said to have told his surgeon that he had still another wound, a deep one in his breast. His losses had been far too great, and for a second time he had been frustrated while trying to help America's land forces. The war would bring him no more opportunities of this nature. However, the fearless count would continue to serve France zealously until that country had its own revolution and he would lose his aristocratic head to the guillotine.

33

CHARLESTON REVISITED

A T THE *time of D'Estaing's departure from Georgia in the autumn of 1779, the war in the North was at a standstill. Sir Henry Clinton, with his eye on the South, had just recalled the British detachment from Newport, Rhode Island, and was consolidating his forces in the New York City area. Washington was preparing to assemble the bulk of his men in New Jersey for the winter. By mid-December, Dr. Thacher was writing:*

General Washington has taken his headquarters at Morristown, and the whole army in this department are to be employed in building log huts. . . . The ground is marked out, and the soldiers have commenced cutting down the timber of oak and walnut, of which we have a great abundance. Our baggage has at length arrived. The men find it very difficult to pitch their tents on the frozen ground, and notwithstanding large fires we can scarcely keep from freezing. In addition to other sufferings, the whole army has been for seven or eight days entirely destitute of the staff of life. Our only food is miserable fresh beef, without bread, salt or vegetables.

It is a circumstance greatly to be deprecated that the army, who are devoting their lives and everything dear to the defence of our country's freedom, should be subjected to such unparalleled privations while in the midst of a country abounding in every kind of provisions. The time has before occurred when the army was on the point of dissolution for the want of provisions, and it is to be ascribed to their patriotism and to a sense of honor and duty that they have not long since abandoned the cause of their country. . . .

Besides the evils above mentioned, we experience another in the rapid depreciation of the Continental money which we receive for our pay. . . . It is from this cause, according to report, that our commissary-general is unable to furnish the army with a proper supply of provisions. The people in the country are unwilling to sell the produce of their farms for this depreciated currency. . . .

The sufferings at Morristown, particularly because of the relentless severity of the weather, were to exceed those of Valley Forge. Judge Jones calls the winter "the severest ever known in the middle colonies." The British, he writes, took an early interest in the American encampment:

. . . information was received at New York that Washington's quarters were in a house . . . at some distance from the huts occupied by the rebel army. The snow was very deep, the winter prodigiously cold, and, as no danger was apprehended, his guards were trifling. Clinton thought the capture of Washington would put an end to the rebellion. I believe it would, as no other person could have kept such a heterogeneous army . . . together. Four hundred horse were dispatched for this purpose. This alert turned out as all others did. It failed. The guides got frightened, the party bewildered. They lost the road, and after a cold, tedious and fatiguing excursion . . . without ever seeing a rebel, returned to New York, all frost-bitten. This manoeuvre was laughed at by the rebel army . . . and cursed by the Loyalists. Thus ended this famous alert . . . that was to have ended the war. . . .

The judge goes on to say that in latter December

. . . General Clinton embarked at New York with a large proportion of the army and went to the southward with intent to attack Charleston, the metropolis of South Carolina, and by its conquest to reduce that colony. Georgia, the adjoining province, was then entirely under the jurisdiction of Britain. . . . Upon Clinton's leaving New York, the command there devolved upon General Knyphausen, Commander-in-Chief of the German auxiliaries. . . . He was nearly seventy, yet able, strong and active, had a good head, a noble soul and a bold heart. As many troops were left at New York as were sufficient for its defence. Nobody repined at the change of commanders. . . . Clinton was in general disliked. He was haughty, morose, churlish, stupid, and scarcely ever to be spoken with.

One of the officers who accompanied Clinton on the southern expedition was Charles Stedman:

The passage might have been expected to be performed in ten days; but such was the uncommon severity of the season that the fleet was very soon separated and driven out of its course by tempestuous weather; and scarcely any of the ships arrived at Tybee [Georgia], the appointed place of rendezvous, before the end of January [1780]. . . . Almost all the horses belonging to the artillery or cavalry perished during the passage; and amongst the ships that were lost was one which contained the heavy ordnance. Fortunately, however, the crews were all saved. Those ships being refitted that stood in need of immediate repair, the fleet sailed from Tybee to North Edisto Sound in the province of South Carolina; and on the eleventh of February the troops were disembarked . . . about 30 miles [below] Charleston. Part of the fleet was immediately sent round to block up the harbour of Charleston by sea. . . .

Charleston was on the point of a narrow peninsula at the junction of the mouthwaters of the Ashley and Cooper rivers, with the Ashley being on the side of Clinton's approach. It was the general's plan to seal up the city and its defenders (who were commanded by General Benjamin Lincoln) by stringing his troops across the peninsula from river to river. He moved northward slowly and cautiously; and, reaching the Ashley, spent several weeks waiting for a reinforcement to march up from Savannah. Included in this reinforcement was Lieutenant Anthony Allaire (of Major Patrick Ferguson's corps), who kept a record of the journey:

Saturday, [March] 11: Crossed the Savannah River. . . . Tuesday, 14th: Found several horses, a quantity of furniture, Continental stores and ammunition hid in a swamp by one John Stafford, a sort of rebel commissary who lives at Coosawhatchie and is . . . a cursed fool, which alone prevents his being a damned rogue. About five o'clock in the afternoon we crossed Tullyfinny Bridge and proceeded about six miles to Mr. McPherson's. Fifty of the [South Carolina] militia on horseback had just left this plantation. . . . A small party of ours pursued them, but could not come up with them. . . . Thursday, 16th: Remained at McPherson's plantation, living on the fat of the land, the soldiers . . . roasting turkeys, fowls,

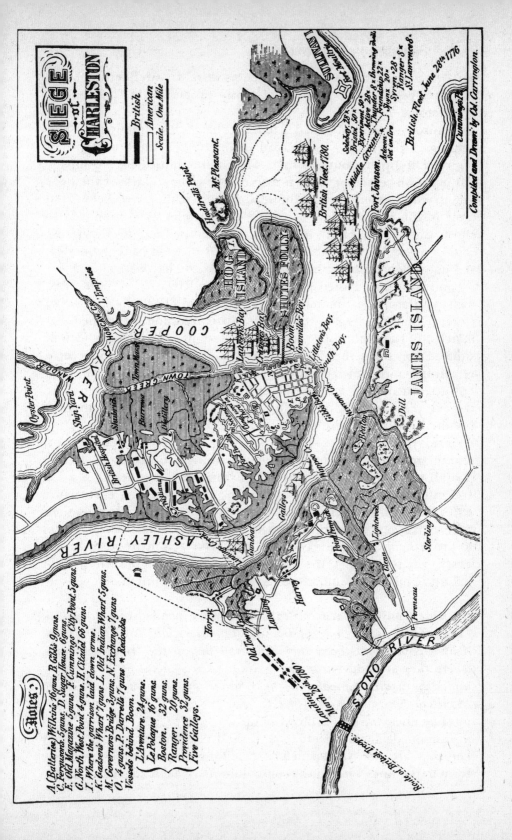

SIEGE of CHARLESTON

British
American
Scale: One Mile

Notes?

A. (Batteries) Wilkie's 16 guns. B. Gibbs 9 guns.
C. Ferguson's 5 guns. D. Sugar House. 6 guns.
E. Old Magazine 5 guns. F. Cummings City Point 5 guns.
G. North West Point 4 guns. H. Citadel 68 guns.
I. Where the garrison laid down arms.
K. Gadsen's Wharf 7 guns. L. Old Indian Wharf 5 guns.
M. Governor's Bridge 3 guns. N. Exchange 7 guns.
O. 4 guns. P. Darrell's 7 guns. * Redoubts
Vessels behind Boom.

L'Aventure. 24 guns.
Le Polaque 16 guns.
Boston. 32 guns.
Ranger. 20 guns.
Providence 32 guns.
Five Galleys.

Compiled and Drawn by Col. Carrington.

British Fleet. June 28th 1776.

British Fleet. 1780.

Solebay 28ₓ   Actæon 28 + burning Hull.
Bristol 50ₓ   Active 28ₓ
Experiment 50ₓ Thunder 8ₓ Friendship 22ₓ
                Sphynx 20ₓ Acteon Æ.
                Syren 28ₓ   Ranger 8ₓ
                            St. Lawrence8.
Middle Ground
Not on fire

Fort Johnson

JAMES ISLAND

STONO RIVER

Route of British Troops

Landing 29th Feb. 1780.
Old Town Creek

Route of British Troops

pigs, etc., every night in great plenty—this Mr. McPherson being a great rebel and a man of vast property, at present in Charleston. . . .

Saturday, 18th: Marched from McPherson's plantation to Salt-ketcher. A rebel party . . . placed themselves on the north side of the river to oppose our crossing. They were amused by a company of the legion returning their fire across the river . . . whilst the light infantry and remainder of the legion crossed the river below and came in the rear of them. . . . Here the bayonet was introduced so effectually that a Capt. Mills and sixteen privates of the rebels could not exist any longer. . . . Four [others] were badly wounded, and one taken prisoner that luckily escaped the bayonet. . . .

Sunday, 19th: Passed [over] Saltketcher River. . . . Wednesday, 22d: The army . . . marched as far as Horse Shoe, where we . . . were detained to repair the bridge. After crossing, continued our march to [Jacksonboro]. . . . [I]t is a pleasant little place, and well situated for trade, but the inhabitants are all rebels—not a man remaining in the town except two, one of whom was so sick he could not get out of bed, and the other a doctor. . . . The women were treated very tenderly and with the utmost civility, notwithstanding their husbands were out in arms against us. . . .

Friday, 24th: . . . This day . . . Ferguson got the [position of] rear guard in order to do his King and country justice by protecting [Loyalists] and widows, and destroying rebel property; also to collect livestock for the use of the army; all of which we effect as we go by destroying furniture, breaking windows, etc., taking all their horned cattle, horses, mules, sheep, fowls, etc., and their Negroes to drive them. . . . Tuesday, 28th: The army . . . marched to Ashley Ferry, where we met the British and Hessians, grenadiers, light infantry and Yagers under command of Sir. H. Clinton.

An American in Charleston said in a letter penned on March 30: "Yesterday a large body of British grenadiers and infantry crossed Ashley River, and today they appeared before the American lines, where they are now encamped." Among the general officers serving under Benjamin Lincoln in the Charleston defenses was William Moultrie, who wrote on April 3:

The enemy are . . . throwing up works very fast. . . . We began to cannonade them yesterday, and shall continue every day. Their batteries are not yet opened. . . . [T]he women walk out from town to the lines with all the composure imaginable to see us cannonade the enemy, but I fancy when the enemy begin they will make themselves pretty scarce.

At this time a formidable British fleet under Admiral Marriott Arbuthnot was lying just outside the range of the guns of Fort Moultrie, the defense at the harbor entrance that had changed the course of the war in the summer of 1776 by mauling the fleet under Clinton and Parker. "As soon as the British [land troops] began to erect batteries against the town," explains England's Charles Stedman, "Admiral Arbuthnot embraced the first favourable opportunity that offered for passing Fort Moultrie. . . ." The decision to hasten past the fort instead of attempting to reduce it proved to be a wise one. According to an American report of April 9:

This afternoon . . . the British fleet passed Fort Moultrie . . . and anchored . . . just out of reach of the guns from the town, where they now continue. . . . One of their frigates had a fore-topmast shot away by a cannon at the fort, and a store ship was so injured in her rudder . . . she went on shore . . . which obliged them to burn her to prevent her falling into our hands. After burning a while she blew up. We had not a man hurt at the fort, though they kept up a brisk fire as they passed.

A number of American warships had been stationed in Charleston Harbor, but their commander, Abraham Whipple, took them into the mouth of the Cooper River as the British approached. There he had sunk several, along with some merchant vessels, to keep Arbuthnot's force from entering the river and making the enemy's encirclement of the city complete. In the meantime, the British on land had continued to make good progress. On April 12 an American diarist recorded:

Day before yesterday the British, having completed their first parallel, summoned the town to surrender, of which General Lincoln took no notice [other than to send a brief note of refusal]; and today Clinton opened his batteries, which are answered . . . with spirit, but not with the effect that will insure success, the enemy's fire being far superior to ours.

Charles Stedman says that the British batteries soon made "a visible impression":

But still the communication between the country and the garrison was kept open across Cooper River. . . . To assist in preserving this communication, General Lincoln had left his cavalry without the lines, with orders to traverse and keep open the country to the eastward of Cooper River, as being that through which he expected to receive his reinforcements [seven hundred of whom had already slipped through, after a forced march from Virginia]; and by the same route he hoped to be able to make good his retreat with the garrison if at last he should find the town no longer tenable.

. . . Sir Henry Clinton . . . was enabled to detach Lieutenant-Colonel [James] Webster with one thousand four hundred men to cut off those of the enemy. By the advanced guard of this detachment, composed of Tarleton's Legion and Ferguson's Corps, the American cavalry, with the militia attached to them, were surprised in the night of the fourteenth of April at Biggin's Bridge, near Monck's Corner, thirty-two miles from Charleston, and completely routed. . . .

With this attack, the youthful, able, and daring Lieutenant Colonel Banastre Tarleton launched himself on a considerable career connected with the war in the South. Patriots would come to fear and hate him wherever he rode, for he was especially aggressive and ruthless. His troops were apt to react to appeals for mercy with bullets and sword hacks; "Tarleton's quarter" became a byword for this kind of inhumanity. Only about thirty Americans were killed or wounded at Biggin's Bridge, but Tarleton's men committed excesses. Charles Stedman, who rarely included his own participation in the occurrences he recorded, made an exception in this case:

Major [Paul Vernier] was mangled in the most shocking manner. He had several wounds, a severe one behind his ear. This unfortunate officer lived several hours . . . even in his last moments cursing the British for their barbarity in having refused quarter after he had surrendered. The writer of this, who was . . . on this expedition, afforded every assistance in his power, and had the major put upon a table in a public house in the village, and a blanket thrown over him. The major, in his last moments, was frequently insulted by the privates of the legion [under Tarleton's command].

Some dragoons . . . attempted to ravish several ladies at the house of Sir John Collington, in the neighbourhood of Monck's Corner. Mrs. ——, the wife of [a Charleston doctor], was most barbarously treated. She was a most delicate and beautiful woman. Lady —— received one or two wounds with a sword. Miss —— . . .

Lieutenant Colonel Banastre Tarleton. Engraving after Sir
Joshua Reynolds portrait. *(Metropolitan Museum of Art, be-
quest of Charles Allen Munn, 1929)*

was also ill-treated. The ladies made their escape and came to Monck's Corner, where they were protected. . . . The dragoons were apprehended. . . . Patrick Ferguson . . . was for putting the dragoons to instant death; but Colonel Webster did not conceive that his powers extended to that of holding a general court-martial. The prisoners were, however, sent to headquarters, and I believe were afterwards tried and whipped.

On April 18, one of Charleston's defenders wrote:

The cannonading on both sides still continues. General Clinton received a reinforcement from New York yesterday, and it is probable he will make a further advance on us soon. He is very cautious and moves with all the care and deliberation of an old Roman, which he certainly is not. Our men are in good spirits, although it seems to be the general opinion that we must at last succumb. . . .

Stedman says that the arrival of the reinforcement from New York enabled Clinton to send a second detachment across the Cooper: ". . . the command of the whole was given to Earl Cornwallis. The force . . . was now so considerable as to cut off from the garrison all reasonable hopes of effecting a retreat." Writing on April 27, General Moultrie admitted that the Americans were now closely blocked up:

I have lost my brave and worthy aid, Philip Neyle (the only child of a crippled and aged father), killed by a cannon ball . . . which took away a part of his head; since which my poor brother Tom was killed. . . . They went out to sally into the enemy's entrenchments. They brought in twelve prisoners, and bayoneted fifteen or twenty more. My brother was the only man killed . . . in this sortie of 300 men. We two days ago had Colonel Parker killed; [otherwise] very little damage has yet happened; not above ten killed and forty wounded, notwithstanding the great number of cannon balls and shells that are thrown into the town.

On April 30, a militiaman in Charleston named Benjamin Smith penned a letter that he tried to have smuggled through the British lines to his wife:

After going through many difficulties, our affairs are daily declining. . . . The enemy have continued their approaches with vigour . . . and are now completing batteries about two hundred yards distance from our lines. . . . [A] short time will plant the British

standard on our ramparts. . . . This will give a rude shock to the independence of America. . . . I hope I shall be permitted to return
home [on parole], where I must stay, as my situation will not permit me to take any further an active part. . . . This letter will run
great risque, as it will be surrounded on all sides; but as I know the
person to whose care it is committed, and feel for your uneasy
situation [regarding my welfare], I could not but trust it. Assure
yourself that I shall shortly see you, as nothing prevents Lincoln's
surrender but a point of honour in holding out to the last extremity. This is nearly at hand, as our provisions will soon fail;
and my plan is to walk off as soon as I can obtain permission. . . .
But a mortifying scene must first be encountered. The thirteen
stripes will be levelled in the dust, and I [will] owe my life to the
clemency of a conqueror.

*This letter was intercepted by the British; and General Clinton,
elated by its admissions, ordered it published.*

*On May 6 the bypassed Fort Moultrie, threatened by a com-
bined land and water assault on its weaker sides, "consented to submission." Shortly General Moultrie noted unhappily from Charleston that "a British flag was . . . flying on the flagstaff."*

*On May 8, under a truce, Lincoln and Clinton began to discuss
terms for the capitulation of the city. The negotiations came to a
deadlock on the ninth, and Clinton sent word that hostilities would
be resumed that evening. In Moultrie's words:*

After receiving the . . . letter, we remained near an hour silent,
all calm and ready, each waiting for the other to begin. At length
we fired the first gun, and immediately [there] followed a tremendous cannonade; and the mortars from both sides threw out an
immense number of shells. It was a glorious sight to see them
like meteors crossing each other and bursting in the air. It appeared as if the stars were tumbling down. The fire was incessant
almost the whole night—cannon balls whizzing and shells hissing
continually amongst us; ammunition chests and temporary magazines blowing up; great guns bursting, and wounded men groaning
along the lines. It was a dreadful night! It was our last great
effort, but it availed us nothing. After this, our military ardor was
much abated. We began to cool, and . . . on the eleventh we
capitulated. . . .

This was a staggering blow to the American cause. Within a week,

Sir Henry sent expeditions fanning out to complete South Caro-
lina's subjugation. Little resistance was encountered, and the job
was accomplished quickly. Banastre Tarleton's mounted troops gave
the Americans another taste of "Tarleton's quarter." Overtaking a
retreating column at the Waxhaws, near the North Carolina border,
the horsemen closed in savagely, ignoring a flag of surrender. "One
hundred and thirteen were killed on the spot," writes Charles
Stedman, "and . . . one hundred and fifty were badly wounded.
. . . The King's troops were entitled to great commendation for
their activity and ardour . . . but the virtue of humanity was totally
forgot."

Clinton now controlled both Georgia and South Carolina. Ac-
cording to Stedman:

. . . the commander in chief, on the fifth of June, embarked for
New York, carrying with him all the troops that could be spared,
leaving Lieutenant-General Earl Cornwallis in the command of
those that remained, with the charge of prosecuting the war in North
Carolina as soon as . . . circumstances would permit.

34

THE SUMMER OF 1780

THE AMERICAN *army quartered in log huts at Morristown, New Jersey, had barely managed to stay intact during the fierce winter months of 1779–1780. That it survived was due in a large part to direct aid in the form of food, clothing, blankets, and other supplies from patriotic civilians, with women's groups being particularly active in the effort. But the camp still suffered from shortages as spring came. The Patriot cause in general was at a low ebb. The South was being systematically conquered, and Washington's northern army was too weak to make any decisive moves. There was a good deal of hope, however. For one thing, it was known that England's outlook, in spite of her recent successes, was none too bright. Her treasury and her manpower were being strained in ways that hadn't been anticipated. The war she had launched to put down a colonial rebellion had got out of hand; its fronts now extended to several parts of the world. Spain had entered on the side of France and America, and Holland was leaning in the same direction. As summed up by an editorial writer in a May issue of* the New Jersey Journal:

When we look to Europe, we there behold the contending parties becoming more and more serious in their determinations. Formidable preparations are making, equally so by Britain as well as all the other belligerent powers. When we turn our eyes to the West India Islands, we there see the same dexterous game playing. Again, when we look to Gibraltar, we find that Britain intends to use her most strenuous efforts in keeping possession of that very important fortress; and, on the other hand, Spain seems to be determined to reduce it under her dominions. . . . The taking of sundry Dutch vessels by the English of late will, it is thought, pave the way to some happy overture. The capital power of Russia . . . conducts in a manner highly foreboding a desire that America may be rendered free and independent. Nay, it is so manifestly the interest of all the European powers to have such an event take place that we may justly unite and say (as Lord North . . . confessed in the House of Commons) Britain is left without an ally.

The Americans were still placing their greatest reliance on the French. On May 10, Dr. Thacher noted in his journal: "The Marquis de Lafayette has just arrived at headquarters, lately from France. The safe return of this respectable personage is a matter of joy and congratulation." Lafayette, who had been on leave from the American army for more than a year, was elated at being reunited with his "beloved and respected friend and general," and brought him some happy news. Another fleet carrying a large land force was on the way from France, and the officers had been instructed to work in close cooperation with Washington. The prime minister of France was reported to have said at this time, "It is fortunate for the King that Lafayette does not take it into his head to strip Versailles of his furniture to send to his dear Americans, as His Majesty would be unable to refuse it." Washington's hope soared. His main problem now, it appeared, would be to secure enough help from Congress and the American people to put his own troops into a suitable condition to work with their great ally. The morale of some of the troops was deplorable. On May 25, according to Dr. Thacher:

Two regiments of the Connecticut line took the liberty to parade without their officers, and in the spirit of mutiny resolved to march into the country to relieve themselves from present difficulties and to furnish themselves with provisions at all hazards. Colonel [Return] Meigs, in attempting to restore order, received a blow from one of the mutineers. A brigade of Pennsylvanians was ordered to arrest their progress . . . and the two regiments . . . returned to their duty. Their complaints are that . . . their sufferings are insupportable, that their pay is five months in arrear and that it is of no value when received. These circumstances are known to be substantially true, and in justice they ought, and undoubtedly will, be admitted in extenuation of the crime which they have committed. It is nevertheless indispensably important that every symptom of insubordination should be crushed as soon as discovered, lest the example become contagious and involve the whole army in ruin.

Washington considered the mutiny, along with its causes, a matter of infinite concern:

This is a decisive moment . . . the most important America has seen. The court of France has made a glorious effort for our deliverance, and if we disappoint its intentions by our supineness we must become contemptible in the eyes of all mankind.

The general had been making every effort to keep his pathetic army well disciplined. This sometimes required the severest of measures. On the day after the mutiny the whole camp was exposed to a demonstration that no man would soon forget. It had nothing to do with the mutiny, occurring only by coincidence at this time. Eleven men had been condemned to die for various crimes—three to be shot and the others to be hanged. With the executions about to begin, the trio received pardons. Dr. Thacher tells what happened to the eight who had been sentenced to the gallows:

This was a most solemn and affecting scene. . . . The wretched criminals were brought in carts to the place of execution. Mr. Rogers, the chaplain, attended them to the gallows . . . impressing on their minds the heinousness of their crimes, the justice of their sentence and the high importance of a preparation for death. The criminals were placed side by side on the scaffold with halters round their necks, their coffins before their eyes, their graves open to their view, and thousands of spectators bemoaning their awful doom. The moment approaches when every eye is fixed in expectation of beholding the agonies of death. The eyes of the victims are already closed [by blindfolds] from the light of this world. At this awful moment, while their fervent prayers are ascending to heaven, an officer comes forward and reads a reprieve for seven of them by the commander-in-chief. The trembling criminals are now divested of the habiliments of death, and their bleeding hearts leap for joy. . . . No pen can describe the emotions which must have agitated their souls. They were scarcely able to remove from the scaffold without assistance. . . .

The [remaining] criminal . . . had been guilty of forging . . . discharges by which he and more than a hundred soldiers had left the army. He appeared to be penitent, and behaved with uncommon fortitude and resolution. He addressed the soldiers, desired them to be faithful to their country and obedient to their officers, and advised the officers to be punctual in all their engagements to the soldiers and give them no cause to desert. He examined the halter and told the hangman the knot was not made right and that the rope was not strong enough, as he was a heavy man. Having adjusted the knot and fixed it round his own neck, he was swung off instantly. The rope broke and he fell to the ground, by which he was very much bruised. He calmly reascended the ladder and said, "I told you the rope was not strong enough! Do get a stronger one!" Another being procured, he was launched into eternity.

The British in New York were well aware of the wretched condition of Washington's army, and early in June five to six thousand men under General Wilhelm von Knyphausen crossed from Staten Island to Elizabethtown Point with the hope of dealing the rebellion a mortal blow. To the elderly German's surprise, he had proceeded only a few miles inland when he began to encounter lively resistance. His army, however, succeeded in burning the village of Connecticut Farms (now Union). During the fighting there, the wife of the Reverend James Caldwell, the mother of a number of children, was killed by a random musket ball. A British officer was later to write: ". . . it appears beyond a doubt that the shot was fired by the rebels themselves, as it entered the side of the house from their direction. . . ." But regardless of how the incident happened, it inflamed the Patriots in the same manner as the murder of Jane McCrea at the hands of Burgoyne's Indians. Knyphausen had intended to press on through Springfield, but American troops began gathering in such numbers that he decided instead to fall back to the coast.

Two weeks later, aided by Sir Henry Clinton, who had just returned from the South, the enemy advanced again. This time they were opposed at Springfield by a detachment of Continentals and some militia units under General Nathanael Greene. Again the Americans showed great spirit. When the men of Colonel Elias Dayton's regiment ran short of wadding for their musket charges, the grieving but unbroken Reverend Mr. Caldwell quickly passed out hymn books to be torn up for this use. After burning a church and a score of houses in Springfield, the invaders again retreated to the coast. On the following day an American soldier wrote: "This

Charles, Lord Cornwallis.

1780 cartoon of Rochambeau reviewing his troops. *(Library of Congress)*

morning some of [our] horsemen have been down to Elizabethtown and find that the British went over to Staten Island last night, took up their [floating] bridge, and bid us farewell." Washington now marched his army northeastward toward the Hudson Highlands. On July 14, Dr. Thacher recorded with elation:

An express has arrived . . . from Rhode Island with the pleasing information of the arrival there of a French fleet accompanied by an army of six thousand . . . French troops who are to cooperate with our army as allies in our cause. They are commanded by [Jean Baptiste Donatien de Vimeur, Comte de] Rochambeau, a distinguished general in the French service.

In a letter dated July 16, General Rochambeau reported to the French government:

Upon our arrival here, the country was in consternation. The paper money had fallen to sixty for one. . . . I spoke to the principal persons of the place and told them . . . that . . . the king was determined to support them with his whole power. In twenty-four hours their spirits rose, and last night all the streets, houses and steeples [of Newport] were illuminated in the midst of fireworks and the greatest rejoicings. . . . You see . . . how important it is to

act with vigor. . . . Send us troops, ships and money. But do not depend upon these people, nor upon their means. They have neither money nor credit. Their means of resistance are only momentary, and called forth when they are attacked in their homes. They then assemble for the moment of immediate danger and defend themselves. Washington commands sometimes fifteen thousand, sometimes three thousand men.

As August began, Dr. Thacher wrote:

It is understood that General Clinton has despatched a part of the British fleet and army on an expedition against our allies, the French fleet and army at Rhode Island. The whole of our army having crossed to the east side of the Hudson, it is conjectured that his excellency contemplates some important enterprise against the enemy at New York, or at least [wishes] to compel General Clinton to recall his expedition from Rhode Island for his own safety. . . .

It is now ascertained (August 4th) that the formidable manoeuvre of our army has effected the object intended. The enemy's expedition to Rhode Island has returned to New York. . . . Orders are now received for our army to recross the Hudson. . . .

The communications that Washington received from the deep South during the latter part of the summer were at first somewhat encouraging. They indicated that the enemy's control of Georgia and South Carolina was not absolute. The spirit of rebellion was being kept alive by Francis Marion, Thomas Sumter, Andrew Pickens, Elijah Clarke, and a number of other elusive southern officers. These men, perhaps the best known of whom was Marion, the "Swamp Fox," had assembled small bands of irregulars and were making repeated hit-and-run attacks on British detachments and on parties of armed Tories. When pursued, the raiders usually vanished into remote swamps or woodlands. They were keeping the enemy on edge, and, in some areas, posed a threat to their security. Washington was basing considerable hope also on some troops he had dispatched from his own army to unite with a gathering of southern militiamen for an organized attack. Congress had sent General Horatio Gates, the hero of Saratoga, to take command of this aggregation. News of the effort's outcome reached the northern army about September 1. In Thacher's words:

Our southern army . . . has been totally defeated in a general action with Lord Cornwallis on the [16th] of August [at Camden, South Carolina]. General Gates, as is reported, retreated with precipitation . . . to escape the pursuit of the enemy. This mortifying disaster gives a severe shock to our army. . . . In his letter to the President of Congress, General Gates says . . . that the Continental troops displayed their usual courage and bravery, but at the first onset of the enemy the whole body of militia became panic-struck, were completely routed and ran like a torrent . . . leaving the Continentals to oppose the whole force of the enemy. . . . Among the killed is Baron de Kalb, a major-general. . . . He was a German by birth. . . . This very unfortunate event has given an impression universally unfavorable to the character and conduct of General Gates, as he has disappointed the high expectations of the public.

Washington was too busy to spend much time brooding over this new setback. One of his oldest problems was giving him special trouble. Dr. Thacher lamented on September 5: "It is mortifying that our stock of provisions is again exhausted. The soldiers have for several days drawn nothing but one pound of flour a man." There were officers, of course, who did not suffer equally with the enlisted men. The doctor admits that on September 8 he and some other officers were invited to dine in style with the Baron von

Steuben: "Notwithstanding the scarcity of provisions in camp, the baron's table continues to be well supplied. His generosity is unbounded."

On September 17, according to Thacher:

His Excellency General Washington with the Marquis de Lafayette and General Knox, with a splendid retinue, left the camp . . . bound to Hartford in Connecticut to have an interview with the commanding officers of the French fleet and army which have lately arrived at Rhode Island.

Meeting in Hartford on September 21, Washington and the two French leaders, the Comte de Rochambeau and Admiral Charles Louis, the Chevalier de Ternay, were "quite charmed with one another," but unable to make any serious plans. A second British expedition had blockaded Newport, and Rochambeau and Ternay were awaiting reinforcements from France. Enough vessels were needed not only to break the blockade but to shatter England's naval superiority. Until this kind of help arrived, the French leaders had little choice but to sit tight. Disappointed in the meeting, Washington began his return to camp on September 23, planning to stop off at West Point, where Benedict Arnold commanded, and inspect the fortifications. This decision landed him in the middle of an astonishing situation.

35

ARNOLD CHANGES SIDES

A T THREE o'clock this morning [wrote Dr. Thacher on September 26, 1780] an alarm was spread throughout our camp. Two regiments from the Pennsylvania line were ordered to march immediately to West Point, and the whole army to be held in readiness to march at a moment's warning. It was soon ascertained that this sudden movement was in consequence of the discovery of one of the most extraordinary events in modern history. . . . The . . . following communication . . . was read by the adjutants to their respective regiments:

"Treason of the blackest dye was yesterday discovered. General Arnold, who commanded at West Point, lost to every sentiment of honor, of private and public obligation, was about to deliver up that important post into the hands of the enemy. Such an event must have given the American cause a dangerous, if not a fatal wound. Happily the treason has been timely discovered. . . . The providential train of circumstances which led to it affords the most convincing proofs that the liberties of America are the object of divine protection. . . . Great honor is due to the American army that this is the first instance of treason of the kind, where many were to be expected from the nature of our dispute. . . ."

West Point is situated in the midst of the Highlands on the west side of the Hudson, sixty miles above New York. . . . It is a strongly fortified castle which, with its dependencies, is considered by General Washington as the key which locks the communication between the Eastern and Southern states; and, of all the posts in the United States, this is the most important. . . .

From the commencement of the American war, General Arnold has been viewed in the light of a brave and heroic officer . . . and it is from his bravery in the field, more than any intrinsic merit, that his character and fame have been established. His meritorious services have been amply rewarded by his promotion to the rank of major-general; but his name will now be transmitted to posterity with marks of infamy, and the pages of our history will be tarnished by the record of crimes of the most atrocious character by a native of our land.

Arnold's switch in allegiance was not a sudden thing. It had been developing over a period of many months. After the British evacuated Philadelphia in June, 1778, he was made the city's military governor. Straining his means to the utmost, he set himself up in a mansion and surrounded himself with the trappings and pageantry of a nobleman. He cultivated associations with the city's wealthier citizens, including Tories. Shortly he met Miss Margaret (Peggy) Shippen, an "elegant and accomplished" beauty not yet twenty years old. Arnold, a widower, was nearly forty and handicapped by the leg wound acquired at Bemis Heights, but he opened a campaign of courtship, and the two were married in 1779. With Peggy's encouragement and aid, Arnold engaged in a secret correspondence with the British in New York, offering to switch sides and help bring the war to an early end—in exchange for a large sum of money. The correspondence was conducted through twenty-nine-year-old John André, whom Peggy had known during the British occupation of Philadelphia and who was now serving as Sir Henry Clinton's deputy adjutant general.

During this whole period, according to Thacher, Arnold had been trying to better his finances in other ways:

Unmindful of his military station, he engaged in various speculations and in privateering [investments], in both of which he was unfortunate. He made exorbitant demands on government in compensation for public services, and made bitter complaints against Congress . . . that he suffered injustice from their hands. The commissioners appointed to liquidate his accounts rejected a large proportion of his demands as being unjust and unfounded. . . . He was charged by the citizens of Philadelphia with gross acts of extortion and of peculating on the public funds; and . . . the gen-

GENERAL ARNOLD.

From a portrait drawn from life during his tour as military governor of Philadelphia.

eral voice demanded an investigation of his conduct. . . . Congress directed that he should be arrested and tried by a court-martial. He was sentenced to be reprimanded by the commander-in-chief, which . . . was carried into execution accordingly.

Washington's words were not severe:

I reprimand you for having forgotten that in proportion as you had rendered yourself formidable to our enemies, you should have been guarded and temperate in your deportment toward your fellow citizens. Exhibit anew those noble qualities which have placed you on the list of our most valued commanders. I will myself furnish you, as far as it may be in my power, with opportunities of gaining the esteem of your country.

But Arnold now had an almost desperate wish to be furnished with an opportunity of an altogether different nature. Thacher explains:

The emoluments of his office, with all his embezzlements, proved inadequate to his exigencies; and, his funds being exhausted, he was unable to meet the demands of his creditors. Thus he evinced a mind destitute of both moral principle and political integrity. . . . At the opening of the campaign in . . . 1780, the commander-in-chief offered him . . . [an important field command], to which his rank entitled him; but this he declined, under the pretext that the wound which he received at Saratoga rendered him incapable of active service. . . . He solicited the station of commander of the garrison at West Point; and in this request he was indulged by the commander-in-chief, who still had confidence in him as a military officer. He was now invested with a situation which furnished him with the meditated opportunity of executing his treasonable purpose. . . .

Arnold went to West Point alone but was soon joined by his wife and a newborn son. In a continuation of the secret correspondence with New York, the agreement was made: Arnold would surrender the post, and Sir Henry Clinton would fill the yawning Arnold purse. Dr. Thacher continues:

The British general . . . selected Major John André . . . to have a personal interview with the traitor to mature the plan. . . . A British sloop-of-war called the *Vulture* came up the . . . river and anchored . . . about twelve miles below West Point. . . . [T]he place chosen for [the interview] was the beach near the house of Joshua Smith, Esquire, who has long been suspected of a predilection for the British interest [but was not, it seems, aware of Arnold's intentions]. In the night of the 21st [of September, 1780] Smith, by the desire of Arnold, went with a boat rowed by some men employed on his farm and brought Major André, alias John Anderson, on shore where he was received by Arnold and [after a long parley] conducted to the house of Smith, within our lines. André remained concealed at Smith's house till the following night, when he became extremely anxious to return on board the *Vulture.*

But during the day the vessel had been fired upon by some alert Americans on the opposite shore, forcing her to change her position; and Smith was now unwilling to risk another trip to her side. Thacher goes on:

. . . it was resolved that André should return to New York by land, to which he reluctantly submitted as the only alternative to escape the danger into which he had been betrayed. For this hazardous attempt, Arnold and Smith furnished him with a horse and with clothes in exchange for his military uniform; and Arnold gave him a passport under the fictitious name of John Anderson, as being on public business. Thus prepared, and accompanied by Smith . . . he proceeded on his journey.

Young André was much of the time quiet and preoccupied as he and Smith traveled first to Stony Point, where they crossed by ferry to the Hudson's east bank, and then faced their horses south toward the Croton River, where Smith planned to turn back. Toward the end of this leg of the trip the major, encouraged to find that his disguise was working, became more cheerful and talkative. Smith relates:

. . I now found him highly entertaining. He was not only well informed in general history but well acquainted with that of America. . . . He had consulted the Muses as well as Mars, for he conversed freely on the belles-lettres. Music, painting and poetry seemed to be his delight. He displayed a judicious taste in the choice of the authors he had read, possessed great elegance of sentiment and a most pleasing manner of conveying his ideas by adopting the flowery colouring of poetical imagery. He lamented the causes which gave birth to and continued the war. . . .

I left [him] at Pine's Bridge, and had pointed out to him the road to the White Plains . . . but he thought the road by the

way of Dobb's Ferry, having the [Hudson] as his guide, would
be much the nearest route; and, having a good horse, he boldly
ventured to take that road. But he . . . was stopped by . . . a scouting
party, between the outposts of the two armies. These men stopped
Major André at a place near Tarrytown and seized his horse by the
bridle in a narrow part of the road. André, instead of immediately
producing his pass, asked where they belonged to? They answered,
"to below" [meaning to New York]. Not suspecting deception, he
replied, "So do I," and, declaring himself a British officer, intreated
that he might not be detained, being on pressing business. . . .
[T]hey took him aside in the bushes and searched him until they
found his papers [which included information about West Point's
defenses] lodged in his boots. . . . The captors then conducted him
to Lieutenant-Colonel [John] Jameson, a Continental officer. . . .

*Failing to grasp the implications of the situation, Jameson decided
to send André, under escort, to Arnold. At the same time, however,
the colonel gave André's papers to a courier and instructed him to
try to find Washington, who was known to be making his return
from his Hartford meeting with the French and was expected to
pass through West Point. André did not complete his journey back
to Arnold. Alert young Major Benjamin Tallmadge rode into
Colonel Jameson's camp soon after the party left, and, learning the
story, urged the colonel to have the prisoner recalled. Jameson did
so. But, unable to believe that Arnold had turned traitor, the
colonel insisted on sending him word of what had happened. Returning to Dr. Thacher's account:*

. . . Arnold . . . received the information . . . on the morning of
the 25th instant. At this moment . . . two of his excellency's aids . . .
[having preceded him to West Point] were at breakfast at
Arnold's table [at his headquarters on the river's eastern bank]. His
confusion was visible, but no one could devise the cause. Struck
with the pressing danger of his situation, expecting General Washington would soon arrive, the guilty traitor called instantly for a
"horse, any one, even if a wagon horse," bid a hasty adieu to his
wife . . . and having repaired to his barge, he ordered the coxwain
with eight oarsmen to proceed down the river, and he was
soon on board the *Vulture* . . . which immediately sailed . . . for
New York.

General Washington arrived . . . and was informed that Arnold
had absented himself, saying he was going [across the river] to West

Point, and should soon return. His excellency passed over the river to view the works there; but, not finding Arnold at his post, he returned in the hope of meeting him at his quarters.

The general met instead Colonel Jameson's courier with André's papers. Though he must have been appalled as the evidence of Arnold's plot presented itself, Washington kept his composure. "Whom can we trust now?" he asked his aides. As for Peggy Arnold, she had earlier taken to her bedroom in a highly nervous state. Everyone believed that her condition was caused by her husband's sudden departure under unaccountable circumstances, but she was doubtless sick over his failure. Covering the real reason for her distress with some splendid acting, she won much sympathy from the American officers. Shortly Washington received a letter from Arnold. It had been written on board the Vulture, *and it contained a request:*

The heart which is conscious of its own rectitude cannot attempt to palliate a step which the world may censure as wrong. I have ever acted from a principle of love to my country, since the commencement of the present unhappy contest between Great Britain and the colonies. The same principle of love to my country actuates my present conduct, however it may appear inconsistent to the world, who very seldom judge right of any man's actions. I have no favor to ask for myself. I have too often experienced the ingratitude of my country to attempt it. But from the known humanity of your excellency I am induced to ask your protection for Mrs. Arnold from every insult and injury that the mistaken vengeance of my country may expose her to. It ought to fall only on me. She is as good and as innocent as an angel, and is incapable of doing wrong. I beg she may be permitted to return to her friends in Philadelphia or to come to me, as she may choose. From your excellency I have no fears on her account, but she may suffer from the mistaken fury of the country.

Washington gave orders for Peggy and her infant son to be escorted safely to Philadelphia. She would presently join her husband among his new associates. As for the luckless John André, he was first brought to West Point and next ordered to be taken down the Hudson to the main army's headquarters, then located at Tappan, in the border country between New York and New Jersey. He was

Major John André, above,
and as sketched by
himself, at right.

in the custody of Major Benjamin Tallmadge, who says that during the trip

. . . he became very inquisitive to know my opinion as to the result of his capture. When I could no longer evade his importunity, I remarked to him as follows: "I had a much-loved classmate in Yale College by the name of Hale, who entered the army in 1775. Immediately after the Battle of Long Island, Washington wanted information respecting the strength of the enemy. Hale tendered his services, went over to Brooklyn, and was taken just as he was passing the outposts of the enemy on his return." Said I with emphasis, "Do you remember the sequel of the story?"

"Yes," said André. "He was hanged as a spy. But you surely do not consider his case and mine alike!"

I replied, "Yes, precisely similar; and similar will be your fate."

He endeavoured to answer my remarks, but it was manifest he was more troubled in spirit than I had ever seen him before.

Sir Henry Clinton, writes Dr. Thacher, had hopes of saving his young assistant and friend:

Accordingly he addressed General Washington, claimed the release of Major André, alleging that he ought not to be considered in the character of a spy, as he had a passport from, and was transacting business under the sanction of General Arnold. But arguments so obviously absurd and futile could have no influence. . . . During the trial of this unfortunate officer, he conducted [himself] with unexampled magnanimity and dignity of character. He very freely and candidly confessed all the circumstances relative to himself, and carefully avoided every expression that might have a tendency to implicate any other person. So firm and dignified was he in his manners, and so honorable in all his proceedings on this most trying occasion that he excited universal interest in his favor. He requested only to die the death of a soldier [before a firing squad] and not on a gibbet. The following is a copy of a very pathetic letter from Major André to General Washington, dated . . . October 1st, 1780:

"Sir: Buoyed above the terrors of death by the consciousness of a life devoted to honorable pursuits and stained with no action that can give me remorse, I trust that the request I make to your excellency at this serious period, and which is to soften my last moments, will not be rejected. Sympathy towards a soldier will surely induce your excellency and a military tribunal to adapt the mode of my death to the feelings of a man of honor. Let me hope, sir, if aught in my character impresses you with esteem towards me—if aught in my misfortunes marks me as the victim of policy and not of resentment—I shall experience the operation of these feelings in your breast by being informed that I am not to die on a gibbet."

. . . This moving letter, as may be supposed, affected the mind of General Washington with the tenderest sympathy, and it is reported that he submitted it to a council of general officers, who decided that, as Major André was condemned as a spy, the circumstances of the case would not admit of the request being granted; and his excellency, from a desire to spare the feelings of the unfortunate man, declined making a reply to the letter. . . .

During his confinement and trial, [André] exhibited those proud and elevated sensibilities which designate greatness and dignity of mind. Not a murmur or a sigh ever escaped him, and the civilities and attentions bestowed on him were politely acknowledged. Having left a mother and . . . sisters in England, he was heard to mention them in terms of the tenderest affection; and in his letter to Sir Henry Clinton he recommended them to his particular attention.

Clinton appealed for André's life by means of a last-minute delegation sent to the American lines, but to no avail. He offered to free any war prisoner Washington might name if the young officer was spared. But the only trade that Washington would have made was André for Arnold; and Clinton, much as he wished to save André, could not do this, since no more deserters were likely to come over to the British if Arnold was sent back to what was bound to be a well-publicized execution. Returning to Thacher:

The principal guard officer, who was constantly in the room with the prisoner, relates that when the hour of his execution was announced to him in the morning [of October 2] he received it without emotion; and while all present were affected with silent gloom, he retained a firm countenance, with calmness and composure of mind. . . . His breakfast being sent to him from the table of General Washington, which had been done every day of his confinement, he partook of it as usual, and having shaved and dressed himself he . . . cheerfully said to the guard officers, "I am ready at any moment, gentlemen, to wait on you."

The fatal hour having arrived, a large detachment of troops

was paraded, and an immense concourse of people assembled. Almost all our general and field officers, excepting his excellency and his staff, were present on horseback. Melancholy and gloom pervaded all ranks, and the scene was affectingly awful. I was so near during the solemn march to the fatal spot as to observe every movement and participate in every emotion which the melancholy scene was calculated to produce. Major André walked . . . between two of our subaltern officers, arm in arm. The eyes of the immense multitude were fixed on him, who, rising superior to the fears of death, appeared as if conscious of the dignified deportment which he displayed. He betrayed no want of fortitude, but retained a complacent smile . . . and politely bowed to several gentlemen whom he knew, which was respectfully returned.

It was his earnest desire to be shot . . . and he had indulged the hope that his request would be granted. At the moment, therefore, when suddenly he came in view of the gallows, he involuntarily started backward and made a pause.

"Why this emotion, sir?" said an officer by his side.

Instantly recovering his composure, he said, "I am reconciled to my death, but I detest the mode."

While [he was] waiting and standing near the gallows, I observed some degree of trepidation—[the] placing [of] his foot on a stone and rolling it over, and [a] choking in his throat as if attempting to swallow. So soon, however, as he perceived that things were in readiness, he stepped quickly into the wagon; and at this moment he appeared to shrink; but instantly elevating his head with firmness, he said, "It will be but a momentary pang."

The provost marshal, Colonel Alexander Scammell, now read the death sentence and asked André whether he had any last words. "I pray you to bear me witness," was the answer, "that I meet my fate like a brave man." Snatching the noose from the executioner (who was trying to avoid public recognition by means of an unshaven and soot-blackened face), André put it in place himself. Then he took a white handkerchief from his pocket and bandaged his eyes. A second handkerchief was used to bind his arms behind him. By this time many members of the crowd were lamenting loudly. Writes Thacher:

The wagon being now removed from under him, he was suspended, and instantly expired. It proved indeed "but a momentary pang." He was dressed in his royal regimentals and boots; and his remains . . . were placed in an ordinary coffin and interred at the foot of the gallows; and the spot was consecrated by the tears of thousands. . . .

Could Arnold have been suspended on the gibbet erected for André, not a tear or a sigh would have been produced, but exultation and joy would have been visible on every countenance.

Thacher goes on to say that the frustrated attempt on West Point made it a place of universal celebration:

. . . the loss of this highly important garrison with some of our best officers and men [and] the immense quantity of ordnance and military stores, together with the prodigious panic and gloom which at this critical period must have pervaded the whole people, could scarcely have failed of being productive of consequences overwhelming the physical powers and energies of our country. But we are saved by a *miracle,* and we are confounded in awful astonishment.

The miscarriage of his plans did not subdue the traitor. Again in Thacher's words:

Arnold had the audacity to remonstrate to General Washington against the execution of Major André [before it was effected] and to attempt to intimidate him by threats of retaliation . . . but his excellency treated both the traitor and his affrontive letters with sovereign contempt. [Arnold] next published an address to the people of the United States, in which he pretended to ascribe his defection . . . to principle. . . . He attempts to vindicate his conduct by the ridiculous pretence that he was actuated by motives favorable to the interests of his country by bringing the war to a speedy termination—as though the destiny of America was doomed to be at his disposal, and that he was authorized to decide the fate of millions. In his artful address he labored to palliate his own guilt and to influence others to follow his vile example. He execrated with peculiar bitterness our alliance with France, and accused Congress of tyranny and usurpation and a total disregard of the interest and welfare of the people.

As the treason story closed, Washington wrote in summation:

In no instance since the commencement of the war has the interposition of Providence appeared more remarkably conspicuous than in the rescue of the post and garrison at West Point. . . . A combination of extraordinary circumstances . . . threw the adjutant-general of the British forces, with full proof of Arnold's intention, into our hands. . . . André has met his fate . . . with that fortitude which was to be expected from an accomplished man and a gallant officer. But I [doubt] if Arnold is suffering . . . the torments of a mental hell. He [lacks] feeling. From some traits of his character which have lately come to my knowledge, he seems to have been so hacknied in crime, so lost to all sense of honor and shame, that while his faculties still enable him to continue his sordid pursuits, there will be no time for remorse.

Washington knew his man. Arnold, paid handsomely by the British despite his failure to deliver West Point to them, also received a commission as a brigadier general under Clinton, and prepared now to fight against the Patriots with the same kind of zeal he had shown in their favor.

36

AMERICA'S FORTUNES BRIGHTEN

WHILE *the events connected with Arnold's treason were rocking the North, Lord Cornwallis proceeded confidently with his plan to complete the British conquest of the South. His lordship's shattering victory over General Horatio Gates at Camden, South Carolina, on August 16, 1780, had eliminated, at least for the moment, all organized resistance to his northward advance. Though his outposts in Georgia and South Carolina were being harassed by Marion, the Swamp Fox, and other irregulars, his over-all grip on these states was secure enough so that he had no misgivings about expanding his effort. He picked Charlotte, North Carolina, as his next target. Writes Charles Stedman, now serving as the main army's commissary, or food procurer:*

. . . Charlotte was taken possession of after a slight resistance from the militia towards the end of September. . . . The vicinity of Charlotte abounded with mills [for grinding grain]; and the army . . . was sufficiently supplied with provisions, notwithstanding the hostile disposition of the inhabitants. So inveterate was their rancour that the messengers with expresses for the commander-in-chief were frequently murdered; and the inhabitants . . . made it a practice to waylay the British foraging parties, fire their rifles from concealed places and then fly into the woods. Nevertheless, Charlotte . . . was a convenient situation to be occupied whenever the army should advance farther into North Carolina; and here, accordingly, Lord Cornwallis intended to establish a post.

At this time there was a British detachment operating in the frontier country about seventy miles west of Charlotte. Composed of a few regulars and about a thousand Tories, the unit was commanded by Major Patrick Ferguson. His dual mission was to protect the main army's left flank by breaking up die-hard bands of Whigs and to try to draw additional Tories into active service. Ferguson's march from South Carolina had carried him toward the foothills of the Appalachian Mountains. He had crossed the border into North Carolina on September 7. Five days later, Lieutenant Anthony Allaire penned in his diary:

. . . got in motion at two o'clock in the morning and marched fourteen miles through the mountains to the head of Cane Creek, in Burke County, in order to surprise a party of rebels we heard lay there. Unfortunately . . . they had by some means got intelligence of our coming . . . [and] thought it highly necessary to remove their quarters. However, we were lucky enough to take a different route from what they expected and met them on their way. . . . On our approach they fired and gave way. We totally routed them . . . after which we marched to their encampment and found it abandoned by those Congress heroes.

In an entry made on September 14, Allaire stated that "the poor deluded people of this province begin to be sensible of their error and come in [to renew their allegiance to the Crown] very fast." But the next day, on a march through Pleasant Gardens, on the Catawba River, Allaire got a different impression: "This settlement is composed of the most violent rebels I ever saw, particularly the young ladies."

Major Ferguson made his headquarters at Gilbert Town (today's Rutherfordton), just east of the Appalachians. This put him at the edge of a section of the Blue Ridge chain that was inhabited by some of America's most independent and self-reliant pioneers. Until lately, the frontier Indians siding with the British had been their chief worry. The war to the east had seemed remote. A few parties of riflemen had made sallies as it began to draw closer. Ferguson was well aware that the people were angered by his presence, and he hastened to spread the word that if they rose against him he would "hang their leaders and lay their country waste with fire and sword." In response, hundreds of buckskin-clad men from both sides of the mountains began banding together for immediate action.

Astonished to find his own force outnumbered at least two-to-one by this "set of mongrels," as he termed them, Ferguson began retreating from the Appalachian country toward Charlotte. He tried to inform Cornwallis that he needed reinforcements, but his communications were poor. At least one messenger was intercepted. On October 5, he wrote:

I am on my march towards you by a road leading from Cherokee Ford, north of Kings Mountain. Three or four hundred good soldiers, part dragoons, would finish the business. Something must be done soon.

His mood improved on the sixth:

I arrived today at Kings Mountain and have taken a post where I do not think I can be forced by [even] a stronger enemy than that against us.

He was on a stony plateau atop a loaf-shaped hill, the sides of which were covered with trees. He assured his men that the position was strong enough to be defended against "God Almighty and all the rebels out of hell."

The rebels out of the mountains, who had enlisted the aid of God Almighty with a mass prayer, were on their way to put Ferguson to the test. They were commanded by Colonel William Campbell of Virginia. According to a report signed by Campbell and two associate leaders:

We marched to the Cowpens on Broad River in South Carolina, where we were joined by Colonel James Williams with four hundred men on the evening of the 6th. . . . He informed us that the enemy lay encamped . . . about thirty miles distant from us. By a council of the principal officers it was . . . thought advisable to pursue the enemy that night with nine hundred of the best horsemen, and leave the weak horse and footmen to follow as fast as possible. We began our march . . . [in a drenching rainstorm] about eight o'clock . . . and marching all night, came up with the enemy about three o'clock p.m. on the 7th.

With the rain having stopped, the Americans surrounded the hill. They planned to attempt an assault to its summit. At this point the various unit leaders made short speeches, of which the following was typical:

My brave fellows: . . . When you are engaged, you are not to wait for the word of command from me. I will show you by my example how to fight. . . . Fire as quick as you can, and stand your ground as long as you can. When you can do no better, get behind trees, or retreat; but I beg you not to run quite off. If we are repulsed, let us make a point of returning and renewing the fight. Perhaps we may have better luck in the second attempt than the first. If any of you are afraid, such shall have leave to retire, and they are requested immediately to take themselves off.

One of the younger men present was James Collins, aged sixteen:

Here I confess I would willingly have been excused . . . but I could not well swallow the appellation of coward. . . . We were soon in motion, every man throwing four or five balls in his mouth to prevent thirst—also to be in readiness to reload quick. The shot of the enemy soon began to pass over us like hail. . . . I was soon in a profuse sweat. My lot happened to be in the center, where the severest part of the battle was fought. We soon attempted to climb the hill, but were fiercely charged upon and forced to fall back to our first position. We tried a second time, but met the same fate. The fight then seemed to become more furious. . . . We took to the hill a third time. The enemy gave way. When we had gotten near the top, some of our leaders roared out, "Hurrah, my brave fellows! Advance! They are crying for quarter!" By this time . . . the enemy was completely hemmed in on all sides, and no chance of escaping. Besides, their leader [Patrick Ferguson] had fallen. They soon threw down their arms and surrendered.

Some of the Americans continued to fire ruthlessly into huddled groups of detested Tories until stopped by their officers. When all of the firing had died, the summit rang with three prolonged shouts of victory. The battle had lasted about an hour. The Americans, whose losses were small, had killed or wounded some three hundred men. Lieutenant Anthony Allaire, who had more than once spoken contemptuously of the rebels in his diary, was one of the survivors. The unit to which he belonged had begun the action with seventy men. They were "all killed and wounded but twenty." The prisoners totaled about seven hundred. James Collins completes the picture:

After the fight was over, the situation of the poor Tories appeared to be really pitiable. The dead lay in heaps on all sides, while the groans of the wounded were heard in every direction. I could not help turning away from the scene before me with horror, and, though exulting in victory, could not refrain from shedding tears. . . . On examining the dead body of their great chief, it appeared that almost fifty rifles must have been leveled at him at the same time. Seven rifle balls had passed through his body, both of his arms were broken, and his hat and clothing were literally shot to pieces.

Their great elevation above us had proved their ruin. They overshot us . . . while every rifle from below seemed to have the desired effect. . . .

Next morning, which was Sunday, the scene became really distressing. The wives and children of the poor Tories came in, in great numbers. Their husbands, fathers and brothers lay dead in heaps, while others lay wounded or dying. . . . We proceeded to bury the dead, but it was badly done. They were thrown into convenient piles and covered with old logs, the bark of old trees, and rocks; yet not so as to secure them from becoming a prey to the beasts of the forest or the vultures of the air. And the wolves became so plenty that it was dangerous for anyone to be out at night, for several miles around. Also, the hogs in the neighborhood gathered into the place to devour the flesh of men. . . .

Charles Stedman describes the American victory as "brilliant," but adds:

. . . they shamefully stained the laurels they had won by cruelties exercised upon the prisoners, ten of whom were hanged. . . .

Much had been expected from the exertions of Major Ferguson . . . and by his unfortunate fall and the slaughter, captivity or dispersion of his whole corps the plan of the expedition into North Carolina was entirely deranged. . . . On the fourteenth of October . . . Lord Cornwallis . . . began his march back to South Carolina. . . . In this retreat the King's troops suffered much. . . . The soldiers had no tents. It rained for several days without intermission. The roads were over their shoes in water and mud. At night . . . the army . . . encamped in the woods in a most unhealthy climate; for many days without rum. Sometimes the army had beef and no bread; at other times bread and no beef. For five days it was supported upon Indian corn, which was collected as it stood in the field. . . . The water that the army drank was frequently as thick as puddle. Few armies ever encountered greater difficulties and hardships. . . .

On the twenty-ninth of October the army arrived at Winns-borough [South Carolina]. . . . Lord Cornwallis, however, did not expect to remain long without such a reinforcement as would enable him to prosecute his further designs. . . . In the meantime the mountaineers, contented with their success against Ferguson, had gone home. . . .

But with the British army off balance, the southern guerrillas were inspired to new vigor. Francis Marion and Thomas Sumter (the "Carolina Gamecock") gathered enough men to operate with persistence, and Banastre Tarleton's horsemen and light foot troops were kept breathless chasing them. In a skirmish at Blackstock's Hill, near Union, South Carolina, on November 20, Sumter was wounded. The Gamecock managed to escape, but the redcoats and their Tory allies were temporarily relieved of the effects of his sharp spurs. Marion maintained his talent for losing his pursuers in the dark swamps.

While Cornwallis was contending with the guerrillas and awaiting a reinforcement from Charleston (just arrived from the northward by sea) that would enable him to make another advance into North Carolina, a new American army was forming at Charlotte, the town Cornwallis had lately vacated. The army's commander was Rhode Island's General Nathanael Greene. According to General William Moultrie, who was then a prisoner-at-large in Charleston, Greene's presence was welcomed by the southern Patriots:

His military abilities, his active spirit, his great resources when reduced to difficulties in the field, his having been quarter-master-general to the army under the commander-in-chief; all these qualities combined together rendered him a proper officer to collect and to organize an army that was broken up and dispersed [by Cornwallis at Camden].

Greene was Washington's personal choice for the southern command after Horatio Gates, picked by Congress, had failed so disastrously. Greene had accepted the appointment with secret reluctance. He was commanding at West Point when his orders came, and had expected to spend the winter there with his wife, to whom he was deeply devoted. "How unfriendly," he lamented to her, "is war to domestic happiness."

At Charlotte, North Carolina, Greene's army numbered only

General Daniel Morgan.

about two thousand effectives, not enough to face Cornwallis boldly. Greene decided to make two divisions of the army and try guerrilla-type tactics. He himself, leading one division, planned to support Francis Marion in eastern South Carolina. The other division, commanded by General Daniel Morgan, veteran of the Quebec expedition and of the campaign against Burgoyne, marched southwestward from Charlotte, crossing South Carolina's Broad River in late December.

Morgan had no definite plan of operations as he established a camp on the north bank of the Pacolet. He sent a detachment to engage some of the smaller forces of the enemy's western outposts but was aware that he would probably have to retreat if confronted by a large force from the main army. Cornwallis acted to meet the threat early in January, 1781:

I . . . directed Lieutenant-Colonel Tarleton to march on the west of Broad River to endeavour to strike a blow at General Morgan, and at all events to oblige him to repass the Broad River. . . . I [had] not the least doubt that General Morgan would retire on our advancing. The progress of the army was greatly impeded by heavy rains, which swelled the rivers and creeks; yet Lieutenant-Colonel Tarleton conducted his march so well and got so near to General Morgan, who was retreating before him, as to make it dangerous for him to pass Broad River, and came up with him [at Cowpens] at eight o'clock of the morning of the 17th instant. Everything now bore the most promising aspect. . . . [T]he . . . quality of the corps [of about eleven hundred men] under Lieutenant-Colonel Tarleton's command, and his great superiority in cavalry, left him no room to doubt of the most brilliant success.

The Americans, of a similar total number, had drawn up in battle formation, three lines deep, with their backs toward the river. The foremost line was made up of militiamen under Colonel Andrew Pickens. Next came a line of seasoned troops, many of whom were Continentals, commanded by Colonel John Eager Howard. In the rear was a mounted reserve, which included a body led by Colonel William Washington. General Morgan had spent much of the preceding night making visits of encouragement among Andrew Pickens's militiamen, whom he did not expect to hold out long against the aggressive Tarleton. Morgan told them that if they stood bravely in the forefront and fired two or three volleys before turning the fight over to the seasoned troops behind

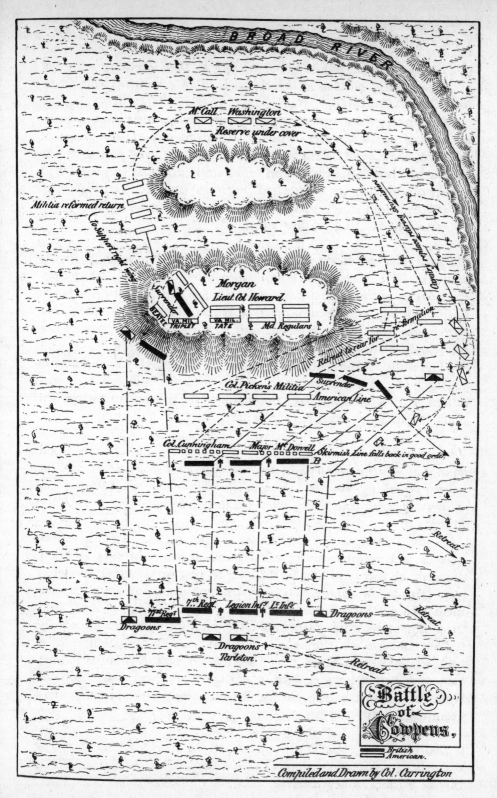

BROAD RIVER

M°Call Washington

Reserve under cover

Militia reformed return

to support right wing

Cavalry Tarleton repulsed

Morgan
Lieut. Col. Howard.

Surrender
BEATIE
TRIPLET

VA. MIL.
TRIPLET

VA. MIL.
TATE

Md. Regulars

re-formation

Retreat to rear for

Surrender

American Line

Col. Picken's Militia

Col. Cunningham

Major M°Dowell

Skirmish Line falls back in good order

B

Retreat

7th Reg.t

Legion Inf.y Lt. Inf.y

71st Reg.t

Dragoons

Dragoons

Retreat

Dragoons
Tarleton.

Retreat

Battle
of
Cowpens,

British
American.

Compiled and Drawn by Col. Carrington

*them they would surely, upon returning to their homes, be blessed
by the old folks and kissed by the girls. The general explains how
the action began:*

The enemy drew up in single line of battle, four hundred yards
in front of our advanced corps. . . . In front moved two pieces of
artillery. Lieut. Col. Tarleton, with his cavalry, was posted in the
rear of his line. The disposition of battle being thus formed, small
parties of riflemen were detached [from our lines] to skirmish with
the enemy, upon which their whole line moved on with the greatest
impetuosity, shouting as they advanced.

*Morgan galloped along the American lines and called out to the
men to "Give them the Indian halloo, by God!" and to refrain
from firing until the last moment. The two British artillery pieces
were booming, and their projectiles tearing through the American
center toward William Washington's cavalrymen in the rear. Then
the small-arms exchange began. Says Banastre Tarleton:*

The militia, after a short contest, were dislodged, and the British
approached the Continentals. The fire on both sides was well supported. . . . The cavalry on the right were directed to charge the
enemy's left. They executed the order with great gallantry. . . .

*The retreating militiamen were at this time swinging around the
flank that was the cavalry's target, and they were appalled to find the
riders pounding toward them with raised swords. Among the
militiamen was youthful James Collins, who had been at Kings
Mountain:*

"Now," thought I, "my hide is in the loft." . . . [T]hey overtook us and began to make a few hacks at some, however without
doing much injury. They, in their haste, had pretty much scattered.
. . . [I]n a few moments Col. Washington's cavalry was among
them like a whirlwind, and the poor fellows began to keel from
their horses without being able to remount. The shock was so
sudden and violent they could not stand it, and immediately betook themselves to flight. . . . [B]oth lines of the infantry [Amer-
ican and British] were warmly engaged, and we, being relieved
from the pursuit of the enemy, began to rally and prepare to re-
deem our credit. . . .

*Tarleton, noting that the main American line was standing fast,
decided to throw in his reserve foot troops. This, he writes, caused
the Americans to begin falling back:*

The British rushed forwards. . . . An unexpected fire at this instant from the Americans, who came about as they were retreating, stopped the British and threw them into confusion. Exertions to make them advance were useless. The part of the cavalry which had not been engaged fell likewise into disorder, and an unaccountable panic extended itself along the whole line. The Americans . . . advanced upon the British troops and augmented their astonishment.

The British were approached from three directions. Bayonets were coming at them in front; Colonel Washington's horsemen were slashing at their right flank; and the militiamen who had retreated at the outset had swung around the rear of the American position and were "redeeming their credit" by swarming in on the enemy's left. Tarleton made a last desperate effort to organize his horsemen and bring them to the charge: "The weight of such an attack might yet retrieve the day . . . but all attempts to restore order . . . proved fruitless." Says American militiaman James Collins: "They began to throw down their arms and surrender themselves prisoners of war. The whole army, except Tarleton and his horsemen, fell into the hands of Morgan. . . ." Only by means of an ignominious flight did Tarleton escape the general destruction. About a hundred of his men had been killed and about two hundred wounded. The New Jersey Gazette *later rejoiced:*

About eight hundred, including the wounded . . . were taken prisoners. . . . Two field-pieces . . . two stands of colors, thirty-five baggage wagons and eight hundred stands of excellent arms, together with all their music, were among the trophies of victory.

General Morgan was able to include in his report that "not a man was killed, wounded or even insulted after he surrendered." Morgan's casualties were remarkably low: twelve killed and sixty wounded. Probably no one in America heard the big news with more satisfaction than Charleston's prisoner-at-large, General Moultrie:

This defeat of Colonel Tarleton's . . . chagrined and disappointed the British officers and Tories in Charleston exceedingly. . . . I saw them standing in the streets in small circles talking over the affair with very grave faces. . . . This great victory . . . changed the face of American affairs. . . . In two actions, soon after each other, the British lost about two thousand men. . . . The latter was of more serious consequence to Lord Cornwallis because it deprived him of nine hundred of his best troops. . . . [H]e was, no doubt, flattering himself that he would receive accounts from Colonel Tarleton of his having defeated General Morgan. . . . His chagrin and his disappointment must have been great indeed. . . .

To young Tarleton, one of his favorite subordinates, Cornwallis wrote consolingly: "You have forfeited no part of my esteem as an officer. . . ." But in his report to Sir Henry Clinton in New York the commander admitted: "It is impossible to foresee all the consequences that this unexpected and extraordinary event may produce. . . ."

37

GREENE AND CORNWALLIS

B Y JANUARY, *1781, the Revolution, now part of a global conflict,*
had been in progress for nearly six years. Since its outbreak
in Massachusetts it had expanded steadily to involve most parts of
the nation-to-be. In the broad forests of the western frontier, Amer-
ica's pioneers strove with Indian warriors and the handful of red-
coats and Tories who urged them on. English and French warships
hovered on the Atlantic coast, with the English still superior.
American vessels, mostly privateers, slipped about warily, engaging
in minor operations. North and South, the land was dotted with
military posts belonging to each side, and the periods between the
explosions of major battles were filled with firecracker raids and
skirmishes. Bands of Whigs and Tories, in alliance with the regular
forces, and also independently, fought each other with special hatred
and cruelty; in the South, it was feared that this strife would soon
depopulate the country.

The French army under the Comte de Rochambeau still waited
at Newport, Rhode Island, for the kind of support from France
that would enable it to attempt a grand stroke in cooperation with
the Americans. Washington continued to keep his army encamped
in such a way as to threaten the British posts in the New York
City area. The American troops were going through another winter
filled with privations, and in January there were two mutinies.
The second was put down harshly. Two of the ringleaders were
ordered to be shot on the spot by a firing squad made up of twelve

of their co-mutineers. Dr. Thacher, who witnessed the proceedings, writes that several men of the firing squad shed tears as they loaded their muskets:

The wretched victims, overwhelmed by the terrors of death, had neither time nor power to implore the mercy and forgiveness of their God. . . . The first that suffered was a sergeant and an old offender. He was led a few yards' distance and placed on his knees. Six of the executioners, at the signal given by an officer, fired—three aiming at the head and three at the breast, the other six reserving their fire in order to despatch the victim, should the first fire fail. It so happened in this instance. The remaining six then fired, and life was instantly extinguished. The second criminal was, by the first fire, sent into eternity in an instant. . . . It is most painful to reflect that circumstances should imperiously demand the infliction of capital punishment on soldiers who have more than a shadow of plea to extenuate their crime. These unfortunate men have long suffered many serious grievances, which they have sustained with commendable patience, but have at length lost their confidence in public justice.

The "public justice" the army wanted was the solid support of the Continental Congress; but the efficiency of that body was suffering because of a lack of real unity among the states. There was hope, however, that the trouble would soon be remedied by the Articles of Confederation, a "glorious compact" in the final stages of ratification.

The attention of both supreme commanders, Washington and Clinton, was focused on the South. Clinton had lately enlarged the southern theater by sending an amphibious force under turncoat General Benedict Arnold to the coast of Virginia. Arnold sailed up the James River and made a quick, destructive raid upon supply dumps and other property in the Richmond area. Then he returned down the river and established a base at Portsmouth. The few American troops in Virginia, commanded by Baron von Steuben, had attempted resistance but were easily brushed aside.

The South's chief contenders continued to be General Greene and Lord Cornwallis. Immediately after Banastre Tarleton's defeat at Cowpens, South Carolina, Cornwallis advanced upon Daniel Morgan with his main army, then consisting of about twenty-five hundred men. Morgan began fleeing northward, and Greene ordered his other wing to follow. All through North Carolina the Americans raced, at length merging at Guilford Courthouse. The British were never far behind. In mid-February the fugitives en-

tered Virginia, crossing the Dan River in Halifax County. Here the pursuit ended, for Cornwallis did not consider himself strong enough to push farther north. Moreover, he had outrun his supply lines. In the words of Colonel Henry ("Light-Horse Harry") Lee, one of Greene's cavalry commanders:

Cornwallis, baffled in every expectation . . . now turned his attention to produce solid advantage out of . . . forcing Greene to abandon [North Carolina]. Selecting Hillsborough as headquarters . . . he . . . proceeded thither by easy marches. Here he erected the King's standard. . . .

In the camp of Greene, joy beamed in every face; and . . . the subsequent days . . . were spent in mutual gratulations; with the rehearsal of the hopes and fears which agitated every breast during the retreat; interspersed with the many . . . anecdotes with which every tongue was strung. . . . The people of Halifax County received us with the affection of brethren. . . . Volunteers began to tender their services. . . .

. . . the General . . . could not long enjoy the agreeable scene, nor indulge his faithful army in its novel state of ease and abundance. On North Carolina his mind was fixed. . . . The Royalists everywhere were preparing to rise, while the well-affected to the cause of America, despairing of protection, began to look for safety in submission.

While Greene was augmenting his strength and preparing to recross the Dan, he sent Colonel Lee and his horsemen, with some attached troops that included Andrew Pickens and his South Carolina militiamen, across the river with orders to watch Cornwallis and try to disrupt the assembling of the Tories.

Lee soon learned that Banastre Tarleton had been assigned the task of hastening the rise of these auxiliary forces and providing them cavalry protection on their march to the British camp. Light-Horse Harry, a commandant of great enterprise, devised a scheme by which he might get close enough to Tarleton to take him by surprise. The American horsemen would be passed off as a British detachment. Such an impersonation was possible because the cavalry of both sides wore green coats. But an opportunity other than the one envisioned soon presented itself.

Lee received word that two mounted Tories were approaching on the road he was using, and that they were looking for Tarleton, having been sent forward by a Colonel John Pyle, who was bringing up about four hundred men. Writing of himself in the third person, Light-Horse Harry relates that he took quick action:

. . . Lee dispatched his adjutant with the intelligence to Brigadier Pickens, requesting him to place his riflemen (easily to be distinguished by the green twigs in their hats, the customary emblem of our militia in the South) . . . out of sight; which was readily . . . done, as we were then in a thick wood. . . .

. . . the two countrymen . . . were received with much apparent cordiality by Lieutenant-Colonel Lee, who listened with seeming satisfaction to their annunciation of the laudable spirit which had actuated Colonel Pyle and his associates, and which they asserted was rapidly spreading through the country. Finding them completely deceived (for they not only believed the troops they saw to be British, but . . . took them to be Tarleton's, addressing the commandant as that officer), Lee sent one of them back . . . to Colonel Pyle with Lieutenant-Colonel Tarleton's gratulations and his request that he would be so good as to draw out on the margin of the road so as to give convenient room for his much-fatigued troops to [ride] without delay to their night position. . . .

. . . [The man] who had been sent to Colonel Pyle returned with his expected compliance, announced in most respectful terms. . . . Colonel Pyle was in . . . the right of the road, drawn up as suggested with his left to the advancing column. . . . Lieutenant-Colonel Lee had concluded to make known to the colonel his real character as soon as he should confront him, with a solemn assurance of his and his associates perfect exemption from injury, and with the choice of returning to their homes [on parole] or of . . . uniting with the defenders of their common country against the common foe.

By Pyle's . . . occupation of the right side of the road it became necessary for Lee to [ride] along the whole line of the Loyalists before he could reach their colonel. . . . They were mounted. . . . Their guns (rifles and fowling pieces) were on their shoulders, the muzzles consequently in an opposite direction to the cavalry. In the event of discovery they must have changed the direction before they could fire—a motion not to be perfomed with a body of dragoons close . . . with . . . their swords drawn. . . .

Lee [rode] along the line, at the head of [his] column, with a smiling countenance, dropping occasionally expressions complimentary to the good looks and commendable conduct of his loyal friends. At length he reached Colonel Pyle, when the customary civilities were promptly interchanged. Grasping Pyle by the hand, Lee was in the act of consummating his plan when the enemy's left, discovering Pickens's militia, not sufficiently concealed, began to fire upon the rear of the cavalry, commanded by Captain [Joseph] Eggleston. This officer instantly turned upon the foe, as did immediately after the whole column.

The conflict was quickly decided, and bloody on one side only. Ninety of the Royalists were killed, and most of the survivors wounded. . . . During this sudden rencounter, in some parts of the line the cry of "Mercy!" was heard, coupled with assurance of being our best friends; but no expostulation could be [heeded] in a conjuncture so critical. [Human nature] even forbade it, as its first injunction is to take care of your own safety; and our safety was not compatible with that of the supplicants until disabled to offend. Pyle, falling under many wounds, was left on the field as dying, and yet he survived. We lost not a man, and only one horse.

Lee was bitterly condemned by the British for this piece of work. Charles Stedman wrote that "humanity shudders at the recital of so foul a massacre." He conceded, however, that "cold and unfeeling policy avows it as the most effectual means of intimidating the friends of royal government." A great many of North Carolina's friends of royal government were indeed intimidated. They suddenly lost all interest in marching to join Cornwallis.

General Greene recrossed the Dan late in February. For more than two weeks, while awaiting additional reinforcements, he maneuvered so as to keep just outside the enemy's reach. Then, with his strength having risen to nearly forty-five hundred men, he encamped at Guilford Courthouse, knowing that the resolute Cornwallis, though now badly outnumbered, would hasten to the spot. This approach was made on March 15, a day that Henry Lee says was "illumined with a cloudless sun" and was of a temperature that kept "the body braced and the mind high-toned."

Early in the morning a detachment under Lee engaged in some sharp skirmishing with the British advance guard under Tarleton several miles out ahead of the American position. Tarleton received a ball in his right hand. Light-Horse Harry almost met disaster when the sun caused a "refulgence from the British muskets" that frightened his horse "so as to compel him to throw himself off." Shortly after remounting, he discontinued the action and fell back to report to Greene.

The general had deployed his army, three lines deep, on rising, wooded ground. The lines were several hundred yards apart. In front were two brigades of inexperienced North Carolina militiamen, bolstered on the flanks by some veteran riflemen and the army's cavalry. The second line was composed of Virginia militiamen, some of whom had seen considerable service. In the third line were Greene's strongest troops, his Virginia, Maryland, and Delaware Continentals.

The general and his army were supported by some unusual "irregulars." The Patriot women of the surrounding countryside, at the suggestion of their pastor, had begun praying, individually and in groups, for the army's safety and success. They would continue these supplications all through the battle.

It was early afternoon by the time the British column drew up a few hundred yards from the first of Greene's lines. As usual, the redcoats presented a picture of smartness and professional spirit. The column, however, contained one man, a Captain Maynard, who, unaccountably, was showing no spirit at all. According to Charles Stedman:

He was naturally of a cheerful disposition and great hilarity; and in several actions during the course of the war he had shewn great gallantry. But a certain presentiment . . . [now] possessed his mind. . . . While the troops were marching on to form the line of battle he became gloomy and gave way to despondency. Not less than two or three different times did he tell Colonel Norton, who commanded the battalion, that he felt himself very uncomfortable and did not like the business at all. . . . Norton endeavoured to laugh him out of his melancholy ideas, but in vain; for even after the cannonade began he reiterated the forebodings of what he conceived was to happen.

With the battle formation completed, Cornwallis passed the order to begin the advance. The drummers and fifers set the pace; and, says Stedman, "the line . . . moved forward with that steady and guarded but firm and determined resolution which discipline alone can confer." The men advancing on both flanks were soon met by long-range rifle fire. The gloomy Captain Maynard, Stedman explains, was on the right:

Early in the action he received a wound in the leg. Unable to proceed, he requested . . . the adjutant of the guards to lend him his horse that he might ride on with the battalion; and when in the act of mounting, another shot went through his lungs. . . .

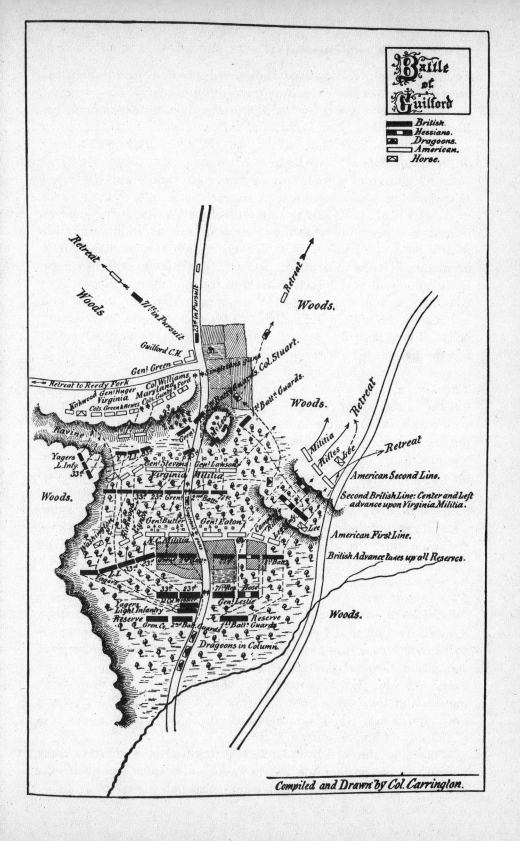

Battle of Guilford

British.
Hessians.
Dragoons.
American.
Horse.

Retreat

Woods

71st in Pursuit

23d in Pursuit

Woods.

Retreat

Guilford C.H.

Gen! Green

Single Gun Tarns

Command & Col. Stuart.

Retreat to Reedy Fork

Col. Williams

Kirkwood Gen! Huger
Virginia Maryland Ford
Cols. Green & Howes Cols. Gunby & Ford

1st Batt! Guards.

Woods.

Retreat

Ravine

Nelson

Militia

Rifles Lee

Retreat

Yagers
L. Infy.
33?

Gen! Stevens Gen! Lawson

Virginia Militia

American Second Line.

Woods.

33? 23? Gren 1st Batt? 71st

Second British Line: Center and Left
advance upon Virginia Militia.

Washington

Gen! Butler Gen! Eaton

N. C. Militia

Lee

American First Line.

33? 23?

1st Batt?

British Advance takes up all Reserves.

Yagers
Light Infantry

71st Reg? Hose

Reserve

Gen! Leslie

Yagers
Light Infantry
Reserve
Gren. Co. 2nd Batt. Guards

Reserve
1st Batt. Guards

Woods.

Dragoons in Column.

Compiled and Drawn by Col. Carrington.

The second wound was a mortal one, but Maynard would labor for breath for two or three weeks before giving his last sigh.

One of the redcoats on the left of the line was Sergeant Roger Lamb, who had been captured by the Americans at Saratoga but had later escaped and was now serving with the Royal Welsh Fusiliers under Colonel James Webster:

. . . the colonel rode on to the front and gave the word "Charge!" Instantly the movement was made in excellent order in a smart run. . . . When arrived within forty yards of the enemy's line, it was perceived that their whole force had their arms . . . resting on a rail fence. . . . They were taking aim with the nicest precision. . . . At this awful period a general pause took place. Both parties surveyed each other for the moment with the most anxious suspense. . . . Colonel Webster rode forward . . . and said . . . "Come on, my brave Fusiliers!" This operated like an inspiring voice. They rushed forward amidst the enemy's fire. Dreadful was the havoc on both sides.

The American units on the flanks of the first line held their ground; but the center of the line quickly collapsed. Henry Lee laments:

To our infinite distress and mortification, the North Carolina militia took to flight, a few only . . . excepted. . . . Every effort was made . . . to stop this unaccountable panic, for not a man of the corps had been killed or even wounded. Lieutenant-Colonel Lee joined in the attempt to rally the fugitives, threatening to fall upon them with his cavalry. All was vain. So thoroughly confounded were these unhappy men that, throwing away arms, knapsacks, and even canteens, they rushed like a torrent headlong through the woods. . . .

This retreat caused a split in the battle formation of both sides. Pressed by a strong body of the British, the men who had been standing fast on the American left began falling back at an angle that carried the action away from the main event. The development worked in General Greene's favor, since it relieved some of the pressure on his two remaining lines. The men who had been fighting well on the right of the first line were now falling back upon the Virginia militiamen who made up the second line. Stedman says of the second-line Americans:

Posted in the woods and covering themselves with trees, they kept up for a considerable time a galling fire which did great execution. At length, however, they were compelled to retreat. . . .

Returning to Lamb, of the Welsh Fusiliers:

Before [the line] was completely routed . . . I observed an American officer attempting to fly. I immediately darted after him; but he, perceiving my intention to capture him, fled with the utmost speed. I pursued and was gaining on him when, hearing a confused noise on my left, I observed several bodies of Americans drawn up within the distance of a few yards. . . . [I]n such moments all fears of death are over. Seeing one of the [British] guards among the slain where I stood, I stopped and replenished my own pouch with the cartridges that remained in his. During the time I was thus employed, several shots were fired at me, but not one took effect.

Glancing my eye the other way [toward the British lines] I saw a company of the guards advancing to attack these parties. . . . On the instant . . . I saw Lord Cornwallis riding across the clear ground [near my position]. His Lordship was mounted on a dragoon's horse (his own having been shot). The saddle bags were under the creature's belly, which much retarded his progress, owing to the vast quantity of underwood that was spread over the ground. His Lordship was evidently unconscious of his danger. I immediately laid hold of the bridle of his horse and turned his head. I then mentioned to him that if His Lordship had pursued the same direction he would in a few moments have been surrounded by the enemy and perhaps cut to pieces or captured. I continued to run alongside of the horse, keeping the bridle in my hand, until His Lordship gained the 23d Regiment. . . .

Adds Henry Lee:

Persevering in his determination to die or conquer, the British general did not stop to concentrate his force but pressed forward to break our third line. The [isolated] action . . . on his right was still sternly maintained . . . so that this portion of the British force could not be brought to bear upon the third line. . . . General Greene was well pleased with the present prospect, and . . . passed along the line exhorting his troops to give the finishing blow.

The Continentals responded with vigor and, according to Banastre Tarleton, "At this period the event of the action was doubtful, and victory alternately presided over each army." But it was the outnumbered redcoats who finally prevailed. General Greene explains:

They having broken the 2d Maryland Regiment and turned our left flank, got into the rear of the Virginia Brigade; and, appearing to be gaining on our right, which would have encircled the whole of the Continental troops, I thought it most advisable to order a retreat.

The Americans were pursued but a short distance. Cornwallis was only too glad to see them go. His own army had been badly hurt. At this time some shots were still sounding from the direction of the isolated action. Light-Horse Harry says that Tarleton was sent to investigate:

The contest had long been ebbing before this corps arrived, and Lieutenant-Colonel Tarleton found only a few resolute marksmen . . . who continued firing from tree to tree. The appearance of cavalry determined these brave fellows to retire and overtake their corps. Thus the battle terminated. It was . . . a day never to be forgotten by the southern section of the United States. . . . The British general fought against two-to-one, but he had greatly the advantage in the quality of his soldiers. . . . The slaughter was prodigious on the side of the enemy, making in killed and wounded nearly one-third of his army. . . . ["About one-fourth of his army" would be more accurate.] Our loss was very disproportionate: only fourteen officers and three hundred and twelve rank-and-file of the Continental troops killed, wounded and missing. . . . Our loss of militia was still less. . . . Many were missing, as is always the case with militia after battle; but they generally are to be found safe at their own firesides. . . . The name of victory was the sole enjoyment of the conqueror. The substance belonged to the vanquished. Truly did the eloquent Fox [later] exclaim in the British House of Commons, "Another such victory would destroy the British army!"

. . . Afflicting were the sensations of the British general when he looked into his own situation after the battle. . . . The night succeeding this day of blood was rainy, dark and cold. The dead unburied, the wounded unsheltered, the groans of the dying and the shrieks of the living cast a deeper shade over the gloom of nature. . . . The ensuing morning was spent in performing the last offices to the dead and in providing comfort for the wounded. In executing these sad duties, the British general regarded with equal attention friends and foes. As soon as this service was over, he put his army in motion for New Garden, where his rear guard . . . met him. All his wounded incapable of moving . . . he left to the humanity of General Greene [who had remained in the vicinity].

. . . His Lordship proceeded . . . by easy marches to Cross Creek [Fayetteville]. . . . The retreat of the British general evinced un-equivocally his crippled condition.

Cornwallis had chosen to withdraw in the direction of Cross Creek because the town was convenient to Wilmington, on the Cape Fear River near the North Carolina coast, which had recently been made the site of a British supply depot by a force sent from Charleston by sea. In Charles Stedman's words:

General Greene followed . . . as far as Ramsey's Mill, on Deep River; and occasional skirmishes happened between the light troops, but nothing of moment between the two armies. Upon the arrival of the British commander at Cross Creek he found himself disap-pointed in all his expectations. Provisions were scarce . . . and the communication expected to be opened between Cross Creek and Wilmington, by means of the river, was found to be impracticable, the river itself being narrow, its banks high, and the inhabitants on both sides, for a considerable distance, inveterately hostile. Nothing therefore now remained to be done but to proceed with the army to Wilmington, in the vicinity of which it arrived on the seventh of April. . . .

The effective force under His Lordship, from sickness, desertion, and the loss sustained at Guilford Courthouse, was now reduced to fourteen hundred and thirty-five men, a number which he con-sidered as totally inadequate to acting offensively in North Carolina. . . . To return to South Carolina by land would be accompanied with . . . hazards. . . . And to return by water would not only be disgraceful but take up much time in waiting for the transports. . . . Upon such a view of the subject, His Lordship determined . . . to march . . . into Virginia and join his force to a strong corps that had been acting there from the beginning of the year. . . .

38

A ROUND OF SWEET REWARDS

GENERAL *Greene, encamped at Ramsey's Mill on North Caro-*
lina's Deep River after discontinuing his pursuit of Corn-
wallis, pondered his options and shortly decided to return to South
Carolina. His intentions were bold and far-reaching. He would at-
tack the British posts that were scattered between Georgetown on
the coast and Ninety Six in the west. He also had designs on Au-
gusta, Georgia. Only Charleston and Savannah, he felt, were too
strong for him, being supported by the Royal Navy. If, however, all
the outposts were taken, reducing British holdings to the two coastal
towns, enemy power in the deep South would be virtually destroyed.
Once again, Greene divided his army. While he himself prepared
to lead the main body toward Camden, South Carolina, he sent Lee's
legion to join Francis Marion, who was farther to the east. Lee re-
lates that he moved first toward North Carolina's Cross Creek:

After advancing in this course . . . [for a time], the . . . corps
turned to the right and, by a very expeditious march, gained
Drowning Creek. . . . In a large field on the southern side of this
stream, Lee encamped for the night, when a very extraordinary
occurrence took place. . . . Between two and three in the morning
the officer of the day was informed that a strange noise had been
heard in front of the picket stationed on the great road near the
creek, resembling that occasioned by men moving through a swamp.
Presently, and toward that quarter, a sentinel fired, which was

followed by a sound of the bugle calling in the horse patrols, as was the custom on the approach of the enemy. The troops were immediately summoned to arms and arrayed for defense. . . .

In a few moments, in a different quarter of our position, another sentinel fired; and soon after, the same report from that point was made as had just been received from the other. . . . A change in the formation of the troops was made to correspond with this last annunciation of the enemy's approach. This was not completed before, in a different direction, we heard the discharge of a third sentinel. Now the most excruciating sensations were experienced. It appeared as if these different feelings of our position were wisely and dexterously made, preparatory to a general assault to take effect as soon as the approach of light should warrant its commencement.

All that could be done was done. The pickets and sentinels held their stations; the horse patrols had been called in; and the corps changed its position . . . upon every new annunciation, having in view the conjoint object of keeping the [camp]fires between us and the enemy, and holding the horse in the rear of the infantry. During our last evolution to this end we were again interrupted by the discharge of the line of sentinels in our rear, along the great road. Thus the enemy had traversed the major segment of our position and had at length fixed himself upon the road of our march. No doubt now remained, not only of the enemy being upon us, but that he was in force and well understood his object. He had reconnoitred with penetration and perseverance, and had ultimately placed himself in the very spot most certainly promising success. . . .

Lee, passing along the line of infantry, made known our condition, reminding them of their high reputation. . . . To the cavalry he briefly communicated the dangers . . . mingled with expressions of his thorough confidence that every man would do his duty. . . . This address was answered by whispers of applause; and, having formed in columns . . . Lee waited anxiously for the break of day, the presumed signal for action. It soon appeared, and the columns advanced to the great road, infantry in front, baggage in the centre, and the cavalry in the rear. . . . The van officer, proceeding a few hundred yards, now got up to the sentinel who had fired last, and received from him the same account so often given before. . . . The . . . corps continued its march, in slow motion, expecting every moment the enemy's fire. In this state of suspense we might have continued long, had not the van officer directed his attention to the road for the purpose of examining the trail of our active foe, when to his astonishment he found the tracks of a large pack of wolves.

It was now evident that the presumed enemy was a troop of wild beasts, collected together and anxious to pass along their usual route, when finding it obstructed they turned from point to point to pass through the field. Everywhere fired upon, they continued widening their circuit until they reached the great road from which they had been originally turned. Our agitation vanished and was succeeded by facetious glee. . . . Never was a day's march more pleasant, being one continued scene of good humor. . . . For a time the restraint of discipline ceased. Every character, not excepting the commandant's, was hit. . . . The pickets, the patrols, the sentinels and the officer of the day were marked as the peculiar objects of derision. Wonderful that not one of the many could distinguish between the movement of wolves and soldiers!

. . . after getting within a day's distance of the Pee Dee, Lieutenant-Colonel Lee dispatched an officer, with a small body of dragoons, to discover in what part of his extensive range Brigadier Marion then was. The officer, on reaching the river, learned that the Brigadier . . . was in the swamps of Black River. . . . Marion received with joy Lee's officer, and furnished boats, which he kept concealed on the Pee Dee, for the transportation of the corps across that river. On the 14th of April [1781] Lee joined the General. These military friends . . . [of the days preceding Cowpens] very cordially rejoiced at being again united in the great attempt of wrestling South Carolina from the enemy. . . .

Active operations now became practicable, and on . . . the 15th Marion and Lee took a position in the open country. . . . Determined to carry [Fort Watson, on the north bank of the Santee River] without delay, Marion and Lee sat down before it early in the evening. . . . The ground selected by Colonel [John] Watson for his small stockade was an Indian mount. . . . It was at least thirty feet high and surrounded by table land. . . . [D]estitute both of artillery and intrenching tools, Marion and Lee despaired of success, when Major [Hezekiah] Maham of South Carolina . . . proposed to cut down a number of suitable trees in the nearest wood, and with them to erect a large strong oblong [tower], to be covered on the top with a floor of logs. . . . To the adjacent farms dragoons were dispatched for axes . . . [and] relays of working parties were allotted for the labor. . . . The besieged was, like the besieger, unprovided with artillery and could not interrupt the progress of [the] work.

. . . A party of riflemen . . . took post in the "Maham Tower" the moment it was completed; and a detachment of musketry, under cover of the riflemen, moved to make a lodgment in the enemy's ditch, supported by the Legion infantry. . . . Such was the effect of the fire from the riflemen, having thorough command of every part of the fort from the relative supereminence of the tower, that every attempt to resist the lodgment was crushed. The commandant, finding every resource cut off, hung out the white flag.

By the date of this victory (April 23) Nathanael Greene had been in the vicinity of his first objective for several days. General William Moultrie, then still a prisoner of war in Charleston, would later record:

The American army . . . took post at Hobkirk's Hill, about one mile from Camden, which . . . was . . . defended with nine hundred men commanded by [Francis] Lord Rawdon, who ordered every man in garrison that could carry a musket to take arms; and on the twenty-fifth marched out to attack General Greene. So little did the Americans expect the British out of their lines that the second-in-command, General [Isaac] Huger, told me that . . . a number of officers with himself were washing their feet, and a number of soldiers were washing their kettles in a small rivulet that run by their camp, when their picket was engaged with the enemy. They ran to camp as fast as they could, and the British was soon after them. . . .

General Greene writes that "the line was formed in an instant" and met the attack with resolution:

. . . I sent Lieutenant-Colonel Washington . . . [with his cavalry] to double the right flank and attack the rear of the enemy. The whole line [of our main body] was soon in action in the midst of a very smart fire, as well from our small arms as from our artillery, which . . . kept playing upon the front of the enemy, who began to give way on all sides . . . when unfortunately two companies on the right of the 1st Maryland Regiment were entirely thrown into disorder; and . . . Colonel [John] Gunby ordered the rest of the regiment, which was advancing, to take a new position towards the rear, where the two companies were rallying. This movement gave the whole regiment an idea of a retreat, which soon spread through the 2d Regiment, which retreated accordingly. They both rallied afterwards, but it was too late. The enemy had gained the eminence, silenced the artillery and obliged us to draw off. . . . The troops rallied more than once, but the disorder was too general and had struck too deep for one to think of recovering the fortune of the day, which promised us at the onset the most complete victory; for Colonel Washington, on his way to double and attack in the rear, found the enemy . . . retreating with precipitation towards the town and made upwards of two hundred of them prisoners . . . before he perceived that our troops had abandoned the field of battle. . . . We . . . retreated two or three miles from the scene of action without any loss of artillery, wagons or provisions. . . .

Returning to General Moultrie's account:

Colonel Washington paroled a number of officers . . . and amongst them eleven surgeons. . . . General Greene immediately sent them in to Lord Rawdon (knowing they would be wanted for the wounded), who was so pleased with General Greene's liberal conduct that he immediately sent to the [British] commandant in Charleston to allow General Moultrie to exchange the like number of his medical line [prisoners since Charleston's fall] . . . and that they should be conducted to any American post that he required. . . .

On the seventh of May . . . Lord Rawdon received a considerable reinforcement . . . and endeavored the next day to bring General Greene to another action, but that could not be effected. General Greene knew that Lord Rawdon was so surrounded that he could not get supplies, and that he must soon quit Camden. . . .

. . . Lord Rawdon, knowing his situation was growing more critical every day . . . determined to . . . retreat to [the vicinity of] Charleston; and on the tenth he burned the gaol, mills and many private houses . . . and retired with his army to the south side of Santee River . . . by which movement he gave up . . . a large extent of country. . . .

Lord Rawdon invited the Tories to accompany him to Charleston . . . but . . . the greater part chose to stay and trust to the mercy of their countrymen. Those who went down with the British were cruelly neglected. After their arrival in Charleston they built themselves huts . . . which was called Rawdontown. Many of these unfortunate women and children, who [had] lived comfortable at their own homes near Camden, died for want in those miserable huts. . . .

Young Lord Rawdon was entering a difficult period. He had served at Bunker Hill and was at first amazed by the quality of American resistance but had soon afterward decided that there was no widespread will to stand against his majesty's superior troops and that the rebellion would be crushed in short order. In November, 1776, when Washington was retreating through New Jersey, Rawdon had stated in a letter to England: ". . . I have not been mistaken in my judgment of this people. The southern people will no more fight than the Yankees." Now, nearly five years later, not only was the despised foe still resisting in all quarters, but the outlook had become gloomy for his majesty's superior troops. Rawdon's own men were expressing such thoughts as "the rebels seem to grow stronger by every defeat" and "I am heartily tired of this country, and wish myself at home."

The day after Rawdon evacuated Camden, the post at Orangeburg surrendered to Thomas Sumter, the Carolina Gamecock. As for Marion the Swamp Fox and Light-Horse Harry Lee: After the surrender of Fort Watson, they crossed to the southern side of the Santee and moved up to Fort Motte on the Congaree. This fort was really a mansion the British had commandeered from a widow named Rebecca Motte, a firm Patriot. According to Lee, the building stood on a high and commanding hill:

It was surrounded with a deep trench, along the interior margin of which was raised a strong and lofty parapet. To this post had been regularly assigned an adequate garrison of about one hundred and fifty men, which was now . . . increased by a small detachment of dragoons which had arrived from Charleston a few hours before the appearance of the American troops. . . . Captain McPherson commanded, an officer highly and deservedly respected.

Opposite to Fort Motte, to the north, stood another hill, where Mrs. Motte, having been dismissed from her mansion, resided in an old farmhouse. On this height Lieutenant-Colonel Lee with his corps took post, while Brigadier Marion occupied the eastern declivity of the ridge on which the fort stood. Very soon the fort was completely invested, and the six-pounder [lately acquired from Greene] was mounted on a battery erected in Marion's quarter. . . . McPherson was unprovided with artillery. . . . [T]he works advanced with rapidity. Such was their forwardness on the 10th [of May] that it was determined to summon the commandant. A flag was accordingly dispatched to Captain McPherson, stating to him with truth our relative situation. . . . To this the captain replied that, disregarding consequences, he should continue to resist to the last moment. . . .

Burning the house [it was concluded] must force their surrender. . . . Marion and Lee determined to adopt this speedy mode of effecting their object. Orders were . . . issued to prepare bows and arrows, with missive combustible matter [for use the next day]. This measure was reluctantly adopted. . . . The . . . house was a large, pleasant edifice intended for the summer residence of the respectable owner. . . . Nevertheless the obligations of duty were imperative. . . . Taking the first opportunity which offered the next morning, Lieutenant-Colonel Lee imparted to Mrs. Motte the intended measure, lamenting the sad necessity. . . . With a smile of complacency this exemplary lady listened to the embarrassed officer, and gave instant relief to his agitated feelings by declaring that she was gratified with the opportunity of contributing to the good of her country. . . . Shortly after, seeing accidentally the bows and arrows which had been prepared, she sent for the lieutenant-colonel and, presenting him with a bow and its apparatus imported from India, she requested his substitution of these as probably better adapted for the object than those we had provided. . . .

. . . a flag was again sent to McPherson for the purpose of inducing him to prevent the conflagration and the slaughter which might ensue. . . . The British captain received the flag with his usual politeness . . . but he remained immovable. . . . It was now about noon, and the rays of the scorching sun had prepared the shingle roof for the projected conflagration. . . . The first arrow struck and communicated its fire. A second was shot at another quarter of the roof, and a third at a third quarter. . . . McPherson ordered a party to repair to the loft of the house and, by knocking off the shingles, to stop the flames. . . . The fire of our six-pounder . . . soon drove the soldiers down; and, no other effort to stop the flames being practicable, McPherson hung out the white flag. . . .

. . . not a drop of blood was shed. . . . McPherson and his officers accompanied their captors to Mrs. Motte's and partook with them of a sumptuous dinner, soothing in the sweets of social intercourse the ire which the preceding conflict had engendered. The deportment and demeanor of Mrs. Motte gave a zest to the pleasures of the table. . . . Conversing with ease, vivacity and good sense, she obliterated our recollection of the injury she had received; and though warmly attached to the defenders of her country, the engaging amiability of her manners left it doubtful which set of officers constituted these defenders.

In the days immediately following, Light-Horse Harry hastened thirty miles farther up the Congaree and secured the surrender of Fort Granby, while Marion moved against Georgetown on the coast. Lee says in summation:

Fort Watson, Fort Motte, Fort Granby and the fort at Orangeburg had . . . yielded. Marion was now before Georgetown, which was sure soon to fall. Thus in less than one month since General Greene appeared before Camden he had compelled the British general to evacuate that important post, forced the submission of all the intermediate posts, and was now upon the banks of the Congaree, in the heart of South Carolina, ready to advance upon Ninety Six (the only remaining fortress in the state, besides Charleston, in the enemy's possession) and to detach against Augusta in Georgia, comprehending . . . the completion of the deliverance of the two lost states, except the fortified towns of Charleston and Savannah—safe because the enemy ruled at sea.

It was the able and energetic Lee himself who was detached against Augusta. First he took a small fort about twelve miles from the town. Then he joined an assemblage of militiamen under General Andrew Pickens and Colonel Elijah Clarke before Fort Cornwallis, the main objective. An outwork commanded by a Colonel Grierson was quickly overrun. Lee laments that

Poor Grierson and several others [were] killed after surrender; and although the American commandants used every exertion and offered a large reward to detect the murderers, no discovery could be made. In no part of the South was the war conducted with such asperity as in this quarter.

The commandant of Fort Cornwallis was Thomas Brown, a Tory colonel. He had gained a reputation for brutal methods, but had himself been a victim of Patriot brutality early in the war. Shrewd as well as courageous, he defended his fort stoutly. It was two weeks before the besiegers triumphed, again aided by a "Maham Tower." When Brown surrendered on June 5 he was paroled and placed in the hands of a special American guard for transfer to the British post at Savannah. According to General William Moultrie:

On his way to Savannah he passed through the settlements

where he had burnt a number of houses and hung some of the relations of the inhabitants. At Silver Bluff, Mrs. M'Koy [of a family among Brown's particular enemies] obtained leave of the American officer who commanded his safeguard to speak to him, when she thus addressed him: "Colonel Brown, in the late day of your prosperity I visited your camp and on my knees supplicated for the life of my son, but you were deaf to my intreaties. You hanged him, though a beardless youth, before my face. These eyes have seen him scalped by the savages under your immediate command, and for no better reason than that his name was M'Koy. As you are now a prisoner . . . for the present I lay aside all thoughts of revenge; but when you resume your sword I will go five hundred miles to demand satisfaction at the point of it for the murder of my son."

Nathanael Greene with the main army was at this time laying siege to Fort Ninety Six, about fifty miles north of Augusta; Light-Horse Harry and his fast-moving legion arrived there on June 8. The fort was a strong one with a large garrison, and the advancement of the siege lines progressed slowly. Greene writes that his persistence was just beginning to gain the advantage when a new concern assailed him:

. . . the enemy had received a considerable reinforcement at Charleston, and . . . I was apprehensive they would march and interrupt our operations. On the 11th I got intelligence they were advancing. . . . We had pushed on our approaches very near to the enemy's work. . . . We had raised several batteries for cannon, one upwards of twenty feet high . . . and a rifle battery [a "Maham Tower"] . . . to prevent the enemy from annoying our workmen. . . . [T]he firing was almost incessant day and night. . . . I found . . . that it would be impossible to reduce the place without hazarding a storm. . . . The disposition was accordingly formed [on June 18]. . . . A furious cannonade preluded the attack. On the right the enemy were driven out of their works, and our people took possession. On the left . . . they were not so successful. . . . Finding the enemy defended their works with great obstinacy, and seeing but little prospect of succeeding without heavy loss, I ordered the attack to be pushed no further. . . . We continued the siege until the enemy got within a few miles of us. . . .

Henry Lee, who of course had taken a leading part in the assault, says that during the night preceding the withdrawal "gloom and silence pervaded the American camp; everyone disappointed—everyone mortified." Lee goes on:

Rawdon had approached our vicinity with a force not to be resisted, and it only remained to hold the army safe by resuming that system which adverse fortune had rendered familiar to us. . . . General Greene, moving [northward] with celerity, gained the Saluda . . . [and] continued his retreat. . . . In the morning of the twenty-first, the British army reached Ninety Six, having for fourteen days been incessantly pressing forward by forced marches. . . . Here followed a delightful scene, and one which soldiers only can enjoy. . . . Officer embracing officer, and soldiers mingling with soldiers, gave themselves up to those gratulations resulting from the happy conclusion of their mutual toils and mutual perils. This pleasing scene lasted only a few hours; for Rawdon, not satisfied with the relief of Ninety Six, flattered himself with adding to the triumph already gained by destroying or dispersing the army of Greene. . . . Passing the Saluda, he pressed forward to the Enoree, on the south side of which his van came up with the American rear under Washington and Lee. . . . No attempt was hazarded against the American rear, which, conscious of its superior cavalry, retired slowly, always keeping the British van in view.

Lord Rawdon now decided that the course he had taken was impracticable. His troops were fatigued and he was entering country that offered him no security. First he fell back to Ninety Six. Then, because of the fort's isolation, he ordered it abandoned and continued his withdrawal to Orangeburg, which placed him within comfortable distance of Charleston. Thus General Greene, who had soon swung about, enjoyed seeing another failure become a success. Ninety Six being the last of the enemy's outposts, the success was particularly gratifying. Greene followed Rawdon to a point near Orangeburg but did not risk an attack. Returning to Lee:

We had often experienced in the course of the campaign want of food . . . but never did we suffer so severely as during the few days' halt here. Rice furnished our substitute for bread. . . . Of meat we had literally none. . . . Frogs abounded in some neighboring ponds, and on them chiefly did the light troops subsist. . . . Even the alligator was used by a few. . . . The heat of the season had become oppressive and the troops began to experience its effect in sickness. General Greene determined to repair to some salubrious and convenient spot to pass the sultry season, and . . . selected the High Hills of Santee. . . .

A brief demonstration toward Charleston by detached troops under Marion, Sumter, and Lee covered Greene's march. The general found the High Hills an excellent haven. Lee concludes:

The troops were placed in good quarters, and the heat of July [was] rendered tolerable by the high ground, the fine air and good water. . . . Disease began to abate, our wounded to recover, and the army to rise in bodily strength. Enjoying this period of rest, the first experienced since Greene's assumption of the command, it was natural to meditate upon the past scenes. . . . The wisdom of the General was manifest; and the zeal, patience and firmness exhibited by the troops could not be denied. . . . Defeat had been changed by its consequences into victory. . . . The conquered states were regained, and our exiled countrymen were restored to their deserted homes—sweet rewards of [our] toil and peril.

39

FINALE AT YORKTOWN

WHEN *Lord Cornwallis decided in April, 1781, to begin marching from Wilmington, North Carolina, for a union with the British forces in southeastern Virginia, that state's role in the war already was expanding. Both belligerents had lately been reinforced. Benedict Arnold had been joined by a detachment from New York under a man he had fought against and helped to capture at Saratoga in 1777, General William Phillips (back with the British after being exchanged for Benjamin Lincoln, taken when Charleston fell). The Americans in Virginia had received help in the form of a detachment from Washington under the Marquis de Lafayette, who shortly became the Virginia army's top commander. There had been no immediate increase in hostilities, since the Americans, still relatively weak, were obliged to practice extreme caution.*

The British were superior not only on land. They controlled also the coastal waterways. The latter circumstance was the source of a personal embarrassment for Washington. A British warship on the Potomac River paid a visit to Mount Vernon and appropriated a number of its slaves; in order to prevent further plundering, Lund Washington, the estate's manager and cousin to the general, met a demand to provide the crew with refreshments. The news of this act of appeasement prompted Washington to inform Lund:

It would have been a less painful circumstance to me to have heard that, in consequence of your non-compliance with their request, they had burnt my house and laid the plantation in ruins.

In late April, Phillips and Arnold left Portsmouth, their coastal base, and made a raid up the James River, soon establishing themselves at Petersburg. Much property was destroyed, and there was some skirmishing. The following anecdote about Arnold was reported by the New Jersey Journal:

. . . he took an American captain prisoner. After some general conversation . . . he asked him what he thought the Americans would do with him if they caught him. The captain at first declined giving him an answer; but upon being repeatedly urged to do it, he said: "Why, sir, if I must answer your question, you must excuse my telling you the plain truth. If my countrymen should catch you, I believe they would first cut off that lame leg which was wounded in the cause of freedom and virtue, and bury it with the honors of war; and afterwards hang the remainder of your body in gibbets."

Lord Cornwallis joined the British troops at Petersburg on May 20. Veteran campaigner William Phillips had just died of a bilious fever. When Cornwallis took over, Benedict Arnold returned to New York. Judge Jones says that he arrived there "as rich as a nabob with the plunder of Virginia." The march that Cornwallis had made was disapproved by Sir Henry Clinton, who continued to direct the war from New York. He had expected the earl to return to South Carolina. Cornwallis had known this, but he believed that the British cause could be better served by a strong move against Virginia, since control of the colony would divide the North from the South. Regarding the deep-southern policy that Clinton had instigated and to which he himself had at first adhered, the earl later stated:

I was most firmly persuaded that until Virginia was reduced we could not hold the more southern provinces; and that after its reduction they would fall without much difficulty.

His lordship, who had lost the better part of one substantial army during his operations in the Carolinas, was now in command of another. Declaring that "the boy cannot escape me," he set out to crush the forces under Lafayette and to destroy whatever stores he could find. Against the stores he enjoyed some success, but the troops were elusive from the start. Lafayette wrote Washington: "I am . . . determined to skirmish, but not to engage too far. . . . I am not strong enough even to get beaten." The game, which was played in the stretch of country between the Lower Chesapeake Bay and Charlottesville, continued for some weeks. Then Cornwallis moved to take up a position on the coast. On July 6, while he was preparing to cross the James River near Jamestown, Lafayette ordered a strike at his rear. "Mad Anthony" Wayne was in charge. According to an unknown member of the American army:

The action was obstinate for the little time it lasted, but the disproportion of numbers was too great. The Marquis arrived in person, time enough to order a retreat. . . . Cornwallis did not pursue . . . more than half a mile. . . . I had the pleasure of seeing the Marquis in a most amiable point of view, visiting the wounded officers and soldiers, going from man to man, examining into their situation, their attendance, their wants, and giving every possible care that all things necessary should be furnished—a conduct which . . . does honor to the humanity and goodness of his heart [and] cannot fail to engage him the affections of the soldiery and endear the name of Lafayette to every American.

The war was now approaching a climax. A strong French fleet under Admiral François Joseph Paul, the Comte de Grasse, was in the West Indies preparing to sail for the American coast. Back in May, when it was learned that De Grasse had left France for the Indies, Washington had met with the Comte de Rochambeau at Wethersfield, Connecticut, to discuss combining the French army at Newport, Rhode Island, with his own forces for a major operation based on the new fleet's support. Washington wanted to attack Clinton at New York, but Rochambeau hedged on this. He had decided privately that a move to the South would be better. In the end, by sending De Grasse a secret message urging him to make his appearance in the Chesapeake, Rochambeau forced Washington into accepting this plan.

The extent of Rochambeau's influence at this time was unknown to most Americans, who believed that Washington was making all the major decisions. In fairness, it must be added that the decisions he made within the framework of Rochambeau's plan were good ones—were, in fact, vital to the operation's success.

In June, Washington had assembled the American army at Peekskill, on the east bank of the Hudson. The ensuing developments were nowhere better recorded than in Dr. Thacher's journal:

July 1st: A division of our French allies are on their march from Rhode Island to unite with us in the service of the campaign. Great preparations are continually making for some important operation, and it is in general conjectured that the object of the campaign is to besiege New York. We are ordered to have four days' provisions cooked, and to march at three o'clock in the morning, leaving all our baggage behind except a single blanket to each man. It is remarkable that we have so much as four days' provisions on hand.

5th: The reveille beat at three o'clock on the 2d instant, when we marched [southward along the Hudson], and reached Tarrytown in the evening. The weather being extremely hot, the troops were much fatigued. Halted at Tarrytown about two hours, and then proceeded. Marched all night, and at sunrise arrived within two miles of the enemy's works at King's Bridge [just north of Manhattan Island]. Having halted about two hours, a firing of cannon and musketry was heard in front, and we were informed that a party of our troops had engaged the enemy, and we were ordered to advance rapidly to their assistance. But before we could reach the scene of action, the enemy had retired within their strong works. . . . We took our repose for the night in the open field; and our tents and baggage having arrived the next day, we pitched our encampment . . . [to the northward] within a few miles of the outposts of the enemy.

The French army under General Rochambeau have arrived and encamped at a small distance on the left of the Americans. The French legion of dragoons and infantry, under command of [Armand Louis de Gontaut, Duc de Lauzun], arrived and took their station near our encampment, and appear in true military style. They are a fine looking corps. . . .

13th: Notwithstanding the active bustle which attends our present situation, I received an invitation, with a number of officers of our regiment, to dine with a party of French officers in their camp. We were politely received under an elegant marquee. Our entertainment consisted of excellent soup, roast beef, etc., served in French style. The gentlemen appear desirous of cultivating an acquaintance with our officers, but being ignorant of each other's language we can enjoy but little conversation. . . . We now greet [the French] as friends and allies, and they manifest a zealous determination to act in unison with us against the common enemy. . . .

In the evening of the 21st, our army and the French were put in motion [southward], marching with great rapidity through a thick, unfrequented wood and swamps, and through fields of corn and wheat. . . . In the morning [after passing to the east of the King's Bridge fortifications] we arrived near the enemy's post at Morrisania [a village at the junction of the East and Harlem rivers], but they had taken the alarm and escaped to New York. Having continued there during the day, we retired in the evening about five or six miles and lay on the hills near King's Bridge, where we remained . . . till the night of the 23d, when we returned to our encampment.

[August] 15th: . . . General orders are now issued for the army to prepare for a movement at a moment's notice. The real object of the allied armies . . . has become a subject of much speculation. Ostensibly an investment of the city of New York is in contemplation. . . .

20th: According to orders, we commenced our line of march yesterday, a party of pioneers being sent forward to clear the road towards King's Bridge, and we expected immediately to follow in that direction. But an army is a machine whose motions are directed by its chief. When the troops were paraded for the march they were ordered to the right about, and, making a retrograde movement up the side of the [Hudson], we have reached King's Ferry and are preparing to cross. . . . Our allies are in our rear, and it is probable we are destined to occupy the ground on the Jersey side. . . .

31st: . . . Our situation reminds me of some theatrical exhibition, where the interest and expectations of the spectators are continually increasing, and where curiosity is wrought to the highest point. Our destination has been for some time [a] matter of perplexing doubt and uncertainty. Bets have run high on one side that we are to occupy the ground marked out on the Jersey shore to aid in the siege of New York, and on the other that we are stealing a march on the enemy and are actually destined to Virginia in pursuit of the army under Lord Cornwallis. We crossed at King's Ferry [on the] 21st instant, and encamped at Haverstraw. . . . [On the] 22d, resumed our line of march, passing rapidly [southward] through Paramus, Acquackanack, Springfield and Princeton. We have now passed all the enemy's posts and are pursuing our route with increased rapidity towards Philadelphia. Wagons have been prepared to carry the soldiers' packs that they may press forward with greater facility. Our destination can no longer be a secret. The British army under Lord Cornwallis is unquestionably the object of our present expedition.

It is now rumored that a French fleet may soon be expected to arrive in Chesapeake Bay to cooperate with the allied army in [Virginia]. The great secret respecting our late preparations and movements can now be explained. It was a judiciously concerted stratagem calculated to menace and alarm Sir Henry Clinton for the safety of the garrison of New York and induce him to recall a part of his troops from Virginia for his own defence. . . . The deception has proved completely successful. . . . [Actually, Clinton sent a recall order, then countermanded to it.] His Excellency General Washington, having succeeded in a masterly piece of generalship, has now the satisfaction of leaving his adversary to ruminate on his own mortifying situation and to anticipate the perilous fate which awaits his friend Lord Cornwallis. . . . Major-General Heath is left commander-in-chief of our army in the vicinity of New York and the Highlands, and the menacing aspect of an attack on New York will be continued till time and circumstances shall remove the delusive veil from the eyes of Sir Henry Clinton, when it will probably be too late to afford succor to Lord Cornwallis. . . .

We crossed the Delaware River at Trenton Ferry on the 1st [of September], and in the afternoon crossed a small river at Shammany's Rope Ferry. Our boats were pulled across with facility by a rope made fast at each shore. We marched nineteen miles and encamped at a place called Lower Dublin. 2d: In the afternoon, marched through the city of Philadelphia. The streets being extremely dirty and the weather warm and dry, we raised a dust like a smothering snowstorm, blinding our eyes and covering our bodies with it. This was not a little mortifying, as the ladies were viewing us from the open windows of every house as we passed through this splendid city. The scene must have been exceedingly interesting to the inhabitants; and, contemplating the noble cause in which we are engaged, they must have experienced in their hearts a glow of patriotism, if not emotions of military ardor. Our line of march, including appendages and attendants, extended nearly two miles. The general officers and their aids, in rich military uniform, mounted on noble steeds elegantly caparisoned, were followed by their servants and baggage. In the rear of every brigade were several field-pieces, accompanied by ammunition carriages. The soldiers marched in slow and solemn step, regulated by the drum and fife. In the rear followed a great number of wagons, loaded with tents, provisions and other baggage, such as a few soldiers' wives and children; though [only] a very small number of these are allowed to encumber us on this occasion. The day following, the French troops marched through the city, dressed in complete uniform . . . and besides the drum and fife they were furnished with a complete band of music, which operates like enchantment.

3d: We crossed the River Schuylkill over a floating bridge and encamped four miles from Philadelphia, where we continued through the day to give the men time to rest and wash their clothes. 4th: Marched through Wilmington [Delaware], eighteen miles. . . . Marched again on the 5th; and on the 6th arrived at the head of Elk River, Maryland . . . having completed a march of two hundred miles in fifteen days. An express has now arrived from Virginia with the pleasing intelligence that Count de Grasse [of the French navy] has actually arrived at the mouth of the Chesapeake Bay with a fleet . . . and three thousand land forces, which are landed and have joined our troops under the Marquis de Lafayette in Virginia.

General Washington was at this time traveling well ahead of his army, and on September 9 he interrupted his journey to pay a visit to Mount Vernon. An approving American officer, Richard Butler, commented in his journal:

He has not been within his own door . . . since he was first a member of Congress in the year 1775, all which time he has been a most faithful patriot and servant of his country. From the citizen, he was a councellor, then a general, and in reality the father of the people.

Dr. Thacher resumes:

The royal army under Lord Cornwallis has taken post in Yorktown, situated on York River in Virginia, where he has constructed strong fortifications for his defence. But his communication [with the sea] by water is now entirely cut off by several French ships stationed at the mouth of the river.

Preparation is constantly making for our troops and our allies . . . to embark at the head of Elk River, whence we shall proceed down the Chesapeake Bay . . . in pursuit of the object of our expedition. About eighty vessels are in readiness, great activity prevails, embarkation has commenced, and our horses are sent round to Virginia by land. It falls to my lot to take passage on board a small schooner with four other officers and sixty men. She is so deeply laden with cannon, mortars and other ordnance that our situation will be attended with considerable danger if rough weather should overtake us.

11th: Sailed at four o'clock p.m. on board the schooner *Glasco*, beat against contrary wind down the Elk River, and at sunrise next morning entered the head of the great Chesapeake Bay. . . . The town of Annapolis . . . is situated on the western shore at the mouth of the River Severn where it falls into the bay. We came to anchor in the harbor at sun-setting, and I accompanied several officers to the coffee house and partook of a handsome supper. A very severe shower of rain, with high winds and extreme darkness, obliged us to spend the night on shore. On the 13th we returned on board at seven o'clock and proceeded on our voyage before a fresh gale, but had not sailed more than four miles when we were recalled by express to the harbor of Annapolis. This is in consequence of intelligence of a naval action between the British and French fleets near the mouth of the Chesapeake Bay. Our safety requires that we should remain in port till the event of the battle is known. Should the British have obtained the victory and should they get possession of the Chesapeake Bay, we shall be unable to proceed on our voyage, and our expedition will be entirely defeated. . . .

In the evening we attended the theatre and were entertained by a Mr. Wall, who exhibited Stephens' Lecture on Heads, greatly to the amusement of the audience; after which Mrs. Wall exhibited a variety of amusing scenes; and her little daughter, of seven years of age, spoke an epilogue and sung several songs, to the admiration of all present.

Information has just reached us that after General Arnold had returned [to New York] from his depredating expedition to Virginia he was despatched on a new incursion to Connecticut, his native state. . . . He landed his troops at the mouth of New London Harbor [which was also the mouth of the Thames River] and proceeded to the town. Fort Trumbull . . . was soon evacuated by our people; but Fort Griswold, on the other side of the river, was courageously defended by Colonel [William] Ledyard and a few militiamen hastily collected. The assault on this fort was made by Colonel Eyre, who . . . finally received . . . a mortal wound; and . . . the command devolved on Major Bromfield, who, by a superior force and much resolution, carried the place at the point of the bayonet. . . . An indiscriminate slaughter by the bayonet of those who had surrendered immediately ensued. . . . Arnold [remained] on the New London side, suffering the town to be plundered; and by a conflagration sixty dwelling houses and eighty-four stores were entirely destroyed. The loss which we sustained was very consider-

able, consisting of vessels, naval stores, European goods, provisions, etc. . . . The militia collected and conducted with great spirit
and alacrity in avenging the murder of their friends, and they
hastened the retreat of the enemy. . . . It is highly probable that Sir
Henry Clinton projected this expedition to Connecticut in the hope
of diverting General Washington from his enterprise against Earl
Cornwallis; but this manoeuvre will not effect his object.

*Arnold's attack on New London, not far from his birthplace at
Norwich, concluded his active part in the war. Detested by the Americans, who had once considered him a great Patriot, he was headed
for exile in England, where, instead of gaining the gratitude he
believed his due, he would meet with little more than toleration.*

*While the Americans at Annapolis fumed over what Arnold did
in the North on September 6, news of a more acceptable nature was
on its way from the deep South. On September 8, about twenty-two
hundred men under Nathanael Greene had made a spirited attack
on a similar number of the enemy under Colonel Alexander Stewart
at Eutaw Springs, South Carolina (about fifty miles from Charleston).
In Dr. Thacher's words:*

The battle . . . was the hottest and the most bloody, for the
numbers engaged, that General Greene ever witnessed. Many of
the officers combated sword to sword, and the soldiers, rushing
together, with the point of the bayonet contended with increased
rage and effort for life, for blood, and carnage. A party of the enemy
possessed themselves of a three-story brick house and a picketed
garden, which gave them considerable advantage and saved their
army from a total rout. . . . Victory is claimed by both commanders,
but the consequences have proved most disastrous to the enemy;
for the next day Colonel Stewart . . . retired . . . towards Charleston.

*The Battle of Eutaw Springs, though somewhat overshadowed by the
momentous developments in Virginia, was by no means an incon-
sequential affair. It brought an end to major hostilities in the deep
South. The British had lost their last measure of power outside the
fortifications that ringed the coastal towns of Charleston and Savannah.*

Writing on September 15, Dr. Thacher rejoiced:

The gratifying intelligence is announced that the naval engagement between the two fleets has resulted in the defeat of the British
with considerable loss, and the French have now the sole command

of the Chesapeake Bay. This event is of infinite importance and fills our hearts with joy, as we can now proceed on our expedition.

Already the enemy troops in Yorktown, the expedition's objective, were beginning to feel the effects of the French blockade. One soldier complained:

We get terrible provisions now, putrid ship's meat and wormy biscuits that have spoiled on the ships. Many of the men have taken sick here with dysentery or the bloody flux and with diarrhea. Also the foul fever is spreading, partly on account of the many hardships from which we have had little rest day or night, and partly on account of the awful food; but mostly the nitrebearing water is to blame for it.

The division of Americans that included Dr. Thacher sailed from Annapolis on September 16, and on the 18th passed the Potomac River, the boundary between Maryland and Virginia:

The bay at this place is about thirty miles wide. The wind this afternoon has blown with all the violence of a gale. The bow of our vessel, in ploughing through the billows, is frequently brought under water, which keeps us in perpetual alarm. We passed York River . . . fifteen miles from the mouth of which stands Yorktown, where . . . Cornwallis is posted. . . . 20th: Passed Hampton Road and entered James River, which is at its entrance about five miles wide. We enjoyed a distant view of the grand French fleet, riding at anchor at the mouth of the Chesapeake. . . . This was the most noble and majestic spectacle I ever witnessed, and we viewed it with inexpressible pleasure; and the warmest gratitude was excited in every breast towards our great ally.

22d: Reached the harbor between Jamestown and Williamsburg, where the greater part of our transports arrived in the course of the day, and the troops disembarked and encamped on the banks of the river within twelve miles of Yorktown. We now congratulated ourselves on having completed our voyage. . . . Vessels with troops are arriving every day. Jamestown is the place where the English first established themselves in Virginia in 1607. Though the most ancient settlement in America, it cannot now be called a town, there being but two houses standing on the banks of the river. 25th: Marched from the landing place through the city of Williamsburg. This is the capital of Virginia, but in other respects is of little importance. . . .

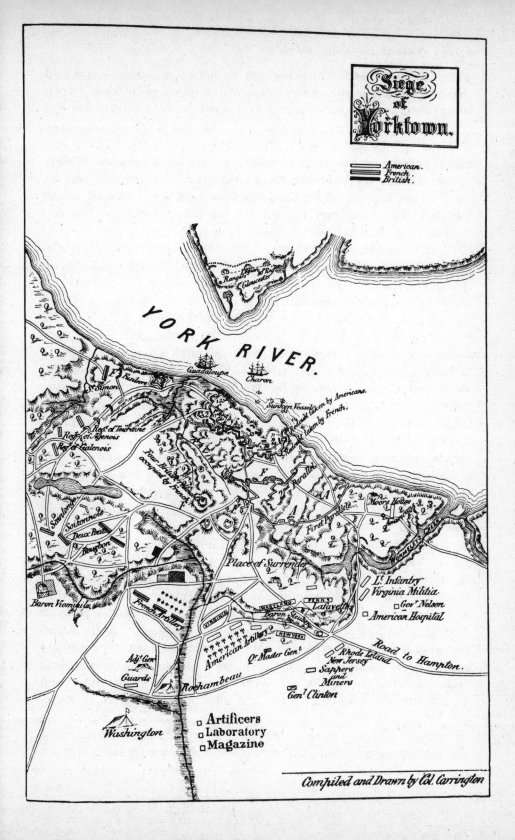

Siege of Yorktown.

American.
French.
British.

YORK RIVER.

Rangers & Reg^t
Gloucester

Guadaloupe

Charon

Sunken Vessels taken by Americans.

Redoubt taken by French.

Fusileers

St. Simon

Reg^t of Touraine

Reg^t of Agenois

Reg^t of Salenois

Four British Redoubts
occupied by French

2^d Parallel

F

Moor's House

Saintonge

Soissonnois

Deux Ponts

Bourbon

First Parallel

WORMLEY'S CREEK

Place of Surrender

Lt Infantry

Virginia Militia

Govr Nelson

American Hospital

Baron Viomenil

French Artillery

MARYLAND

Baron Steuben

PENN^a

Lafayette

VIRGINIA

NEW YORK

American Artillery

Q^r Master Genl

Road to Hampton.

Adj^t Gen

Guards

Rochambeau

Rhode Island

New Jersey

Sappers
and
Miners

Genl Clinton

Washington

□ Artificers
□ Laboratory
□ Magazine

Compiled and Drawn by Col. Carrington

27th: We arrived at Yorktown yesterday . . . and have encamped within one mile of the enemy's line of redoubts. 28th: The French troops have arrived and encamped on our left. Yorktown is situated on the south bank of the river. . . . In this little village, Lord Cornwallis, with about seven thousand troops, has taken his station and is endeavoring to fortify himself against the impending danger of our combined operations. His communication [with the sea] by water is entirely cut off by the French ships of war stationed at the mouth of the river, preventing both his escape and receiving succor from Sir Henry Clinton at New York.

The allied army is about twelve thousand strong, exclusive of the [Virginia] militia under Governor [Thomas] Nelson. [The total number of troops exceeded sixteen thousand.] The Americans form the right, and the French the left wing of the combined forces, each extending to the borders of the river, by which the besiegers form a half-circle round the town. His Excellency General Washington commands in person, and is assisted by Major-General Lincoln, Baron Steuben, the Marquis de Lafayette, General Knox, etc. The French troops are commanded by General the Count Rochambeau, a brave and experienced officer having under him a number of officers of distinguished character. Unbounded confidence is reposed in our illustrious commanders; the spirit of emulation and military ardor universally prevails; and we are sanguine in our expectations that a surrender of the royal army must be his lordship's fate. A cannonade commenced yesterday from the town, by which one man was wounded, and I assisted in amputating his leg.

30th: We are agreeably surprised this morning to find that the enemy had, during the preceding night, abandoned three or four of their redoubts and retired within the town, leaving a considerable extent of commanding ground which might have cost us much labor and many lives to obtain by force. Our light infantry and a party of French were ordered to advance and take possession of the abandoned ground and to serve as a covering party to our troops who are employed in throwing up breastworks. Considerable cannonading from the besieged in the course of the day, and four militiamen were wounded by a single shot, one of whom died soon after. . . . October 1st and 2d: Our troops had been engaged in throwing up two redoubts in the nighttime. On discovery, the enemy commenced a furious cannonade, but it does not deter our men from going on

vigorously with their work. Heavy cannon and mortars are continually arriving, and the greatest preparations are made to prosecute
the siege in the most effectual manner.

3d and 4th: A considerable cannonading from the enemy. One
shot killed three men and mortally wounded another. While the
Rev. Mr. Evans, our chaplain, was standing near the commander-
in-chief, a shot struck the ground so near as to cover his hat with
sand. Being much agitated, he took off his hat and said, "See here,
General!"

"Mr. Evans," replied his excellency with his usual composure,
"you had better carry that home and show it to your wife and
children."

. . . The enemy, from the want of forage, are killing off their
horses in great numbers. Six or seven hundred of these valuable
animals have been killed, and their carcasses are almost continually
floating down the river.

The British are in possession of a place called Gloucester, on the
north side of the river nearly opposite Yorktown. Their force consists of one British regiment and Colonel Tarleton's legion of horse
and infantry. In opposition to this force, the French legion under
the command of the [Duc de Lauzun] and a detachment of French
infantry and [American] militia are posted in that vicinity. Tarleton is a bold and impetuous leader and has spread terror through
the Carolinas and Virginia for some time past. In making a sally
from Gloucester yesterday they were attacked by the French and
defeated. . . .

The British have sent from Yorktown a large number of Negroes
sick with the smallpox, probably for the purpose of communicating
the infection to our army. . . .

7th: A large detachment of the allied army, under command of
Major-General Lincoln, were ordered out last evening for the purpose of opening intrenchments near the enemy's lines. This business
was conducted with great silence and secrecy. . . . Our troops were
indefatigable in their labors . . . and before daylight they had
nearly completed the first parallel line of nearly two miles in
extent, besides laying a foundation for two redoubts within about
six hundred yards of the enemy's lines. At daylight the enemy, having discovered our works, commenced a severe cannonade, but our
men, being under cover, received no injury.

A French soldier deserted to the enemy; after which [presumably with the deserter pointing out targets] there was a constant firing against the French lines, and one officer was killed and fifteen men were killed or wounded. . . .

8th and 9th: The duty of our troops has been for several days extremely severe. Our regiment labors in the trenches every other day and night, where I find it difficult to avoid suffering by the cold, having no other covering than a single blanket in the open field. We erected a battery last night in front of our first parallel without any annoyance from the enemy. Two or three of our batteries being now prepared to open on the town, His Excellency General Washington put the match to the first gun, and a furious discharge of cannon and mortars immediately followed, and Earl Cornwallis has received his first salutation.

On the following day, one of the earl's soldiers wrote:
Early this morning we had to change our camp and pitch our tents in the earthworks, on account of the heavy fire of the enemy. . . . One could . . . not avoid the horribly many cannon balls either inside or outside the city. . . . Many were badly injured and mortally wounded by the fragments of bombs which exploded partly in the air and partly on the ground, their arms and legs severed or themselves struck dead.

Dr. Thacher continues:
From the 10th to the 15th, a tremendous and incessant firing from the American and French batteries is kept up, and the enemy return the fire, but with little effect. A red-hot shell from the French battery set fire to the *Charon,* a British 44-gun ship, and two or three smaller vessels at anchor in the river, which were consumed in the night. From the bank of the river I had a fine view of this splendid conflagration. The ships were enwrapped in a torrent of fire, which, spreading with vivid brightness among the combustible rigging and running with amazing rapidity to the tops of the several masts, while all around was thunder and lightning from our numerous cannon and mortars, and in the darkness of the night, presented one of the most sublime and magnificent spectacles which can be imagined. . . .

We have now made further approaches to the town by throwing up a second parallel line and batteries within about three hundred yards. This was effected in the night, and at daylight the enemy were roused to the greatest exertions. The engines of war have raged with redoubled fury and destruction on both sides—no cessation, day or night.

Among the casualties at this time was a French gunner, who had a foot torn off. Writes the Abbé Robin, a chaplain with the French forces:

I tried to console the unhappy man in the first moments of his anguish, when he gave me for answer, "I am less afflicted for the loss of my foot than for being so unfortunate as not to have had time, before it happened, to discharge the cannon I had pointed with so much care!" He soon after died of his wound, and never ceased to complain, till the last, of the failure he had made in firing the piece.

Returning to Dr. Thacher:

The siege is daily becoming more and more formidable and alarming, and his lordship must view his situation as extremely critical, if not desperate. Being in the trenches every other night and day, I have a fine opportunity of witnessing the sublime and stupendous scene which is continually exhibiting. The bombshells from the besiegers and the besieged are incessantly crossing each other's path in the air. They are clearly visible in the form of a black ball in the day, but in the night they appear like a fiery meteor with a blazing tail, most beautifully brilliant, ascending majestically from the mortar to a certain altitude, and gradually descending to the spot where they are destined to execute their work of destruction. . . . When a shell falls, it whirls round, burrows, and excavates the earth to a considerable extent, and, bursting, makes dreadful havoc around. I have more than once witnessed fragments of the mangled bodies and limbs of the British soldiers thrown into the air by the bursting of our shells; and by one from the enemy, Captain White of the Seventh Massachusetts Regiment and one soldier were killed, and another wounded, near where I was standing. About twelve or fourteen men have been killed or wounded within twenty-four hours. I attended at the hospital, amputated a man's arm and assisted in dressing a number of wounds.

The enemy having two redoubts about three hundred yards in front of their principal works, which enfiladed our intrenchment and impeded our approaches, it was resolved to take possession of them both by assault. The one on the left of the British garrison, bordering on the banks of the river, was assigned to our brigade of light infantry under the command of the Marquis de

Lafayette. The advanced corps was led on by the intrepid Colonel [Alexander] Hamilton. . . The assault commenced at eight o'clock in the evening, and the assailants bravely entered the fort with the point of the bayonet. . . . We suffered the loss of eight men killed and about thirty wounded. . . . [British] Major Campbell, who commanded in the fort, was wounded and taken prisoner, with about thirty soldiers. The remainder made their escape. I was desired to visit the wounded in the fort even before the balls had ceased whistling about my ears, and saw a sergeant and eight men dead in the ditch. . . . During the assault, the British kept up an incessant firing of cannon and musketry from their whole line. . . .

The other redoubt, on the right of the British lines, was assaulted at the same time by a detachment of the French commanded by the gallant [Antoine-Charles du Houx] Baron de Viomenil. Such was the ardor displayed by the assailants that all resistance was soon overcome, though at the expense of nearly one hundred men killed and wounded. The cause of the great loss sustained by the French troops in comparison with that of the Americans in storming their respective redoubts was that the American troops, when they came to the abatis, removed a part of it with their hands and leaped over the remainder. The French troops, on coming up to theirs, waited till their pioneers had cut away the abatis . . . which exposed them longer to the galling fire of the enemy. To this cause also is to be ascribed the circumstance that the redoubt assailed by the Americans was carried before that attacked by the French troops.

Before the simultaneous attacks had been launched, the Baron de Viomenil and the Marquis de Lafayette had exchanged some light words, with the baron maintaining that his Frenchmen would doubtless outdo Lafayette's Americans. Dr. Thacher says that as soon as the Americans had gained their victory, Lafayette sent one of his aides, a major, to inform the baron that he, Lafayette, was already in his redoubt and was wondering where the baron was:

The major found the baron waiting the clearing away [of] the abatis . . . [and was given] this answer: "Tell the marquis I am not in mine, but will be in five minutes." He instantly advanced and was [in], or nearly so, within his time. Of the defenders of the redoubt, eighteen were killed, and one captain and two subaltern officers and forty-two rank-and-file captured.

Our second parallel line was immediately connected with the two redoubts now taken from the enemy, and some new batteries were thrown up in front of our second parallel line, with a covert way and angling work approaching to less than three hundred yards of their principal forts. These will soon be mantled with cannon and mortars, and when their horrid thundering commences it must convince his lordship that his post is not invincible and that submission must soon be his only alternative.

Cornwallis had lately received word from New York that Sir Henry Clinton was preparing to come south with a rescue fleet. In reaction, the earl wrote Sir Henry: "I cannot recommend that the fleet and army should run great risk in endeavouring to save us." The earl says of the siege:

Being perfectly sensible that our works could not stand many hours after the opening of the batteries of [their second] parallel, we not only continued a constant fire with all our mortars and every gun that could be brought to bear upon it, but a little before daybreak in the morning of the 16th, I ordered a sortie of about three hundred and fifty men . . . to attack two batteries which appeared to be in the greatest forwardness, and to spike the guns.

These batteries were in the French sector. The Abbé Robin writes that the British managed to make their attack a surprise and that they

. . . nailed up seven pieces of cannon, killed some soldiers, made a few prisoners, and wounded about thirty. A lad of fifteen years old (servant to an officer) who was sleeping just by was stabbed with a bayonet in thirteen or fourteen different parts of his body.

Being soon driven away, the British left behind several killed and wounded. The wounded were carried by the French to one of their own hospitals. Robin comments that "the men who a moment before had been cutting each other's throats were now collected under the same roof and received . . . the same care and attention." Cornwallis goes on:

This action . . . proved of little public advantage, for the cannon having been spiked in a hurry, were soon rendered fit for service again; and before dark the whole parallel and batteries appeared to be nearly complete. At this time . . . there was no part of the whole front [under attack] in which we could show a single gun, and our shells were nearly expended. I had therefore only to choose between preparing to surrender next day, or endeavouring to get off [by water to Gloucester Point] with the greater part of the troops; and I determined to attempt the latter. . . . Sixteen large boats were . . . ordered to be in readiness to receive troops precisely at ten o'clock [that night]. . . . After making my arrangements with the utmost secrecy, the light infantry, the greatest part of the guards, and part of the 23d regiment embarked at the hour appointed; and most of them landed at Gloucester; but at the critical moment the weather from being moderate and calm, changed to a most violent storm of wind and rain, and drove all the boats, some of which had troops on board, down the river. . . . In this situation, with my little force divided, the enemy's batteries opened at daybreak. The passage between [Yorktown] and Gloucester was much exposed. But the boats having now returned, they were ordered to bring back the troops that had [crossed] during the night, and they joined us in the forenoon without much loss.

"Thus," laments Banastre Tarleton, "expired the last hope of the British army." Tarleton and his detachment had remained at Gloucester. The date was October 17; and Dr. Thacher recorded:

The whole of our works are now mounted with cannon and mortars. Not less than one hundred pieces of heavy ordnance have been in continual operation during the last twenty-four hours. The whole peninsula trembles under the incessant thunderings of our infernal machines. We have leveled some of their works in ruins and silenced their guns. They have almost ceased firing. We are so near as to have a distinct view of the dreadful havoc and destruction of their works, and even see the men in their lines tore to pieces by the bursting of our shells. But the scene is drawing to a close. Lord Cornwallis, at length realizing the extreme hazard of his deplorable situation and finding it in vain any longer to resist, has . . . come to the humiliating expedient of sending out a flag requesting a cessation of hostilities for twenty-four hours that commissioners may be appointed to prepare and adjust the terms of capitulation. . . .

18th: . . . At an early hour this forenoon General Washington communicated to Lord Cornwallis the general basis of the terms of capitulation which he deemed admissible, and allowed two hours for his reply. Commissioners were soon after appointed to prepare the particular terms of agreement. The gentlemen appointed by General Washington . . . have this day held an interview with the two British officers on the part of Lord Cornwallis. The terms of capitulation are settled; and, being confirmed by the commanders of both armies, the royal troops are to march out tomorrow and surrender their arms. . . .

19th: This is to us a most glorious day; but to the English one of bitter chagrin and disappointment. . . . At about twelve o'clock the combined [Franco-American] army was arranged and drawn up in two lines extending more than a mile in length. The Americans were drawn up in a line on the right side of the road, and the French occupied the left. At the head of the former, the great American commander, mounted on his noble courser, took his station, attended by his aids. At the head of the latter was posted the excellent Count Rochambeau and his suite. The French troops, in complete uniform, displayed a martial and noble appearance. Their band of music, of which the timbrel formed a part, is a delightful novelty, and produced, while marching to the ground, a most enchanting effect. The Americans, though not all in uniform nor their dress so neat, yet exhibited an erect soldierly air, and every countenance beamed with satisfaction and joy. The concourse of spectators from the country was prodigious . . . but universal silence and order prevailed.

It was about two o'clock when the captive army advanced through the line formed for their reception. Every eye was prepared to gaze on Lord Cornwallis, the object of peculiar interest and solicitude; but he disappointed our anxious expectations. Pretending indisposition [or, perhaps, being truly indisposed as the result of his weeks of unrelieved strain], he made General [Charles] O'Hara his substitute as the leader of his army. This officer was followed by the conquered troops in a slow and solemn step, with shouldered arms, colors cased, and drums beating. . . .

When General O'Hara reached the head of the Franco-American line, he tried first to make his surrender to Rochambeau, but was directed to Washington. Thacher continues:

. . . General O'Hara, elegantly mounted, advanced to his excellency the commander-in-chief, taking off his hat, and apologized for the non-appearance of Earl Cornwallis. With his usual dignity and politeness, his excellency [declining to accept O'Hara's surrender] pointed to Major-General Lincoln [O'Hara's counterpart among the American officers] . . . by whom the British army was conducted into a spacious field, where it was intended they should ground their arms.

The royal troops, while marching through the line formed by

the allied army, exhibited a decent and neat appearance as respects arms and clothing. . . . But in their line of march we [perceived] a disorderly and unsoldierly conduct. Their step was irregular and their ranks frequently broken. But it was in the field, when they came to the last act of the drama, that the spirit and pride of the British soldier was put to the severest test. Here their mortification could not be concealed. Some of the platoon officers appeared to be exceedingly chagrined when giving the word "ground arms," and I am a witness that they performed this duty in a very unofficer-like manner; and that many of the soldiers manifested a sullen temper, throwing their arms on the pile with violence as if determined to render them useless. This irregularity, however, was checked by the authority of General Lincoln. After having grounded their arms and divested themselves of their accoutrements, the captive troops were conducted back to Yorktown and guarded by our troops. . . . The British troops that were stationed at Gloucester surrendered at the same time and in the same manner to the command of the [Duc de Lauzun]. . . .

20th: In the general orders of this day our commander-in-chief expresses his entire approbation and his warmest thanks to the French and American officers and soldiers of all descriptions for the brave and honorable part which they have acted during the siege. He congratulates the combined army on the momentous event which closes the campaign and which crowns their heads with unfading laurels and entitles them to the applause and gratitude of their country. . . .

. . . In the design and execution of this successful expedition, our commander-in-chief fairly out-generaled Sir Henry Clinton, and the whole movement was marked by consummate military address, which reduced the royal general to a mortifying dilemma that no skill or enterprise could retrieve. . . . Lord Cornwallis is a very distinguished warrior. He possesses an exalted spirit, is brave and intrepid; and never was there a more zealous champion of his tyrannical master. . . . But Cornwallis has fallen! And our country is not subjugated.

The news of the great victory spread rapidly in all directions from Yorktown. During the earliest morning hours of October 22 a public watchman and crier, "an honest old German," was walking his lonely beat in Philadelphia when he heard a clatter of hooves approaching. He raised his lantern as a breathless messenger drew up

*and asked at what door he could find Thomas McKean, the presi-
dent of the Continental Congress. After obliging the rider the old
German continued on his way, calling out protractedly in broken
English, "Basht dree-e-e o'glock, und Gornva-a-a-allis isht da-a-a-
aken!"*

*Not since Burgoyne's surrender at Saratoga, four years before,
had there been such genuine reason for joy among America's Patriots. A New Jersey newspaper reported that*

. . . our illustrious Washington . . . like the meridian sun, has
dispelled those nocturnal vapors that hung around us, and put the
most pleasing aspect upon our political affairs that any era of the
present war has ever beheld.

*The grand accomplishment was marked by religious observances,
the ringing of bells, the firing of cannons, the building of bonfires,
and by feasting, drinking, dancing, and singing.*

*Though an official peace was still two years away, a great many
people on both sides recognized the fall of Cornwallis as the virtual
close of the war. All of England's policies—northern, southern, and
central—had ended in failure. There seemed nothing else she could
try. Moreover, she was being worn down by her struggles with
France, Spain, and Holland in other parts of the world.*

*Perhaps no one put the spirit of Yorktown into better words
than America's good friend, the young Marquis de Lafayette: "The
play is over. . . . I was somewhat disturbed during the former acts,
but my heart rejoices exceedingly at this last. . . ."*

APPENDIX

From Lexington to Yorktown

A Chronology of the Book's Chief Events

1 7 7 5

APRIL 19   First shots fired at Lexington and Concord.

MAY 10–17   Mastery of Lake Champlain secured by Ethan Allen and
                Benedict Arnold.

JUNE 15   Second Continental Congress elects George Washington com-
                mander in chief of the Patriot army.

JUNE 17   Battle of Bunker Hill.

JULY 3   Washington assumes command of the army at Cambridge,
                Massachusetts.

OCTOBER 10   Sir William Howe succeeds Thomas Gage as supreme com-
                mander of British forces.

OCTOBER 18   British burn Falmouth, Maine.

DECEMBER 9   Battle of Great Bridge, Virginia.

1776

JANUARY 1	American assault on Quebec repulsed.
JANUARY 1	Royalist Governor Dunmore sets fire to Norfolk, Virginia.
JANUARY 1	Washington raises first union flag of thirteen stripes at Cambridge.
JANUARY 9	First publication of Thomas Paine's "Common Sense."
FEBRUARY 27	Battle of Moore's Creek, North Carolina.
MARCH 17	British evacuate Boston.
MARCH 23	Privateering authorized by Congress.
JUNE 28	British fleet repulsed at Charleston, South Carolina.
JULY 4	Congress adopts Declaration of Independence.
AUGUST 27	Battle of Long Island.
AUGUST 29–30	Washington withdraws his defeated troops across East River to Manhattan.
SEPTEMBER 15	Americans routed at Kip's Bay and abandon New York City to British.
SEPTEMBER 16	Skirmish at Harlem Heights.
SEPTEMBER 21	Part of New York City burned.
SEPTEMBER 22	British execute Nathan Hale.
OCTOBER 11–13	Battle of Lake Champlain.
OCTOBER 28	Engagement at White Plains, New York.
NOVEMBER 16	British assault and capture Fort Washington on Manhattan.
NOVEMBER 20–21	Americans evacuate Fort Lee, New Jersey, and begin retreat to Pennsylvania.
DECEMBER 8	British occupy Newport, Rhode Island.
DECEMBER 13	General Charles Lee captured by British patrol.
DECEMBER 26	Washington crosses the Delaware and surprises Hessians at Trenton.

1777

JANUARY 3	Battle of Princeton.
JANUARY 6	Washington makes Morristown his headquarters for winter operations in New Jersey.

APRIL 26   British raid Danbury, Connecticut.

JUNE 14   Congress adopts Stars and Stripes.

JUNE 30   British evacuate New Jersey, crossing to Staten Island.

JULY 1   British army from Canada under John Burgoyne appears be-
                  fore Ticonderoga.

JULY 6   Americans retreat from Ticonderoga.

JULY 7   Battle of Hubbardton, Vermont.

JULY 23   Expedition under Howe sails from New York, bound for
                  Pennsylvania.

JULY 26   Jane McCrea killed by Indians.

JULY 30   Americans retreat down Hudson Valley, leaving Fort Edward
                  to Burgoyne.

JULY 31   Congress commissions Lafayette a major general.

AUGUST 6   Militiamen under Nicholas Herkimer ambushed near Fort
                  Stanwix.

AUGUST 16   Battle of Bennington, Vermont.

AUGUST 19   Horatio Gates succeeds Philip Schuyler as commander of the
                  northern army.

AUGUST 22   Barry St. Leger lifts siege of Fort Stanwix as Arnold approaches
                  with relief force.

AUGUST 25   Howe expedition disembarks in Maryland.

SEPTEMBER 11   Battle of Brandywine.

SEPTEMBER 19   Battle of Freeman's Farm.

SEPTEMBER 21   Troops under Anthony Wayne surprised at Paoli.

SEPTEMBER 26   British occupy Philadelphia.

OCTOBER 4   Battle of Germantown.

OCTOBER 6   British capture Forts Clinton and Montgomery on the Hudson.

OCTOBER 7   Battle of Bemis Heights.

OCTOBER 17   Burgoyne surrenders at Saratoga.

NOVEMBER 10–20   British operations reduce Forts Mifflin and Mercer on the
                  Delaware.

DECEMBER 18   Americans go into winter quarters at Valley Forge, with the
                  "Conway Cabal" having been added to Washington's concerns.

1 7 7 8

JANUARY 5	Battle of the Kegs.
FEBRUARY 6	French government declares for an alliance with America.
APRIL 5	Charles Lee, on parole pending his exchange for Richard Prescott, is welcomed at Valley Forge.
MAY 18	Howe feted with "Mischianza" as he turns his command over to Sir Henry Clinton.
JUNE 18	Clinton evacuates Philadelphia to march to New York, and Americans launch pursuit.
JUNE 28	Indecisive Battle of Monmouth, New Jersey, resulting in Charles Lee's suspension from command.
JULY 1–5	Tories and Indians ravage Wyoming Valley settlements on the Susquehanna.
JULY 29– AUGUST 30	Unsuccessful attempt on British base at Newport by Americans cooperating with French fleet under D'Estaing.
SEPTEMBER 5	British amphibious force under Sir Charles Grey begins punitive raid along southern coast of Massachusetts.
NOVEMBER 11–12	Cherry Valley, New York, assaulted by Tories and Indians.
DECEMBER 29	British capture Savannah, Georgia.

1 7 7 9

FEBRUARY 3	William Moultrie defeats British detachment at Beaufort, South Carolina.
FEBRUARY 14	Andrew Pickens victorious at Kettle Creek, Georgia.
MARCH 3	British rout Americans at Briar Creek, Georgia.
JUNE 20	Benjamin Lincoln repulsed at Stono Ferry, South Carolina.
JUNE 21	Spain declares war against England.
JULY 5–12	Connecticut coast raided by British amphibious force under William Tryon.
JULY 16	Anthony Wayne assaults Stony Point, on Hudson River.
JULY 25– AUGUST 14	Americans make unsuccessful effort against British post in Penobscot River, Maine.
AUGUST 19	British fort at Paulus Hook, New Jersey, assaulted by Henry Lee.
SEPTEMBER 23	John Paul Jones wins naval battle off English coast.

SEPTEMBER 30	John Sullivan concludes punitive expedition against the Iroquois.
OCTOBER 9	Franco-American attack on Savannah repulsed.
OCTOBER 25	British evacuate Newport.
DECEMBER 26	Expedition under Clinton leaves New York for Charleston.

1 7 8 0

MARCH 29	Siege of Charleston begins.
APRIL 14	British rout American force at Monck's Corner, South Carolina.
MAY 11	Charleston capitulates.
MAY 29	Banastre Tarleton falls upon retreating Americans at the Waxhaws, near North Carolina border.
JUNE 5	Clinton sails for New York, leaving Lord Cornwallis in command of southern operations.
JUNE 6–24	Americans in New Jersey withstand incursion by General Knyphausen.
JULY 10	French army under Rochambeau arrives at Newport.
AUGUST 16	Battle of Camden, South Carolina.
SEPTEMBER 21– OCTOBER 2	Arnold treason episode, ending with death of Major André.
OCTOBER 7	Battle of Kings Mountain, South Carolina.
OCTOBER 14	Nathanael Greene appointed commander of American forces in the South.

1 7 8 1

JANUARY 17	Battle of Cowpens, South Carolina.
JANUARY 20	British amphibious force under Arnold occupies Portsmouth, Virginia, after raid up James River to Richmond.
FEBRUARY 1–14	Greene retreats through North Carolina, pursued by Cornwallis, to refuge in southern Virginia.
FEBRUARY 20	Henry Lee decimates band of Tories marching to join Cornwallis at Hillsborough, North Carolina.
MARCH 15	Battle of Guilford Courthouse, North Carolina.

APRIL 6	Greene begins return to South Carolina for campaign against British outposts.
APRIL 25	Battle of Hobkirk's Hill, South Carolina.
MAY 9	British under Generals Phillips and Arnold occupy Petersburg, Virginia.
MAY 20	Cornwallis reaches Petersburg.
JUNE 5	Augusta, Georgia, falls to Americans.
JULY 3	Lord Rawdon abandons Fort Ninety Six, South Carolina.
JULY 6	Lafayette repulsed by Cornwallis near Jamestown, Virginia.
AUGUST 22	Cornwallis concentrates his forces at Yorktown and Gloucester.
AUGUST 25	Army under Washington and Rochambeau begins march from Hudson River to Chesapeake Bay.
AUGUST 30	Fleet under Comte de Grasse arrives in Chesapeake.
SEPTEMBER 5	French establish naval superiority in engagement with British.
SEPTEMBER 6	Arnold attacks New London, Connecticut.
SEPTEMBER 8	Battle of Eutaw Springs, South Carolina.
SEPTEMBER 28– OCTOBER 19	Siege of Yorktown, ending with surrender of Cornwallis.

ACKNOWLEDGMENTS

While assembling this history the author, of course, got help from many quarters. In the first place, his publisher conceived the project and early encouragement was provided by the editors of *American Heritage,* who published the book's first chapter in article form in April, 1971. Several other particular debts must be acknowledged. The extraordinary collection of eyewitness accounts, *The Spirit of 'Seventy-Six,* edited by Henry Steele Commager and Richard B. Morris, and the detailed and veracious *Rebels and Redcoats,* by George F. Scheer and Hugh F. Rankin, not only pointed the way to much good eyewitness material (and provided directly a few brief items from writings in the public domain) but also offered for study a wealth of factual information and scholarly insights. Deep obligation is acknowledged also to The New York Times & Arno Press for their *Eyewitness Accounts of the American Revolution* (called to the author's attention by his friend Peter Rado). This series, produced under the general editorship of Malcolm Decker, has made many rare old writings readily available. Thirty-four of the books on the following list are Arno reissues. Finally, the author wishes to express his appreciation for the genial aid provided by Dr. Robert Bray Wingate, chief of Rare Books and Special Collections at the Pennsylvania State Library. Most of the book's maps, incidentally, are from the Centennial edition of Henry B. Carrington's *Battles of the American Revolution.*

BIBLIOGRAPHY

ADAMS, JOHN. *Familiar Letters of John Adams and His Wife Abigail Adams During the Revolution.* Edited by Charles Francis Adams. New York: Hurd and Houghton, 1876.

ALDEN, CARROLL S. *A Short History of the United States Navy.* Philadelphia: J. B. Lippincott Company, 1939.

ALDEN, JOHN R. *A History of the American Revolution.* New York: Alfred A. Knopf, 1969.

ALLEN, ETHAN. *The Narrative of Colonel Ethan Allen.* New York: Corinth Books, 1961.

ANBUREY, THOMAS. *Travels Through the Interior Parts of America.* 2 vols. London: William Lane, 1789. (Reprinted by The New York Times & Arno Press, 1969.)

ANDRÉ, JOHN. *Major André's Journal.* Tarrytown, N.Y.: William Abbatt, 1930. (Reprinted by The New York Times & Arno Press, 1968.)

ANDREWS, WILLIAM LORING. *An Essay on the Portraiture of the American Revolutionary War.* New York: Dodd, Mead & Co., 1896.

BARBER, J. W. *United States Book.* New Haven: L. H. Young, 1834.

BARTLETT, W. H., and WOODWARD, B. B. *The History of the United States of North America.* New York: George Virtue & Co., 1856.

BOLTON, CHARLES KNOWLES. *The Private Soldier Under Washington.* New York: Charles Scribner's Sons, 1902.

BOUDINOT, ELIAS. *Journal or Historical Recollections of American Events During the Revolutionary War.* Philadelphia: Frederick Bourquin, 1894. (Reprinted by The New York Times & Arno Press, 1968.)

BURGOYNE, JOHN. *A State of the Expedition from Canada as Laid Before the House of Commons.* London: J. Almon, 1780. (Reprinted by The New York Times & Arno Press, 1969.)

CALDWELL, CHARLES. *Memoirs of the Life and Campaigns of the Hon. Nathanael Greene.* Philadelphia: Robert and Thomas Desilver, 1819.

CARRINGTON, HENRY B. *Battles of the American Revolution.* New York: A. S. Barnes & Company, 1877. (Reprinted by The New York Times & Arno Press, 1968.)

CHASE, ELLEN. *The Beginnings of the American Revolution.* 3 vols. New York: The Baker and Taylor Company, 1910.

COBURN, FRANK WARREN. *The Battle of April 19, 1775.* Lexington, Mass.: Published by the author, 1912.

———. *Fiction and Truth About the Battle on Lexington Common.* Boston: F. L. Coburn & Co., 1918.

CODMAN, JOHN, 2ND. *Arnold's Expedition to Quebec.* Edited by William Abbatt. London: The Macmillan Company, 1903.

COLLINS, VARNUM LANSING (ed.). *A Brief Narrative of the Ravages of the British and Hessians at Princeton in 1776–77.* Princeton, N.J.: The University Library, 1906. (Reprinted by The New York Times & Arno Press, 1968.)

COMMAGER, HENRY STEELE, and MORRIS, RICHARD B. *The Spirit of 'Seventy-Six.* New York, Evanston, Ill., and London: Harper & Row, 1967.

CUTTER, WILLIAM. *Life of Israel Putnam.* New York: George F. Cooledge & Brother, 1848.

DAWSON, HENRY B. *Battles of the United States by Sea and Land.* 2 vols. New York: Johnson, Fry and Company, 1858.

DRAKE, SAMUEL ADAMS. *Bunker Hill: The Story Told in Letters from the Battlefield by British Officers Engaged.* Boston: Nichols and Hall, 1875.

———. *Burgoyne's Invasion of 1777.* Boston: Lothrop, Lee & Shepard Co., 1889.

DRAPER, LYMAN C. *King's Mountain and Its Heroes.* Cincinnati: Peter G. Thomson, 1881.

ELLIS, GEORGE E. *History of the Battle of Bunker's (Breed's) Hill.* Boston: Lockwood, Brooks and Company, 1875.

FANNING, NATHANIEL. *Fanning's Narrative; Being the Memoirs of Nathaniel Fanning, an Officer of the Revolutionary Navy.* Edited by John S. Barnes. New York: Naval History Society, 1912. (Reprinted by The New York Times & Arno Press, 1968.)

FISHER, SYDNEY GEORGE. *The True History of the American Revolution.* Philadelphia: J. B. Lippincott Company, 1902.

FITZPATRICK, JOHN C. (ed.). *The Writings of George Washington.* 39 vols. Washington, D.C.: Government Printing Office, 1931–1944.

FLEXNER, JAMES THOMAS. *George Washington in the American Revolution (1775–1783).* Boston: Little, Brown and Company, 1967.

FORCE, PETER. *American Archives,* Fourth and Fifth Series. Washington, D.C.: M. St. Clair Clarke and Peter Force, 1837–1853.

FRENCH, ALLEN. *The Day of Concord and Lexington.* Boston: Little, Brown and Company, 1925.

———. *The First Year of the American Revolution.* Boston and New York: Houghton Mifflin Company, 1934.

———. *The Siege of Boston.* New York: The Macmillan Company, 1911.

————. *The Taking of Ticonderoga in 1775: The British Story.* Cambridge, Mass.: Harvard University Press, 1928.

FROST, JOHN. *Pictorial Life of George Washington.* Philadelphia: Leary & Getz, 1854.

FROTHINGHAM, RICHARD. *History of the Siege of Boston.* Boston: Charles C. Little and James Brown, 1849.

————. *Life and Times of Joseph Warren.* Boston: Little, Brown & Company, 1865.

GIBBES, ROBERT W. *Documentary History of the American Revolution.* 3 vols. New York: D. Appleton and Company, 1853–1857.

GOSS, ELBRIDGE HENRY. *Life of Colonel Paul Revere.* 2 vols. Boston: Joseph George Cupples, 1891.

GRAHAM, JAMES. *Life of General Daniel Morgan.* New York: Derby & Jackson, 1856.

GRAYDON, ALEXANDER. *Memoirs of His Own Time.* Edited by John Stockton Littell. Philadelphia: Lindsay & Blakiston, 1846. (Reprinted by The New York Times & Arno Press, 1969.)

GREEN, SAMUEL A. (ed.). *Three Military Diaries Kept by Groton Soldiers in Different Wars.* Cambridge, Mass.: University Press, 1901.

Harper's Encyclopaedia of United States History. New York: Harper & Brothers, 1915.

HATCH, CHARLES E., JR. *Yorktown and the Siege of 1781.* Washington, D.C.: United States Department of the Interior, 1957.

————, and PITKIN, THOMAS M. *Yorktown, Climax of the Revolution.* Washington, D.C.: United States Department of the Interior, 1956.

HEADLEY, J. T. *Illustrated Life of Washington.* New York: G. & F. Bill, 1860.

HEATH, WILLIAM. *Memoirs of Major-General William Heath, by Himself, to which is added the Accounts of the Battle of Bunker Hill by Generals Dearborn, Lee and Wilkinson.* New York: William Abbatt, 1901. (Reprinted by The New York Times & Arno Press, 1968.)

HENRY, JOHN JOSEPH. *Account of Arnold's Campaign Against Quebec.* Albany: Joel Munsell, 1877. (Reprinted by The New York Times & Arno Press, 1968.)

HIGGINBOTHAM, DON. *The War of American Independence.* New York: The Macmillan Company, 1971.

HUDSON, CHARLES. *History of the Town of Lexington.* 2 vols. Boston and New York: Houghton Mifflin Company, 1913.

HULTON, ANN. *Letters of a Loyalist Lady.* Cambridge, Mass.: Harvard University Press, 1927.

JONES, CHARLES C., JR. (ed.). *The Siege of Savannah in 1779 as Described in Two Contemporaneous Journals of French Officers in the Fleet of Count d'Estaing.* Albany: Joel Munsell, 1874. (Reprinted by The New York Times & Arno Press, 1968.)

JONES, THOMAS. *History of New York During the Revolutionary War.* Edited by Edward Floyd de Lancey. 2 vols. New York: The New York Historical Society, 1879. (Reprinted by The New York Times & Arno Press, 1968.)

LAMB, ROGER. *An Original and Authentic Journal of Occurrences During the Late American War.* Dublin: Wilkinson & Courtney, 1809. (Reprinted by The New York Times & Arno Press, 1968.)

LAURENS, JOHN. *The Army Correspondence of Colonel John Laurens in the Years 1777–8.* New York: The Bradford Club, 1867. (Reprinted by The New York Times & Arno Press, 1969.)

LEE, HENRY. *Memoirs of the War in the Southern Department of the United States.* New York: University Publishing Company, 1869. (Reprinted by The New York Times & Arno Press, 1969.)

LESTER, C. EDWARDS. *History of the United States.* 2 vols. New York: P. F. Collier, 1883.

LOSSING, BENSON J. *Story of a Great Nation.* New York: Gay Brothers & Company, 1893.

MACLAY, EDGAR STANTON. *A History of the United States Navy.* 2 vols. New York: D. Appleton and Company, 1897.

MARTIN, JOSEPH PLUMB. *A Narrative of Some of the Adventures, Dangers and Sufferings of a Revolutionary Soldier.* Hallowell, Me., 1830. Reissued as *Private Yankee Doodle.* Edited by George F. Scheer. Boston and Toronto: Little, Brown and Company, 1962. (Reprinted by The New York Times & Arno Press.)

MOORE, FRANK. *Diary of the American Revolution; from Newspapers and Original Documents.* 2 vols. New York: Charles Scribner, 1860. (Reprinted by The New York Times & Arno Press, 1969.)

MOULTRIE, WILLIAM. *Memoirs of the American Revolution, so far as it Related to the States of North and South Carolina and Georgia.* New York: David Longworth, 1802. (Reprinted by The New York Times & Arno Press, 1968.)

MURDOCK, HAROLD. *Bunker Hill.* Boston: Houghton Mifflin Company, 1927.

NILES, HEZEKIAH. *Principles and Acts of the Revolution in America.* New York, Chicago, and New Orleans: A. S. Barnes & Co., 1876.

PAUSCH, GEORG. *Journal of Captain Pausch, Chief of the Hanau Artillery During the Burgoyne Campaign.* Translated by William L. Stone. Albany: Joel Munsell's Sons, 1886. (Reprinted by The New York Times & Arno Press, 1971.)

PETERSON, CHARLES J. *The Military Heroes of the Revolution.* Philadelphia: Jas. B. Smith & Co., 1859.

PONTGIBAUD, CHEVALIER DE. *A French Volunteer of the War of Independence.* Translated and edited by Robert B. Douglas. Paris: Charles Carrington, 1898. (Reprinted by The New York Times & Arno Press, 1969.)

POTTER, ISRAEL R. *Life and Remarkable Adventures of Israel R. Potter.* Providence: J. Howard, 1824.

RIEDESEL, BARON FRIEDRICH ADOLPH VON. *Memoirs and Letters and Journals.* Translated by William L. Stone. 2 vols. Albany: J. Munsell, 1868. (Reprinted by The New York Times & Arno Press, 1969.)

RIEDESEL, BARONESS FRIEDERIKE VON. *Letters and Journals Relating to the War of the American Revolution.* Translated by William L. Stone. Albany: Joel Munsell, 1867. (Reprinted by The New York Times & Arno Press, 1968.)

ROBERTS, JOHN M. (ed.). *Autobiography of a Revolutionary Soldier* [James Potter Collins]. Clinton, La.: The Feliciana Democrat, 1859. (Reprinted by the Naylor Printing Co., San Antonio, Tex., 1930.)

ROBERTS, KENNETH. *March to Quebec.* New York: Doubleday, Doran & Company, Inc., 1938.

ROBERTS, LEMUEL. *Memoirs of Captain Lemuel Roberts.* Bennington, Vt.: Anthony Haswell, 1809. (Reprinted by The New York Times & Arno Press, 1969.)

ROBIN, ABBÉ. *New Travels Through North America in a Series of Letters.* Philadelphia: Robert Bell, 1783. (Reprinted by The New York Times & Arno Press, 1969.)

SAWTELL, CLEMENT C. *The Nineteenth of April, 1775.* Lincoln, Mass.: Sawtells of Somerset, 1968.

SCHEER, GEORGE F., and RANKIN, HUGH F. *Rebels and Redcoats.* Cleveland and New York: The World Publishing Company, 1957.

SENTER, ISAAC. *The Journal of Isaac Senter on a Secret Expedition Against Quebec.* Philadelphia: Historical Society of Pennsylvania, 1846. (Reprinted by The New York Times & Arno Press, 1969.)

SHERBURNE, JOHN HENRY. *Life and Character of the Chevalier John Paul Jones.* Washington, D.C.: 1825.

SMITH, JOSHUA HETT. *An Authentic Narrative of the Causes which Led to the Death of Major André.* London: Mathews and Leigh, 1808. (Reprinted by The New York Times & Arno Press, 1969.)

SPARKS, JARED (ed.). *Correspondence of the American Revolution.* 4 vols. Boston: Little, Brown and Company, 1853.

SPEARS, JOHN R. *The History of Our Navy.* 4 vols. New York: Charles Scribner's Sons, 1897.

STEDMAN, CHARLES. *The History of the Origin, Progress and Termination of the American War.* 2 vols. London: Printed for the author, 1794. (Reprinted by The New York Times & Arno Press, 1969.)

STONE, WILLIAM L. *The Poetry and History of Wyoming* [Pennsylvania]. New York: Wiley & Putnam, 1841.

TALLMADGE, BENJAMIN. *Memoir of Col. Benjamin Tallmadge.* New York: Thomas Holman, 1858. (Reprinted by The New York Times & Arno Press, 1968.)

TARLETON, BANASTRE. *A History of the Campaigns of 1780 and 1781 in the Southern Provinces of North America.* London: T. Cadell, 1787. (Reprinted by The New York Times & Arno Press, 1968.)

THACHER, JAMES. *Military Journal of the American Revolution.* Hartford, Conn.: Hurlbut, Williams & Company, 1862. (Reprinted by The New York Times & Arno Press, 1969.)

TOWNSEND, JOSEPH. *The Battle of Brandywine.* Philadelphia: Townsend Ward, 1846. (Reprinted by The New York Times & Arno Press, 1969.)

UPHAM, WILLIAM P. *Letters Written at the Time of the Occupation of Boston by the British.* Salem, Mass.: Salem Press, 1876.

WALTON, JOSEPH S., and BRUMBAUGH, MARTIN G. *Stories of Pennsylvania.* New York: American Book Company, 1897.

WEBB, SAMUEL BLACHLEY. *Correspondence and Journals.* Collected and edited by Worthington Chauncey Ford. 3 vols. Lancaster, Pa.: Wickersham Press, 1893–1894. (Reprinted by The New York Times & Arno Press, 1969.)

WILKINSON, ELIZA. *Letters of Eliza Wilkinson During the Invasion and Possession of Charlestown, S.C., by the British in the Revolutionary War.* Edited by Caroline Gilman. New York: Samuel Colman, 1839. (Reprinted by The New York Times & Arno Press, 1969.)

WILKINSON, JAMES. *Memoirs of My Own Times.* 3 vols. Philadelphia: Abraham Small, 1816.

WILLETT, MARINUS. *A Narrative of the Military Actions of Colonel Marinus Willett.* New York: G. & C. & H. Carvill, 1831. (Reprinted by The New York Times & Arno Press, 1969.)

WORTLEY, MRS. E. STUART (ed.). *Correspondence of 3rd Earl of Bute and of Lt. Gen. The Hon. Sir Charles Stuart.* London: John Murray Company, 1923.

INDEX